The 10
Companies To Work For In The UK

Millennium Edition

Nightingale Multimedia

TEACH YOURSELF BOOKS

Dedication

To Bob, Ben, Verity, my parents.

And to anyone who gave a hand along the way.

Orders: please contact Bookpoint Ltd, 39 Milton Park, Abingdon, Oxon OX14 4TD. Telephone: (44) 01235 400414, Fax: (44) 01235 400454. Lines are open from 9.00–6.00, Monday to Saturday, with a 24 hour message answering service. Email address: orders@bookpoint.co.uk

A catalogue record for this title is available from The British Library

ISBN 0 340 73739 5

First published 1997
Second edition 1999

Impression number	10	9	8	7	6	5	4	3	2	1	
Year	2005		2004		2003		2002		2001	2000	1999

Cover illustration by Tim Kahane
Typeset by Transet Limited, Coventry, England.
Printed in Great Britain for Hodder & Stoughton Educational, a division of Hodder Headline Plc, 338 Euston Road, London NW1 3BH by Cox & Wyman, Reading, Berks.

Contents

Contents

Acknowledgements

Warm thanks to the many hundreds of human resources and public relations professionals in the 100 Best Companies and beyond who gave their full support to this project.

Special thanks are due to: Ruth Spellman, Chief Executive of Investors in People; Hilary Simpson, Chair of Parents At Work; Roger Adams, Head of Research and Technical Services at ACCA; Richard Medley at Countrywide Porter Novelli; Kirstie Upton at Parents At Work; Angela Giveon at Executive Woman; John Kelly, European Quality Publications; Pipi Sappal, Human Resources magazine; and Joanne Osborn and Sue Hart at Hodders.

To the principal writers and journalists on the team: Mark Taylor, Peter Welbourn, Mike Griffiths, Nigel Dudley, Gavin McGuire and Keith Walker.

Introduction

A decade of The 100 Best Companies To Work For In The UK

This edition of *The 100 Best Companies To Work For In The UK* marks the Millennium. Readers who make employment decisions based on the profiles of the companies in this book will be making career choices for the twenty-first century. Human resources, which was largely a Cinderella function in businesses when we put together the first edition for publication in February 1989, has blossomed into the key internal strategic discipline. Companies have recognized that employee motivation and morale is an essential ingredient in their success.

In the research for the edition which is now before you, identical messages resonated from every corner of the corporate world. People are the defining factor for success. Human resources has entered the current corporate lexicon and emerged as an unalienable aspect of conducting business in the modern world. Global economics and strengthening international competition has forced many companies down strategic routes which embrace positive employment practice. Almost every company argues that it now owes its success to the quality, determination, energy and expertise of its people.

Recognition – both in the material and social senses of the world – has developed into a key determinant of the nature of the employee response. The trends which we noted in the 1997 edition of *100 Best Companies* have been underscored and their impact is deeper. Lifetime employment with a single employer is a minority ambition. Both recruits and bosses speak – conventionally – of a sequence of assignments. Portability of skills which was a concept restricted to a few employers at the time of the last edition is accepted as commonplace today. Therefore the emphasis for many businesses and their employees is training.

More than any other manifestation of the employment relationship, training is seen as the greatest source of attraction for most candidates. For employees, training must meet the twin aims of being leading edge and relevant to long-term career ambitions. For employers conscious of an environment which is in constant turmoil, training must be sufficiently flexible and adaptable to meet changing demands while delivering today's services. It is a tall order. The most pressing consideration for CEOs is Where will my company need to be in two years? He or she will be aware that the chief executives of companies which are serious rivals will be posing the same question. This embraces the status of the market and the capacity of the employer to meet anticipated market demand. Against this environment, the CEO knows that IT systems and products will change alarmingly quickly and that in six months or a year, technology will be able to perform wonders which are perhaps understood today only by IT people.

Introduction

The scope of the business organization of two years hence, the nature of the services which it will need to provide and the structure which is necessary to deliver that service are all crucial aspects of the CEO's dilemma. This immediately prompts a series of questions about a company's people policies. The hypothetical chief executive will want to be aggressively pragmatic about the sort of qualities and talents which will be needed in the vision of the corporate future. Some defined plan about the competencies which are required to meet the commercial objectives of the business will be needed. That will shape decisions about the people requirement.

Many of the companies in this selection have made considerable progress in defining the competencies needed in specific individuals and teams. Rather fewer have achieved a universal picture of the total sum of competencies in the business as a whole and determined what the composite skill requirement will be. It is not an easy task as many businesses have discovered. First, a robust system to define and record defined competencies is needed. Some departments or divisions in some companies are quicker than others in delivering their complete appraisal. Once the tally is made, it needs to be matched with what perceived requirement is likely to be. The process is often cathartic. But many HR professionals say that once it is in place, they do not know how they survived without it.

These initiatives regularly betray rigidity of thought between departments or functions. Heads of department speak boldly of their flat, flexible structures when in practice they may be open only in name. Since 1989 and even 1997 organizations have decidedly moved from hierarchies to flat structures. The former preserve of the Californian high tech company is now the norm for the vast majority of businesses. The speed of change has forced even the most inelegant corporate dancer to be lighter on the feet. Even the monoliths – especially from mainland Europe – have cut their layers of management from 30 or 40 to 10 or 12.

Much of the pioneering work in companies is being done in the area of corporate structure where, as Andersen Consulting predicted five years ago, the workforce is seen as a single pool of labour. Teams are created and disbanded as demand dictates. The consultants would argue that they have been doing something similar for several years. In practice, what they mean is they have encouraged greater fluidity in structure. This is a positive move, but it is not quite the same thing. The last ten years have embraced the most significant upheaval in corporate structure for a century. The move to core and non-core and the inevitable growth of outsourcing means that businesses are now more focused on their primary business aims. The pace of competition has obliged them to seek highly talented people and to grant them much greater operational freedom than even ten years ago. The growth in the team concept, the rise in importance of customer service and the devolution of decision making to those in the best position to make the most effective judgement are all examples of the trend.

The effectiveness of companies in the new decade will be determined by the proficiency of their teams and the quality of dialogue among employees and with customers. It is small surprise that the key disciplines being taught in companies are communications skills, people management, negotiation skills and customer service delivery.

Companies now invest vast sums of money on training. The global corporate training market is estimated at $100 billion. Businesses spend $12 billion on executive education, a quarter of which goes to the business schools. Most international companies worth their salt are running bespoke MBA programmes and the extent of training in some blue chips for all staff has risen to at least two weeks a year.

The growth of greater personal responsibility for career development is another key facet of the changes in process. A menagerie of buddies, mentors, partners and more exotic creatures are available to assist employees with their career choices. But the emphasis has moved from the company dictating the potential of a career to the individual employee playing the central role. In many progressive companies the employee is equipped with a dizzying array of tools with which to make choices. One of the great advantages of technology is access. And in many companies this is put to good use to explore career routes. In some of the case studies in this book, businesses allegedly leave everything to the staff member concerned. In others, employees work with line managers to define work priorities and training and development targets. In yet more the manager has the upper hand.

In most businesses there has been a standardization of the appraisal and assessment systems which lead to reward adjustments, targets and objectives and developmental planning. Across the patch the average is still a formal annual review with informal appraisals at various times in the year. Informal appraisals which are recognized as part of the assessment process have increased dramatically. In the last 18 months companies have become increasingly excited by feedback. This started as managers giving employees feedback on their performance. Two concepts have changed the shape of the appraisal. One is the growth in the flexible team as the principal structural vehicle, meaning that employees interact with a much wider pool of people. The second is the adoption of formalized competency-based measurement. Both of these have encouraged the soliciting of formal feedback from a much wider group than was formally common. In its ultimate expression this has emerged as the 360 degree feedback. A small group of companies were providing this approach in 1997. Now it is normal practice in many businesses, certainly for managers. And its application will increase.

Another important development in the last decade has been the widespread quest for accreditation under Investors in People. The process has obliged companies to create a recognizable and demanding structure for expressing commitment to good employee relations. IIP accreditation has great commercial value for businesses. Mercury Asset Management mentioned in its interview for this book the importance which its clients attach to the IIP accreditation. Mercury's customers regard the IIP award as convincing evidence that the firm is serious about developing and motivating its people. The continued expansion of IIP and its role in progressing management attitudes towards staff is important for creating a culture of awareness and responsiveness to employee issues.

Among the 23 new entries in this edition are several largely non-graduate employees. Among the companies which fall into this category are Pret A Manger, Richer Sounds, Carphone Warehouse and Whitbread. These companies rely heavily on generating high employee morale and enthusiasm. They are not among the upper echelon for reward packages but they impress by their flair for energizing their workforce, their commitment to training and development and their opportunities for early promotion. Whitbread is the leader in this field. It is extremely creative devising techniques to help employees discover their own personal strengths and character qualities.

In the last edition, Coopers & Lybrand and Andersen Consulting were included for the first time. During the research cycle of this book, Coopers merged with Price Waterhouse to become a dominant UK employer. We have also selected Deloitte & Touche for its freshness and humanity, KPMG for the quality of opportunities which it provides and Ernst & Young for its originality. This means that for the first time all Big Five accountancy-led practices are included. These are each major employers in their own right and combined they account for a sizeable proportion of the graduate hires.

Financial services which, as one company in the sector commented, does not have a formidable reputation for best employment practice, is better represented. The powerful escalation is also represented with first time appearances by Nokia, Cable & Wireless, Motorola and Vodafone. Some of the businesses omitted from this year's list are undergoing restructuring. Others are engaged in mergers or takeovers. British Aerospace would most certainly have been included in this edition but at press date it was unclear if BAe was merging with GEC or DASA or anyone. Similarly, Astra Pharmaceuticals is a business which is highly regarded by the editorial team and it announced a merger with Zeneca. The employment implications of this merger were not clear and so Astra-Zeneca did not make it this time. Many of the companies which were omitted are very good businesses but face rapid changes.

Many companies wonder how the selection of the 100 Best Companies is made. The research process begins with the existing 100 and companies we examined for the previous edition. We have an informal editorial board of senior human resources directors and advisers in a range of businesses and consultancies who generously give their nominations. Also, the core team of journalists consult editors of influential sector publications in human resources and market sectors.

We also consult published and online information sources about companies and we have access to specialist information on reward packages of particular companies. This enables us to make detailed comparisons. The nominations for inclusion these days rarely run to more than 200 businesses, whereas in the early days it was more like 2000. This is because the names of the better employers are increasingly well known.

We seek companies which genuinely respect and encourage their people. These are businesses where the dialogue is developed and appropriate and the outcome is clear for everyone to see. It is fascinating to watch companies like Colgate-Palmolive enjoying such a positive return from innovative communications ideas and businesses like HHCL+Partners experimenting with unusual work environments.

For all the genuine exponents of improved employee relations, there are regrettably some who pay lip service and nothing more to the idea of empowering employees. Many believe their own publicity and we have met some of these. The standardization of language into a kind of meaningless corporate speak is still prevalent across industry and it is a disturbing trend. Equally unwelcome is the affirmation in an increasing number of companies that they must see their entry in the *100 Best Companies* prior to publication and pass it through their legal departments. The case studies in this book are pieces of journalism and although they reflect companies in a positive light are not pieces of company puff.

The challenge for businesses in the new century is to anticipate customer demand and understand what this will mean for their people. Employees with talent can be choosy about where they will conduct their careers. Less supremely gifted people can take heart from the high number of businesses which have learned the value of people with energy and vitality. The scope for best employment practice has never been higher. Corporate bosses have learned, as we said in 1989, that motivated people mean greater profits. It is never more true today.

New entrants to this edition

Abbey National
Air Products
Allied Irish Bank
Cable & Wireless
Carphone Warehouse
Colgate Palmolive
Deloitte & Touche
Diageo
Ernst & Young
Goldman Sachs
Kelloggs
KPMG
Lloyds TSB
McKinsey
Mercury Asset Management
Motorola
Nokia
Pret A Manger
PricewaterhouseCoopers
Richer Sounds
Standard Chartered
Vodafone
Whitbread

Notes: Diageo is the merger of Guinness and Grand Metropolitan. Guinness was selected for the last edition but Grand Met was not. PricewaterhouseCoopers includes Coopers & Lybrand which was in the last edition.

The following companies were included in the 1997 edition, but have since been succeeded.

Allied Dunbar
Astra Pharmaceuticals
AT&T (due to restructuring)
Brann
BSkyB
Burmah Castrol
Coats Viyella
Dresdner Kleinwort Benson
Green Flag
Hoseasons
Iceland
ICI
Kwik Fit
LucasVerity
Monsanto
Mulberry
Pearson
Pilkington
RAC
Rover
Siemens
Texas Instruments
Western Provident Association

Judge a Business by the Company it Keeps

Ruth Spellman, Chief Executive, Investors in People (IIP), discusses why a skilled and motivated workforce is central to success in business.

Who, today, begins employment with the view to remaining in that organization for the next five years, let alone until retirement? We are living in a time in which short-term employment and self-managed careers are the norm. Employees have taken charge of their own destiny, often moving from company to company to advance their careers, and employers are having to fight harder to keep their staff.

Without a capable and motivated workforce, an organization will struggle to survive in today's fiercely competitive business climate. The only truly original asset an organization can ever have is its people. Whatever your product or service, someone, somewhere will eventually have something very similar to offer. The workforce *is* the competitive edge every organization is trying to achieve – but it needs careful cultivation to bring to fruition.

Winning the competition for skills is the first step to winning the competition for customers and, to do this, an organization has to prove that it has more to offer the discerning individual.

This is why I welcome a publication such as *The 100 Best Companies to Work For*. It is a clear acknowledgement of the fact that organizations can no longer fail to focus on the continuous need to recognize the contribution of the individual. The bright, capable and enthusiastic employees for whom organizations are competing are more switched on than ever. They actively seek out organizations that will bring out the best in them, that will help them develop new skills and aptitudes, that will encourage their involvement in decision making, and that will further their development and acknowledge their contribution to the business goals. To today's career-focused employees, the guarantee of self development and good training can be as motivational as a bonus.

But of course, today, no business can afford to invest time and money for the sake of showing that it is a 'nice' company. Companies that are good to work for are those that are wise to the fact that a motivated workforce is the surest way to business success. In motivating its workforce, such companies create a win-win situation – a win for the employee who will spend his or her working time in an encouraging, supportive environment that takes personal development seriously, and a win for the company which will reduce turnover and absenteeism and improve client satisfaction and competitiveness.

This, in a nutshell, is the foundation of the Investors in People Standard which has proven its validity in over 31,000 organizations. A study from the Hambleden Group found that Investors in People companies perform seven times better than non-Investor companies in terms of profit per employee and the return on human capital. The message is simple – invest in your staff and they will look after your bottom line.

Further hard evidence to demonstrate the impact that investing in people can have is shown through research carried out in the UK and in Europe. A survey by the European Foundation for the Improvement of Living and Working conditions concludes that economic performance increases and sickness and absenteeism reduce as employees become more involved in company issues.

Similarly, a recent study by the Institute of Personnel and Development found that job satisfaction and organizational commitment can each make a five per cent difference in the profitability of companies.

What happens though when the reverse is true and employee participation is not taken seriously? Investors in People UK's own recent research found that one in four workers in Britain feels under-utilized, bored, demotivated or stressed. This happens when employees are not involved with the company's goals or when they feel that their ideas are not wanted or listened to. Staff turnover increases as employees leave for more interesting jobs, and this impacts on the morale of those left behind, levels of customer service and quality – both key areas of success in today's competitive environment.

Despite the progress made by many companies in the UK, there is still work to be done. While 80 per cent of chief executives recognize that investment in people is key to business success, Coopers and Lybrand and Investors in People UK together found that only one in three has a written human resource strategy aligned to corporate objectives and 20 per cent of boards do not have a member with responsibility for people issues.

The study also found that some 62 per cent of CEOs fear that their employees are ill-equipped in terms of skills. Nearly half of the chief executives questioned said that they were concerned about the levels of training. Yet it is in the hands of the CEOs to change this situation The answer lies in analysing what people skills are needed to meet the changing demands of the workplace and then putting a framework in place to fill the gaps.

Far from being a soft benefit, it should be clear that investing in people instead provides hard bottom line business benefits, with the Standard as the one tool that delivers these benefits time and time again.

Most employees during the 1990s were downsized, de-layered, restructured or re-engineered. Many experienced unemployment for the first time and currently work the longest hours in Europe. If more is to be delivered it must be through working smarter rather than working harder.

We are suffering from corporate anorexia, but slimmer organizations are not necessarily fitter. To quote Gary Hamel, Chairman of Strategos and Visiting Professor of Strategic and International Management at the London Business School, 'Too often cuts and more cuts leave old ways of thinking and leading intact.'

Success breeds success, and the brightest and best people will want to work for the best, most successful companies with just such bottom line success and the infrastructure to ensure success is a constant. However, the UK as a nation does not shout about it's successes enough. Instead we all too often have a culture of dignified failure, and when we are successful, we hide it.

The best examples of British business are those that not only succeed in terms of results, but which recognize the need to be proud of both their individual employee and collective corporate achievements, and take a positive stance to let others know of their success – an Investor in People organizational trait I am committed to increasing.

This 'corporate state of mind' has to be a business constant. In times of boom, they will need to compete with other organizations to recruit and retain the best employees for future growth.

In times of recession they will need to act as standard bearers for the UK, self-promoting to win more business, and delivering customer service excellence to retain an edge in their respective market.

In between, they will focus on increasing individual employability and transferable skills, recognizing the role of the individual in their own success, and living a sense of duty to help their people gain new employment more easily if redundancies become a reality.

As Gary Hamel says, 'Modern business is building a new market for talent. Successful enterprise will concentrate on getting the best people and getting the best out of them.'

Future business success will belong to attractive organizations rather than aggressive ones, in which direction is clear but the route map is flexible, and in which employee involvement, innovation and creative thinking and learning are encouraged and rewarded.

These organizations will be the long-term best companies to work for in the UK. The simple rule is better people mean better business, and in assessing a potential employer as one of the best, this area is one of the first you should consider.

Creating a Lifestyle Balance

Hilary Simpson, Chair, Parents At Work.

It has become a cliché to talk of the rapid change taking place in the world of work, but it is difficult to exaggerate the revolution that has occurred in many jobs as a result of new technology and the higher consumer expectations which accompany it. Many jobs can now be done anywhere and at any time, and services are increasingly being provided around the clock. Work is always there and can never really be said to be 'finished'.

For many people, their work no longer has clear boundaries and it becomes increasingly difficult to define what constitutes 'enough' in terms of work time: in theory you could work for ever and never fully achieve the objectives of your job. British men work longer hours than any of their European counterparts and in many occupations working long hours is a badge of commitment and success. Yet working consistently long hours has been shown to damage long-term health, and stress is now the second most common work-related health problem.

The dilemma of striking an acceptable balance between work and home was pushed up the organizational agenda over the last decade by parents and others with caring responsibilities as they began to make up a growing percentage of the workforce. A significant number of organizations responded by adopting what are commonly called 'family-friendly' employment policies, including a range of part-time working patterns, provision for various kinds of family leave and practical support in the form of assistance with childcare.

It is now becoming more widely accepted that all employees, not just those with children or other dependants, benefit from a healthy balance between work and non-work activities, and this has led some organizations to adopt the wider concept of 'work-life balance'. Alternative working patterns, personal development, sabbaticals and community involvement are promoted for all. Often this is accompanied by an increased emphasis on employee health, with access to counselling, fitness centres and alternative therapies being provided at the workplace. It may also incorporate a menu-based or 'cafeteria' approach to benefits which recognizes that employees' needs and preferences change over a working lifetime, allowing them to tailor their own package of, say, annual leave, health care, childcare support and reduced hours.

Companies with this kind of approach clearly regard their employees as a long-term investment rather than as a short-term cost, and there is increasing awareness of the business advantages of such working practices, which include not only tangible, bottom-line results in areas such as retention, productivity and attendance, but also benefits in the less tangible but equally important areas of motivation, satisfaction and creativity.

But to be a leading-edge employer, it is no longer enough just to have a portfolio of 'work-life' or 'family-friendly' policies. Often these remain at the level of pious intentions in the staff handbook, because in practice the organization sends out strong counter-messages, and employees may be reluctant to take up such options because they fear that they will be seen as lacking in commitment. The best employers therefore recognize the need to take positive steps to help their employees make sense of the shifting boundaries in the world of work and to create working patterns which provide a 'best fit' between the needs of the individual and the needs of the organization. In addition, their top managers practise what is preached so that there can be no doubt about the organization's values.

In essence, the approach of the best employers can be summed up as 'holistic' and 'sustainable' – New Age terminology which reflects sound business practice. Best practice in employment is holistic in the sense that it recognizes that employees bring their whole selves to work, and cannot be expected to leave their personal circumstances – health, relationships, family, and so on – conveniently at the door.

Contrary to popular mythology, companies that accept and engage the whole person reap corresponding rewards in terms of commitment and quality. Best practice in employment is sustainable in the sense that it regards employees not as a commodity to be used until 'burnt out', but as a resource which, properly managed, is renewable. The employers in this book have succeeded – at least partly – in measuring up to this high standard.

The Importance of Environmental and Social Issues for the Job Market

Roger Adams, Head of Research and Technical Services, Association of Chartered Certified Accountants (ACCA).

Many of the latest recruitment surveys show that there has been a dramatic shift in the issues which are important for prospective employees when seeking their first work assignment. In particular, graduate recruitment and human resources consultancies point to a movement away from lifelong careers with one employer towards a series of high profile or in-depth assignments with keynote employers.

Three principal factors dominate the reason why undergraduates, for example, apply to particular businesses: the status and reputation of a specific business, its policy towards training and development, and the environmental and social policies which it pursues. The corporate image of a business has always been a factor especially among the better qualified graduates. In a world where two- to three-year assignments are now commonplace, the greater number of brand name employers on a CV the better. This feeds into the second point which embraces the quality of training and development. Ambitious employees plan their careers in stages and seek to gain particular skill sets and marketable experience in each assignment with a top flight employer.

There is a great deal of talk in the human resources world about portability of skills. This means that companies do not guarantee a job for life but instead attempt to increase their attractiveness to recruits by offering training and development which is leading edge. The argument runs that when an employee re-enters the job market at the end of an assignment he or she will be fully equipped to compete with the best of the field.

The first two points – corporate reputation and quality of training – are intensely practical issues and relate directly to short-term and long-term employment prospects. The third factor – the environmental and social profile of a business – has become a consideration in the last five years. Whereas five to ten years ago, environmental and social policy was an emerging interest for companies, it was hardly a key strategic determinant. Also employees might have asked some questions about the profile of companies in their communities but often these were unclear and unfocused.

But in the last few years environmental and social factors have entered the mainstream. Employers report that at milk round or face to face interviews candidates are asking detailed and informed questions about the environmental and social policies of their companies. Candidates are genuinely knowledgeable about a wide range of environmental factors and will be aware of the achievements – or lack of them – of specific corporates.

There is a sequence of processes at work. For school children and teenagers, environmental factors – specifically – are areas of major concern. From a very early age, tuition at school often focuses on protecting the environment and classes regularly run projects on the damage caused by waste products, degenerative gases and environmentally unfriendly policies operated by major companies. Schools have created a generation which is aware of corporate policies which are injurious to the Earth.

As they grow older, information sources such as television news programmes and magazine articles feature reports on world environmental conferences such as Rio and Kyoto. Many web sites are dedicated to the environment and provide a constantly updating resource for people interested in and studying the environment. Many young people display considerable impatience with their elders on poor performance on emission standards and destruction of the rain forests. Some industrialists regard concerns such as this as a passing fad. They would be wrong to do so. For the present generation green issues are a matter of life and death.

At the same time that environmental and social issues have risen to the top of the agenda for many young people, regulators and corporate bosses have begun to take action. Businesses which regularly pollute have come to realize that they must take steps to show that they are alert to their social responsibilities. In 1991, the Association of Chartered Certified Accountants (ACCA) launched the first UK environmental report awards. An independent panel of accountants, environmental specialists, and Government authorities reviewed the quality of reports issued by the small group of companies that then reported on their environmental performance. Eight years later these reports are far more numerous, produced to a much higher standard and convey extremely detailed information.

Some of the reports are presented as printed documents, others are dedicated web sites. Some are stand alone documents, others are included as part of wider social reports. The depth of reporting is a recognition that environmental issues have come to centre stage. In fairness, some of the reporting is statement of objectives rather than achievement but it shows vision, enterprise and a perception of potential goals. In 1999, ACCA joined with other professional accountancy bodies in France, Germany, The Netherlands, Belgium and Denmark to make an award for the Third European Environmental Reporting Awards. Certain companies, like BT and British Airways, are regular winners in the UK and in the last ceremony Anglian Water, Eastern Group, BAA, Vauxhall Motors and the Co-operative Bank were recipients.

Since 1996 certain companies have moved to social reporting. The Body Shop International and BP (now BP-Amoco) are prime examples. These aim to show the activities of their publishers in the much wider context of their relationships with their communities. ACCA has created the first international framework for social reporting. Making Values Count was published in autumn 1998. It provides a systematic approach to evaluating the quality and relevance of social reporting.

Businesses may feel considerable pressure in the coming decade to enhance the quality of their environmental performance. In the UK a substantial element of this will come from the Government which is determined that performance will improve. Some of the stronger pressure groups in the sector will also exert an influence. But perhaps the greatest impetus will come internally as businesses recruit greater numbers of environmentally and socially committed employees.

THE 100 BEST COMPANIES TO WORK FOR IN THE UK

A–Z Listing

ABB

Few multinationals are as highly respected among chief executive officers as ABB. The European engineering and technology giant is the world's largest company in its sector. ABB is a resilient business which has earned an enviable reputation for integrity, quality, managerial excellence and superior technical initiative. CEOs polled for publications such as the *Financial Times* regularly cite ABB as the European company which they admire the most. It combines a global presence with substantially autonomous local operations and in particular is noted for its capacity to react swiftly to changing market conditions. ABB takes career development extremely seriously and its willingness to delegate authority to the lowest possible level in the company is characteristic of the organization.

ABB at a glance

Employees: 240,000 worldwide, 13,000 UK
Annual staff attrition: 3 to 4 per cent
Key locations: London (HQ), 25 manufacturing and more than 120 customer service centres across the UK
Annual graduate intake: 35
Annual intake: ABB has grown by acquisition with – on average – six new companies joining the group each year in the UK

An inside view

ABB was formed in 1988 by the merger of Asea, the Swedish industrial group, and the Brown Boveri Company, of Switzerland. At the time it was the largest industrial or commercial merger ever seen. Ten years later more than 1,000 companies had been brought into the combine which is the world's biggest engineering and technology group.

The challenge of combining the founding partners in ABB was complex. The sheer diversity of interests in the group encouraged the then chief executive, now chairman, Percy Barnevik to introduce a form of matrix management which since has become the hallmark of ABB. It has been emulated widely in many companies and many countries. The ABB matrix reflects the business drivers of the operation. It divides, on one axis, the management of the group into clusters or segments, according to client or market groups. These segments are based on products and services and include: power generation, power transmission, power distribution, oil and gas, automation, and industrial products and contracting. The group also has an independent financial services function which forms the seventh segment. The heads of the individual segments come together in the global executive council or board of ABB.

Each segment has further sub-divisions or business areas. These correspond to specific products or services offered by the group internationally, for example, motors of a certain size or the construction and management of gas-fired power stations. The annual turnover of ABB is $35 billion and there are more than 30 business areas. So each business area is a substantial enterprise in its own right. Each business area manager, who is normally based in group headquarters in Zurich, has a global perspective. He or she travels extensively to monitor progress internationally. Business area products and services are sold in many markets worldwide. The second axis of the ABB matrix is the scope of the country manager. Country managers have day-to-day responsibility for the ABB companies in their territories and they liaise with managing directors to set turnover and profit targets.

ABB's policy of thinking globally and acting locally is a key element of its commercial success. It means that strategy is set by current chief executive Goran Lindahl and the executive council (the segment managers plus certain large country managers). Delivery is firmly in the hands of local operating companies. This management style – of devolving decision making to lowest effective level – creates adept and able managers throughout the organization. It also means that individuals become real managers often at an age that less confident companies would consider impractical. ABB's growth in the UK during the last decade from £100 million to £2 billion in annual turnover is testimony to its belief in its managers and its willingness to let them achieve.

The Barnevik philosophy of devolving authority and responsibility, and keeping close to the customer, means that ABB profit centres normally do not exceed 300 people. Managers are responsible for and benefit from their commercial results. There is an absolute minimum of bureaucracy. The UK headquarters employs only 17 people to look after the needs of 13,000 employees. Business units, therefore, have the freedom and motivation to run their own affairs.

One defining characteristic of ABB is its constant success in process and product improvement. An emphasis on productivity and high technology makes for a stimulating and active culture where rewards for success are very high and a talent for competitiveness is valued. To maintain its critical edge over competitors, ABB invests heavily in the development of its people and offers them an opportunity to participate in real decision making from the outset.

How does ABB rate?

Pay:	very good
Benefits:	very good
Communications:	very good
Training:	excellent
Career development:	excellent
Morale:	excellent

People and personnel policies

For ABB, if empowerment is to be successful for the company and the employee, then both individual and team development must each play a role. At the core of this is ABB's benchmark training agenda. Training is business-sector driven and extensive, focusing primarily on an individual employee's knowledge of technology and its application within the team. The training approach for each employee is tailored by his or her operating company, although where appropriate the business area or country management can take a lead, particularly in senior management development or succession planning. The UK operates a senior programme through Henley Management College which fits with more advanced programmes run by the global management team in Zurich.

The group in the UK does not run a central graduate recruitment, but many of the larger operating companies attend career fairs at universities and seek to attract graduating students. ABB Ltd, however, does monitor potential high fliers.

Remuneration is primarily the responsibility of the country head. However, in the UK, the general policy is that salary should be set at the median level, with incentive payments based on performance increasing total remuneration to the upper quartile. Similarly to many other leading companies, ABB is moving to a structure where incentive payments for good performance are increasingly important and typically in some companies all employees are part of a business-wide incentive scheme. In the UK, the company has an excellent pension plan.

Like many engineering companies, ABB has a paucity of women at senior levels. Most of its recruits tend to be men and, although many of the constituent parts of the group are tolerant of flexible working arrangements, ABB does not believe in pursuing a policy of positive discrimination. Racially, however, the group is much more diverse. This is due not least to its somewhat complex ownership structure, which means that ABB is not particularly identified with any one set of national characteristics.

The UK group head office does not recruit graduates. All employment applications need to be made to the specific ABB operating company.

Contact address

Ian Donald
Group Human Resources Manager
ABB Ltd
Orion House
5 Upper St Martin's Lane
London WC2H 9EA.
Telephone: 0171 753 2000
Fax: 0171 753 0205
Web site: http://www.abb.co.uk

Abbey National

Abbey National plc is a key player in the UK personal financial services industry. The business encompasses a wide range of traditional and non-traditional areas of the industry from savings and retail banking to joint ventures and wealth management. One of the best-known names in the industry, Abbey National has always shown concern for the welfare and development of both its employees and clients and is committed to involving employees as financial stakeholders. The company achieves its stated corporate purpose, of above-average growth in shareholder value over the long term, by meeting the needs of its customers, employees and other stakeholders in its business. It has outstanding equal opportunities policies. Seventy-five per cent of its workforce and 55 per cent of its managers are female.

Abbey National at a glance

Employees: 28,000
Annual staff attrition: n/a
Key locations: London (HQ), branches throughout the UK
Annual graduate intake: 100
Annual intake: 3,000

An inside view

Historically, Abbey National focused on mortgage and savings activities but in recent times has diversified into areas such as Finance House, General Insurance, Life Assurance, Treasury and Offshore and Wealth Management. The company upholds strong management of and control over risks and secures and maintains competitive advantage through superior customer service, particularly in the retail business. Remaining a low cost operator is important to Abbey National as is preserving and continuously enhancing its strong brand name in the market place. Many are familiar with the Abbey National 'Because Life's Complicated Enough . . .' advertising campaign, which reinforces its policy that customers' needs always come first. Overseas operations are relatively small, with branches in France, Italy and Spain.

Abbey National is a major UK provider of mortgage and savings deposit products, current account banking, short-term and long-term protection insurance and investment offerings. The UK Retail Banking division is increasingly broadening the range of services offered to customers in order to diversify profits away from traditional sources. The savings division benefited from the launch of the highly competitive Bonus Postal Account, which has taken over £4 billion of funds, and the Group now has the second largest remote ATM network in the UK. The current focus is to encourage more customers to make greater use of self-service facilities for simple transactions, thus leaving employees free to provide added value service face-to-face.

By the end of 1997 nearly half of Abbey National's pre-tax profit, excluding exceptional items, derived from non-traditional areas. Acquisitions are crucial to the diversification process and the latest purchase of Cater Allen Holdings Plc, a wholesale banking group with offshore and onshore retail businesses, has strengthened Abbey National's position in offshore and private banking. Key joint ventures and partnerships also consolidate the company's stature in the industry. A general insurance joint venture with Commercial Union and a recent private medical insurance joint venture with Norwich Union increase the proportion of non-mortgage related revenue. Scottish Mutual and Abbey National Life provide life assurance and pensions. Their ability to grow organically is demonstrated by the growth of funds under management, which recently exceeded £10 billion. Abbey National is the sixth largest unit trust provider by PEP fund value.

In a constantly changing industry, Abbey National has acquired a reputation for flexibility in its outlook and policies. Abbey National was the first to introduce Performance Related Pay in the UK. The company recognizes the importance of the ability to adapt in a marketplace, which is the subject of ever increasing regulation. Its innovative approach has set trends amongst the competition. Abbey National competes in an industry where customer care is a high priority and has nurtured an environment that satisfies the needs of both clients and employees.

Abbey National recruits 3,000 employees each year. In pursuance of its policy of diversity, the annual recruitment intake includes 100 graduates of a variety of subjects for the graduate trainee scheme. A significant proportion of the annual intake is engaged in the area of information technology for which A-level qualifications are needed. Flexibility is an important attribute and Abbey National looks for people who are able to respond well to change and are willing to undertake the challenge of movement within the company.

How does Abbey National rate?

Pay:	good
Benefits:	good
Communications:	very good
Training:	very good
Career development:	very good
Morale:	good

People and personnel policies

Industry regulations demand a certain level of training and qualification of employees and in addition to the graduate trainee scheme, various in-house and outside courses are provided as well as distance learning. The company has a bespoke training centre in North London and further education continues throughout the career of employees. As aspects of the industry change, employees receive frequent training on new products and new processes. Management development is targeted, and specifically designed for the individual.

Remuneration is linked closely to performance development and constitutes an important part of company management. Abbey National strives to identify the market rate for jobs but as the company diversifies it becomes increasingly difficult to define a typical salary. The salary benchmark is the median for the industry, and depends in which area of the business the employee works. The three main salary determinants are comparison to market rate, performance, and available budget. Abbey National operates a profit share scheme throughout the company and various bonus schemes appropriate to individual parts of the business. The objective of remuneration is to put cash into the employee's hands. To align the interests of shareholders and staff, Abbey National is keen on increasing employee share ownership.

There is great opportunity for movement within Abbey National – all positions are advertised and the company believes in moving people up the ladder quickly, if talent is evident. The company is keen to place graduates in a prestigious job as soon as possible. The relatively young workforce lends itself to mobility within the company and the number of jobs available has expanded since conversion from a building society. An appraisal of every employee is performed annually and compared with pre-determined objectives. Salary awards are made in accordance with the results of the annual appraisal.

Abbey National is proud of its strong commitment to diversity and takes part in the Equal Choices Schools Initiative, which aims to broaden the career aspirations of ethnic minority students. This innovative initiative, which operates in partnership with three other Milton Keynes-based employers, won the silver medal in 1997 for the British Diversity Awards. As a user of the Department of Employment Service 'Positive about Disabled People' symbol, Abbey National continues to encourage applications from people with disabilities and takes all practical measures to assist in the recruitment, retention and career development of disabled people. Over 55 per cent of managers are women, and there is a maternity leaver's bonus to inspire women to return to work at Abbey National. Flexible working arrangements are easily accommodated.

Contact address

John King
HR Director
Abbey National plc
Abbey House
201 Grafton Gate East
Milton Keynes MK9 1AN
Telephone: 0870 607 6000
Fax: 01908 343 687
Web site: http://www.abbeynational.co.uk

Air Products plc

Air Products plc is part of a global manufacturer of industrial gases, speciality chemicals and equipment, with operations in more than 30 countries. Throughout the world people unknowingly use products in their daily lives which have been made with the aid of industrial gases like those manufactured by Air Products plc, such as alarm clocks, food products, pharmaceuticals, calculators and glassware. Air Products plc sees a direct link between the wellbeing of individuals and the wellbeing of the company, demonstrating its commitment to its employees by winning the Human Resources Contribution to Employee Wellbeing Award in the Human Resources Excellence Awards in 1998.

Air Products plc at a glance

Employees: 16,000 worldwide, 2,000 UK
Annual staff attrition: 10 per cent
Key locations: offices in 13 European countries including head office at Walton-on-Thames, Surrey, European R&D at the European Technology Centre, Basinstoke, Hampshire and chemicals manufacturing sites in Teesside and Manchester
Annual graduate intake: 25
Annual intake: 200

An inside view

Founded in Detroit, Michigan, USA in 1940, Air Products plc established operations in Europe in 1957. The company manufactures and supplies industrial gases and chemicals, cryogenic and non-cryogenic process plant and services to markets worldwide. With an annual turnover of $4.6 billion worldwide, Air Products plc is the fourth largest gas supplier and one of the leading suppliers of chemicals in the world.

It supplies a broad range of gases – primarily oxygen, nitrogen, argon, hydrogen, carbon monoxide and helium – and related production services and equipment to a diverse range of industries including the chemical and refining, oil/gas production and recovery, food and metals processing, semiconductor manufacture, healthcare, aerospace, pulp and paper, as well as chemicals to customers in the adhesives, agriculture, furniture, automotive products, paints and coatings, textiles, paper and building products industries. Air Products plc is the world leader in the supply of helium and hydrogen and in advanced technology for food freezing applications as well as being the number one supplier of gases to the European electronics industry.

Air Products plc believes that ensuring the wellbeing of employees, customers, shareholders, suppliers and communities is fundamental to its success and prosperity. It manages remarkably well to combine these, perhaps conflicting, interests, with the needs of the company. Alan Carver, human resources director of Air Products plc, stated when receiving the Human Resources Contribution to Employee Wellbeing Award, 'You can only be the first choice of customers if you're able to demonstrate that you're the first choice for employees, too.' The enduring nature of Air Products plc's commercial relationships, the unusually large number of long-term shareholders and the retention of many employees for their entire careers, demonstrates that the company has gained the trust of those inside and outside the company.

The company carries out its activities ethically and with integrity. Given the potentially hazardous nature of the company's products, it is particularly significant that Air Products plc enjoys a well-deserved reputation as an industry leader in safety. The company attributes its achievements to the fact that it has built its health, safety and environmental objectives into its culture. Air Products plc is committed to open and honest communication at all levels as a way of promoting high-quality performance as well as making the workplace more pleasant.

How does Air Products plc rate?

Pay:	good
Benefits:	superb
Communications:	very good
Training:	good
Career development:	very good
Morale:	excellent

People and personnel policies

Air Products plc's employee development programme forms a direct link between individual and business goals. It is seen as a partnership between employees and managers in that training enables people to further their own career goals at the same time as increasing their contribution to Air Products plc. The identification of training needs is an integral part of the annual performance planning review.

Most training is job specific and takes place on the job. Training courses are provided in-house or by external agencies and are divided broadly into two categories: modules for core skills, such as communication or presentation skills, and company programmes designed to support particular business objectives and aimed at specific groups. Air Products plc's leadership education initiative is designed to create an atmosphere where all employees can contribute and develop to their full potential, building an organization that can thrive in a competitive marketplace increasingly characterized by change.

Employees are encouraged to take responsibility for their career development, with Air Products plc demonstrating its own commitment by assessing and rewarding managers, in part, on how well they support individuals' career planning and development initiatives. The annual performance planning review plays a key part in assessing an employee's achievements, in setting business objectives and dealing with training and career development issues. Through a number of processes, such as the 360 degree feedback review, Air Products plc also assesses employees' skills against a range of competency profiles, including leadership, marketing, engineering and finance.

Air Products plc has identified four key competencies which occur in all types of work. These are the ability to build relationships, a drive for results, innovation and being able to influence others. Air Products plc expects people to change and grow during their careers with the company and provides opportunities for excellent people to grow and be successful wherever they choose.

Air Products plc rewards its employees with a competitive remuneration package together with a superb range of other benefits and schemes including fitness programmes, safety schemes and health policies. The Human Resources Contribution to Employee Wellbeing Award in the Human Resources Excellence Awards in May 1998 recognized that Air Products plc's investment in the wellbeing of its staff exceeds that of major competitors, even though the company is one of the youngest in its field.

Air Products plc has impressive facilities and services including an occupational health centre, with rehabilitation facilities, and an extensive on-site fitness centre where staff can take part in fitness programmes such as lifestyle and health assessments. Yoga is a recent addition – and, following employee surveys, the fitness centre has plans to introduce beauty treatments and assorted therapies, such as massage, physiotherapy and reflexology. The company also has its own sports and social club where employees can relax, socialize and organize out of work activities including team sports and weekend trips.

Air Products plc truly believes that everyone can contribute to, and be part of, the success of the company and makes this clear in practical ways through its policies towards employees. The company offers flexible contracts for fixed-term and part-time workers, home working and flexible retirements, where retired staff are used for training and outsourcing from time to time. These are the sort of policies which make Air Products plc attractive to women and, indeed, anyone with family commitments, as well as older people. Air Products plc is equally positive in its policies towards the disabled. With operations worldwide, the company is culturally and racially diverse and the ability to move from country to country can be a definite advantage to an individual's career prospects.

Contact address

Human Resources Department
Air Products plc
Hersham Place
Molesey Road
Walton-on-Thames
Surrey KT12 4RZ
Telephone: 01932 249200
Fax: 01932 249565
Web site: http://www.airproducts.com

Allied Irish Bank

Allied Irish Bank (AIB) is Ireland's largest commercial bank. It opened its retail network in Britain in 1970 to serve the needs of the Irish Diaspora but in recent years has become acknowledged as a leader in innovative practice and AIB has established a niche position in the owner-managed businesses market. It has three times won the award for the Best Business Bank from the Forum of Private Business, the latest occasion being 1998. AIB has had a presence in London since 1825 and it has the largest branch network of any non-UK owned banking group. In 1997 the Group reported profits of I£580 million. Some 24 per cent of these profits were made in the UK.

Allied Irish Bank at a glance

Employees: 23,000 worldwide, 1,100 UK
Annual staff attrition: 8 per cent
Key locations: Greater London, M25 ring and major population centres in the Midlands, North and Scotland. Some 35 branches in Great Britain plus 77 in Northern Ireland as First Trust Bank
Annual graduate intake: 25
Annual intake: 100

An inside view

The owners and managers of small and growing businesses are famously critical of their banks. Any survey among directors of small to medium-sized enterprises (SMEs) shows widespread discontent about attitudes of managers and staff, understanding of small business issues and quality of customer service. Yet there is one bank which stands head and shoulders above the pack in terms of the dialogue with customers. The Allied Irish Bank consistently wins prizes from the SME community for its willingness to listen and act upon customer demand. It is a shrewdly managed operation which demonstrates a remarkable capacity to achieve profitability while, at the same time, being popular with its customers.

In 1994, 1996 and 1998, it collected the prestigious Forum of Private Business award for the Best Business Bank. Considering that the award is made only every two years, AIB has dominated the selection for the better part of a decade. Stan Mendham, chief executive of the Forum, said at the time of the latest award, 'AIB is able to deliver in areas that are important to small business. It has shorter lines of communication, can move faster and is better able to detect businesses in trouble at an earlier stage.'

The award is made after a comprehensive survey of the small business market in terms of attitude to bankers. In the latest analysis, AIB was substantially ahead of its rivals in knowledge and understanding of the market, appreciation of the dynamics of individual businesses, efficiency, quality of the product and pricing. Notably, AIB scored twice as high as its nearest competitor on the ranking for 'My bank manager inspires confidence'. Only 16 per cent of the sample had cause to complain about AIB services whereas the average among larger banks was about 30 per cent.

AIB is a part of the AIB Group, which is based in Ballsbridge, Dublin. AIB is Ireland's largest private sector employer and is a key force in the Irish economy with branches of the bank in most towns and cities across the Republic. It has a market capitalization, at time of writing, of I£10 billion. AIB Group is listed in Dublin and London, and its shares are traded on the New York Stock Exchange. AIB has assets of I£40 billion, 900 branches and 23,000 staff worldwide. Its principal markets are Ireland, the UK, United States, Central Europe and Asia.

Its 1997 financial results show that AIB Group made pretax profits of I£580 million. Around 40 per cent of this profit was made in the Republic, 30 per cent in the US, 24 per cent in the UK and six per cent elsewhere. AIB Group operates through three major divisions: AIB Bank, AIB Capital Markets and USA Division. AIB Bank operates 317 locations in the Irish Republic and 77 branches in Ulster. It has 35 branches in Britain plus activities in the Channel Isles and the Isle of Man. In Ireland it trades as AIB Bank, in Northern Ireland as First Trust Bank and in Great Britain as Allied Irish Bank (GB). In total the division has 9,500 employees.

The British operation covers England, Wales and Scotland. AIB offers day-to-day banking facilities, money transmission, international trade services, corporate treasury, asset finance and investment banking. Private banking facilities are also available. The character of AIB is defined by a high degree of autonomy for local branches. AIB argues that its managers and staff have much greater freedom on lending and customer account management than any of its principal rivals. Also it prides itself on speedy decision making on complex customer problems. Allied Irish achieved the Investors in People Award in 1995. IIP's assessors concluded that 'Allied Irish's corporate strategy is based on excellence of service, integrity and professionalism, and these are values around which it plans and runs the business.'

How does Allied Irish rate?

Pay:	good
Benefits:	very good
Communications:	very good
Training:	excellent
Career development:	very good
Morale:	very good

People and personnel policies

'We are a niche business supplying bespoke full service banking to a market which is predominantly owner-managed businesses,' says John Kilty, Head of Business

Marketing in Great Britain. 'We operate from a national network of 35 specialist branches. Our primary locations are Greater London and the M25 ring moving up through the major population centres in the Midlands and North. We also have branches in Edinburgh and Glasgow.'

AIB in Britain has a very low attrition rate and as a consequence its annual intake is comparatively small at around 100. About 25 of the 100 are graduates but there is no active graduate recruitment programme because AIB does not need one. Some of its specialists will come in any event from Ireland and it will actively seek people from other leading financial institutions to fulfil particular roles. This means that AIB can be extremely selective about the new people which it draws in.

Kilty says that AIB has a defined cultural personality which attracts certain types of individuals. 'We are looking for a high degree of commerciality and developed people management skills. We would value those skills more than the simple ability to crunch numbers. Some people come in as graduates, others are recruited post-A levels, others are experienced professionals. Some go directly to branches to develop first-hand retail banking experience, others will be assigned to specialist support units. There is a well-structured induction pack and programme which is designed to help them understand and get to know the organization. Each new recruit receives, on the day he or she joins, a very clear job description.'

Allied Irish is justifiably proud of its achievements in training. It is widely regarded in the banking sector for the quality of its training approach. 'It is a combination of on-the-job training and in-house training courses. Our on-the-job training features skill enhancement from a basic level upwards. These processes will lead to outside verification such as NVQs. We also have a calendar of courses called The Learning Curve. These are circulated annually in advance and individual staff members can apply to join specific courses. Each individual will examine The Learning Curve calendar and plan – in association with the line manager – attendance on relevant courses.'

Since AIB focuses heavily on customer service, it tracks the performance of branches and individuals on several customer service performance criteria. It encourages feedback from customers in this process. The results of performance are discussed with the branches and employees and they are are used to shape objectives and development training.

Contact address

Simon Boulcott
HR Manager
Allied Irish Bank (GB)
Bankcentre – Britain
Belmont Road
Uxbridge
Middlesex UB8 1SA
Telephone: 01895 272222
Fax: 01895 238600
Web site: http:///www.aib.ie

Andersen Consulting

Andersen Consulting is the world's largest business and technology consultancy. In recent years, it has been growing at an annual rate of 20 per cent and has established an enviable reputation for professionalism among clients and rivals alike. Whether at graduate or more experienced levels, the company prides itself on recruiting the best and the brightest talent available and providing them with a challenging environment to develop their skills. Andersen offers unrivalled training and development prospects for those seeking a career in management consultancy.

Andersen Consulting at a glance

Employees: 65,000 worldwide
Annual staff attrition: 12 per cent
Key locations: offices throughout the UK and worldwide
Annual graduate intake: 300
Annual intake: 700

An inside view

Andersen Consulting is commonly acknowledged to be one of the most successful management consultancies in the world. Growing at more than 20 per cent a year, it has consistently increased its share of the fast-growing and lucrative consultancy market. It is currently structured into five business competencies – strategy, technology, change management, process and practice management – and is built around an ethos of providing the very highest level of client service. More recently, it has been particularly successful in winning outsourcing contracts, whereby it takes wide-ranging responsibility for the operation and management of client systems and facilities.

Notwithstanding its rapid rate of growth, management consultancy is a highly competitive industry and Andersen Consulting recognizes that it needs to constantly stay ahead of its rivals. One of the key ways in which it does this is through recruiting and retaining the best available staff. Increasingly, the company is looking to recruit experienced staff with particular industry expertise, although graduates still constitute the majority of recruitment.

For all employees, intellectual capacity is clearly a key consideration in selection. However, Andersen Consulting also places considerable emphasis on a candidate's interpersonal skills and, in particular, his or her ability to work within teams. It is looking for people with a demonstrable record of achievement – 'doers' rather than 'talkers' – capable of showing initiative and enterprise, and able to carry their colleagues with them.

Inevitably, for a business so often involved in managing the business of change, Andersen Consulting is itself a fast-moving environment, with client assignments and priorities changing at short notice. This may frequently involve staff being assigned to new clients in out-of-town locations, perhaps overseas. Adaptability, flexibility and the capacity to learn quickly are all key attributes which Andersen Consulting seeks in its staff, particularly in the early years of their careers.

Rivals of the business like to characterize Andersen as a somewhat ruthless organization. Andersen concedes that staff tend to be very highly motivated, but argues that this is a function of client requirements. It is actually no different from most other professional service firms in this respect, although possibly more open about it. Furthermore, recognizing that its employees work in a demanding environment, Andersen Consulting is keen to be as supportive as possible. Accordingly, it has developed a series of initiatives such as its Help Desk (which can organize various household tasks such as house-sitting and shopping) and in-house travel service to make life easier for its employees. Nonetheless, it should be noted that the atmosphere at Andersen Consulting may not be to everyone's taste.

How does Andersen Consulting rate?

Pay:	good
Benefits:	good
Communications:	good
Training:	very good
Career development:	excellent
Morale:	good

People and personnel policies

One of the key ways in which Andersen Consulting strives to maintain its edge over its rivals is through its training policy. The company has a world-famous training centre in Chicago, to which virtually all recruits are sent on an induction course, and these are supported by other training centres in London and Eindhoven. At higher levels, training courses are specially structured and all professional staff have a specially devised training plan throughout their time at the company. Andersen Consulting invests very heavily in training and it forms a central part of an employee's development.

Continuous development is very much part of the culture at Andersen Consulting and the company believes that its success in this field is one of the main reasons for high staff retention rate, particularly at a time when staff turnover in the industry is running at record levels. All professional staff have regular quarterly reviews where they are assessed against agreed criteria.

All employees have a career counsellor assigned to them from their first day in the organization. It is their responsibility to ensure that employees remain on track in terms of career development

Andersen Consulting has also developed a network of 'communities'. The purpose of a community, is to develop a feeling of belonging for its staff. Regular get-togethers are organized to allow staff to network with others in different parts of the firm and share experiences.

Not surprisingly, Andersen Consulting is prepared to pay well in order to recruit and retain staff. Nonetheless, the company finds that it is not only financial benefits which makes the firm attractive to employees. Andersen Consulting is also keen to provide a supportive environment for all its employees – including those looking to combine work and family commitments. The firm has a generous maternity programme, childcare support and offers flexible voluntary working arrangements.

Contact address

Liz Mills
EMEA Director of Recruitment
Andersen Consulting
2 Arundel Street
London WC2R 3LT
Telephone: 0171 438 5000
Fax: 0171 831 1133
Web site: http://www.ac.com

ASDA

ASDA has become a challenger in the fiercely competitive sphere of food retailing. Its primary achievement has been to force a fourth place at the top table of supermarket retailing, where previously there had been but three senior players. At a time when Tesco ousted Sainsbury from the UK market leadership, ASDA rivalled – and some say surpassed – Safeway for the number three spot. Energy, vision and vitality have enabled ASDA to be seen as an attractive business for up and coming managerial talent as well as employees on the shop floor. The chain was founded by a group of Yorkshire farmers in a former music hall in Leeds. A key facet of its market strategy is to offer quality products at low prices. A few years ago the company was a short step away from bankruptcy; its turnaround has been equally dramatic with a determined focus on expansion.

ASDA at a glance

Employees: 78,450
Annual staff attrition: 28 per cent
Key locations: HQ at Leeds employing 1,200 with 220 stores throughout the UK
Annual graduate intake: 50
Annual intake: 25,000

An inside view

In less than a decade the mechanics of Britain's high streets have changed irrevocably. Retailing is no longer the province of local owners and managers, but of national groups competing on thousands of product lines, represented by substantial outlets either off the high street or out of town. In days past, some 80 per cent of food retailing was done through local shops. Today the exact opposite is true – some four-fifths of food shopping nationwide is done at Tesco, Sainsbury, Safeway and ASDA. The benefit to customers has been seen in lower prices, greater range of goods, enhanced customer facilities and a series of related services such as financial products.

Commentators often say that retail – and especially supermarket retailing – is the purest form of capitalism. And all the characteristics of a vigorously competitive market are seen in the retail environment. ASDA – of all the main players – has had the toughest task in carving out an identity for itself. Tesco and Sainsbury were consistent features of the British high street for decades, Safeway a high quality US operator. Managers at ASDA have fashioned a distinctive identity that is at once a challenging, exciting and enjoyable place to work and a commercial formula which meets and exploits latent market demand.

But this dynamic success is a relatively recent phenomenon. Chairman Archie Norman put the company back on its feet in the mid-1990s. In the last edition of *The100 Best Companies To Work For In the UK* we reported an ASDA director who said 'the business was basically bust' in the early 1990s. Norman understood there is limited growth in demand. Therefore ASDA needed to be different to attract, maintain and improve market share. He reversed the trend of decades and reduced the role of the impressive head office to a support centre. Real power was devolved to the stores. Each was an autonomous profit centre where the store management was responsible for meeting targets and decision making.

This one act convinced potential recruits and analysts that ASDA meant business. The turnround has been dramatic: sales in 1998 reached £7.6 billion up from £4.8 billion in 1994 and operating profit more than doubled to £413.7 million in 1998 from £196.7 million in 1994. This is clearly a transformation. Another facet of the change was to turn ASDA into the consumer's champion. ASDA has fought for customers' rights on a panoply of issues from taxation, through Resale Price Maintenance on medicines and vitamins, to the abolition of the Net Book Agreement.

The company has embarked on its Formula for Growth, its current internal and external campaign focus. Its aim is to be Britain's best value fresh food and clothing superstore retailer. To meet this target it relentlessly seeks innovation. 'Delivering growth successfully and consistently requires focus. We focus on innovation not diversification, simplification not complication,' says chief executive Allan Leighton. Key aspects of the plan are: larger stores, its own clothing brand, and enhancing traditional craft skills in its own academy of excellence.

In the quest to be different, the stores are designed to appear distinctive. During the year to summer 1998, ASDA opened 12 new market hall superstores including five rebuilds. The hypermarkets division had 15 outlets, all with more than 50,000 square feet, in summer 1998 and expected to build more as the year progressed. Sales in the hypermarkets have grown 34 per cent over the 12 months to mid-year 1998. Demanding performance criteria have been set for new stores. The average post tax cashflow, for example, is more than 16 per cent. To achieve performance targets in new stores, ASDA is working with a team of design and build contractors. So far this has enabled the company to cut lead times from 32 to 27 weeks.

ASDA's watchwords are pace, motivation and simplicity. These central themes are supported by a series of approaches. They are: truly different stores, up to ten per cent better value, stunning fresh food delivered by craftsmen, an unmatchable mix of goods, serious clothing offers, all backed by selling and service with verve and personality.

How does ASDA rate ?

Pay:	fair
Benefits:	good
Communications:	excellent
Training:	excellent
Career development:	very good
Morale:	excellent

People and personnel policies

In the early years of the ASDA recovery, the company recruited predominately from outside. This was necessary to bring in flexible and talented people to rebuild the company. Now it is principally concerned with growing its own. Norman says 'It is immensely important to us that we can grow our own people from within. ASDA people committed to our business and the ASDA Way of Working. We have established our colleague culture based on the belief that recruiting the right people and motivating them well is the prerequisite to good customer service.'

In the ASDA annual review Norman says that by all serious measures of attitude and commitment to the business, ASDA employees each year outperform their previous year's best. 'We believe in real colleague stakeholding. More than 42,000 ASDA colleagues hold share options as part of our Colleague Share Option Plan. The first 26,000 received their shares in July 1998.' The company believes that employee ownership creates a level of commitment to ASDA which rarely exists without a shareholding.

Supermarkets generally have a high annual turnover of staff. ASDA prides itself on the fact that its attrition rate is 12 per cent better than those of the company's main rivals. An average of 450 work in each store and the plan is to extend that overall capability by ten a year. The management structure is founded on individual and group tiers of responsibility with retail managing directors each taking the reins of overseeing up to 38 stores.

ASDA develops its own talent from within the business. And in theory anyone who joins the company at whatever level can end up in the boardroom. But the annual graduate intake is on a fast track to promotion, and the company picks the cream of an average of 2,500 applicants for the few places available. The thrust of the HR policy is of necessity directed at female workers who make up 80 per cent of the workforce. Most of those are part-time, balancing their lives between store and family, and ASDA has enshrined a flexible working policy directed towards part-timers. There is a flexible shift swap system because, as Smith insists, 'We try to make our system work for the people who work with us.'

Contact address

David Smith
Retail Personnel Director
ASDA
ASDA House
Southbank
Great Wilson Street
Leeds LS11 5AD
Telephone: 0113 243 5435
Fax: 0113 241 7634
Web site: http://www.asda.cu.uk

BAA plc

BAA is the world's largest commercial operator of airports. It owns and operates seven UK airports, which handle 70 per cent of UK air passenger traffic and 82 per cent of air cargo including Heathrow, the world's busiest international airport. It also manages four overseas airports and serves 104 million passengers in the UK and 25 million overseas. The company has diversified from its core business into retailing (mainly duty free), rail transport (the Heathrow Express) and property management and development. The group's employment policies are adapted to meet local requirements and to take account of best practices in the countries in which the group operates. They are designed to promote the group as 'preferred employer' and enable it to attract and retain high quality employees from the diverse communities in which it operates.

BAA at a glance

Employees: 12,300
Annual staff attrition: n/a
Key locations: Heathrow, Gatwick, Stansted, Glasgow, Edinburgh, Aberdeen and Southampton in the UK. Melbourne/Launceston, Newark, Pittsburgh, Indianapolis, Harrisburg and Naples overseas. Corporate HQ in central London
Annual graduate intake: n/a
Annual intake: n/a

An inside view

BAA (formerly British Airports Authority) was privatized in 1987 and has become the largest commercial airport operator in the world. The majority of sales – 52 per cent – derives from retailing, mainly duty free goods, throughout the world. The group has 200 duty free shops in the UK and USA as well as the newly acquired World Duty Free Inflight, the world's leading concessionaire for the sale of duty free goods on board aircraft. BAA also financed, built and operates the £450m Heathrow Express, which provides a high speed train service from Paddington in the centre of London to Heathrow airport. It is one of the UK's largest private sector infrastructure projects.

BAA's property and related activities (including baggage handling) generate 14.7 per cent of total revenues. Its aim is to develop more and better space for customers and commercial properties on or near airports, which are not an integral part of airport sites.

The dynamic growth of the company since privatization is attributed to the leadership of Sir John Egan, the chief executive appointed in 1990. Since his appointment annual sales have increased from £746m to £1,679m. The latest annual report indicates another highly successful year for the business. A fundamental priority of the business is airport safety and security. One third of all BAA employees work in security, mainly screening passengers and hand baggage. £175m has been invested in the world's most advanced screening technology for handling hold baggage.

A key issue for the company continues to be an additional terminal at Heathrow. BAA stated in its case to a public inquiry that there is no alternative to Terminal 5 if airline and passenger demand and expectations are to be met. A Government decision is expected in the year 2001. If approved, a five-year building programme to the opening of phase 1 will follow.

The mission statement of BAA continues to be to make BAA the most successful airport company in the world by focusing on customers' needs and safety, achieving continuous improvements in costs and services and enabling employees to give of their best. The company continues to make progress in the environmental sphere. In February 1999 it was commended for its site reports in the 1998 ACCA Environmental Reporting Awards.

How does BAA rate?

Pay:	good
Benefits:	good
Communications:	very good
Training:	very good
Career development:	very good
Morale:	good

People and personnel policies

BAA seeks to create an environment which enables employees to give of their best. A good and safe working environment is provided to attract and retain committed employees. Training and two-way communications allows employees to fulfill their potential and contribute directly to the success of the company.

A high priority is the provision of adequate training and development facilities and opportunities to enable all employees to maximize their contribution to the business and achieve their ambitions within the group. The company estimates that five per cent of its payroll costs are invested in staff training. The group has recently reviewed its equal opportunities policy and reinforced its commitment to providing equality of opportunity, free from unfair discrimination and harassment.

Employee commitment to the improvement of business processes and to innovation continues to be seen as a priority by the company. The development of the innovative 'Freedom to Manage' programme increases the involvement of employees in decisions within their workplace to improve efficiency and customer service.

The group has comprehensive arrangements for providing employees with information on matters affecting them and financial and economic factors affecting the performance of the company. Regular roadshows presented by senior management are held as forums for communication with employees.

Remuneration levels within the group are very competitive in relation to job equivalents in other leading companies in similar locations. A fairly standard range of benefits is provided for employees and all members of the workforce participate in annual bonus schemes.

The company actively encourages employees to participate in the success of the business by means of Inland Revenue-approved share save and share option schemes. It estimates that 90 per cent of its employees own shares in BAA.

BAA is very conscious of its environmental responsibilities and a special board committee deals with safety, security and the environment. BAA acknowledges the concerns of its local community neighbours, sets itself targets and institutes audits against these targets. There is a fine balance between its aim of providing passengers with the best and most efficient service and the effects on local communities of noise, pollution and traffic congestion. BAA is fully committed to meeting in full all legal and regulatory requirements, acts resolutely to minimize environmental impacts and acts positively as a good corporate citizen in the wider community. BAA circulated, with its annual report, an additional Environment and Community report entitled 'Managing Responsibility . . . our contract with the community'. The report charts BAA's progress in putting its principles into practice and its performance as a corporate citizen.

The public inquiry into the proposed Terminal 5 at Heathrow will be a very open review of policies and practices and the company's ability to increase capacity of the overstretched facilities at Heathrow. There is a fine and delicate balance between the need to provide a comprehensive and efficient service for an ever-increasing number of passengers and the environmental and infrastructure rights of the large local communities which surround Heathrow.

Contact address

Group HR Director
BAA plc
130 Wilton Road
London SW1V 1LQ
Telephone: 0171 834 9449
Fax: 0171 932 6699
Web site: http://www.baa.co.uk

Bass plc

Bass is a leading international hospitality and leisure group, operating in the hotels, leisure retailing and branded drinks industries. The constituent parts of Bass and its subsidiaries are the result of the amalgamation of more than 80 companies over 200 years. Founded in Burton upon Trent in 1777, it is now a £5 billion-plus business operating on the world stage. People in more than 90 countries enjoy Bass products and the group operates more than 450,000 hotel rooms in every corner of the globe. Bass can offer a wide variety of stimulating and rewarding careers for those who identify with the company and who can add value.

Bass at a glance

Employees: 80,500 worldwide
Annual staff attrition: 20 per cent
Key locations: London (HQ) and various locations around the UK, Atlanta, Brussels
Annual graduate intake: 200 (35–40 on graduate programmes)
Annual intake: 5,000

An inside view

Bass is one of the top FTSE 100 public limited companies in the UK. Traditionally, the name Bass was closely associated with beer and pubs, but in the last two decades a new and diverse Bass has emerged. It now operates in three distinct business areas: hotels, through the franchising, ownership, management and leasing of hotels and resorts; leisure retail, through the management and ownership of public houses and restaurants, bars, venues and entertainment centres; and branded drinks, through the production and marketing of alcoholic and soft drinks. In a people-oriented business, Bass invests heavily in the development and welfare of its employees.

Bass Hotel and Resorts is the Group's hotel division, based in Atlanta, Georgia, USA. It operates or franchises more than 2,700 hotels, with more than 450,000 guest rooms in more than 90 countries. Approximately 80 per cent of the hotels are located in the US and are mostly branded as Holiday Inn and Crowne Plaza Hotels and Resorts among others. The Bass Leisure Retail division is responsible for the 2,500 pubs, bars, restaurants and venues owned and managed by the Group. These include Harvester Restaurants, O'Neill's Irish Bars, All Bar One and Dave and Buster's entertainment venues.

For more than 30 years, Bass has been at the forefront of the UK brewing industry.

Its principal brands are Carling, the most popular beer in Britain with sales of 870 million pints in 1997, Caffrey's, Tennent's and Worthington. Bass owns and operates eight breweries in the UK. Bass also manages Britvic Soft Drinks, the second largest producer of soft drinks in the UK. Its brands include Tango and Robinson's and it has the exclusive right to package and sell the Pepsico brands.

The Bass culture is based on experience and excitement. Life at Bass is about having the expertise, energy and imagination to turn new ideas into great customer experiences. But it is also about creating interesting career experiences for employees. 'Delivering experience' can be said to be the group's philosophy and the training programme is designed to be flexible to deliver against an individual's requirements. It is a vibrant work environment with stimulating daily challenges and the anticipation that each day is never routine.

The company is one of the top FTSE employers in the UK with 80,000 people worldwide. When recruiting, Bass looks for initiative, intelligence and commitment to the company and its customers. Employees must have the determination to meet the challenges posed by the business, the intelligence to thrive in an ever-evolving business environment and the ability to balance day-to-day managerial responsibilities and advanced business learning. Bass is in the 'enjoyment' business so it seeks people who are young and dynamic, with energy, vision, fresh thinking and the ability to easily establish a rapport with those around them.

How does Bass rate?

Pay:	very good
Benefits:	very good
Communications:	excellent
Training:	very good
Career development:	excellent
Morale:	very good

People and personnel policies

The training programme for graduate recruits is structured but flexible to an individual's requirements. From day one and throughout the time spent on the programme, newcomers work in a real commercial job with demanding, practical challenges. Working development is measured by regular performance reviews. On- and off-job training relevant to the graduate's position is a continuing feature of working life. It will focus on such areas as critical work processes, quality improvement, problem solving and project management.

By year three, an employee is likely to have progressed to a substantial management role in his or her chosen function. If nominated and supported by excellent performance results, the individual may follow a tailored Diploma in Management Studies (DMS) course. Specific to Bass, this offers the chance to explore thinking and practice in areas Bass particularly wishes to develop, such as international branding and customer service.

Depending on performance and career ambitions, employees can experience different jobs throughout the company as

Bass aims to have a high percentage of employees coming through the organization to fill senior management roles. Increasingly, there is potential for international moves. Development can also continue through further academic studies of a Bass-specific MBA. Participation is again performance-related and focuses on key issues such as M+A, globalization and innovation.

The management philosophy of such a vast corporation emphasizes devolution of power to the management division of each company. The Bass board determines the outline operational structure and financial target for subsidiary management to implement. Beyond that, company directors are able to determine the principles and direction of their specific business. The group maintains that giving responsibility to those in senior positions produces better results, because employees feel they are playing an active part in the development of the company.

Bass considers internal communications to be essential to effective business management. The internal communication system allows employees to give feedback and receive up-to-date company news. Group-wide frameworks are in place for communicating on corporate issues, and local information and consultation procedures meet the needs of each division. For example, an electronic suggestion box is posted on the group-wide service, inviting innovative ideas from within the company, and a corporate video is produced regularly and made available to the entire workforce.

Contact address

Graduate Recruitment
Bass plc
PO Box 31
Richmond
Surrey
TW9 2FB
Telephone: 0171 409 1919
Fax: 0171 409 8503
Web site: http://www.bass.com

Bettys and Taylors of Harrogate

Awarded two of the Tea Council's 'Awards of Excellence' in 1996 (the Oscars of the tea world) for its tearooms in Harrogate and Ilkley, Bettys is truly a grand day out for any beverage connoisseur or gastronome. People travel from all over the world to Harrogate, not to take the waters, but to visit one of the best café-tearooms in the world. Behind a Victorian façade of glass and hanging baskets there is a traditional English tearoom which is also totally European. The secret of this family-run company's success is its commitment to the highest standards of service and quality that were brought to England from Switzerland in the early 1900s by founder Frederick Belmont. His family have continued the tradition ever since.

Bettys and Taylors at a glance

Employees: 640
Annual staff attrition: 10 per cent
Key locations: Harrogate, York, Ilkley and Northallerton
Annual graduate intake: six or more
Annual intake: 60

An inside view

The Swiss confectioner Frederick Belmont arrived in Yorkshire by mistake after boarding the wrong train. But soon after his arrival in Bradford, he realized that the city was home to more millionaires within one square mile than anywhere else outside London. He also discovered fashionable Harrogate, opening the first Bettys Café Tea Rooms there in 1919. With gleaming silver, flowers, music and tea served to perfection, it became a safe haven for townswomen who were limited in where they could respectably and comfortably meet.

Today, Bettys offers the same splendour and respectability. The merger between Yorkshire-but-Swiss Bettys Café Tea Rooms and another Yorkshire institution, Taylors of Harrogate, tea and coffee merchants, has created a £45 million business which is now one of the county's main employers.

HR director Sue Symington says the culture and the business approach can be summarized simply. 'We strive continuously to be the best; we treat people as we would wish to be treated ourselves; we actively involve every single member of staff in how the business is run; and we share our success.' Above all, quality, the desire to be the best, sharing and mutual respect drives this intriguing company forward, as it has done for the past 80 years. It has a tightly controlled culture – its shared language and values are evident among staff in each of the company's tea rooms and manufacturing operations.

The company's business plan is totally integrated within the human resources plan, and vice versa. Bettys & Taylors was one of the first businesses to apply for the Investors In People (IIP) standard in 1991 which proved to be the catalyst for what has become a firm and clear management structure within the company. 'I needed the business plan to progress the IIP application,' says Symington. 'It was only when our managing director pulled it out of his desk that we both had a blinding realization that only the directors were aware of its content and objectives.'

An annual staff questionnaire gives directors a fair idea of where Bettys & Taylors' staff see strengths and weaknesses. This taken into account, the completed annual operational plan and strategic aims are displayed throughout the company. Each year is named; 1999 is the Year of the Yorkshire Rose, during which Bettys & Taylors is focusing on nurturing growth.

How does Bettys and Taylors rate?

Pay:	competitive
Benefits:	excellent
Communications:	excellent
Training:	superb
Career development:	good
Morale:	very good

People and personnel policies

Each of the company's 640 employees contributes to the business plan through a matrix of 104 teams, consisting of not more than five or six people and a leader, trained in people management skills. Everyone who joins the company, irrespective of where they will eventually work, undertakes the same training, at the same level. This includes how to handle food safely, look after themselves safely and how not be a liability to others. In addition, they are given a group induction day to understand the company as a whole. And, occasionally, groups of high flyers will be given specific training for a year or so. All training is carried out in-house with the exception of professional certification which provides the opportunity to meet colleagues in other businesses.

Each month, staff teams demonstrate – to senior management – the results of benchmarking exercises where they have compared their activities with their competitors'. Sometimes these examine new products, packaging and environments. 'There's a great sense of respect for others within our business,' Symington comments. 'There is so much to learn from other people. Our customers perceive Bettys as non-changing when, in fact, behind the scenes, it changes all the time.'

There is no formal policy regarding graduate recruitment but due to Bettys & Taylors' popularity among the Yorkshire working population, graduates will apply to Bettys & Taylors sometimes having had several years' experience already. During

1997, five management trainees were recruited, 'but it can be more if we find people who interest us.' The company involves local schools on a regular basis, being an active member of the North Yorkshire Business & Education Partnership.

Potential staff are 'those with a ready smile and a desire to please. We need people who can work hard for the company with grace and commitment.' Once on board, employees each receive their own skills training booklet and are assigned to a team. During their employment, the booklet is a record of competence in core skills for their specific job, extra training for first aid or fire officer duties, and a comprehensive tasting list – everyone is expected to know and have experience of the products produced by Bettys & Taylors. Personal appraisals are carried out quarterly and give staff the chance to discuss career progression. If new blood is needed, they may be seconded to other areas of the business. The sharing culture extends to an attractive employee bonus scheme, paid out quarterly. After 20 years, employees are provided with free health insurance. And, on top of staff restaurant facilities and discounted products, every member of staff receives a Christmas present of £100 for a personal gift for themselves.

Communications within the company are excellent. A monthly newsletter reports on events, training and 'good customer relations' and includes a back page packed with personal congratulations on births, certificates, promotions, new appointments and 'champagne moments'. Socially, staff involve themselves in fund-raising events for a specific charity democratically elected each year. In 1997, they raised £12,000 which was then matched by the directors. As one would expect in such a people conscious and locally focused firm, community relations figure highly. Among many examples is a mentoring project with local schools where pupils with learning disabilities are paired with company staff. The project encourages the children to develop valuable job skills whilst experiencing the joys of working with culinary materials. Another is the 'Trees for Life' appeal which, although launched eight years ago, is still going strong.

Contact address

Ms Susan Symington
Human Resources Director
Bettys and Taylors of Harrogate Limited
Pagoda House
Prospect Road
Harrogate
North Yorkshire HG2 7NX
Telephone: 01423 889822
Fax: 01423 881083
Web site: the company has no web site

Black & Decker

Black & Decker is a global marketer and manufacturer of products that have become famous for their quality and application in the home and factory in more than 100 countries worldwide. The company is the world's largest producer of a diverse range of power tools, power tool accessories, residential security hardware, and fastening and assembly systems. 1998 registered record sales of almost $5 billion, and is currently implementing a strategic repositioning plan to attain new levels of operating and financial performance.

Black & Decker at a glance

Employees: 4,700 Europe, 2,000 UK
Annual staff attrition: 5 per cent
Key locations: European HQ: Slough, manufacturing at Spennymoor, County Durham
Annual graduate intake: 10–20
Annual intake: 70–100

An inside view

Black & Decker (B&D) is perhaps best known in the UK for its home improvement tools, in particular the famous power drill. However, the company's success is built on a much wider range of products, supported by successful marketing and distribution strengths. In addition, B&D has a reputation for quality, innovation, design and value. Seventy years of growth ended in the early 1980s but by the middle of that decade the company had revitalized itself and was performing strongly again, emphasizing new products and speed to market. B&D has created a product development process which gives the company a significant competitive advantage in consumer and commercial markets around the world.

Its philosophy today is predicated on business improvement through quality, using what it accepts as its enormous 'people potential'. The company's mission statement says, 'We know that there is enormous people potential within our business – intelligence, commitment, loyalty, innovation, motivation, creativity, initiative – we will harness this fantastic power and apply it in a single forward direction, towards our customers. As a result, our customers will be satisfied, market share gains will be made, profits will be increased, employees will be fulfilled and our shareholders will be satisfied because our performance will be superb. We are dedicated to exceeding the expectations of all our customers with uncompromising integrity. In a teamwork environment of continuous improvement, our commitment is to satisfy our customers by continuously providing error-free products and value-added services at the right price. Total quality is the most important drive of our business. We will be consistently focused on the customer, and the subsequent recognition and success will be the main contributor to employee satisfaction.'

Of B&D's worldwide sales, the European operations contribute a fifth, and the UK a fifth of that – at $200 million. The UK is the company's main consumer product manufacturing base through a plant at Spennymoor, in the north-east of England. Here some 14 million items a year, such as lawnmowers and power drills, are produced.

How does Black and Decker rate?

Pay:	very good
Benefits:	excellent
Communications:	good
Training:	good
Career development:	very good
Morale:	very good

People and personnel policies

Like many other aware and assertive companies, B&D's employee policies have grown out of visits that senior executives made to study Japanese industry a decade ago, and they are very apparent at Spennymoor. They had gone to that country with the belief that the Japanese won on technology, but came back with the conclusion that what the Japanese did so well was to get its employees to believe in, indeed, become obsessed by, success. B&D already had good employee relations, partly because it committed itself to the job-hungry northeast part of the country, where the closure of coal mines and shipyards had created massive unemployment.

Today B&D is well known in industry for caring for its people. In 12 of 14 professional categories, it rates above average – and in particular it is noted for a generous pension allocation. Someone who has worked for the company for 30 years, with a final salary of £30,000, and retired at age 55, will command a pension of £20,000. In many companies, you would have to have worked another ten years to gain that level of pension. All employees, after one year's service, are provided with permanent health insurance.

In particular, over the past ten years, the company has made a determined attempt to implement progressive practices that are closely aligned to business objectives and needs. 'Human resource "people policies" are not separate from the other objectives of the company,' says Rowena Vale, human resources manager. 'They are tied in with the whole business plan. HR plays a pivotal role in the running of the whole business.'

The company, with headquarters in Baltimore, Maryland, is culturally American; but serious efforts have been made to distil a mixture of philosophies into its human resource policy. 'We have always been interested in what people do, but now we are interested in how they do it. Some years back all we cared about was selling our products. Now, we support and help our customers in order to do the selling, by explaining how they can get the best from our products. For example, we send our staff to retail outlets to demonstrate the products, and work in partnership with our customers. The consumer needs to be helped to get a feel for the product, and this is how we try to differentiate ourselves from our competitors. In this way we are developing a relationship with our customers.

'Our human resource policy is full, rounded, progressive and business aligned,' he says. 'We have a very supportive culture, quite paternal. If we lose people – or have to lose people – we pay redundancy that is far in excess of any statutory requirements. We are renowned for the support we give in outplacement. You are not thrown on the scrap heap, you are looked after – and psychologically, as well.'

While the company is extremely profit driven, the workforce has deliberately been given its own empowerment. 'We are not hierarchical any longer,' he says. 'Management levels have been reduced and we are continuously giving more responsibility to the employees to use their initiative and apply their knowledge. Opportunities are increasing for gaining wider experience with the focus now firmly on pan-initiatives, which are taking the business well into the twenty-first century.'

Contact address

Mrs Rowena Vale
Human Resources Manager
Black & Decker
210 Bath Road
Slough
Berkshire SL1 3YD
Telephone: 01753 500732
Fax: 01753 576811
Web site: http://www.blackanddecker.com

The BOC Group plc

Industrial gases is a highly competitive global business sector – and The BOC Group is among only a handful of key players able to compete worldwide. This highly resilient organization has built on its traditional strengths in the UK, North America, South Africa, Australia and India to create a business that draws its income from all corners of the globe. It is highly active in the Far East and China and has invested heavily in local partnerships. Despite challenging markets, The BOC Group continues to demonstrate its inherent strengths and is currently engaged in the most substantial overhaul of the group since the late 1970s. It is widely respected for the integrity of its management culture and is determined to capitalize on its full potential to meet increasing levels of expert competition in all markets.

The BOC Group at a glance

Employees: 37,000 worldwide, 13,300 Europe
Annual staff attrition: 3 per cent
Key locations: Windlesham (HQ), Guildford (Gases), Crawley (Vacuum), Aldershot (Distribution)
Annual graduate intake: 400 globally
Annual intake: n/a

An inside view

August 1998 was the most significant turning point for The BOC Group in more than two decades. Faced by a series of challenges to its inherent profitability, the company's chief executive Danny Rosenkrantz decided to reconstruct the group to ensure that it was able to take full advantage of the market's potential in the future. BOC has been a formidable world class player for many years and enjoyed particular strengths in key regional markets. But in the last few years, it has encountered competition from its principal rivals in every important territory across the world.

The purpose of the restructuring was to tackle this series of challenges and to create a business which offered all of its products and services to a consistently high level anywhere in the world. It demanded focus on the core business – industrial gases – and the creation of streamlined global teams to address key areas of business need.

BOC is making the shift to a completely global operation against a background of challenging times. Four key external factors have had a direct bearing on its recent development. First, the company has been hit by the strong pound sterling. Second, the Asian meltdown caused a difficult period for the group. Around one-third of its sales come from Asia-Pacific so analysts, in particular, were concerned and The City marked down BOC's share price considerably. In practice, the exposure was not nearly as great as brokers feared. In most cases, BOC's Asian activities were joint ventures so the risk was substantially less than feared and a good deal of the business is on longer term contract.

Third, BOC has suffered through the recent steep downturn of the semiconductor industry. BOC supplies vacuum pumps and also industrial gases to the industry. Demand should, however, pick up again from mid-1999.

Fourth, the industrial gases market has become increasingly competitive. The process of globalization has underlined the need for players in this industry to be excellent in all their products and services and in every territory worldwide.

Chief executive Rosenkrantz has set out to achieve greater efficiencies from the business. He reported in 1998 that he wanted to see much greater return on investment and improved earnings per share. On 11 August 1998, he introduced a restructured BOC. His structure has created lines of business which operate on a global basis. 'The new BOC is being built around four lines of business each pursuing its own strategy at global and local level. This is a major shift for BOC, which historically has been organized and operated on a largely regional basis,' says Rosencrantz.

The four lines of business are: Industrial & Special Products, which focuses on thousands of customers who buy packaged gases; Process Systems, which concentrates on the chemicals, petroleum and metals industries where demand is in large volumes and produced on the customer's own site; BOC Edwards, dedicated exclusively to serving the semiconductor industry; and Applied Gas Solutions, aimed at bulk consumers such as the glass and food processing sectors.

New organization models in information management, finance and human resources functions are being developed to reduce costs permanently, eliminate duplication and provide new levels of service. In practice, this means that service delivery will be better co-ordinated in the major geographies which will also allow the development of functional expertise and greater leverage of best practice both within the geography itself and across the world. BOC expects this will remove 1,500 posts from the company across the world.

'The scale of the change is revolutionary. I say revolutionary because the job of every person in BOC will be affected. I set a target of one year (to August 1999) for the bulk of the changes to be accomplished. And also the leap in performance which we are looking for will mean considerable change in approach. This is not about incremental growth, it is about getting into a different league in terms of sales and profit, and return for our investors. It is about a complete change in our culture,' says Rosencrantz.

How does BOC rate?

Pay:	very good
Benefits:	very good
Communications:	excellent
Training:	good
Career development:	superb
Morale:	good

People and personnel policies

Rosencrantz says that one of the aims of the restructuring is to release the potential of its people. 'We want to liberate managers and their teams, and make them more accountable – providing them with far more opportunity to be true entrepreneurs – actively building their businesses.

'This shift will be achieved by devolving profit responsibility down the lines of business to the individual business units. They will be accountable for their own targets and profits – releasing the potential of their people and providing the stage for an emerging generation of managers to prove their worth – and be rewarded for their successes.'

Don Beattie, chief executive HR, comments, 'In the last 18 months there has been some of the most significant changes that have occurred in the history of BOC. It began with the disposal of Ohmeda and has now moved on to the restructuring of the broader business. In terms of Ohmeda, we announced our intention to make the disposal in July 1997. We informed all 5,000 employees in the healthcare companies within 24 hours of the announcement. We kept them informed during the sales process and for many of our staff we established effective retention packages to ensure that they stayed with the business and continued to perform during the sales negotiation period. BOC also ensured that all employees were protected going forward in terms of either continuity of employment or honourable redundancy arrangements.'

There has been a similar approach in launching the new BOC and the new business unit focused organization. Much time and effort has been spent in staffing the top jobs in the business units and in HR, finance and IM functions to ensure that only the very best people are appointed. Beattie says 'that for this purpose all our senior managers are rated against clear criteria that we have developed to build a high performance organization.

'Our aim is to breed a performance culture inside BOC and I believe that we will use increasingly sophisticated techniques against which to assess managerial performance.'

Personal performance reviews are conducted annually. 'We changed the emphasis a couple of years ago. It used to be a review of performance by management objectives. Now it is more behavioural. We define the key competencies of the job. We look at the strengths of the individual. We identify the development gaps and draw up an action plan. There will also be a discussion about the person's potential and aiming point in the organization.'

On human resources employees can expect a greater consistency of delivery across the company. Human resources will continue to be close to the businesses but new processes are being developed to ensure a more systematic approach. Training is a prime example. Beattie says 'In the past, training policy and delivery has lacked consistency.' In the new BOC, a core induction course will be created and this will flow through to common programmes on topics such as negotiation, processing, time management and project management.

Similarly, in the recruitment process higher standards are being demanded and duplication will be removed. Beattie sees a convincing argument to create centres of excellence for recruitment and more consistent application of more demanding selection criteria. The assessment of applicants against a rigorous catalogue of competence criteria is being extended across all levels in the business.

BOC is also reshaping its executive education. Currently, managers in the UK often go to Ashridge for development and training and BOC expects shortly to embark on management training online. In addition, it sponsors employees' MBAs and degree courses at a range of universities. Middle managers attend operations workshops which give them access to leading edge strategic thinking. These are run with institutions such as Cranfield and Columbia University in the US.

Contact address

Alf Turner
Director, HR
The BOC Group plc
UK Services
Priestley Centre
Priestley Road
Surrey Research Park
Guildford
Surrey GU2 5XY
Telephone: 01276 477222
Fax: 01276 471333
Web site: http://www.boc.com

The Body Shop International

Founded by Anita Roddick in 1976 when she opened her first small shop in Brighton, The Body Shop International has grown to a worldwide business of about 1,600 shops in 47 countries of which just over 300 are owned and almost 1,300 are franchises. The company manufactures, distributes and sells skin and hair care products and is well known for its social and environmental policies with a vehement opposition to animal testing. Its headquarters are in Littlehampton, West Sussex, close to its Brighton origins.

The Body Shop at a glance

Employees: 5,000
Annual staff attrition: 23 per cent
Key locations: Littlehampton (HQ and manufacturing plant), two further manufacturing plants in Glasgow and Wake Forest, North Carolina
Annual graduate intake: n/a
Annual intake: 950

An inside view

The Body Shop International has a high profile public image as a specialist retailer with high principles on ethical issues such as animal testing and environmental protection. At the same time it has a strong commercial base with competitive pricing, product quality and simple but attractive recyclable packaging. To protect its ethical policies, research and development and the majority of manufacturing are carried out internally. The company regularly audits compliance with its environmental and social policy.

The latest annual report of the company shows an improvement in financial results after two years of stagnation. The company's top four trading countries, in terms of retail outlets, are USA 290, UK 263, Canada 119 and Japan 116. There are 527 European outlets outside the UK. Korea recently became country number 47 on the Body Shop trading map.

The company recently undertook a comprehensive strategic review of its activities, which identified the need for fundamental changes in order to develop the business in the future. In July 1998 the task of realizing the strategic plan and developing the Body Shop brand while retaining its philosophy and business ethics, was given to a new chief executive officer, Patrick Gournay. The founder, Anita Roddick, and her husband, Gordon, now co-chair the company.

The Body Shop's human resources policy is based on the company's overall objective 'to create and sustain a successful community of individuals actively committed to meeting each other's needs.' The success of attaining this goal leads to achievement of business goals in terms of both profit and values. The company believes that a community has a common purpose, but at the same time encourages individuals to contribute their own unique qualities and aspirations. By meeting each other's needs, the community achieves its objectives and creates an environment of mutual trust and respect, which ultimately sustains the successful community.

There is also recognition that there are rights and responsibilities of both individuals and the community which are framed in a 'Bill of Rights and Responsibilities' embodied in The Body Shop Employee Handbook.

How does The Body Shop rate?

Pay:	good
Benefits:	excellent
Communications:	superb
Training:	good
Career development:	very good
Morale:	excellent

People and personnel policies

In 1996 The Body Shop International Human Resources Department developed a strategy for the subsequent four years and called it 'Vision 2000'. It set out five main priorities:

First, to develop and pilot a learning programme in six markets, which would significantly increase levels of motivation, confidence and knowledge of shop staff, local franchisees and head franchisee staff.

Second, to cascade the business plan into departmental objectives and to implement the new organizational capabilities to drive cultural and behavioural changes necessary for successful implementation of the business plan.

Third, to research, collate and agree major key performance indicators that will be used to measure the company's performance against the business plan.

Fourth, to determine an appropriate remuneration and rewards strategy divided into profit share, pay review strategy, bonus system, long-term incentives and a job evaluation system.

Fifth, to fine tune the appraisal system and align it with the key elements of the business plan.

Body Shop places strong emphasis on equal opportunities for employees of whatever gender, nationality, religion or ethnic origin. Forty-four per cent of employees in the top half of the company's salary bands are female. The company aims to recruit hard-working energetic employees with the right qualifications who support the company's values and to enable a diversity of people to succeed within their key capabilities.

The company has no specific graduate recruitment policy. It aims to recruit the best person for the job and new employees are selected on merit and measures, which are relevant and appropriate to individual jobs and future promotion and succession requirements. The company has a universal informal dress policy and an open, honest and friendly atmosphere.

The company actively encourages career development and provides counselling and sponsorship to enable employees to realize their full potential within the business and to provide the organization with a more effective succession plan. Body Shop believes that its culture encourages individuals to take responsibility for their own learning. At the same time senior managers are committed to the learning and personal development of all employees and are actively involved in development programmes and support individual learning and development.

The remuneration package is comprehensive and progressive and the company places it in the medium to upper quartile compared with similar businesses. Jobs throughout the organization are evaluated against the same seven-band pay structure.

In addition, there is a flexible benefits package called 'Choices' covering pension, holidays, death in service cover, private medical insurance and contributory health scheme. Each employee is invited annually to choose from a menu of benefits, which gives them a certain amount of flexibility to choose benefits to suit their individual needs. Holiday and pension can be topped up.

Fixed benefits cover basic holiday entitlement, new product samples, interest free season ticket loans, factory local transport, service awards and staff discounts. The company also provides childcare (crèche or voucher depending on the location), maternity and paternity entitlements and adoption leave.

A recent innovation is the launch of an advocacy process to advise, support, and independently represent employees in grievance and disciplinary proceedings within the company.

Contact address

Mark Barrett
Head of Human Resources
The Body Shop International plc
Watersmead
Littlehampton
West Sussex BN17 6LS
Telephone: 01903 731500
Fax: 01903 726250
Web site: http//www.the-body-shop.com

The Boots Company plc

Boots is one of the most well-known names in the high street. It is the UK's leading chain of chemist shops, and the group also includes Halfords, Boots Opticians, Boots Healthcare International, Boots Contract Manufacturing and Boots Properties. The company employs 84,000 people – the vast majority of them in its shops around the UK. It has a long tradition as a thoughtful and active employer that seeks to attract high calibre people, and has some of the highest numbers of employees who have been through National Vocational Qualification schemes. Since 1995 a number of group businesses have received the Investors in People award. Boots The Chemists (BTC) spends at least £25 million on training. In 1998 the company reported sales of £5 billion with an operational profit of £538 million.

Boots at a glance

Employees: 84,000
Attrition rate: n/a
Key locations: Nottingham (group HQ); 2,000+ stores and offices throughout the UK
Annual graduate intake: 500
Annual intake: n/a

An inside view

Boots The Chemists is one of the best-known names in the UK high street. Most people will be familiar with it, even if they are not daily shoppers in the company's chemist stores. It is also highly regarded by the City, giving the fourth highest shareholder return against a range of peer group companies in the period to March 1998.

Deputy chairman Sir Michael Angus says, 'We continue to maintain a high level of investment focused on our existing operations and directed to maximizing long-term value. Increasing focus on core businesses is a common theme across the group. Boots The Chemists is concentrating space and product development on healthcare and beauty products. Halfords is shifting its emphasis from high street branches to superstores, and increasing its own brand ranges. Boots Opticians continues to build its own brand business. Boots Healthcare International is building and extending its strong brands internationally in the self-medication market. Boots Contract Manufacturing is expanding internationally in Europe to meet growing demand there. Boots Properties, our second largest business, manages the property portfolio by selective purchases and developments.'

In the last few years, Boots has expanded from being a UK business into certain acquisitions around the world. In Europe in particular Boots Contract Manufacturing (BCM) has acquired a series of companies and its customers now include major retailers from France, Spain, the Netherlands and Portugal. In 1995 BCM acquired Croda International's cosmetics and toiletries manufacturing businesses in France and Germany, and in 1997 it added the Roval toiletries businesses in France and Spain. Boots Healthcare International has greatly strengthened its European presence through the acquisition of Lutsia (France) in 1996 and Hermal Kurt Herrman in 1977.

Boots measures its performance in terms of total shareholder returns. The key driver is the long-term cash flows generated by high levels of investment throughout the group. In 1997/98 the company reinvested more than £276 million in capital expenditure in its various businesses. The biggest net beneficiary was Boots The Chemists itself. Boots The Chemists has more than 1,350 stores, Halfords 412 stores, Boots Opticians 285 practices, Boots Healthcare International has 18 businesses operating around the world, Contract Manufacturing runs seven factories and one major development laboratory, and Boots Properties holds some 800 retail properties.

The largest number of employees is in Boots The Chemists where it has 58,369 employees, the next largest being Halfords which has a little over 9,500. Boots The Chemists accounts for £3.6 billion of the group's £5 billion sales. It is clearly the largest part of the enterprise and continues to expand, reporting a profit increase of over four per cent in 1997/98. Dispensing sales are the heart of the business. The authority of its pharmacists and their expert advice secure the trust and authority which Boots demands.

How does Boots rate?

Pay:	very good
Benefits:	very good
Communications:	good
Training:	excellent
Career development:	very good
Morale:	very good

People and personnel policies

Boots has a long-standing reputation as a forward-thinking employer. This helps the company to attract the best people and enables its managers to demand high standards of performance encouraged by incentives and strong rewards. In 1997/98 four of its businesses enjoyed Investors in People status. It is one of the largest participants in the National Vocational Qualifications scheme, and some 21,000 staff are currently working for NVQs. It has a policy of actively encouraging people to transfer between its businesses, and its management development programme is aimed to give them broad experience and perspective and to aid the spread of ideas and best practice throughout the group.

The recruitment of high quality people is vital for Boots as the company trades on the quality and excellence of its advice. Particularly in Boots The Chemists in its pharmaceutical operations and Boots Opticians, it makes high demands on the quality of the people that it recruits. Boots is increasingly successful in retraining its skill base. Investment in training leads to reduced staff turnover. In Boots The Chemists three-quarters of store staff who take maternity leave return to work. The company supports staff retention through a variety of family friendly policies, including flexible working, term-time working, job shares and career breaks.

One of the most important strategic aims is to maximize the affiliation benefits that each business gains from being part of the wider group. The transfer of people is effective in disseminating ideas and best practice from business to business, creating more rounded managers and enriching their careers in the process. The company is working to increase the number of transfers.

Clear and consistent two-way communication is a priority through the organization. To monitor its effectiveness MORI has been commissioned to conduct group-wide employee attitude surveys. The results guide future personnel activity and provide benchmarks for subsequent research. Significantly, MORI has found that the proportion of staff claiming to understand the business and objectives is exceptionally high compared with other organisations. As well as communicating through line management and award-winning staff news magazines and videos, the company has a well-established formal structure of staff councils. This complements the relationships with trade unions and is a key to good industrial relations.

Contact address

The Boots Company plc
Group Personnel
Group Headquarters
Nottingham NG2 3AA
Telephone 0115 9506111
Fax: 0115 9592280
Web site: http://www.boots-plc.com

BP Amoco plc

BP Amoco is the UK's largest company formed from BP of the UK and Amoco of the US in the second biggest industrial merger in history. The new company is one of the world's three largest oil, gas and chemical companies, operating in 100 countries across the globe. In the UK, BP had long been seen as one of the better companies to work for, a reputation enhanced by outstanding recent performance and the extra opportunities created by the merger with Amoco. The new company builds on the high standards of integrity and respect for health, safety and the environment which were characteristics of both BP and Amoco. The new company is a believer, like its founders, in partnership with customers, communities and the environment. BP Amoco is a major recruiter of graduates, offering early development through real jobs and the opportunity to build world class careers in business and technology.

BP Amoco at a glance

Employees: 99,000
Annual staff attrition: n/a
Key locations: London (HQ) with several sites across the UK; BP Amoco also operates in 100 countries
Annual graduate intake: 400
Annual intake: n/a

An inside view

Under the leadership of Lord Simon, now a Government minister, and his successor Sir John Browne, BP focused its business and created a performance-driven culture. Growth through expansion in East Asia, Eastern Europe and South America was supplemented by an innovative joint venture with Mobil in Europe and the merger with Amoco.

BP Amoco seeks to combine global muscle with local responsiveness through organization in 120 business units. These cover four sectors: exploration and production of oil and gas; refining and marketing; petrochemicals; and solar energy. The company seeks to be distinctive through its constructive engagement in major business, environmental and social issues. Sir John Browne has stood out from other oil industry leaders in tackling the issue of global warming, actively through public debate, research and the development of a leading solar business.

Openness is a value which has come to the fore in recent years. Much of BP Amoco's business is carried out in partnership with governments and joint venture operators. BP Amoco believes that being open about its health, safety and environmental record and the steps it needs to take to improve and maintain standards in these areas helps to build trust. Likewise, the company has extended the same approach to its suppliers and developed closer relationships with them.

The desire for good relationships extends to a large community programme and BP Amoco employees are encouraged to give of their time and skills to the community in which they work. The company will match employees' private donations to good causes and it offers grants to groups supported by BP Amoco employees. In 1997, BP alone invested more than £19 million in community programmes with £7.5 million being spent in the UK.

How does BP Amoco rate?

Pay:	good
Benefits:	very good
Communications:	good
Training:	excellent
Career development:	excellent
Morale:	very good

People and personnel policies

Working effectively with other people is at the heart of a successful career with BP Amoco, whether it is in a team tackling a project together or in a worldwide network sharing ideas through video links. There are five key qualities sought in recruits: business sense (which includes viewing activities as a means to an end, rather than as an end in itself); drive (taking the initiative, persistence); thinking; working together (including seeing things from someone else's perspective and building relationships); and influence (such as developing teamwork while leading a group).

BP Amoco recruits around 400 graduates a year worldwide. These employees are seen as a pool from which many of the company's future leaders will emerge. Graduates, in general, are expected to be mobile and there is a European recruitment programme specifically for people speaking at least two European languages who seek international careers starting in a foreign country.

Graduates join an early development programme in which they start either in a technology role, applying a technical degree, or a commercial role, including a scheme for the human resources function. Over their first few years they gain a variety of experience in real jobs, supported by training and mentors. Towards the end of the programme, graduates from all over the world meet on a two-week group induction event. In one of five locations, each on a different continent, about 20 people from every part of the business teach each other about the breadth and opportunities of BP Amoco.

Starting in their early development programme, all BP Amoco employees are encouraged to plan their own personal development, helped by their manager, their mentor, the company Intranet and a personal development framework. After further experience, some aspire to the highest positions in the company. If their performance matches their aspiration, there are outstanding opportunities in a very international and socially prominent industry.

To reach the top requires sustained commitment as well as ability: long hours and much travelling are the norm even though the company is striving for a better balance between work and family life. Knowledge management techniques and desktop video communications are helping to cut travel.

Pay is linked to performance and the total package is in the top quarter of the industry range. There are employee share ownership schemes and a long-term performance plan which links the rewards of top executives to the performance of the company over a long period.

Contact address

BP Amoco plc
Britannic House
1 Finsbury Circus
London EC2M 7BA
Telephone: 0171 496 4000
Fax: 0171 496 4630
Web site:
http://www.bpamoco.com/recruitment

British Airways plc

British Airways has always been regarded as one of the top tier of UK employers. Its commitment to excellent customer service is mirrored in its determination to provide its staff with a challenging and rewarding place to work. It is respected throughout industry for the quality of its training and the more recent creation of an efficient performance management culture. Like most large international carriers, the company sees itself as a global enterprise which must be world class in all areas of its operation.

British Airways at a glance

Employees: 63,000 worldwide, 50,000 UK
Annual staff attrition: 2 per cent
Key locations: Heathrow Airport (HQ), Gatwick Airport, London and various locations around the UK and the world
Annual graduate intake: 130
Annual intake: 4,500

An inside view

The reputation of British Airways as a quality organization which exudes reliability, commitment to customer service and high technical standards is matched by another equally valuable but scientifically less verifiable factor. It is a glamour company. For many young people, employees are engaged in a romantic, exciting and fascinating business. British Airways specifically and the airline sector generally is splendidly attractive and the company is never short of potential recruits. And, despite some internal tensions in the last couple of years, employee attrition is tiny. Non one, it seems, wants to leave BA.

This is hardly surprising since by many measures British Airways is a phenomenally successful organization. In the 12 years since privatization it has transformed into one of the world's most polished and aggressive companies. In the year to March 1998, the company carried a record 41 million passengers. Its route network is one of the most extensive in the world, serving some 166 destinations in 85 countries. In a *Financial Times* survey among CEOs of European companies, BA was voted the second most respected company in Europe, after ABB.

The company argues that in many parts of the world the airline industry is still highly regulated. However, the trend is toward deregulation. Where this has occurred it has encouraged competition between existing operators and has enabled easier entry by new low-cost operators. British Airways, itself, has also launched a low-cost airline under the brand Go. The overall effect is that in most developed markets there is strong competition and these competitive pressures are increasing.

The company's chief executive Bob Ayling argues that there is a new spirit of optimism and confidence in the company. In mid-year 1998 he told shareholders, 'Thanks to the efforts of our people and our continued evolution as a company we will be recruiting 15,000 new employees over the next three years. They will come from all parts of the world. More than 60 per cent of our customers come from outside the UK and we anticipate that this will soon rise to 80 per cent. Savings in operating costs have enabled us to plan the investment of £6 billion over three years on new services, products, aircraft and training.

In late 1996 British Airways announced a four-year business efficiency which is on track to improve efficiency by £1 billion a year by the year 2000. It is important to understand that this programme consists of a wide range of measures designed to improve efficiency and is not simply a cost-cutting initiative. Staff numbers have increased during the period of the programme.

BA's mission is to be the undisputed leader in world travel. In order to achieve this, the company believes that two factors are critical: the safety and security of passengers; and the quality of customer service is a key source of competitive advantage. In addition, BA is trying to create an atmosphere of greater openness within the company. This is especially true in current trading conditions which demand greater operational flexibility.

How does British Airways rate?

Pay:	good
Benefits:	good
Communications:	very good
Training:	excellent
Career development:	excellent
Morale:	good

People and personnel policies

BA has made a major ongoing investment in training and development and regards itself as a leader in training in the industry. The company is widely respected across the commercial and industrial landscape for the relevance, integrity and high quality of its training. Consistent with its policy of continuously improving customer service, many of the training initiatives are focused on this area. For example, a new two-and-a-half-year corporate programme for all employees, based on customer service, started in Spring 1999.

BA has started a major programme of investing in people management, introducing a new performance management system and a new management induction system. It believes that an essential part of its success is the motivation and commitment of its employees. This is rewarded through the airline's profit share scheme. At senior levels, further incentive payments become an increasingly large element of total remuneration. Employee ownership in the company is encouraged and it is estimated that currently 83 per cent of the workforce are shareholders.

The airline has a comprehensive internal communications programme to ensure that employees are well informed about the business and its industry in general. As well as formal methods of communication, line managers are encouraged to regard communication as an integral part of the job and are assessed accordingly. A particularly innovative development is that the company holds an annual business fair where employees can learn more about the company and question senior directors face-to-face. The employee newspaper *BA News* is published weekly and the company has also launched its own television channel.

BA is also working on a major theme for the company's HR approach: diversity. The airline is a champion member of Opportunity 2000 (a campaign working to improve the representation of women in management), and is a founder member of Race for Opportunity, which aims to encourage businesses to invest in the diversity of Britain's ethnic minorities. BA has also created its own equal opportunities steering group.

In an industry which can be associated in the public perception with the problems of noise, pollution and congestion, BA understands the importance of the need to consider the environment in all aspects of its business. It sets itself annual environmental objectives (for example, to reduce the number and frequency of noise infringements). These results are published in an annual environmental report. British Airways has been a winner in the benchmark annual ACCA Environmental Reporting Awards.

Contact address

Mr Mervyn Walker
Director of Human Resources
British Airways plc
Waterside (HEB 1)
PO Box 365
Harmondsworth UB7 0GB
Telephone: 0181 738 5265
Fax: 0181 738 9686
Web site: http://www.britishairways.com

British Steel plc

The steel manufacturing sector is one of the most competitive and truly global of any industrial market. External producers benefit from massive government subsidies. British Steel has succeeded as a top low-cost high quality steel producer without access to any public sector funding. Its achievement has been due to a strong management culture, an understanding of the real economics of steel production and a commitment to cost-effective excellent quality output. In spite of the strong pound and the economic crises in the Far East, British Steel made pretax profits of £315 million on a turnover of more than £6.9 billion in the financial year 1997–98. The company has around 48,000 employees worldwide (20 per cent of them outside the UK) and is the second largest steel producer in Europe – and the fourth largest in the world. It is consistently among the UK's top ten exporters and independent analysts rate it as the world's most cost-efficient integrated steel producer, and among the most profitable.

British Steel at a glance

Employees: 48,000 worldwide, 38,000 UK
Annual staff attrition: n/a
Key locations: Brinsworth, Corby, Dalzell, Ebbw Vale, Hartlepool, Llanwern, Lye, Newport, Port Talbot, Rotherham, Scunthorpe, Sheffield, Shelton, Shotton, Skinningrove, Stockton, Teesside, Templeborough, Trostre, West Midlands and Workington
Annual graduate intake: 200
Annual intake: n/a

An inside view

The challenge for the company today is sharply defined. It competes with national producers worldwide and must meet global standards for cost-effective, innovative and excellent production. Many of its rivals are heavily subsidized by national governments but British Steel enjoys no such benefits. It nevertheless is widely regarded as the most efficient and effective low cost general producer in the world.

Some 70 per cent of the steels in use today have been generated within the last ten years and British Steel is at the forefront of this development. It has created world-renowned technology centres, employing approximately 1,000 scientists in research and development, including metallurgists, engineers, designers, physicists, chemists, mathematicians and computer scientists. These scientists develop products for diverse markets.

The largest is the construction industry which accounts for 25 per cent of the steel used in the UK. Products include piling for foundations, tubes and sections for structural frames, plates for bridgework, metallic and organic coated steels for cladding, roofing and internal partitions, profiled sheets for cladding and roofing systems, and steel framing for domestic housing.

The second largest market is the automotive sector which accounts for 22 per cent of the UK's steel. As well as supplying flat rolled steel for car bodies, the company works closely with the automotive industry to produce finished, forged and machined components, from crankshafts and hubs to axle beams, brake parts, gears, transmission and suspension parts. British Steel is also a leading member of a worldwide consortium of steel companies which is developing technologies to reduce the weight of today's typical car body.

Industrial plant accounts for 12 per cent of the UK's steel, and packaging eight per cent – from the thinnest of materials for the food trays used in microwave ovens to steels for giant 210 litre drums. The company says that four out of five cans of all types are made of steel and that every steel can contains 25 per cent of recycled metal. In fact, steel is the most recycled material in the world. In all, British Steel has 57 per cent of the UK market which accounted for 43 per cent of its turnover in 1997–98.

With more than 50 per cent of its business outside the UK, distribution is vitally important for British Steel. The company has developed a network of more than 70 sales and distribution companies throughout Europe, North America, Asia Pacific, the Middle East, South Asia and Australasia.

How does British Steel rate?

Pay:	very good
Benefits:	excellent
Communications:	very good
Training:	excellent
Career development:	very good
Morale:	excellent

People and personnel policies

The culture of British Steel can be described as competitive, demanding, merit-based, product-orientated and with a high level of commitment. Nevertheless, the company recognizes that as the leading player in the UK steel market it has few competitors from which to acquire staff and that it must encourage, train and nurture its own talent. In 1997–98 it spent £53 million on the training and development of employees, involving an average of 11 days for each UK employee. It is expected that even higher levels of investment will be made in this area over at least the next three years.

Forty-four per cent of employees are now working in businesses with Investors in People recognition and a further two National Training Awards were received in 1997–98. British Steel has won more training awards than any other UK company – 50 in total.

The aim of the company is to get the best out of people by making full use of their individual abilities, to develop senior managers for the future, and to provide fulfilling and challenging careers. For graduates this means competitive pay and benefits, superior training, the opportunity of accelerated management development, the possibility of a business-school designed programme which includes the option of an in-company MBA, and an international management programme to equip managers with the necessary business skills to meet the increasingly international nature of the Company's markets.

The international nature of British Steel needs to be emphasized. It has a growing requirement for its managers to understand the global business environment of which the company is a part. To aid this process it uses international business schools (such as INSEAD in France and IMD in Switzerland as well as schools in North America) and provides in-house language training facilities. The company stresses that it is keen to develop a culture where it is natural for every manager to speak at least one foreign language.

'We definitely encourage early exposure to other countries and cultures,' says David John, manager, Management Development and Selection, 'and we operate an exchange scheme with a number of foreign steel producers. There are also opportunities for secondments, especially in commercial functions, to our businesses overseas.'

Other management development initiatives include two assessments in the first four years of the potential of each graduate and regular performance appraisals. Selected graduates also have the opportunity of an accelerated management development programme.

Contact address

John Carson
Manager, Management Selection and Graduate Resourcing
British Steel plc
Ashborne Hill Management College
Leamington Spa CV33 9QW
Telephone: 01926 488000
Fax: 01926 488024
Web site:
http://epic.wcn.co.uk/bsteel/intro.html

BT plc

The transformation of BT from inefficient state monopoly to one of the most dynamic modern businesses is a classic business school case study. BT is one of the world's largest telecommunications companies. It is – by far and away – the biggest telecoms provider in the UK operating commercial and domestic services and running a vast network. The company has experienced massive change since its privatization, transforming its reputation from slow and bureaucratic to an alert, innovative and efficiently managed operation. As part of this cathartic change, the company has substantially improved its standing as an employer. BT is now a highly attractive business for all grades of employee, especially graduates.

BT at a glance

Employees: 124,700 worldwide
Annual staff attrition: 14 per cent
Key locations: London, plus every major city in the UK
Annual graduate intake: 500
Annual intake: 1,100

An inside view

BT is one of the great players in worldwide telecommunications. It is the industry's dominant force in the UK and is one of the handful of companies which is a serious operator on the global stage. For the last few years the business has been attempting to exploit all its opportunities and this has meant global merger proposals. In 1994 it formed an alliance with the US telecoms giant MCI to create Concert Communications Services. Concert is a focused business, providing networking solutions to multinational clients, some 40 per cent of which are based in the US.

BT wanted a closer relationship with MCI but in the end it was outbid by WorldCom and sold its 20 per cent stake in MCI to the successful bidder. BT's chairman Sir Iain Vallance was disappointed but not fazed by the decision. He told shareholders 'Concert has not been compromised and continues to lead the world in providing global managed services to multinational clients.' Overall BT is continuing to grow in all its markets. In 1998 it reported sales up to £15.6 billion and pretax profits were up seven per cent to £3.2 billion.

Sir Peter Bonfield, chief executive, is upbeat about the company's immediate prospects. 'In the UK we support around 27 million customer lines and, through our 60 per cent stake in Cellnet, more than three million mobile connections. Our main services are local, national and international calls, and supplying telephone lines, equipment and private circuits for homes and businesses. Outside the UK our strategy is to expand by developing a series of alliances and joint venture partnerships. We are also in the forefront of the development and marketing of a comprehensive range of advanced data and interactive multimedia solutions and technologies of the future.

Today's BT is much smaller in employee terms than in its public sector days. In 1991 it employed 227,000 people, compared with less than 125,000 now. The company has clinically removed whole sections of its management and workforce – a process which its senior directors said was necessary to be an effective competitor in world markets. The service which it now provides to its domestic customers is widely agreed to be manifoldly more effective, cheaper and diverse. The quality, cost effectiveness and responsiveness to which the customers of US telecoms companies have long been exposed is becoming a reality in the UK. Spurred by competition initially from Mercury and now from a range of operators in different market sectors, BT has enthusiastically embraced the challenge of high quality customer service. It also aims to be a technology leader and is the largest business in the world to receive company-wide accreditation under the ISO9001 quality standard.

BT has also changed radically in structure and approach to staff. Much of the old-fashioned public sector culture has been removed – and although BT is probably more centrally directed than many modern businesses, the comparison between now and 15 years ago is light years apart. Possibly because BT had further to travel than many of its competitors in revolutionizing the business, it remains a steely organization with drive and determination. This is hardly an easy going West Coast emergent-technology company basking in the Californian sunshine. It is a resolute, structured business which equips its people with the skills to take on the world's finest. This is now a customer-orientated organization, managed professionally, which emphasizes quality and continuous improvement.

How does BT rate?

Pay:	very good
Benefits:	very good
Communications:	very good
Training:	superb
Career development:	excellent
Morale:	very good

People and personnel policies

BT is enormously proud of its achievements in the area of people management. 'At BT we understand the link between our customers' supplier-of-choice and our people's employer-of-choice. That is why we have such a deep commitment to our people. During the last year we recruited more than 500 high calibre graduates and 500 modern apprentices. BT is a key supporter of the UK Government's New Deal programme and plans to help 250 unemployed people back to work in the next year. We seek to promote real equality of opportunity throughout the company and actively encourage the employment, training and career development of people with disabilities,' comments Sir Peter Bonfield.

One of BT's strongest achievements in recent years is its emergence as a management culture, respected globally for its tenacity and its capacity to build on its strengths as a business while moving relatively quickly to eliminate some of the handicaps which had held the company back. The fact that it is now a primary choice by undergraduates demonstrates how effective BT has been in introducing a positive, objective-orientated environment. In a survey conducted by employment specialists Pearn Kandola, BT emerged as the second most favoured choice for graduates after long-term top selection ICI. The study also showed that the same group also enjoyed a detailed appreciation of the company's operations and business objectives. It ranked fourth best known business among the control group. Its dexterity in planning makes a key contribution to the corporate achievement and nowhere is this more apparent than in the field of human resources.

John Steele, director of human resources at BT, emphasizes the care and attention that is given to selecting, retaining and developing a workforce which is robust, articulate and skilful. Two of its five corporate values focus on HR issues: 'we respect each other' and 'we work as a team'. In their entirety the values give a graphic snapshot of a business on the move. Steele says, 'we have moved from a single, unitary company to a series of autonomous businesses which operate within a common framework. Each business has its own people requirements and recruits personnel to meet its own specific needs. The way in which people are employed in the separate businesses will vary and we have adopted a range of flexible contracts to suit the demands of the time.' BT used to be a *job for life* company but now Steele talks about improving the employability of its workforce. Many will be on assignment with the company for a limited period during which they will enhance their skills substantially to offer to other organizations after their BT work has been completed.

'BT will move progressively to even greater decentralization,' he comments. The common feature in all the BT businesses is its attitude towards personnel and its management style. There is an increasing drive towards strengthening personal leadership talents. Steele sees BT people as leaders and coaches who work in teams to manage designated business areas, technical developments or customer initiatives. He places great store by the company's policy to create and manage teams to address every key commercial, technical and administrative issue. Structurally, BT's companies are based on flexible teams which are made and remade in response to market conditions.

Contact address

Andrew Harley
BT Group Personnel
81 Newgate Street
London EC1A 7AJ
Telephone: 0171 356 5000
Fax: 0171 356 6077
Web site: http://www.bt.com

Cable and Wireless plc

Cable and Wireless is one of the world's most prominent international telecommunications groups, operating in more than 70 countries worldwide. It provides a variety of services, including telephone, facsimile, telex, Internet, cable television, multimedia and data transmission, to both business and domestic users, using the most modern fixed line and mobile technology available. The Cable and Wireless vision is to lead the world in integrated communications. Cable and Wireless has an unrivalled global presence and is now the third largest carrier of international traffic.

Cable and Wireless at a glance

Employees: 45,000 worldwide and 12,000+ in the UK
Annual staff attrition: 12 per cent
Key locations: Central London (HQ), 70 countries worldwide
Annual graduate intake: 25 – 50 on international graduate development programme (IGDP) and 25 at Cable and Wireless Communications
Annual intake: n/a

An inside view

Cable and Wireless products and services span the technological spectrum from basic, first-time connections to sophisticated global telecoms services. Operating throughout the world, its interests include Hongkong Telecom, Cable and Wireless Panama, Cable and Wireless OPTUS (Australia), Cable and Wireless USA and businesses situated as far afield as Indonesia, the Caribbean and the Falkland Islands.

In the UK, Cable and Wireless's operations consist primarily of its 52 per cent interest in Cable and Wireless Communications (CWC), a company formed in 1997 through the merger of its Mercury subsidiary with Nynex Cable Communications, Bell Cablemedia and Videotron. The Cable and Wireless vision is to lead the world in integrated communications, bringing together fixed and mobile telephones, data, Internet connectivity, broadband services, entertainment and television.

Cable and Wireless Global Mobile reached a customer base of more than 3.3 million during 1998. In the UK, One 2 One is now the country's fastest-growing mobile service, reaching almost two million customers at the end of 1998. When the downturn hit Asia in 1998, Hongkong Telecom took the opportunity to buy the mobile business, Pacific Link, consolidating its number one position in the Hongkong mobile market, where it is also the market leader in interactive multimedia services.

The launch of the Cable and Wireless Communications brand in the UK in September 1997 was highly successful with 125,000 new customers signed up in the first 90 days. Awareness of the Cable and Wireless name in the UK has gone from virtually zero to a current rating of 90 per cent.

Cable and Wireless regards the recruitment of high potential graduate entrants as vital for the future management population of the company. Selection criteria include the minimum of a 2.1 degree, strong analytical ability, and a real interest in the telecommunications industry.

There are graduate trainee opportunities in five areas or streams: finance; marketing; electronic/ telecommunications engineering; human resources management; and information technology. Graduate trainees must be comfortable with change, enthusiastic about a challenge, with a 'can do' attitude and the ability to make things happen. For most positions other than at entry or graduate trainee level, Cable and Wireless are usually interested in people who already have telecoms experience.

How does Cable and Wireless rate?

Pay:	very good
Benefits:	good
Communications:	good
Training:	very good
Career development:	excellent
Morale:	very good

People and personnel policies

There is a range of formal development programmes for high performing employees with leadership potential, of which the two graduate recruitment schemes are an important element. There is a team inside CWC which provides a variety of general training as well as courses in management skills, customer services, systems and process training. The Cable and Wireless College delivers sales, product and technical training, and management development within CWC. Graduate trainees are sponsored to work towards gaining membership of the relevant professional institute, for example, chartered engineer status, where one exists.

All graduate trainees are allocated a mentor from the company's Leaders of Tomorrow management population. Support and encouragement are provided to graduates by managers, mentors and senior figures from across the business who support and champion the graduate schemes.

Work placements are at the heart of both graduate schemes. Placements last between six months and a year and are designed to give the graduate real hands-on experience in preparation for the first line role at the end of the training period. Graduates entering the CWC scheme must be willing to relocate to any of the CWC office locations in the UK. Graduates on the International Graduate Development Programme (IGDP) spend three years on the programme living and working abroad.

Cable and Wireless has deliberately created an environment where individual performance is recognized and rewarded. At all levels of the company, open and honest communication is promoted and all managers are encouraged to adopt an open management style. The company's values promote high performance with a strong focus on customer service.

Cable and Wireless operates a series of performance related incentive schemes. Not all employees are eligible for membership of such a scheme, but every employee is encouraged to maximize his or her salary through individual high performance. Pay for high performers is benchmarked towards the upper quartile. Performance reviews occur twice a year and salaries are reviewed once a year. The exception to this stipulation are graduate trainees whose salary is reviewed every six months while they are on a graduate training scheme.

The company operates a flexible benefits programme which allows employees to adjust certain benefits to better match their own lifestyle. The healthcare scheme provides cover for employees only, although it can be extended, and the pension benefits equates to matched contributions between two and five per cent. Accident insurance, employee assistance programmes and 23 days' holiday a year, not including bank holidays, are some of the benefits employees can expect. Benefits vary between Cable and Wireless plc and CWC with additional benefits in some businesses including increased holiday allowance, car lease purchase opportunities and assisted health club membership. Cable and Wireless companies outside the UK have their own benefits programmes.

The Cable and Wireless website is growing in importance as a means of communication within the company. A newspaper, *Cable and Wireless World*, is circulated to every employee worldwide, and CWC has its own sister paper.

Contact address

Cable and Wireless plc
124 Theobalds Road
London WC1X 8RX
Telephone: 0171 315 4000
Fax: 0171 315 5000
Web site: http://www.cwplc.com

Cadbury Schweppes

In 1783 in Geneva Jacob Schweppe perfected his process for the manufacture of mineral water, while in 1824 John Cadbury began selling tea and coffee in Birmingham. These two long-established operations merged in 1969 and Cadbury Schweppes began a programme of worldwide expansion. The acquisition of the US soft drinks company Dr Pepper/Seven-up in 1995 heralded the most substantial move for the group since its merger. Further acquisitions took place in 1996, 1997 and 1998, while in February 1997 the group sold its 51 per cent interest in Coca-Cola & Schweppes Beverages to focus on being a brand owner rather than bottler. Today Cadbury Schweppes is number three in global soft drinks and the world's fourth biggest supplier of chocolate and sugar confectionery.

Cadbury Schweppes at a glance

Employees: 41,320 worldwide, 10,052 UK
Annual staff attrition: n/a
Key locations: Cadbury Ltd, Birmingham; Reading Scientific Services Ltd, Reading; Trebor Bassett Ltd, Maple Cross, Herts; Cadbury Schweppes Africa, India, Middle East and Europe Beverages, Watford
Annual graduate intake: n/a
Annual intake: n/a

An inside view

The confectionery side of Cadbury Schweppes is a major global force in both chocolate and sugar confectionery, and produces a mix of international, regional and local brands. It has manufacturing plants in 25 countries and sales in a further 170. The beverages arm of the company has sales in 162 countries, mainly through local licensing and distribution arrangements, and including 13 countries through its own bottling and partnership operations. Key international soft drink brands are Schweppes, Dr Pepper and Crush, while the Cadbury masterbrand is the largest confectionery brand in the world. In 1997 the company reported sales of almost £4.2 billion and pretax profits of £575 million.

Full results for 1997 show it to have been an excellent year for the group. Branded sales volumes from continuing operations increased by four per cent in both beverages and confectionery. This performance was stimulated by higher levels of marketing investment behind the brands, as well as the continued successful introduction of new products and international expansion of existing brands. Trading margins grew again, to 14.5 per cent.

The UK operation is divided into beverages and confectionery, and around 10,000 people are employed within sales, manufacturing, marketing and head office functions. Cadbury Schweppes' governing objective is growth in shareholder value. In April 1997 a major new initiative was launched to meet this objective, called Managing for Value (MFV). The five interrelated key elements of the MFV programme are: raising the bar of financial performance; applying the principles and techniques of Value Based Management to the development of strategy throughout the group; sharpening the group's culture through greater accountability, aggressiveness and adaptability; developing an outstanding management team with the required qualities of leadership; and aligning the financial rewards of employees with those of shareholders.

Managing for Value is a long-term philosophy to which the whole organization is committed. However, as group chief executive, John Sunderland, has emphasized: 'Managing for Value is not just about financial management. It is 20 per cent about numbers and 80 per cent about the people and culture, because people create value.'

Cadbury Schweppes was voted 'Britain's Most Admired Company' in 1995 through a widely supported poll of peer companies. The criteria for the award included quality of management, quality of products/services, capacity to innovate, quality of marketing, community and environmental responsibility and financial soundness. In 1998, for the third year running, Cadbury Schweppes was named one of the world's best managed companies by the US magazine *IndustryWeek*, voted by a panel of over 80 business leaders, analysts, and academics from around the world.

How does Cadbury Schweppes rate?

Pay:	very good
Benefits:	very good
Communications:	very good
Training:	very good
Career development:	very good
Morale:	very good

People and personnel policies

The belief that achieving commercial objectives and meeting the needs of customers in a profitable and competitive manner is dependent on the contribution of all employees, is central to company philosophy. Employees are encouraged to develop their contribution to the business wherever they happen to work. Continuing programmes on quality and customer service are run in the UK and provide an opportunity for all employees to be involved in making improvements within their own operations. Employees are also encouraged to participate financially through a variety of share schemes which provide them with a direct stake in the growth and prosperity of the business.

Chairman Sir Dominic Cadbury believes that the company's ability to sustain a competitive advantage over the long-term is dependent on the continuous development of employees. 'The company is committed to providing an environment which values continuous learning and which provides learning and development opportunities within individual business units and across the entire group. Development is a shared responsibility and employees for their part must possess the drive and initiative to take advantage of the available learning and development opportunities,' he says.

Business units within the group provide the relevant systems and programmes to meet the differing development needs of employees which vary significantly from business to business. For instance, National Vocational Qualifications have been adopted in the UK by Cadbury Ltd and Trebor Bassett in order to suit their individual business needs.

Although graduates are recruited from a wide variety of disciplines, there is no specific graduate programme in the UK. Rather, the company prefers to put graduates into 'real jobs' with the emphasis on gaining experience of different functions, markets and businesses in the UK and abroad. To cope with the constantly changing aspects of the marketplace, the company also develops ongoing programmes for its senior executives. International assignments are also encouraged through an Accelerated Development Programme.

A remuneration committee of non-executive directors reviews and approves annual salaries, incentive arrangements, option grants, service agreements and other employment conditions for executive directors. In setting basic salaries for directors, the committee takes into account the pay practices of other companies and the performance of each individual director. Salaries are competitive with those of other similar companies which trade on a worldwide basis.

Cadbury Schweppes contributes actively to the communities in which it operates around the world. During 1997 contributions within the UK to charities or equivalent organizations through corporate giving, or as part of the activity of UK operating companies, amounted to over £1¼ million.

Cadbury Schweppes is a member of the Per Cent Club. As well as donations and sponsorship, activities include employee involvement or secondment and help with facilities in addition to direct financial support. Increasingly the Group is building partnerships with projects or organizations in local communities to ensure that contributions are as effective as possible.

Contact address

Human Resources Department
Cadbury Schweppes
25 Berkeley Square
London W1X 6HT
Telephone: 0171 409 1313
Fax: 0171 830 5200
Web site:
http://www.cadburyschweppes.com

Cap Gemini

With a worldwide turnover of more than £2 billion, Cap Gemini is the largest European computer services company. Headquartered in France, the group provides IT services such as IT consultancy, systems integration, software development and information systems management (ISM). Founded more than 30 years ago, the group employs around 37,000 people in 16 European countries, Asia and the US. The company prides itself on its ability to develop bold solutions to complex problems for a broad range of clients and market sectors including travel, insurance, telecoms, pharmaceuticals, finance and transport.

Cap Gemini at a glance

Employees: 37,000 worldwide, 8,000 UK
Annual staff attrition: 12 per cent
Key locations: London (HQ), and 14 other locations in the UK and Ireland
Annual graduate intake: 300+
Annual intake: 2000

An inside view

Cap Gemini's success in one of today's fastest-growing industries is founded on its in-depth understanding of each of its customers' businesses and markets and its ability to find innovative solutions to client problems. It provides a wide range of IT products and services including information systems management, which includes responsibility for all or part of a customer's IT function; project services, such as systems integration, software development and migration; the provision, implementation and continuous support of software and software products; and consulting, as well as education and training.

The group's focus on the needs of its clients is reflected in its organizational structure, which aligns closely to market sectors. The sectors include finance, transport, insurance, telecommunications, utilities, process, public, retail and manufacturing. In addition, specialized service delivery staff are responsible for the management and quality delivery of service to the customer. Within the company, business support services staff assist the customer-facing staff.

Cap Gemini's overall strategy is to help people use IT to run their business better. It aims high, having the courage to challenge the accepted way of doing things, giving honest advice without shrinking from difficult assignments. It has the energy and professionalism to deliver complex business solutions – on time and above clients' expectations. By listening twice as much as it talks, Cap Gemini builds an in-depth understanding of its clients' businesses. Multi-functional and multi-disciplinary teams not only add value for Cap Gemini and its clients, but provide mutual support through shared experience and knowledge.

The company has gained the trust and respect of its clients through its open-minded, pragmatic approach to doing business. Not only does Cap Gemini respect a client's culture and business approach, dealing with them in a genuine and straightforward manner, but it also appreciates that its own employees have lives outside work and that family comes first. It believes that a person will be more interesting, relaxed and productive at work if they are not always working. Throughout all, Cap Gemini sees humour as an essential element in a challenging, often pressurized work environment, believing that people who enjoy what they do and like the people they work with perform better.

How does Cap Gemini rate ?

Pay:	good
Benefits:	good
Communications:	very good
Training:	excellent
Career development:	very good
Morale:	good

People and personnel policies

Cap Gemini is renowned for the excellent training with which it provides its people. It has invested £1.5 million in the Cap Gemini Academy which handles seven graduate intakes a year, each revolving around a six-week residential course developing business, interpersonal and core technical skills to be immediately effective in one of the Cap Gemini business units – delivering real solutions to real customers. Individuals continue their training by learning from more experienced colleagues.

Every year, around 1,000 graduates from across the worldwide Cap Gemini Group with 12–18 months' experience take part in multi-cultural exchanges and a special international Discovery Programme at the Cap Gemini University, housed in a twelfth-century French château at Behoust, Paris. Participants share best practices and experience and become part of an international graduate network. Cap Gemini has set up an intranet to pool collective knowledge and share experience and has established Centres of Technical Excellence which focus on latest industry trends.

Cap Gemini actively promotes the commercial and technical development of its employees through an individually structured career path and the support of a mentor who advises on career and personal issues. The company promotes on merit – responsibilities and the level of client contact, as well as opportunities to progress into other areas of the company, increase in line with the individual's skill and experience. The Cap Gemini Academy is a unique facility for all graduate entrants. It demonstrates the company's commitment to the careers and long-term personal development of Cap Gemini employees. The Cap Gemini Academy is the first step in a number of development programmes, others include 'Young

Professionals' and the 'International Discovery Programme' at the Cap Gemini University. All jobs and training opportunities are publicized on the Cap Gemini intranet.

Remuneration and rewards are based on the performance and achievements of both the individual and the company. Cap Gemini fully appreciates the necessity for a competitive pay and benefits package in order to attract, recruit and retain the talented and skilled people it needs in an industry known for a high rate of movement between jobs. Designed to reward excellent performance and enable all employees to share in the company's profitability, the package includes competitive basic salaries, performance and profit-related pay schemes and motivational bonus schemes. There is a long list of other attractive benefits including a final salary pension plan, private medical cover and interest-free loans for employees to purchase a PC at a discounted rate.

Naturally enough, the better an individual reflects the Cap Gemini company culture, the better they will fit in. Cap Gemini is looking for people with confidence, decisiveness and initiative who will set themselves high professional standards, thinking and acting like the business is their own. Many of the project teams are multicultural, so employees need to be flexible, able to handle a great deal of change and mobile enough to work wherever they are needed – either at a Cap Gemini office or at a client site.

Cap Gemini expects individuals to treat colleagues and clients with courtesy and respect, as well as being open-minded and honest, for instance, asking questions if they don't know and not using jargon. People who embody the company values of courage, excellence, teamwork, respect and humour have the chance to work with leading edge technologies and forward thinking people on some of Cap Gemini's most ground-breaking projects around the world.

Contact address

Mr Robert Ingram
Human Resources Director
Cap Gemini UK plc
Dukes Court
Duke Street
Woking GU21 5XP
Telephone: 01483 248574
Fax: 01483 248902
Web site: http://www.capgemini.co.uk

The Carphone Warehouse

The Carphone Warehouse is one of the UK retailing success sensations of the last decade. It has expanded rapidly from its inception in 1989 to become the largest independent mobile phone retailer in the UK, entirely autonomous of all manufacturers and networks. This puts it in an ideal position to provide extensive and impartial information to today's consumer and support their standpoint in the complex and continually changing market. Recently, the company has expanded across Europe and its operations now encompass France, Spain, Ireland, Sweden, Belgium and Germany.

The Carphone Warehouse at a glance

Employees: 1,155
Annual staff attrition: 18 per cent
Key locations: 172 stores in the UK, 100 branches in seven major European countries
Annual graduate intake: 200+
Annual intake: 300+

An inside view

The Carphone Warehouse was founded by the entrepreneurial Charles Dunstone, who identified a niche in the market for an entirely novel type of mobile phone retail outlet. Observes Dunstone, 'During the 1980s the majority of mobile phones were purchased by big businesses and organizations so corporate clients got good deals and were well looked after. But small businesses, the self-employed and Joe Public – for whom mobile phones would be the most useful – had to go to some tacky car stereo shop under the railway arches. And that's where we came in.' Currently there are 172 stores in the UK, making 41 per cent of all high street connections and acquiring 49 per cent of all mobile communication sales by value. As a frontline retail business, The Carphone Warehouse recognizes that its success is built on the quality and commitment of its staff in whom substantial resources are invested.

One of the core principles behind the accomplishments of The Carphone Warehouse is to ensure its customers receive candid and objective recommendations and thus enable them to make the most suitable selection for their individual needs. It does not advocate any specific network, tariff or model of handset over any other, and as a result customers can choose from products that comprise all four networks, more than 20 types of tariff and over 100 phones and accessories. Other important services promoted by The Carphone

Warehouse are comprehensive back-up facilities including insurance; battery performance checks; Express Repairs and While-U-Wait Repairs and in-car installations.

The predominant culture of The Carphone Warehouse has the employees and customers at its hub. The company prioritizes first-rate customer services and has formed five fundamental rules that are conveyed on a daily basis to both employees and business partners. These include, 'If we don't look after the customer someone else will', 'Always deliver what we promise. If in doubt, under promise and over deliver', and 'The reputation of the whole company is in the hands of each individual.' To reinforce these principles, they are made obvious in day-to-day operations, appearing on computer screen savers and business cards. Employee opinion is highly valued and many opportunities are made available for them to express their views and have them implemented.

The Carphone Warehouse seeks out people who are highly motivated, enthusiastic, dedicated and looking for a company in which they can get personally involved. As results of the annual survey show, employee turnover is at 18 per cent, markedly lower than the retail average of 39 to 40 per cent. This illustrates high job satisfaction amongst employees, a reflection on the positive work environment that has been created at The Carphone Warehouse.

How does The Carphone Warehouse rate?

Pay:	very good
Benefits:	very good
Communications:	very good
Training:	excellent
Career development:	excellent
Morale:	excellent

People and personnel policies

The Carphone Warehouse is highly regarded for its training programme and financial investment in employee development – around £1,500 is spent on the training of each member of the workforce, eight times more than the average high street retailer. The training process begins with a two- to three-week induction course. This entails learning about the structure of the communications industry – product and procedures – as well as the company ethos and most importantly, customer care. A key factor in the training is making certain that the employees have a full understanding of the product so they can relate helpful and educational information and advice to customers.

Every member of the workforce undergoes an annual appraisal during which the employee and manager pinpoint key objectives. The implementation of these are reviewed after six months and a training course is then agreed upon by both the manager and employee that satisfies training needs and learning objectives. Once this training course is completed, the employee fills out an action plan outlining what they have learnt and what they will do differently, to be reviewed two months later by the manager to make sure they are on track.

The Carphone Warehouse encourages the promotion of employees and there are appropriate development programmes that are tailored to the specific requirements of employees, such as Pre management and Branch Management. Opportunities are exceptional for career advancement as the positions of Assistant Manager, Branch Manager and Area Manager are all appointed internally. The Carphone Warehouse promotes development in a broader context as well. For example, it will subsidize the MBA degree's tuition fee to a maximum of 50 per cent of the course costs. The recent successful pilot scheme of a Modern Apprenticeship programme in Customer Service has meant it is now extended to employees in branches throughout the country.

One of the more unusual benefits at The Carphone Warehouse is an Employee Benefits Trust Fund, which works as an umbrella for the entire company. Everyone is able to draw on the fund's capital and it provides financial aid in times of emergency as well as sending gifts when an employee has a baby or gets married.

Another important method which The Carphone Warehouse uses to keep a close watch on the state of employee morale, job satisfaction and needs of its workforce, is an annual postal survey. It is a comprehensive document that requests employees to evaluate the company on a vast range of areas including skills and training, career development, communication, the working environment, pay and benefits, decision making and management style. The findings are used to obtain an overall representation of employee opinions and satisfaction and are presented at the annual Company Day. At this gathering, which the whole organization attends, employees' efforts are recognized and rewards given for outstanding achievement within the business.

Contact address

Peta Clifton
HR Manager
The Carphone Warehouse Limited
North Acton Business Park
Wales Farm Road
London W3 6RS
Telephone: 0181 896 5000
Fax: 0181 896 5005
Web site:
http://www.carphonewarehouse.co.uk

Coca-Cola & Schweppes

Coca-Cola & Schweppes (CCS) is the leading soft drinks bottler and distributor in the UK, selling more than two billion litres of soft drinks in a year. CCS was founded in 1987 as a joint venture between Cadbury Schweppes and Coca-Cola, but in February 1997 Cadbury Schweppes sold its interest to Coca-Cola Enterprises for more than £600 million. A 15-year licensing agreement (with a ten-year extension option) for the bottling and distribution of Cadbury Schweppes soft drinks brands in Great Britain formed an important part of the deal. CCS offers significant opportunities for people to fashion their own careers in a fast-moving, yet supportive, environment.

CCS at a glance

Employees: 4,700
Annual staff attrition: 5 per cent
Key locations: HQ Uxbridge, six manufacturing sites, four regional service centre, seven vending depots and eight regional sales offices
Annual graduate intake: n/a
Annual intake: 200

An inside view

CCS products account for nearly one-quarter of the UK soft drinks market, although this is an industry which it describes as a 'sleeping giant' compared with that of the US or Germany. Under its new ownership, CCSB intends to wake this sleeping giant in an industry challenge to customers, manufacturers, brand owners and suppliers alike. Its parent organization is the world's largest bottler and distributor of soft drinks, so CCS has the benefit of a wealth of corporate background and experience to fall back on.

CCS is the market leader in the UK with top brands Coca-Cola, Diet Coke, Sprite, Lilt, Fanta, Five Alive, Dr Pepper, Schweppes Tonics and Mixers and Kia Ora. It also has the Nestlé franchise in the UK and distributes Perrier and Vittel from France as well as handling the Schweppes water brands of Ashbourne, Buxton and Malvern. Critical to the company's success is product availability be it in the shop, supermarket or off-licence in the retail market, on premises in the leisure industry, or from machines and/or refrigerated cabinets in the convenience sector.

There is a young fast-paced culture in the company to match its high profile position in the FMCG sector, but an informal friendly atmosphere prevails. Nonetheless, there is also a long-term view characterized by a current programme of investment designed to further develop the company's infrastructure. The most recent example of this has been felt in the regionalization of the commercial function to follow the decentralized autonomy and accountability approach of the new American parent company. This is designed to provide the flexibility which will allow each individual business operation the opportunity to adapt to different market demands and requirements.

The change in ownership marks a fundamental watershed in the history of CCS. The company has embarked on a major recruitment campaign and is prepared to spend money to recruit the right people who will succeed and grow with the company supported by strong training and development programmes.

Most senior managers have risen through the ranks of the company, many in a relatively short period of time, and it is the stated policy of the company to encourage all new recruits to progress as fast as their personal capabilities will permit them.

How does CCS rate?

Pay:	excellent
Benefits:	superb
Communications:	excellent
Training:	very good
Career development:	superb
Morale:	very good

People and personnel policies

The change of ownership from a UK to a wholly US base has been the golden opportunity to fashion personnel policies to coincide with the overall aims and concepts of the business. The company is known to be open and direct, and honesty in all aspects of the business is considered the foundation of success.

As befits a service-based company, CCS strives not only to meet and exceed customers' needs but to anticipate them first. This responsiveness means an adaptable approach is paramount as changes are frequent. Trying something new and rushing to meet tight deadlines is the norm. The pace creates a lot of energy, but gives individuals the opportunity to reach their full potential and get a buzz about their achievements.

Coaching from line managers ensures individuals are capable of achieving success by taking ownership of their own development. Individual members of staff are encouraged to challenge their own performance to search for best practice solutions to problems and to make things happen. Wherever possible, decisions are passed right down the line. This means individuals tend to learn directly from their own experiences.

In 1998, CCS recruited more than 700 people and this is anticipated to be exceeded in 1999. A campaign to recruit the right people in the right locality is a keystone of the planned dynamic expansion of the company, and this has necessitated a major investment in the recruitment budget.

Highly innovative elements of the recruitment programme are SkillStart and Frontline. Working with City and Guilds, the University of Bradford and the National Extension College, CCS has developed combined work and study programmes that allow recruits to take on a job while studying for a City and Guilds Progression Award in Manufacturing and Distribution or a four-year business studies degree programme in sales. At the end of the programmes recruits have work experience with a successful company and a nationally recognized qualification. The schemes also have the benefit that what is learned at work can be applied to the study course and vice versa. In-house training and development are integral elements of the initiative. The programmes are designed for young people aged 18 to 23 and all study related costs are picked up by the company. There is no commitment on either side after the course is completed.

CCS believes it is strong in reward packages. Basic pay is considered good, while almost every employee has a variable element in their pay. In addition, the company offers fully flexible benefits in a cafeteria-style facility. Certain benefits such as pension, life insurance, sick pay and holidays are standard, then a value is put on the remainder of an individual's package. The employee can select from a number of options to draw up their own benefits package. Employees are even allowed to take a lower basic pay to enhance their personal benefits package.

It is very apparent that CCS is keen to secure the best available staff for its long-term future and is willing to incur costs and be ahead of the market in recruiting new staff and rewarding current employees.

Contact address

Jim Couton
Vice President
Coca-Cola & Schweppes
Charter Place
Uxbridge
Middlesex UB8 1EZ
Telephone: 01895 231313
Fax: 01895 230493
Web site: http://www.ccsb.com

CMG

CMG plc is one of Europe's leading information technology services groups, founded in 1964 but now operating in more than 30 countries from bases in the UK, the Netherlands, Germany, France and Belgium. It supplies systems development, management consultancy and advanced technology services to the finance, transport, trade and industry, energy, telecommunications, information processing and public sectors. It specializes particularly in providing information solutions to help customers achieve their business objectives. The company has developed many long-term relationships with commercial and government organizations; its clients range from Shell to BUPA and bankers Dresdner Kleinwort Benson. It is renowned for a unique human resource culture developed around a strong employee share ownership policy.

CMG at a glance

Employees: 6,000
Annual staff attrition: 15 per cent
Key locations: London, Amsterdam, Brussels, Paris and Frankfurt
Annual graduate intake: 100 (UK); 300 (Netherlands)
Annual intake: 2,000 (across the group)

An inside view

CMG has never made a loss since it was established, largely because it recognised early on that the company and its clients were operating in a world where the only constant was change, and that the rate of change – particularly in this decade – would only increase, providing enormous challenge for commercial and government organizations alike.

All have faced competitive pressure and the need to reduce costs and grow at the same time. Companies have realized that as well as meeting the needs of global customers, they must meet economies of scale that global markets provide, and the flexibility and potential cost savings afforded by using suppliers and resources all over the world. They have delayered their management structures and increased local autonomy so that customer service is optimized at local level while global contracts can still be secured.

In recognizing this sea change of almost constant upheaval, CMG has concentrated its strategy on long-term relations with large companies which must satisfy three basic criteria: fast growth, sharply changing business environment, and sufficient size. It is particularly known for work with the banking sector and its development of risk management systems and software packages for central bank reporting.

From the start, CMG's founders intended to build their company by staying close to their customers, doing exactly what their customers wanted of them and growing as their customers grew. 'We knew that by helping to make customers more successful, the company would become more successful,' says Cor Stutterheim, chairman of CMG. 'Over a period of time, we would build a relationship that would develop into a partnership and mutual trust difficult to break.'

This apparently simple business philosophy has been the cornerstone of more than 33 years of profitable growth. The group's growth has been largely organic although a number of strategic acquisitions have been made mainly to gain access to individual software packages or to enhance CMG's position in certain geographical markets.

CMG's work with leading banks throughout Europe has become a company trademark. It works for the leading banks in each of the Netherlands, the UK and Germany, for eight of the top ten international oil companies, 27 European telecom operators, ten of Europe's leading transport companies, and 18 government departments in the Netherlands and the UK. Recent projects range from developing an early warning system to prevent flooding in the Rotterdam port area to developing a mobile data gathering system for British Gas. It has developed world class products in areas such as mobile telephony, central bank reporting and direct insurance.

The company's year end results for 1997 reflect outstanding performance, with profit after tax up 44 per cent to £24.7 million, and the 24 per cent growth in group turnover to £303 million being virtually all organic. The company now employs around 6,000 people, an increase of 36 per cent on the same period last year.

How does CMG rate ?

Pay:	very good
Benefits:	excellent
Communications:	good
Training:	very good
Career development:	excellent
Morale:	very good

People and personnel policies

The most important facet of CMG, which was established at its inception and has continued to this day, is the involvement and commitment of its employees. This factor is remarked upon by outside business observers as much as those who work for the company. The founders felt strongly that all employees should share in the success of the company, be involved in decisions about the company, and also be shareholders. Until its public flotation in December 1995, CMG was primarily owned by its directors and employees. Today, more than half of its 6,000 employees have an equity interest in CMG, either through direct shareholdings or share options. Furthermore, all CMG employees reaching the first level of management are required to hold CMG shares equal to the value of one half of their annual salary five years after appointment. Higher levels of management are required to hold a year's salary in shares.

Barbara Ward, group director for human resources, says that CMG is run on a family basis, but it is a family that no one joins by accident. 'It's very difficult to get in. The company wants to be convinced that anyone who wants to work at CMG is a CMG person. Unlike many other companies, we want people to come here for the duration.' But once inside, an employee discovers a workplace that is distinctive, if not unique. There are, for example, no offices – and there are also no pay-slip envelopes. CMG operates in 'open plan' that embraces all aspects of the work environment. The monthly salary slip is left on everyone's desk in a totally open plan physical environment. 'Everyone knows what everyone else earns. Traditionally, you know another person's grade by the size of their desk or their chair. Everyone has the same size desk and the same type of chair,' she says. 'And there is no kowtowing to rank, either. This is a can-do company in which everyone is encouraged to have a go. And if you don't do well in your job, you are not fired but demoted. We have an overt concern for our people. The person who was promoted and didn't do well in the new position obviously did well in the previous position, otherwise they wouldn't have been promoted. So, this is our fault as much as anyone's.'

There are five sectors of the CMG Group, in five countries, and the company's board of directors visits each sector twice a year. This is extremely time consuming, but essential to the culture of openness. The directors always have lunch with the people who have just joined the company. 'We try and spend as much time on staff matters as on business matters,' says Barbara Ward. 'This all comes from the belief that you treat people as you would wish to be treated. Our balance sheet is filled with people, not buildings, and they earn the company's living.'

CMG has only one work contract, from directors down to graduates; and there is no one employed part-time. 'We want people who live to work, not people who work to live,' says Stutterheim, 'and full-time people deliver better quality work.'

The benefits package is among the top in the industry, and there is no variable or performance-related pay. 'We don't want our people to worry about their annual income; we want them to know what they will be getting – we only want them to worry about doing the job properly.'

Contact address

Mrs Barbara Ward
Group Director
CMG
Parnell House
25 Wilton Road
London SW1V 1EJ
Telephone: 0171 592 4000
Fax: 0171 592 4804
Web site: http://www.cmg.com

Colgate-Palmolive

Colgate-Palmolive enjoys a formidable reputation as one of the great US multinationals. In many ways it is a quintessential American corporate. It is often the subject of case study and profiles as an excellent manufacturer and sales and marketing operation. Colgate is regularly quoted in the American business press. But the UK company rarely features. And yet it is a role model for an innovative, participative and commercially astute organization which deserves much wider recognition. By standards of many US-owned businesses here, Colgate is comparatively small in the UK: it employs around 588 people. But these 588 are among the most effective employees in the British Isles.

Colgate-Palmolive at a glance

Employees: 588 (UK and Ireland) – 430 in manufacturing in Salford, 132 in HQ and sales and marketing in Guildford, 22 in Dublin, four in the research facility tied to the University of Manchester
Annual staff attrition: 8 per cent
Key locations: Guildford (HQ), Salford, Dublin
Annual graduate intake: no active graduate recruitment
Annual intake: 45

An inside view

Colgate-Palmolive is often mentioned in the same breath as Procter & Gamble and Unilever. Colgate's British managers are secretly very pleased at the comparison. Procter & Gamble employs 5,500 here and Unilever more than 20,000. In contrast, Colgate currently has 588 members of staff in the UK and Ireland. The company characterizes its approach as lean and productive, and says that given its market shares it is apparently more effective than its rivals.

Colgate is a unique enterprise which is rigorous in selection, offers copious opportunities internationally and promotes a culture of active teamwork and learning. It is strong on process, especially continuous improvement, and has a formidable work ethic. Staff loyalty is consistently high and some units have been together for years. Getting into Colgate can be difficult. Once inside people do not want to leave. This is one of the least political environments in British industry. This is partly a function of size – everyone knows everyone else – but also of its essential team orientation, friendly atmosphere and sense of pragmatism.

The two main locations of the business are in Guildford and Manchester.

The atmosphere in headquarters is inevitably different from the factory in Salford but they are guided by the same principles. Progress in the 1990s has been strong. The company was losing money in the last decade and took important steps which included significant strategic refocusing of its business portfolio and how Colgate commercially manage their products to consumers and customers. It is Colgate's focus on the consumer that has allowed it to generate insights that have led to strong innovative brands like Colgate Total, Palmolive shower gels, Soft & Gentle and many others. Such consumer knowledge has enabled Colgate to enjoy a strong consultative role with most major retailers where they are highly respected for their expertise in oral care. This remarkable achievement has been underlined since early 1997 by considerable progress in its Salford factory. Colgate UK now makes up a considerable portion of European Division's profit.

This facility was bought by Colgate in 1938 and in the 1990s was fully modernized with the latest computer technology. This has given Colgate the opportunity to capitalize on innovative human resources practices to provide people with greater scope in their careers. The international company decided to create what it called European focus factories, which means that certain product lines are concentrated in single units. The Manchester facility produces 90 per cent of Colgate's European toothpaste requirements, 100 per cent of its aerosol needs and 100 per cent of its mouth rinse products.

The factory has only 430 employees and demonstrates how effective use of technology combined with participative people approaches can have a dramatic impact on productivity. The entire business – and especially the Salford plant – is modelled on a flat structure. The factory's human resources manager Turner Atkinson says, 'Manchester is a traditional area. When we first proposed the changes which we introduced in early 1997 we were told that they would be too complex and too hard to be introduced. That makes the achievement much more satisfying in a way. The traditional concept of the roles had started to be eroded but we put forward a completely new proposal and this met some initial resistance.'

The new approach was based on skill blocks. Skills are defined as core, support and boundary. Core skills are those essential to the daily operation and delivery of the business, support skills are those normally performed by quality inspectors or engineers and boundary skills those functions provided by managers. The focus in the new structure was on building a progression of skills from core through support to boundary. Each individual is responsible for both personal development and contribution to the team. Colgate, as a matter of business philosophy, devolves decision-making as far down the chain as makes commercial sense.

So the individual plays an active part in the running of the business and identifying the skills which he or she needs to function effectively. After the initial concern, employees have embraced the new structure with enthusiasm. The extent to which the company was prepared to empower them came as a surprise but it was welcomed.

The skills block system has transformed the working practices of the Salford site. Within the scope of overall targets and a basic production schedule, teams make all the key operational decisions which lead to a constantly improving process. 'When we introduced the skills block system we also brought in an excellence programme and this too has had a great impact. The level of motivation was always good but morale is now exceptional.' Every single member of the workforce was retrained for the programme and as part of the company's individual assessment scheme has taken part in monthly one-to-one sessions with their managers since.

How does Colgate-Palmolive rate?

Pay:	very good
Benefits:	excellent
Communications:	superb
Training:	excellent
Career development:	excellent
Morale:	superb

People and personnel policies

In the 1980s, Colgate in the UK went through a bad time. It was poorly managed and it lost money. Two years ago when its long-standing finance director retired, the European President asked him why the British business is now so successful. 'There were several factors which he cited. First the way in which we recruit people changed radically. We looked seriously at the characteristics which successful people share and applied these competences to our recruitment processes. Colgate has always recognized that people have a life outside work and so many of our approaches are flexible. Beyond this there is a strong work ethic.'

It is the dramatic movement in people management policies which has underpinned the transformation to profitability. Colgate has chosen to create an alert, appropriate, articulate and capable workforce who receive competitive basic pay but outstanding bonuses, and a remarkably good benefits policy. There is quite a lot of structure about the Colgate human resources approach but it does not limit. It provides a flexible framework to make personnel initiatives fully effective. For example, rivals often attempt to draw Colgate people away to work in their companies. 'They do this by comparing the basic pay levels. So we created a comparative benefits sheet for each employee which shows the true value of their own total reward package.'

Colgate's pay becomes outstanding when it includes the performance related elements. Performance related pay is awarded on achievement against personal, team and company goals. Since the company is doing extremely well, performance bonuses are generally high. The reward package includes private health insurance, a share matching scheme, staff restaurant, long-term disability insurance, subsidized sports and social club membership, pensions, and five weeks a year holiday. The company operates a cafeteria approach to benefits which means that people can pick and choose to suit themselves. This is particularly important for Colgate's many company car drivers.

The business is especially supportive to its women who leave to have children. Colgate is very generous on maternity pay and is highly flexible, which allows women to come back to work if they wish to return. 'We will consider any appropriate solution if it is part-time working or job sharing or whatever is suitable,' says Annette Pettman.

The shift in recruitment policy has created a truly scientific approach to identifying the right people. 'We spend a lot of money on recruitment but in the end it is less expensive than recruiting the wrong people,' she says. 'Many companies use assessment centres but in most cases they rely on gut instinct in the final analysis. Every aspect of the assessment centre is scored and the successful candidates are those who achieve the top scores. There is no rationalization. The tests are constructed to reveal the qualities which we seek.'

In 1997, Colgate launched a new management development programme with new applicants. From 1,000 possibles, it chose four and has since taken another one. The successful people complete three nine-to-fifteen months cross-functional assignments in the business to give them a good commercial grounding. Colgate has a long tradition of moving people around and being adaptable is a core trait for success in the business. It is also extremely creative in its use of development assignments. If someone needs more experience in a specific discipline or exposure to a line of work then opportunities created by maternity leave or study leave will be fully exploited.

The UK business provides more employees to overseas Colgate companies than any other subsidiary. 'We could do more and it is a definite pre-requisite for success in the UK company.' The UK sales director was a UK entrant who became sales director in Portugal before being promoted to a similar position here. One British woman went to New York before becoming head of a global product division. The UK company has a long tradition of providing excellent people to the global corporation. 'When people have reached a certain level then we believe that international experience is extremely valuable.'

Colgate runs a values-driven employee attitudes initiative which is central to its diverse communications programme. The business is among the most innovative internal communicators in British industry with team briefings, flexible cross functional taskforces and creative use of communications media. For some of the research team, this is the best company in the book.

Contact address

Denise Cross
HR Co-ordinator
Colgate-Palmolive (UK) Ltd
Guildford Business Park
Middleton Road
Guildford
Surrey GU2 5LZ
Telephone: 01483 302222
Fax: 01483 464448
Web site: http://www.colpal.com

The Corporate Services Group plc

The Corporate Services Group is a leading international employment services organization. It provides workforce logistics at all levels throughout industry and commerce, and to a growing international client base. Whether sourced and placed from the UK or from its companies in continental Europe, its contract workers are to be found working throughout the world: from Europe to Japan, from the Middle East to South America – and in such far-flung outposts as the Falkland Islands and Ascension Island.

Corporate Services Group at a glance

Employees: 4,000+
Annual staff attrition: n/a
Key locations: UK, US and France. Head office in Glaston (Rutland)
Annual graduate intake: 50
Annual intake: n/a

An inside view

Less than ten years ago founder and current executive chairman, Jeffrey Fowler, identified a developing market in the employment industry that he has since utilized to become the foremost supplier of innovative workforce logistics to companies. The company is recognized as a leader in all of the key markets in which it operates – technical, industrial logistics, building services, commercial, catering and healthcare. The company provides skilled and semi-skilled contractors, ranging from aeronautic designers to process engineers, from electronic assemblers to telecommunication technicians, from HGV drivers to warehouse operatives, from data input personnel to call centre staff, from head waiters to catering assistants, and from doctors to carers. Corporate Services Group manages the payroll, benefits and career paths of its contract workers.

Since its inception, Corporate Services has expanded rapidly in the UK and continental Europe. With the recent acquisition of Corestaff Services Inc., one of North America's largest national providers of employment services, the group now has a major US presence. The UK operation comprises 260 offices, the US has 167 offices including on-site operations, France has 85 and Spain has seven.

The industrial, technical and building services division accounts for 52 per cent of sales and 37 per cent of operating profit. The Healthcare division achieved a turnover of £52.8 million in 1997, up from £26.6 million the previous year. While this dramatic growth included the acquisition in 1996 of Medacs, the UK's largest supplier of locum doctors to the NHS, organic revenue growth was 18 per cent up on 1996. CSG now owns one of the largest databases in the industry and have pioneered the development of long-term contract business with NHS Trust hospitals.

Corporate Services has a strong commercial and catering division. It has successfully established itself as one of the UK's largest suppliers of commercial staff to three key target markets: banking and financial services; public utilities; and local authorities. The division's catering arm concentrates on four main markets: contract catering, hotels and restaurants, hospitality and the public sector. The company is the largest provider of event and catering staff, having moved into long-term contracted arrangements with catering firms.

The Corporate Services Group recognizes that people are its principal asset. The culture of the group focuses therefore on ensuring that employees are well looked after, well trained and committed to customers. It seeks employees who are professional with a high degree of personal integrity, because the reputation of the group depends on its representatives. Flexibility is an essential attribute of employees as they must be able to handle the demands of different clients and new responsibilities and be prepared to learn new skills.

How does The Corporate Services Group rate?

Pay:	very good
Benefits:	very good
Communications:	good
Training:	superb
Career development:	excellent
Morale:	excellent

People and personnel policies

The Corporate Services Group currently employs more than 4,000 permanent employees and places approximately 100,000 contract and temporary staff each week. The group's training and development function is therefore crucial to the maintenance of high standards and a quality team of employees. All employees attend an induction course and thereafter have a structured training programme specific to individual needs. Throughout the year, employees benefit from a range of training programmes designed to increase their core competencies and improve their business skills. As a result the company consistently achieves enhanced levels of productivity which are above the industry average. The Training and Enterprise Council-administered National Training Award for excellence, awarded to the group, recognizes the high quality training offered to employees.

The company has a graduate recruitment programme, taking on 50 recent graduates a year and placing them in different operations around the country to train as recruitment consultants. When they have acquired the rudimentary skills needed to become an accomplished consultant, they are given the opportunity to develop a fast-track career within the group. The dedicated in-house training centres enable employees to have on-going training as needed.

The divisional structure of the company gives substantial freedom to the directors of each division and requires effective company communication channels. Monthly meetings within each division provide a forum for the exchange of information between its senior management, directors and employees. A training and quality assurance director ensures best practice across the group and regular internal communications throughout the company.

Remuneration rates in the company vary widely due to the diverse nature of the business and the wide range of industries in which it operates. In order to attract high quality employees committed to Corporate Services, the company ensures that its employees receive competitive rates of pay and an extensive benefits package.

Contact address

Rhiannon Smith
Director
Human Resources
The Corporate Services Group plc
Alexandra House
7 Alexandra Road
Hemel Hempstead HP2 5BS
Telephone: 01442 247697
Fax: 01442 254979
Web site:
http://www.corporateservices.co.uk

De La Rue plc

The De La Rue Group is synonymous with banknotes but has recently restyled itself as the Cash-to-Cards Group. The heartland of its business lies in the security printing of banknotes for up to 150 countries worldwide. In recent years it has also integrated a banknote paper manufacturer and enjoys dominant global market shares in both printing and paper manufacture. But the scope of the group does not stop here. It has rapidly growing divisions in the SMART cards areas, it prints certificates of authentication for Microsoft, advises central and retail banks on cash management, makes and sells cash handling devices for banks and shops, and provides passport and electoral systems for governments worldwide. The group has a mixture of mature businesses and activities in high growth sectors. Its challenge in tough trading is to gain greater efficiency from its traditional strengths and to secure significant positions in its newer enterprises.

De La Rue at a glance

Employees: 10,000 worldwide, 4,000 UK
Annual staff attrition: 10 per cent
Key locations: HQ and divisions at Basingstoke, operates in 30 countries
Annual graduate intake: 30
Annual management intake: 100

An inside view

De La Rue is a group in transition. It did extremely well from its traditional businesses in the early 1990s and is now facing challenging competition in these core areas. But the group's management perceived the trend of future opportunities and it created new initiatives which offer great potential. The group is the world's largest security printer of banknotes. Some 150 countries use De La Rue's security printing division, which makes it by far the largest operator in this sector.

John Gilkes, director of human resources, says that despite a market share of more than 50 per cent of the available market, De La Rue is facing stiff competition in banknote manufacturing and needs to achieve better returns. In 1995, the group bought a banknote paper manufacturer. This is the dominant player in global markets and has been fully integrated into the group.

De La Rue also prints a wide variety of non-banknote security products. Among these are stamps, cheque books, bonds and passports. A contract of major significance is its assignment to print the security covers for Windows 98 as an anti-counterfeiting measure for Microsoft. Given the number of Microsoft software packages which are sold worldwide, this is extremely important for the group. Within its security paper and printing division, De La Rue also has a function devoted to brand protection.

Around a half of group turnover comes from Cash Systems, a division which has invested heavily in technology in the past two years. Trading conditions have also been demanding but nevertheless, De La Rue continues to lead key global markets. It is the most significant player in cash handling equipment for banks. De La Rue makes and markets equipment to supply cash to tellers in banks and building societies. It also produces equipment which sorts and counts banknotes and coins. In addition, it advises retail banks on cash handling and the management of cash cycles. The division has 20 new products in the global market and has invested in IT to improve margins and service delivery.

Card Systems is the world's leading supplier of Visa and Mastercard products, and is dominant in magnetic swipe cards and SMART cards. SMART cards are the new growth area in the sector and De La Rue is positioning itself to exploit the most relevant opportunities. In 1997 it bought Philips' SMART card operations in France which will enable De La Rue to make a mark in this sector. Card Systems also produces passports and electoral systems for governments around the globe. By 2005, De La Rue hopes that ten per cent of the world's population will possess a card made by the group. This would include banking and credit cards, Pay TV cards and other high security cards.

The group and the divisions combine a mixture of established, mature businesses and areas of high growth potential. In the last couple of years, the group has invested in acquisitions and technology, disposed of non-core activities, and worked to achieve higher returns from its traditional sources of businesses. Group management recognizes that in order to become established as a major player in emerging business sectors it needs to make worthwhile commitments to investment.

Culturally the group is changing. It was grounded in the values of the security printing operation: absolute integrity, quality and technical excellence.

How does De La Rue rate ?

Pay:	good
Benefits:	good
Communications:	good
Training:	excellent
Career development:	excellent
Morale:	good

People and personnel policies

The group employs a head office corporate team of around 70 people and the rest of the 10,000 employees work for one of three divisions: Cash Systems, Security Printing and Paper and Card Systems. To bring the head office closer to the divisions, it was moved in December 1998 from central London to Basingstoke where the divisional headquarters are based.

The divisions each run under a managing director who enjoys considerable autonomy but is responsible to the group for the performance and management of his or her sector. 'The group has a strategic direction, it has core values and a philosophy of the way in which it does business. The centre provides the glue which holds the group together,' says John Gilkes.

Recruitment is done largely by the operating companies but the group also runs a central graduate recruitment programme. This brings in around six people a year who are viewed as future general manager candidates. They spend 16 months on a centrally funded induction course and are then given assignments in the division. 'We produce a recruitment brochure which goes around all the universities but in practice we attract candidates from a more limited number of universities.'

He says that traditionally De La Rue has employed people with language skills, strong leadership potential, high intellect and a global outlook. 'We are now trying to do two more things. We are looking at people with a broader mix of academic disciplines, for example scientists and engineers. Ideally, we seek linguists with a science or engineering degree. Also we want to recruit more non-Brits.'

The change is indicative of the cultural movement that is taking place in the group as a whole. 'Our culture until comparatively recently was that of the security printing operation. This has tended to be hierarchical, highly respected and blue chip with many clients in banking and government. Our culture tended to reflect that of our clients. Neither of these sectors is particularly leading edge in terms of employee empowerment. But we now have many businesses at the leading edge of technology and communication. These are flexible, responsive organizations where employees at the front line have a strong say in how the company runs. What we are trying to do is transform the culture of the group.'

Inevitably, De La Rue will emerge as a much more diverse organization. Some 87 per cent of its sales are drawn from markets outside the UK. Much of the currency printing is completed for third world countries. So there is logic in moves which will capitalize on its international identity to create a broader culture composed of traditions from various intellectual disciplines and geographical regions.

The group does not offer spectacular salaries in comparison with the investment divisions of its banking clients. It benchmarks against a set of comparable companies in its field and seeks to provide a median. The basic salary package is overlaid by a pattern of bonus payments, related to group financial performance, team or unit contribution and individual achievement. A contract is drawn up for each manager in the group which best reflects his or her capacity to make a contribution. 'The objective is to tailor an incentive contract which is relevant to a specific individual in a particular job,' says John Gilkes.

Contact address

John Gilkes
Director of Human Resources
De La Rue plc
De La Rue House
Jays Close
Viables
Basingstoke RG22 4BS
Telephone: 01256 329122
Fax: 01256 842509
Web site: http://www.delarue.com

Dell Computer Corporation

Dell Computer Corporation was founded in 1984 – it is now the world's leading direct computer systems company. It is also the fastest-growing computer company worldwide. The UK subsidiary, Dell Computer Corporation Ltd, which is based in Bracknell, is responsible for Dell sales and support in the UK and the vast call centre operation in Dublin. The Europe, Middle East and Africa headquarters are also based in Bracknell. Dell offers well rewarded and attractive career prospects in a fast changing technological business and, for those who can keep pace, represents an exciting work environment.

Dell at a glance

Employees: 23,000 worldwide, 1,100 UK
Annual staff attrition: 10 per cent
Key locations: global HQ, Austin, Texas, US; Dell Europe, Middle East and Africa HQ, Bracknell, Berks; Telesales: Dublin, Ireland
Annual graduate intake: variable
Annual intake: c.400

An inside view

Michael Dell founded Dell Computer Corporation in 1984 from his dormitory in the University of Texas. He was armed with $1000 and an original idea: to bypass the middle man and sell PCs directly to end users.

Dell Computer Corporation went public four years later. In 1987, Dell opened its first overseas office – in the UK. It has about 23,000 employees worldwide and sales value for fiscal 1999 $18.2 billion. It has sales offices in 33 countries worldwide and it serves customers in more than 170 territories.

Dell is acknowledged as the largest online commercial seller of computer systems, with an average turnover of $14 million a day. It is also redefining the role of the web in delivering faster, better and more convenient service to customers.

Dell is well known to the general public for its direct selling through media advertising. It also has a strong market presence in the business community, supplying businesses of all sizes and providing a dedicated account management team to large businesses. In recent years the company's performance has been outstanding. Earnings per share for fiscal 1999 increased 64 per cent over 1998. In January 1998, *Business Week* identified Michael Dell as one of the top 25 managers of the year. On the top ten of America's most admired companies, Dell reached number four.

Dell attributes its success to direct customer contact. Direct selling eliminates the unnecessary time and cost of retailers and other resellers, and permits a greater understanding of customer expectations. It also allows latest relevant technology to be introduced in its product lines more quickly than through slow-moving indirect distribution channels. The company builds custom made systems and uses the knowledge gained from direct contact before and after the sale to provide a tailored customer support service.

Dell endeavours to develop goodwill with its customers by means of competitive pricing and an emphasis on customer care. The benefit of this goodwill translates fairly rapidly into bottom line profits as rapid technological advances severely limit the life of PCs. The company is continuously refining its direct approach to manufacturing, selling and servicing computer systems. Current initiatives include achieving even greater volumes of product sales via the Internet and expanding its range of value-added services.

How does Dell rate?

Pay:	good
Benefits:	very good
Communications:	very good
Training:	excellent
Career development:	very good
Morale:	very good

People and personnel policies

The company's employment culture and philosophy are determined in Texas based on global and corporate targets, although the UK operation has some autonomy in order to meet local requirements. Dell recognizes that, to meet its goals as a corporation and to continue to grow and flourish, it must continue to attract and retain talented people. Its profit sharing and stock purchase plans are designed to reward the people who have made the company successful with financial success of their own.

Dell is committed to attracting and retaining high calibre employees. It aims to secure the right recruits and make their jobs and rewards attractive in order to retain their services in the long-term. Dell looks for self-starters, who are also team workers. The company is heavily customer-led and many roles are customer-facing, making strong interpersonal skills essential. The company's business environment is rapidly changing, therefore flexibility and an ability to cope with change and challenge are also important qualities.

Employees are assessed annually as part of a formal appraisal process, which is updated regularly during the year. The company has developed a management leadership model, which identifies key management competencies. Management appraisals are based on the achievement of objectives derived from the leadership model.

New employees go on a comprehensive induction course, the length of which depends on the nature of the job. It comprises a core element for all recruits, which outlines the business, its philosophy and how it operates, and the remainder is technical training. Subsequently training is a mix of on-the-job training and courses covering specific management skills and techniques.

As one of the world's fastest-growing computer companies, Dell acknowledges that its success depends on knowledge and education. The aim of its education policy is to put the right people in the right training at the right time. It promotes business, team and individual success by anticipating and meeting the educational needs. It offers on-line training, CD-ROM delivery options, orientation kits and web-based tools to enable employees to learn and apply new information, processes and technologies.

Dell offers all permanent employees competitive basic pay and a comprehensive package of employee benefits, designed with the employees and their families in mind. All employees participate in either a profit sharing plan or incentive bonus plan. They may also participate in a stock purchase plan, which gives staff the opportunity to invest between one and fifteen per cent of monthly earnings in Dell stock. The latter has been a very lucrative benefit in recent years due to Dell's strong stock market performance. There is a voluntary contributory pension scheme, life assurance, private medical insurance and long-term sickness benefits from day one of employment. A more unusual benefit is the Dell Employee Assistance Programme, which is a personal support programme that provides a completely independent and confidential off-site professional counselling service for employees and their immediate families for emotional, legal and financial problems.

Contact address

Vikki Sly
Human Resources Department
Dell Computer Corporation
Dell Plaza
Western Road
Bracknell
Berks RG12 1RD
Telephone: 01344 748000
Fax: 01344 714423
Web site: http://www.dell.com/uk

Deloitte & Touche

Deloitte & Touche is one of the world's largest firms of accountants and business advisers. It is one of the Big Five accountancy-led practices worldwide and is the UK practice of Deloitte Touche Tohmatsu. In 1998 D&T celebrated the centenary of its founders by reporting its highest ever fee income (turnover) of £563 million which was a 27 per cent rise on 1997.

Deloitte & Touche at a glance

Employees: 72,000 worldwide, 7,000 UK
Annual staff attrition: 21 per cent
Key locations: London, Birmingham, Manchester, Leeds, Edinburgh, Glasgow
Annual graduate intake: 500
Annual intake: 1,000

An inside view

Amid the welter of mergers and attempted mergers at the top end of the accountancy spectrum, Deloitte & Touche has remained apart. It has determined that clients do not want a shrinking number of full service firms and has therefore concluded that its growth will come primarily from organic development. The increase in performance in key business areas appears to give credence to its strategy: Deloitte Consulting, for example, improved its income by 78 per cent in the last year to reach £117 million. The tax division advanced 15 per cent and corporate finance put on 31 per cent.

Outgoing senior partner John Roques commented, 'We concluded in 1997 that major mergers in the Big Six (as it was then) were not in the interests of our clients, our people and the profession. Our focus has continued to be on our clients and we believe that this has played a part in our most successful year to date.'

The firm has significant presence in the UK, employing around 7,000 people. In round terms, some 3,000 are auditors, 1,000 are consultants, 1,000 are in support functions, and 2,000 are engaged in outsourcing. The model for organic growth applies across the business, but primarily in the traditional accountancy and consultancy businesses.

There is a distinction between advisory work done by the people in the audit and tax areas and the assignments undertaken by employees and partners in Deloitte Consulting. The advisory services are bolt-ons to Deloitte & Touche's audit and tax compliance work while the consultants tend to handle projects in change management and IT implementation. The firm draws in around 1,000 people a year. Some 500 are recent graduates though some new consultants may have worked in industry for the early part of their careers.

'Our key HR strategy is attracting and retaining outstanding people – that's what we are selling to our clients,' says Steve James, national HR manager. 'We have a dual focus – our clients and our people. Graduates are key to our HR model – they are central to our business. We train and develop them and promote them quickly. So they become the mainstay of our practice.'

Deloitte & Touche's research shows it is consistently seen as the friendliest of the Big Five. Throughout its literature it emphasizes a combination of intellectual achievement with direct straightforward people skills. In addition, it categorizes a series of qualities which the firm looks for in successful candidates. These embrace passion, dedication, confidence, ambition, loyalty and consistency in a changing environment.

These values are benchmarks against which to assess progress as careers develop. 'They have not been arrived at in isolation but represent key aspects of the relationship with our clients. As a firm we are especially keen on feedback as a principal tool in developing all the main areas of our business. We did an extensive investigation into client attitudes towards the firm – a client service analysis. We asked for feedback – what do we do well and what can we improve upon. Out of that came a set of core skills and competencies and a blueprint for the model firm and the model professional within the firm.'

Like all major accountancy practices, the battle is to retain the better newly qualified professionals. 'This is a common theme among all accountancy practices and we work very hard to keep them. But there are great attractions for newly qualified in industry, in finance and in consultancy. Our attrition rate overall is about 21 per cent which is very good.'

How does Deloitte & Touche rate?

Pay:	very good
Benefits:	very good
Communications:	good
Training:	excellent
Career development:	excellent
Morale:	very good

People and personnel policies

Training is the central element of the Deloitte approach. There is a three-day national induction programme for graduates where new recruits learn about the firm and its processes, get to know each other and their training and work programmes for the following three years, and the range of options available to them in study. Running parallel with this is a local induction scheme which is designed to familiarize them with the format of Deloitte & Touche offices in the area and their work.

Trainee accountants then start their formal studies and attend courses run by Deloitte & Touche's service providers FTC (Financial Training Company) or ATC (Accountancy Tuition Centre). They also join a support network within the firm. 'One of the things which is important to us is the quality of support which trainees can rely upon as they proceed through their three-year training. We are now the only firm that has four key players as part of our development network. This includes a staff partner responsible for that particular office, a counselling partner who is an objective third party to whom the student can talk, a mentor who is one of the management group, and then an academic partner who will be one of the HR department. Their induction includes meetings with all these people.

'We have recently launched a new induction programme for non-graduate entry, which replicates parts of the graduate induction. It includes a schedule of workshops and introductions to local practices.'

Training is ongoing for everyone. Qualified accountants, who make up the bulk of the professional staff, need to be updated on new technical standards. This is done in a variety of different ways from newsletters to face-to-face presentations and software products. When the new audit approach AS2 was introduced all relevant staff were briefed on its content. Since then they have been regularly brought up to speed on new aspects and developments of AS2. The firm has a national audit and accounting department which liaises with the professional bodies and makes members of the firm aware, through electronic communication, of changes in technical direction and policy. There are equivalent groups in tax and other divisions.

These workshops can lead to a plethora of options including secondments, distance learning, and MBAs. The workshops are a key part of the employee's review process. 'Alongside this we have an annual appraisal round and that is built around the same core skills and generating feedback on them. Our policy is that everyone gets an appraisal at least once a year. The appraisal includes 360 degree feedback and measures performance against objectives set. As part of that every individual sets his or her own development agenda based on the appraisal and feedback.'

The opportunities for migration to other sectors of the business are quite high. 'Many of our business areas are dependent on our qualifieds in assurance and advisory for their future employees.' For example, corporate finance and corporate recovery rely very heavily on this route for their resourcing. In tax it is less so because tax has developed a new model and it is recruiting and training its own people.'

Six months before people qualify they are all brought together in an internal careers fair. There are presentations from partners and stalls from all the divisions and functions. Employees can then understand where opportunities lie within the firm, which can counteract tempting offers from outside.

Contact address

Steve James
Human Resources Department
Deloitte & Touche
Hill House
1 Little New Street
London EC4A 3TR
Telephone 0171 303 3760
Fax: 0171 353 0807
Web site: http://www.deloitte.co.uk

Diageo plc

Diageo, created in December 1997 by the merger of GrandMet and Guinness, is one of the world's leading consumer goods companies. Its ambition is to be one of the top five global players in this sector – a goal that its management believes can be achieved through the creation of a totally new corporate culture and identity. Diageo, whose portfolio of internationally respected food and drinks products includes Smirnoff, Johnnie Walker, J&B, Gordon's, Pillsbury, Haagen-Dazs, Guinness and Burger King, made a profit of £1.9 billion on a turnover of £12 billion in the year to June 1998. All the businesses are growing profitably and nearly £2.8 billion has been returned to shareholders. Diageo aims to build on this performance by setting demanding challenges for its managers and employees, employing and developing the careers of those who can achieve these targets and providing the marketing support – currently £1.7 billion – to enable them to succeed.

Diageo at a glance

Employees: 77,000 worldwide; 12,000 UK
Annual staff attrition: n/a in 1998 due to merger
Key locations: London (HQ), Miami, Minneapolis and operations in 70 countries
Annual graduate intake: n/a in 1998 due to merger
Annual intake: n/a in 1998 due to merger

An inside view

The decision to use the name Diageo rather than take the traditional route of amalgamating GrandMet and Guinness was the clearest evidence of the board's determination to transform two groups containing some of the world's most famous brand names into a totally new international company. Just as important was the public statement that its goal is to become one of the five leading consumer goods companies in the world, which requires setting tougher challenges than executives had faced in the past.

'The targets which Diageo set were more demanding and completely different to what those who had worked for Guinness and GrandMet were used to. By setting such daunting levels, we are already making a break with the past', says Phil Radcliff, group organization planning and development director. A third change was to base investment decisions and calculate rewards for senior executives on a completely new system called economic value added (EVA). Diageo is the largest

British firm to use EVA, which requires major decisions to be taken on the basis of a formula which takes into account expected profits and the cost of capital, including equity.

This enables managers to assess the real economic cost and the real value creation of an acquisition or investment. In contrast, traditional measures such as earnings per share and pretax profit don't take account of the balance sheet so cannot assess returns on invested capital, and growth in turnover does not always mean increased value for shareholders. 'Managing for value is our core business philosophy. It is about having the creativity and commitment to make sure that all our decisions maximize value for our shareholders', says group chief executive John McGrath.

EVA is particularly important in an organization as diverse as Diageo which is split into four businesses and a group headquarters, as it provides strategic direction. The largest business is UDV, the wine and spirits company which comprises IDV from GrandMet and United Distillers from Guinness. With sales of more than 100 million nine litre cases a year to 200 countries, it produced operating profits of more than £1.1 billion last year. UDV has seen some of the most radical changes since the merger with new sales and marketing teams created in 55 of its most important markets and it has generated £260 million annual merger cost savings (plus a further £30 million from head office cost savings).

Although its brands include world class names such as Johnnie Walker, J&B and Bells whisky, Gordon's, Tanqueray and Gilbey's gin and Smirnoff vodka, UDV still accounts for only five per cent of total world spirits volumes. It has also had to cope with the downturn in sales in Asian emerging markets in recent months. A second business is headed by Guinness, one of the world's most famous brand names with 10 million glasses of stout drunk every day in 150 countries, and includes Kilkenny Irish beer and other beer brands. The third, the branded foods group, includes Pillsbury dough products, Haagen-Dazs ice cream and Green Giant vegetables. The fourth is Burger King, which is second only to McDonald's in the fast food market.

These four businesses will remain the core of Diageo, whose strategy will be to ally the traditional and romantic Celtic images of its leading spirits and beers such as Guinness to the demands of a modern market where the greatest growth potential comes from a younger generation with high disposable income. The key to this, says McGrath, is efficient marketing. 'Our strategy is to deliver profitable organic growth by investing marketing expenditure and capital behind our most powerful brands with the greatest value-creating opportunities', he says.

How does Diageo rate?

Pay:	good
Benefits:	very good
Communications:	superb
Training:	very good
Career development:	excellent
Morale:	good

People and personnel policies

One of the toughest challenges for Diageo in its first year has been to select the new executive team and to ensure that its members saw themselves as representing the new company rather than the merger partner they previously worked for. These are still aspirations though Phil Radcliff says the revolution is far more advanced than had been predicted a year ago.

One reason for the rapid success is that the company saw human resources as one of the strategic imperatives and put great emphasis on finding managers and senior staff who understood and were able to implement Diageo's new values. These are the freedom to succeed, to be the best, to be passionate about consumers and to be proud of what the company does.

'We want a company of highly motivated, well rewarded people. We were and are looking for people who are intolerant of mediocrity and who are innovative and prepared to take calculated risks but are ready to learn. We give a lot of leeway but they must understand the importance of teamwork and brand building', says Radcliff.

All managers in the parts of the business that were being integrated (i.e. the UDV spirits/wines business and the corporate HQ) had to apply for their own jobs which meant that more than 5,000 appointments had to be made. The top 200 appointments were made rapidly which, says Radcliff, sent a clear signal to the rest of the company that decisions would be made on the basis of ability.

'We developed a global resourcing framework with ground rules and policies which have been applied extremely well. We have filled the 5,000 jobs with very few complaints. We have been fair and professional and we went for the best people not just former GrandMet or former Guinness people. Things have gone a lot better than I expected', he says.

This approach was particularly important in the spirits sector where there was most overlap between the two merger partners. Differences were flushed out and a leadership group established to ensure that the division had a new identity and was not an amalgam of fiefdoms.

One significant change has been a conscious attempt to move the drinks division away from its traditional white middle class, middle aged, male image. A start has been made on attracting staff more in tune with a market which has a growing proportion of young, female and cosmopolitan consumers.

Diageo is still preparing its longer term recruitment strategy. While some parts like Pillsbury do recruit graduates, Diageo does not yet have a graduate scheme. Future recruitment will see a mix of graduates and experienced executives with emphasis on sales and marketing skills and those who are prepared to manage their own development and ready to work across the whole Diageo group.

'The merger has created in Diageo a larger and more varied business which is in four different sectors. One of the key benefits for individuals is the chance to develop their career across the whole company – our recruits are joining Diageo not just a particular division of the company. They must be seen as a group resource and be prepared to move between functions and regions. We have good performance assessment which will enable us to breed better managers and track them for advancement,' says Radcliff.

In addition there is a management development programme in which young managers who are deemed to have growth potential will, after five or six years of their career, go through tests and exercises designed to give them insights into their own development and where their future lies in the organization. Considerable emphasis is put on the training at all levels. During 1999, the company is continuing to hold regular strategy and leadership workshops designed to build up the strategic decision-making abilities for the 280 senior executives. 'Instead of the classic training where you just teach people about strategy, this is intended to show people how they can work together to develop a strategy. There will also in the next year be great emphasis on developing high class marketing skills. This will touch everyone from senior managers to graduate entrants and will be carried out on a Diageo-wide basis,' says Radcliff.

The intention to shape a new company is also reflected in the innovative reward package. Introducing EVA visibly changed business behaviour and, using it as the basis for assessing bonuses for the top 1,000 executives, is intended to reinforce the new approach. Next year's bonuses will be based on EVA targets and could be the equivalent of 30 per cent of salary. Top managers will have a long-term incentive plan based on shares but bonuses will depend entirely on EVA.

Contact address

Human Resources Department
Diageo plc
8 Henrietta Place
London W1M 9AG
Telephone: 0171 927 5200
Fax: 0171 927 4600
Web site: http://www.diageo.com

Electronic Data Systems (EDS)

Since its formation in 1962, EDS has grown into one of the world's leading information technology and consultancy providers. In the UK it has tripled in size over the last four years, and now employs more than 12,000 people, ranking as the UK's largest computer services company in terms of revenue. Much of its growth has been driven by its winning of a series of high-profile outsourcing contracts. With the demand for its services continuing to increase rapidly, EDS offers access to an unrivalled range of opportunities for those who wish to pursue a career in IT.

EDS at a glance

Employees: more than 110,000 worldwide, 12,000 UK
Annual staff attrition: n/a
Key locations: UK HQ near Uxbridge, Middlesex; 140 sites with major presence in Bristol, Sheffield, Telford, Derby, Hampshire-Surrey border
Annual graduate intake: more than 500
Annual intake: more than 3,000

An inside view

Founded in 1962, EDS became a subsidiary of General Motors in 1984, but became an independent company once more in 1996. During the 1980s and early 1990s EDS established itself as a provider of IT-related services to third parties. Its success was such that it now employs in excess of 110,000 staff worldwide and operates in more than 40 countries. EDS's operations in the UK began to gather pace after its acquisition of SD-Scicon, another large software and services group, in 1991. Today, it has a workforce of more than 12,000 operating from 140 sites, some of which are client sites.

The company spans a wide variety of business areas: systems and technology services; developing, integrating and managing systems to achieve recognized business goals; Internet and electronic markets, enabling customers to exploit the opportunities of the electronic marketplace; business process management, taking responsibility for a customer's whole business process (sometimes including non-IT functions); and management consulting, focusing on improved business performance, by linking income directly to the customers' performance. Movement from both within and across these business areas is actively encouraged, especially where it is felt that this will broaden the individual' s skills base.

The growth of the IT services industry over recent years has been well documented and EDS has participated in this process fully. In addition to its organic growth (from 1 January 1998 to 30 October 1998 there were 2,780 new hires, of which two-thirds are newly created jobs), the company has also enjoyed substantial growth through winning outsourcing contracts. Recent successful contracts include BP and the Employment Service, to add more than 70 separate contracts since EDS entered the UK marketplace. These contracts reflect the fact that EDS has major customers in both the private and public sectors, including such prestigious names as Rolls-Royce and the Inland Revenue. Indeed, more than 50 per cent of the UK workforce has transferred in from other organizations. This means that EDS has developed what it describes as a 'kaleidoscope of cultures' , where diversity is seen as a positive asset.

In addition to the appropriate technical and academic skills, EDS places an emphasis on candidates who have a high level of business awareness and are therefore capable of communicating effectively with clients. Given that the majority of EDS's staff are located at client sites, or at least spend considerable portions of their time there, it is imperative that they understand the customer' s business issues and problems.

How does EDS rate?

Pay:	good
Benefits:	very good
Communications:	very good
Training:	excellent
Career development:	very good
Morale:	very good

People and personnel policies

IT is a growing and dynamic industry. In recognition of this, and in common with other leading firms, EDS has developed a strongly performance-driven culture. However, it is also an organization that stresses communication and open, two-way discussions are encouraged, which is typical of the company which places great emphasis on teamwork.

In recognition of the many countries and industries in which EDS operates, the corporate policies are sufficiently flexible to reflect the local environment and cultural expectations of employees and customers alike.

EDS expounds the view that pay and benefits are only part of the picture when attracting and retaining staff. A key additional factor is EDS's ability to offer significant opportunities for career development. The company' s size and growth mean that there is a constantly changing series of opportunities becoming available, appropriate to a wide range of skills.

While EDS is happy to facilitate employee movement wherever appropriate, individuals own their own careers and are encouraged to be pro-active in identifying the opportunities available. To encourage this process, EDS operates a system of regular two-way communication between an employee and his or her manager, including, but not relying entirely upon, formal performance reviews to discuss individual goals and development needs. Wherever possible, promotion is from within and an important part of this is a level playing field for all employees, based on ability and aptitude.

For IT professionals, the opportunities are especially exciting, because the range of businesses with which EDS works offers a range of technical environments and industries from which to choose. This is of special significance for those employees who have joined from other organizations as a result of transfer, as they become part of an organization where IT is a core function rather than a peripheral role.

EDS provides quality training and training support service which will enable staff to fulfil their job requirements and maximize their potential. Technical, management and leadership training are offered throughout the individual' s career with EDS, from initial entry to Modern Apprenticeships in IT and a full graduate training programme, to senior levels in the company. In particular, there is close liaison with external bodies for the provision of special programmes tailored in the company' s needs.

Training normally takes place at one of two internal training centres and is designed to balance individual and business needs. EDS is committed to training its workforce to high standards and is recognized as providing training which is among the leaders in industry.

EDS is a major and permanent employer in the UK and as such is able to offer its employees exciting opportunities across the country, and in a wide variety of careers.

Contact address

Robert Bowler
UK Recruitment Manager
EDS Ltd
4 Roundwood Avenue
Stockley Park
Uxbridge
Middlesex UB11 1BQ
Telephone: 08000 747077
Fax: 0181 754 4277
Web site: http://www.career.eds.co.uk

Eli Lilly & Company

Eli Lilly & Company is a global pharmaceutical company with a world class reputation for developing its employees. After some restructuring, the company is focusing on producing innovative pharmaceuticals and on demand realization. The company is US owned but 50 per cent of its activity is conducted outside America. It is probably best known in the UK for manufacturing and marketing the antidepressant Prozac, which has been one of the company's most successful products. Its new high flyer is Zyprexa, used to treat schizophrenia, which was discovered in the UK and won the Prix Galien award in 1997 and Millennium Product in 1998.

Eli Lilly at a glance

Employees: 30,000 worldwide, 1,950 UK
Annual staff attrition: 4–5 per cent
Key locations: Basingstoke, Windlesham, Speke
Annual graduate intake: 100
Annual intake: 150

An inside view

Pharmaceutical companies are probably the paramount exponent of global economics. They were among a handful of business sectors which realized – at an early stage – that the scope of their operations would need to be worldwide. This appreciation has dominated their thinking ever since and percolated through their businesses. In order to be sufficiently agile for world markets, their structures would need to be flexible but tough, and their people would need to be the best.

Since emerging as global player, Lilly has shaped and reshaped its businesses. In the mid-1990s Lilly discovered that it was active in too many market areas. The changes which were occurring throughout the healthcare sector did not favour a company with such diverse interests. It decided to narrow its focus and invest heavily in the discovery and development of innovative molecules (new drugs) and in demand realization (getting the product out to the customer).

The impact has been startling. Since early 1994 the company has increased shareholder return by more than 500 per cent. It has helped that Lilly has a portfolio of innovative products in numerous therapy areas which has assisted this process. Management also initiated an efficiency programme which led to the manufacturing division producing 57 per cent more output at 1993 prices.

Lilly wanted an employee-led revitalization. The company encouraged group-wide discussion on how to tap the pool of talent within the organization based on its founding values of respect for people, excellence and integrity. A series of programmes inside departments and business units has encouraged people to shape their own careers and to influence the destiny of the company. The engine of change has been innovation.

The climate which this approach has engendered extends far beyond the laboratory. It has also cultivated a fresh approach in the sales and marketing of products, finding new ways to establish brands and to meet market needs. For employees this has meant greater opportunities to build relationships, to express novel ways of doing things, and ultimately to carry them out.

The UK company's human resources director Steve Fry says that although the company is a matrix operation, it adapts its structure to suit business needs. In some cases the team is central, in other areas individuals play a more prominent role. Lilly is an exceptionally pragmatic organization in that it is entirely driven by the needs of its customers.

How does Lilly rate?

Pay:	very good
Benefits:	very good
Communications:	good
Training:	excellent
Career development:	excellent
Morale:	excellent

People and personnel policies

Lilly recruits a thoughtful and articulate workforce. In 1997, around 150 graduates including six MBAs joined the company. Fry says that 150 was unusually high and in 1998, he anticipated, it would bring in more like 100. Nevertheless graduate entry accounts for the majority of the newcomers. And although he recognizes that people will move on, Lilly's objective is to recruit individuals who will stay for the length of their careers. Much of this recruitment is done by the traditional method of visiting universities and competing with other companies to locate the most attractive graduates.

Fry says that building relationships with prospective candidates and their colleges is his preferred approach. There are certain universities which are on Lilly's preferred list but visiting all the relevant places of learning is the only way to ensure that the best candidates are located.

The UK operation is based in Basingstoke where 400 people work in manufacturing. Another 650 are employed in sales, marketing and administrative support. Some 350 people work in research and development in Windlesham in Surrey, and a further 400 are located in Speke in Liverpool in a second manufacturing facility. Both the R&D and sales divisions are expected to grow in the next 12 months.

Personal objectives are set from team goals and divisional targets. These are directed by overall corporate goals. There is a framework but each individual's personal goals are determined by what the business unit demands. 'Teamwork is a discipline which we all value but if outstanding customer service is the principal aim of an individual's job then that will be his or her first objective,' says Fry.

He adds that the company wants open, honest and direct relationships. Clearly, if an issue – either positive or negative – arises then managers will not wait for an interim review but will discuss it immediately. Reward is determined by performance review. It is also linked to business unit performance.

Lilly was among the first pharmaceuticals companies to offer global stock option plans for its workforce. In April 1993 it issued the first grant to all employees and repeated the exercise in 1995. 'Now when we have employee meetings they ask questions about the share price. Many of our employees have benefited significantly from this programme.'

Lilly is particularly responsive to the needs of female employees and has won awards for its willingness to be responsive to career needs of women. It is hosting a job share programme, it also offers term-time working, reduced hours, career breaks and sabbaticals. Its WorkLife programme encourages employees to balance the needs of the job with those of a healthy home life.

The company is an active proponent of diversity. Lilly manages diversity so that it reflects its three core values of respect for people, integrity and excellence. The company's stance on this matter permeates everything it does. Lilly's managers use it not only as an internal tool but also as a key to commercial success.

Contact address

Mr Steve Fry
UK Human Resources Director
Eli Lilly & Company
Dextra Court
Chapel Hill
Basingstoke RG21 5SY
Telephone: 01256 315000
Fax: 01256 315858
Web site: http://www.lilly.com

Ernst & Young

Ernst & Young (E&Y) is a global accountancy and business advisory firm – one of the so-called Big Five. It was created from the merger of Ernst & Whinney and Arthur Young in 1989. E&Y has a wide spread of professional and advisory activities. Ernst & Young has always been strong in the US and by some measures it is the largest operator in America. UK fee income is around £600 million.

Ernst & Young at a glance

Employees: 86,000 worldwide, 8,000+ UK
Annual staff attrition: 19 per cent
Key locations: London (3,500), Reading, Bristol, Manchester, Birmingham, Glasgow
Annual graduate intake: 500
Annual intake: 1,500

An inside view

At the time of writing, there are five global accountancy-led business advisory firms. The Big Five has emerged from a process of merger, assimilation, product and service innovation and competitive advantage. The demand for consistently high and uniform service standards worldwide from multinational clients has led to the creation of businesses with sufficient critical mass to supply their services anywhere in the world.

The current Big Five emerged from a Big Eight and then a Big Six but neither could command enough strength in depth to meet client expectation. Also the accelerating pace of global competition among clients means that service provision from advisers needs to scale similarly more demanding standards. The global operators are obliged to make heavy investment in IT, people and product development.

Ernst & Young is itself the outcome of a series of mergers over many years. Ernst & Ernst was a top five US practice which merged in the 1980s with the UK's Whinney Murray to create Ernst & Whinney. Another Big Eight practice Arthur Young, which was strong on mainland Europe and in Scotland, united with E&W to create Ernst & Young. In the autumn of 1997, following the announcement of an ultimately successful proposal to merge Price Waterhouse with Coopers & Lybrand, E&Y announced that it was planning to join with KPMG, another prominent Big Five firm. After serious talks, it was clear that this was not going to work and there were some shared concerns about clearing regulatory hurdles.

E&Y, though has emerged strengthened from the encounter. The firm now has an enhanced internal conviction in its strategic force. It has driven the business forward during the last three years and continues to report annual increases in fee income –

equivalent to turnover – of around 20 per cent. The vast bulk of the UK operation is concentrated in London. The firm operates from Becket House, opposite St Thomas' Hospital in Lambeth Palace Road, and Rolls Buildings, off New Fetter Lane in the City. There are five key areas of business: audit, management consultancy, tax, corporate finance and corporate recovery.

Nicolas Mabin, director of recruitment, Management Consultancy, says, 'We are very strong in the US in terms of sheer numbers and client list. We are also strong in Europe. In the UK, which is the second largest E&Y practice after the US, we have grown – in fee income – by 57 per cent in the last three years. This is because we have concentrated heavily in three different markets. One is global clients, who need a one-stop shop so we can look after their needs in any country. We also have a whole area of activity based on companies in the top 350. There is a third group of activities looking at entrepreneurial companies, emphasizing owner-managed businesses.'

An international group co-ordinates the diverse activities of the practices in each territory where service requirement is often different. The representatives agree on an overarching worldwide approach and provide a coherent global network.

How does Ernst & Young rate?

Pay:	very good
Benefits:	very good
Communications:	very good
Training:	excellent
Career development:	very good
Morale:	very good

People and personnel policies

There are 11 different schemes for graduate entry into Ernst & Young, including one for the consultancy. One of the most popular is the process which brings graduates into a number of E&Y businesses to train and qualify as professional accountants. There is, additionally, a policy to recruit experienced hires who are almost all inevitably graduates or professionally qualified people.

Pam Evans, director of human resources, Management Consultancy, says, 'The entry requirements for the consultancy scheme are very clear. We are looking for candidates with a minimum of a 2:1 and preferably a first. They must be fluent in a second language and hold 24 UCCA points. For the rest of the firm a 2.2 and 22 UCCA points are acceptable. The subject of the degree is not of great interest to us. The qualities that we look for in prospective recruits include lateral thinking, communications skills, analytical and objective thinking, and self-confidence.

E&Y spends around $20 million a year on training. There are formal processes where recruits train to be accountants leading to different professional qualifications and, in addition, a series of ongoing developmental training. New recruits to the management consultancy enter a two-year programme which includes two weeks of induction and a sequence of developmental training throughout the initial period of employment.

There is an annual appraisal system. Mabin says, 'This is very much an objective setting session. Objectives are reviewed in terms of the experience, knowledge or competency of the individual. This is done in a tight framework so at the end of 12 months it is obvious whether or not someone has met their objectives. Everyone has a counselling manager who is vital to the process. The counselling manager will gather feedback from clients and colleagues alike. The aim is to discover how the employee is doing, what the perceptions are of his or her work, and what he or she needs to do to move forward. You have a responsibility to move ahead in your own learning and experience, to seize opportunities for learning and to contribute to the development of people around you.'

'In the last few years we have absorbed much greater capacity to provide learning opportunities. For example, electronic communication provides several platforms for easy access learning programmes, much of which is interactive. This also gives people greater opportunity to access the areas which they want to learn. In our larger offices we have learning centres where people can go. In November we had Learning Week in the management consultancy where there were 30 different programmes running. Other parts of the business have replicated this. Three-day career development workshops are run periodically to help individuals explore their career paths.'

Learning Week brought 400 consultants together to attend a variety of programmes including keynote speakers. 'Normally consultants work in small groups on assignment. They will come in for one training programme when they will be part of a group of no more than 20. In Learning Week, 400 came together to meet and talk as well as learning in formal gatherings. It was enormously powerful,' says Mabin.

Contact address

Nicolas Mabin/John Cornish
Directors of Recruitment
Ernst & Young
Becket House
Lambeth Palace Road
London SE1 7EU
Telephone: 0171 928 2000
Fax: 0171 928 1345
Web site: http://www.eyuk.com

Esso & Exxon Group of Companies

The Exxon Corporation is one of the world's largest and most successful companies. It is a key standard setter for the energy sector, enjoys a triple A financial rating and combines excellent technical and marketing skills. In 1997 it posted record earnings for the third consecutive year and raised its dividend payment for the fifteenth year in a row. The UK business is composed largely of Esso, the oil refining and marketing company, and Exxon Chemical. If these two main UK operating arms were to be quoted separately from the main corporation their combined revenues would place them among the top UK companies. Both provide long-term careers in a stable, challenging and diverse environment with a high emphasis on operational safety, quality, teamwork and innovation. Staff attrition is well below average and the rewards package is among the best in industry.

Esso & Exxon at a glance

Employees: 4,000
Annual staff attrition: 5 per cent
Key locations: Four in Esso and three in Exxon Chemical. Esso UK's HQ is in a purpose-built complex in Leatherhead, Surrey and a refinery at Fawley, Hampshire. The Exxon Chemical HQ is based at Fareham, Hampshire.
Annual graduate intake: 40–50
Annual intake: 100

An inside view

Exxon enjoys a commanding reputation among global businesses. One of the oldest and most impressive multinational corporations, it has consistently outperformed competitors while setting demanding standards for quality and excellence. In Britain, it is known as the Esso & Exxon Group of Companies. Its principal manifestation is Esso UK which is composed of two major operations – Esso Exploration and Production, which explores for and extracts crude oil and natural gas (upstream activities), and Esso Petroleum Company, which refines, distributes and markets petroleum products (downstream activities). Its upstream company is one of the largest investors in UK offshore oil and gas, while the downstream refinery operation processes 300,000 barrels of crude oil a day, and every day produces enough petrol to keep a million cars on the road for a week. Its sister company Exxon

Chemical researches, markets, manufactures and distributes chemicals which are found in everyday products from wallpaper to traffic cones, and food packaging to car oils.

In the report on Esso in the first edition of this book (this is the third edition), we commented on the high degree of distinction between the parent and the UK business. The core values of integrity, quality, safety and tight financial controls are replicated in the British operation but they are expressed in different ways. The UK operation still has a predominately national focus. As Sara Vann, manager of the UK recruitment centre explains, 'Oil is expensive to ship and so most countries will have their own refineries and a marketing policy which is driven by local needs.' Esso and Exxon Chemical derive benefits as key components of the Exxon Corporation but they are also granted significant freedom to achieve financial and operational targets.

Despite an increasing international orientation away from long-term careers with a single employer (which Esso recognizes), Esso & Exxon is keen to recruit people for the duration of their working life. Vann says that the company has a high rate of retention, with 50 per cent of graduate entrants staying for longer than ten years. Traditionally this has been a culture of science, engineering and technology graduates. The intake today comes from a broader range of disciplines – including marketing, logistics and human resources – but Esso & Exxon is still a highly attractive career option for mechanical and chemical engineers. The careers of graduate managers are planned as part of job families – or disciplinary groups – within the UK businesses. An individual recruited to work in the refinery, for example, can expect assignments in the supply, planning, upstream, manufacturing or distribution departments.

Another area where Esso and Exxon are pleased with progress is their Graduate Development Programme (EGDP) which is a three-year training and development programme run at the London Business School – one of the leading business schools in the world. The EGDP aims to develop within each graduate a comprehensive awareness of the petrochemical business, the skills to put that understanding within the context of the latest management theories, and the opportunity to learn and develop the personal skills needed to succeed in a chosen career.

How does Esso rate ?

Pay:	good
Benefits:	good
Communications:	excellent
Training:	excellent
Career development:	excellent
Morale:	very good

People and personnel policies

Esso & Exxon aims to be a quality employer which maximizes the potential of its people to generate positive returns for the group. It is strong on financial controls and sees its people as chief among its resources for reaching its targets. In order to ensure that it fully understands what its employees and potential recruits regard as key issues, the company conducts regular surveys among cross-sections of staff and undergraduates.

The feedback from these exercises shows that the single biggest issue for employees and potential recruits is training and development. The company responded by extending and enhancing its continuous learning processes, and has gone significantly further than many other leading businesses in devoting time and money to building its expertise in training – hence the EGDP with the London Business School which it started in September 1996. Further back down the recruitment line it also runs summer courses, of about eight weeks length, for penultimate year students who want to know more about careers in the oil and petrochemical industry, and Christmas courses for finalists.

Item number two on Esso & Exxon's slate of issues which influence commitment to an employer is the provision of challenging work. The company says that its drive for superb performance in all areas of its operation means that its people are faced with key challenges on a daily basis. It also suggests that its activities are so diverse that individuals can move to a new discipline, take an assignment overseas or seek another posting elsewhere in the UK. People are also looking for long-term commitment by the business which reflects Esso & Exxon's own desire to find individuals who are keen to have the option of staying with one employer.

Prospective employees are also concerned about the quality of the pay package and standing of the company in its communities. Although the industry as a whole may not always win plaudits for its approach to the environment, Esso & Exxon has always taken its responsibilities as a petrochemical company seriously. Where problems have occurred the company has acted ethically and won respect.

Esso & Exxon has evolved since we first examined the company in the late 1980s. One of the major changes is the rise of women within the culture. As recently as 1985, there were few women chemical engineers emerging from universities. At that stage, Esso & Exxon took a long-term decision to encourage young women to enter science, engineering and technology courses at university. Part of this process involved working with primary school teachers to adopt a positive attitude towards science and engineering. At the secondary stages active projects are in place to capitalize on a greater awareness of these disciplines and to foster interest among girls and boys. The strategy has paid off because by 1995 some 45 per cent of graduates recruited into Esso & Exxon were women.

Contact address

Sara Vann, Recruitment Manager
Esso & Exxon Group of Companies in the UK, Recruitment Centre
Administration Building
Fawley
Southampton SO45 1TX
Telephone: Freephone 0800 373 518
Fax: 01703 896038
Web site: http://www.exxon.com

Federal Express

Headquartered in Memphis, Tennessee, Federal Express – more commonly known as Fedex – is the largest express transportation company in the world, employing 143,000 people and delivering more than three million packages every single working day to over 211 countries. Fedex enjoys an excellent reputation for its approach towards its employees, summed up by its People-Service-Profit philosophy, which considers that looking after the wellbeing of its people is a crucial link in the process of providing a good service to customers, who in turn generate profit for the company. Fedex completes the People-Service-Profit circle by reinvesting profits back into the people and the business infrastructure.

Fedex at a glance

Employees: 143,000 worldwide: 5,500 Europe; 1,500 UK & Ireland
Annual staff attrition: 10 per cent
Key locations: central London, Heathrow, Enfield, Stansted, High Wycombe, Birmingham, Manchester, Leicester, Bishops Stortford, Coventry, Nuneaton, Prestwick
Annual graduate intake: n/a
Annual intake: 300

An inside view

A subsidiary of FDX Corp, Fedex was founded by Fred Smith, and began worldwide operations in April 1973, since when it has grown into the largest express carrier in the world, generating revenues of US$13.3 million in fiscal 1998. Fedex currently employs around 143,000 people worldwide, 1,500 of whom are located in the UK and Ireland business district, which is part of the Europe, Middle East and Africa (EMEA) region.

The way in which Fedex runs its business is based on Fred Smith's idea of a central operational hub situated close to an airport, hence the company has key hub locations at Stansted and other airports in the UK, with the administration of the business being concentrated mainly in the Midlands. The workforce is divided on a ratio of 60:40 between operational staff, such as couriers, those involved in depot management and workers at the hubs; and functional staff, including customer service people and central support functions such as administration, finance and HR.

In the express carrier business, competitive environment companies compete with one another by offering a combination of reliability, speed of delivery and efficiency in their efforts to service businesses around the world.

Fred Smith's HR ideas are still reflected in Fedex's HR policies today with

Fedex maintaining its competitive edge by genuinely acting out its PSP philosophy in its day-to-day business operations. It fully recognizes that the prosperity of the company is dependent on its ability to attract and retain key business accounts. Employees need to be good teamworkers demonstrating a willingness and capacity to meet clients' requirements and solve their delivery problems through a combination of energy, determination and intelligence.

How does Fedex rate?

Pay:	good
Benefits:	good
Communications:	good
Training:	superb
Career development:	very good
Morale:	very good

People and personnel policies

Helen Hutchins, Fedex personnel manager, states that the company HR goal is 'to provide the necessary programmes and services for a knowledgeable, safe, productive and motivated workforce which will support the People-Service-Profit philosophy.' The company achieves these aims admirably, fully deserving its reputation for the superb training, career and personal development opportunities with which employees are provided. Fred Smith was the first at Fedex to tackle the issue that many managers who were good at operations were less successful when it came to the management of people. As a result, he introduced a competency-based readership development process. The use of competencies is now the foundation for Fedex's drive to utilize leading edge selection, training, development, motivation and appraisal methodologies.

In order to ensure its people have the capacity to perform at the demanding level required in a competitive business environment, Fedex invests heavily in training, not only for work skills but also personal development. The emphasis on strong leadership means every manager is encouraged to complete 40 hours or more training every year. Various training media are suggested including videos from Fedex's own FXTV Leadership series.

Many people begin with Fedex at entry level in positions such as couriers, customs clerks or customer service agents, where little formal qualification is needed, although candidates must possess good communication and interpersonal skills. As far as the recruitment of managers is concerned, although academic qualifications – perhaps to degree level – are preferable, personal qualities are viewed by the company as being of more interest in the selection procedures. Other key recruitment areas include Sales and IT.

Fedex is remarkable in that this attitude still holds true when it comes to the career development of individuals, believing that personal qualities like drive, commitment to the customer and the imagination and initiative to actually make an impression on the company are more important than paper qualifications. In addition, most people in the company will have to deal with customers at some time in their careers and therefore need to be confident, co-operative and helpful.

Where possible, Fedex prefers to promote from within and its people can take advantage of some very good opportunities to develop their careers. However, the company's expansion programme will continue to make it necessary for people to be taken on externally. Fedex is currently establishing a European Management Development Centre which will be responsible for tailoring the company's Leadership development series to the specific needs of the region.

Aware that the company's prosperity is fundamentally entwined with the quality of its people, the overall remuneration package provided by Fedex is competitive, allowing the company to recruit and retain people of the necessary calibre. For most employees the compensation package consists of a combination of basic pay, variable pay and benefits, although Fedex HR is focusing on areas of critical skills where it recognizes the fact that the company must offer enhanced rewards. Exceptional performers can be rewarded through a number of different recognition programmes.

Contact address

Helen Hutchins
Personnel Manager
Federal Express
Bond Gate
Nuneaton
Warwickshire
Telephone: 01203 343333
Fax: 01203 681559
Web site: http://www.fedex.com

F.I. Group plc

F.I. Group is one of Britain's longest-established suppliers of business technology services. Started in the early 1960s, it is now one of the top ranked companies providing applications management and outsourced IT services. It has experienced outstanding growth, quadrupling turnover and increasing pretax profits five-fold in the last five years. The company has an exceptionally high level of employee shareholdings and is acknowledged for the quality of its training.

F.I. Group at a glance

Employees: 3,000 (including about 1,000 contractors) + 1,000 in India
Annual staff attrition: 10 per cent
Key locations: Hemel Hempstead (HQ) and around the UK with new operations in India and US
Annual graduate intake: 100
Annual intake: 400

An inside view

F.I. is UK market leader in applications management – the fastest growing sector of the IT industry. Its blue chip client base now includes Bank of Scotland, Barclays Bank, BT, Co-operative Bank, DHL, Lloyds TSB Bank, Legal and General Insurance, Sainsbury, Tesco, Thames Water, Whitbread and Yorkshire Electricity. F.I. operates in three industry sectors – financial services, retail and leisure – and seeks to create a balance of business across these three sectors. The company has used its base market of applications management to develop longer-term, more comprehensive outsourcing contracts. This has at times resulted in the absorption of client workforces by F.I.

At the end of 1997 F.I. took its first strategic step in international development to meet the global demands of its customers. It acquired IIS Infotech, a leading software house, operating from three centres in India, the United States and Singapore.

The company actively encourages employee participation as workers and through share ownership. Employee share ownership reflects the culture of the company rather than a fringe benefit of employment. The workforce is consulted on key management issues and is a fundamental element in the decision-making processes. Indeed, prior to the flotation of the company on the London Stock Exchange, the workforce were asked to vote on whether they wanted the flotation to go ahead.

The company attracts lively minded, articulate and intelligent individuals, which has given rise to a culture where debate is commonplace. It is now a thriving PLC but the workforce continues to regard the company as its own creation. Their high level of shareholding ensures that they have significant influence.

F.I. has progressive equal opportunities policies. Of the six executive directors, four are female including the deputy chairman and chief executive, Hilary Cropper. The company has achieved outstanding results under her leadership.

The company has a high number of freelance contractors who comprise approximately 30 per cent of the workforce. They are mainly specialists engaged for particular assignments.

How does F.I. Group rate?

Pay:	very good
Benefits:	excellent
Communications:	superb
Training:	very good
Career development:	good
Morale:	superb

People and personnel policies

The company recognizes that its workforce provides skills and energy and is a fundamental factor in the growth and success of the company in recent years. The reward structure is designed to give full recognition to workforce input. The basic philosophy is to reward people fairly and competitively with packages that are both performance related and flexible. The workforce is encouraged to contribute to discussion on reward provision and improvement in individual performance.

F.I. prides itself on having rewards, benefits and share ownership packages which are amongst the most progressive and flexible currently on offer. In addition to basic rates of pay comparable with other IT organizations, the reward structure recognizes achievement by means of profit share allocations and management bonuses once significant year on year growth targets have been met. The maximum potential allocation is ten per cent of salary per employee and this was paid out in full in the 1998 financial year because of the superb year on year growth achieved in that period.

Morale and company loyalty is so high that in 1997, 96 per cent of the allotted bonuses was taken in the form of shares in the company and only four per cent as cash. The company also has a Share Save Scheme and a Share Option Scheme. Employee share schemes are operated through two trusts and currently own 22 per cent of the company between them. This compares with the holding of the largest individual institutional shareholder at a mere 4.2 per cent.

In addition to remuneration packages the group operates a flexible benefits scheme which allows each individual employee the opportunity to select from a range of benefits according to personal needs. The benefits include pension scheme choices, life assurance, permanent health, medical and dental insurances and holidays. There is even an option to express a preference to receive the value of some of the benefits in cash.

Flexibility also extends to working arrangements. F.I. is renowned for its Flexible Employment Contract by which all the benefits of working full time are extended to those who wish to work only part-time.

Communications within the group are top of the range of any UK companies and there is a culture of openness, integrity and active feedback from the workforce. Most recent initiatives include open lunches with board directors and structured feedback programmes giving everyone the chance to input ideas. There is an eight-page quarterly professionally produced house magazine *Insight* issued free to all of the workforce which covers personal interest stories from local branches as well as major company news stories.

The group invests heavily in training, some of which is handled by its own training company F.I. Training. In the fast-moving IT business it is essential to have staff at the leading edge of the latest technology and innovation, in order to maintain long-term relationships with clients. The company has a structured career development programme, with personal development plans for all employees. All managers have a mentor – a more experienced manager – to provide guidance and act as a sounding board. There is a proactive graduate recruitment programme. F.I. seeks graduates who see things differently – lateral thinkers capable of developing colourful solutions to some of the most complex business challenges.

Employees are encouraged to develop their own career at their own pace of progress. The company provides a firm foundation for personal growth through business, technical and personal skills training. This balanced approach has been rewarded by Investors in People re-accreditation.

F.I. tries to put something back into local communities across the UK by using skills and energy to help both individuals and organisations. Its primary focus is the use of IT to help young, disadvantaged people, but skills are also made available to other needy local projects.

Contact address

F.I. Group plc
Campus 300
Maylands Avenue
Hemel Hempstead
Herts HP2 7TQ
Telephone: 01442 233339
Fax: 01442 238400
Web site: http://www.figroup.co.uk

Finelist Group plc

The Finelist Group is the UK's largest motor vehicle parts distributor. It was originally based on a perception that a highly fragmented sector could be consolidated, and disparate businesses – with widely varying standards of service – could be assembled into an integrated group. An appetite for aggressive acquisition is a cornerstone of the Finelist approach. It is matched by strong organic performance in core businesses and a markedly entrepreneurial culture. Finelist values commitment, drive and intelligence and has emerged as one of the fastest-growing businesses to be based in the West Midlands and is the top growth company in Europe.

Finelist at a glance

Employees: 7,500
Annual staff attrition: 10–15 per cent
Key locations: 790 throughout the UK; head office in Stratford-upon-Avon
Annual graduate intake: 20
Annual intake: 850

An inside view

In the late 1980s few market sectors remained as disparate as motor vehicle parts distribution. Typically, distributors were family-owned with perhaps two or even three branches. The quality of service offered would be dictated by the extent and approach of competitors. No economies of scale applied because managers possessed no substantial purchasing power.

Chris Swan, one of the leaders of a management buy-out at Autela Components in Warwickshire, saw things differently. By rapid acquisition, standardization of reliable customer service and with a degree of financial muscle, he could create a national network. A decade later, Finelist is the UK market leader. But the Finelist achievement is not defined by corporate finance and management skills alone. It is characterized by a strong belief in the capacity of employees – given support and enthusiasm – to mould commercial success.

In recent years the pace of expansion has accelerated. Alongside the major purchases of networks of distributors, Finelist has bought, almost on a daily basis, tiny operations often owned by single proprietors. Each of these has been assimilated into the group's developing operational base. The impact of each new acquisition is seen quite quickly because after ten years of adding businesses, the integration programme is smooth. The strategic direction of the group is firmly controlled from the centre. It establishes tight financial targets but also allows local management a high degree of operational freedom. Year on year the financial health of the business appreciates. Its latest financial results show sales of £388.1 million with an operating profit of £37 million.

More than 60 companies have been bought since the group floated in 1994. This policy of aggressive acquisition will continue. There is still plenty of room for manoeuvre; although it is now the largest player in its sector, it commands ten per cent of the market. The parts distribution sector is estimated to be worth £4.7 billion. At present Finelist comprises a wide range of businesses, catering to every possible need of the motor industry, apart from total vehicle manufacture. Among the brands within the business are Tuberex, Autostart, Autela, LSUK, SDL, Veco, Truckline, Engine Express, First Line, Ferraris Piston Service, AutoGem, Panther Products, Genex, Maccess, Edmunds Walker, Motor World, Charlie Browns, Motor Store, Road User and XL Components.

How does Finelist rate?

Pay:	very good
Benefits:	good
Communications:	excellent
Training:	very good
Career development:	very good
Morale:	excellent

People and personnel policies

In a phrase which reveals volumes about the Finelist business approach, its head of human resources Jerry Hayter describes personnel policy as 'the minimum of fuss but the maximum of total accountability'. The human resources operation is about people, not structures or things. Hayter looked at what other companies were doing in his field. In the main he was not impressed, but derived some benefit from this benchmarking exercise and trimmed sails accordingly.

People policy is about allowing employees sufficient support to do the job but also space to make their own mark. Hayter emphasizes the need to free line management from bureaucratic trivia. Management in all separate companies and branches is encouraged to manage with complete autonomy. In practice, the use of small, fast moving teams is characteristic of the group and their application can be seen in all of its businesses.

Swan is firm in his employee-centric view of the future of the group. Although staff empowerment has been in vogue generally in the last few years, it has been a cardinal value in promoting organic growth in Finelist since the start. He argues that it is a self-evident requirement of any business which seeks long-term success and stability. In Finelist, as with many other areas of its commercial philosophy, HR policy is directly expressed and straightforward. Swan and Hayter give people opportunity. They train them well, they give them good pay and benefits for the sector and set them free. New talent is actively recruited from the shop floor.

Finelist is rigorous in its selection of candidates for their first assignments in the group. It is in fact probably a good more thorough than many businesses. Hayter holds the view that if it is careful about its newcomers and spends a proportionately greater time in initial selection, the group will benefit from a higher retention of candidates. Finelist's staff attrition rate is relatively low for the sector. Also those who stay tend to do so for longer than the market average.

One of the main reasons for employee loyalty is Finelist's express commitment to openness and information flow. Responsibility is devolved down to branch managers who are expected to release energy against a background of a clear framework of objectives, financial information and control systems. In other words everyone is seen as a key player in the organization, and without each player the team does not function. Once ability is spotted, promotion is rapid. Finelist has little time for unnecessarily rigid structures and so talented people – having proved themselves – are given fresh challenges.

Training is a catalyst for accelerated promotion. Most attention is focused currently on management development with the ultimate aim of a downwards cascade. Graduates are regarded as the management of the future and are trained accordingly but there is a dual strategy in the future wellbeing of the company. Some of the organization's best managers joined under the youth training scheme or in junior roles. A core tenet of open access underpins its recruitment and promotion policy.

All companies within the group are seen as individual businesses and free to negotiate their own hourly basis pay rates. Managers are on salaries but there is a profit related pay scheme across the group and performance bonuses too. The package is made more attractive by share saving schemes and the company matches employee contributions into a money purchase pension scheme.

Contact address

Jerry Hayter
Head of Human Resources
Finelist Group plc
Birmingham Road
Stratford-upon-Avon
Warwickshire CV37 0BN
Telephone: 01789 414545
Fax: 01789 414526
Web site: http://www.finelist.co

Glaxo Wellcome plc

Glaxo Wellcome plc is one of the world's largest pharmaceutical companies and was formed in 1995 when Glaxo launched a successful takeover bid for the Wellcome Foundation. Since then, Glaxo Wellcome has been among the UK's biggest companies in terms of stock market capitalization. Over the years it has built up a strong and well-earned reputation as one of the UK's best employers. With a well-developed human resources policy and a high-profile graduate recruitment programme, it has long been the first choice of many graduates emerging into the job market for the first time.

Glaxo Wellcome at a glance

Employees: 54,000 worldwide, 13,000 UK
Annual staff attrition: 5 per cent
Key locations: HQ in Greenford, Middlesex with nine other sites in the UK
Annual graduate intake: 125
Annual intake: n/a

An inside view

When Glaxo acquired Wellcome for £9 billion in March 1995, it was at that time the largest acquisition in the UK by any company. The deal created the third largest UK company and the largest pharmaceutical company in the world. For the first year or so, the main priority of the then chief executive Sir Richard Sykes was inevitably rationalizing and integrating the two businesses, as well as devising a strategy for Glaxo Wellcome to become a consistent leader in the world pharmaceuticals industry. Rationalization and amalgamation, where appropriate, of research and development programmes was essential to realize the full benefits of the merger.

Glaxo had been spurred into takeover action by the widespread change in the pharmaceutical sector. The industry had developed from national markets and spheres of operation to an increasingly international industry. Competition had intensified, regulation had been tightened by many countries and financial pressures were prevailing. Glaxo's management took the decision that a major acquisition of a company with a similar culture based on science, sound research, a complementary range of products and a high calibre staff was needed and homed in on Wellcome.

The result is a full service company which provides healthcare solutions in continuous dialogue with sector professionals and prescribers. It operates in a phased progression of discovery, development, manufacture and marketing of its pharmaceutical products. The merged companies have moved from

Glaxo's heavy reliance on one major product (Zantac – the anti-ulcerant) to a broad portfolio of pharmaceutical products.

The style and culture of the company is decentralized with each business run as an autonomous unit, with its own managing director reporting directly to a main board director. Inevitably, in the commercial aspects of the business there is still a strong national structure as there is a need to work with local healthcare professionals on local priorities. However, in the Research and Development discipline it is the global entity which is autonomous, even though there are R&D operations in the UK, US, Canada, Australia, Switzerland, France, Italy and Spain. On the manufacturing side of the business, Glaxo Wellcome has concentrated on the areas where it has expertise but has also formed alliances where there are other established companies with their own specialist operations.

How does Glaxo Wellcome rate?

Pay:	very good
Benefits:	excellent
Communications:	good
Training:	superb
Career development:	excellent
Morale:	very good

People and personnel policies

The autonomous unit style of the Glaxo Wellcome group, with each business having its own human resources requirements, has been the basis of the Glaxo Wellcome personnel policy. However, in mid-1997 a UK Human Resources Policy Manual was issued to promote a consistent approach and understanding of human resource policies across all UK businesses. The manual was a product of a joint working party drawn from all UK business units. The manual is the first attempt at introducing policies on core issues and will be updated in the light of experience and changing legislation. Embodied within the policy is a group grading structure which relates to any individual company grading structures so that group benefits can be applied evenly and fairly across the group.

Glaxo Wellcome tries to reward employees competitively according to the criteria of each marketplace. It seeks to recruit highly motivated, intelligent and well-skilled staff who will be with the group for the long-term. Naturally, as talented people they will demand top rate rewards and remuneration. The aim is to create the strongest relationship between the employee and the company. This is not designed to be a paternalistic relationship, but one where employees recognize that the rewards and social ambiance of the company are designed to engender a comfortable and supportive feeling towards the group.

In terms of remuneration, clearly the motivation for a scientist will be vastly different from that of a salesman.

Therefore, a key concept in designing reward packages is flexibility, so that all disciplines receive their rewards and motivation by the method best suited to their discipline and individual needs. One example of this flexibility is to be found in the pension plan. This, in its basic form, is non-contributory but has three elements: the core element, which is provided by the company; the partnership element, where the employee's voluntary contribution is matched by GW; and a savings element which is purely an employee's voluntary contribution. This hybrid pension scheme is commonly regarded as a benchmark scheme for many others.

Another example of flexibility is in the car policy. Any employee who establishes a qualification for a car by management grade, market relationship or business need can opt for a cash alternative and provide his or her own transport. Healthcare cover is provided for all employees, with additional cover for families paid for by the company for managerial grades and at the employees' voluntary cost for lower grades. There are also voluntary group Share Option and Sharesave schemes.

The philosophy of Glaxo Wellcome on career development is that the fundamental emphasis must be on self-development, although the group will provide considerable assistance to employees in developing their career plans. The company wishes to help individuals to make a greater contribution to the group by selecting and developing the careers of those who wish to and are capable of succeeding. One of the greatest challenges in such a diverse group is cross-fertilization between disciplines and businesses, as it recognizes that with a highly educated workforce, restrictions on opportunity will have a negative effect on the individual and the company.

A possible solution being tested is team-based projects where groups of unrelated employees are being used to broaden individual skills and give greater exposure to challenges. There is a fundamental belief that the most talented people are flexible, adaptable, highly motivated and better able to handle change. This philosophy is going to need a continuous throughput of talented and positive recruits who are people who do not walk away from a problem and the recruitment procedures are under way.

Glaxo Wellcome is a forward-thinking and diverse group where career opportunities will be created for the talented, industrious and self-developing recruits. It has a good track record for training and development of recruits and is high in the league of the major employers for pay and benefits.

Contact address

Dr David Findley
Director, Human Resources
Glaxo Wellcome plc
Glaxo Wellcome House
Berkeley Avenue
Greenford
Middlesex UB6 0NN
Telephone: 0171 493 4060
Fax: 0181 966 8330
Web site: http://www.glaxowellcome.com

Goldman Sachs

Goldman Sachs is a leader in virtually every field of investment, finance and research, as well as in mergers and acquisitions. It is a member of major securities and commodities exchanges worldwide, including the New York Stock Exchange, Tokyo Stock Exchange and the London Stock Exchange. Goldman Sachs is headquartered in New York, has regional headquarters in London, Tokyo and Hong Kong, and offices throughout the Americas, Europe and the Asia-Pacific region. The firm serves clients through teams of professionals who provide state-of-the-art services and products in local markets and have distinctive capabilities to help them capitalize on opportunities worldwide. In April 1999 it announced a share-out to staff which will make many millionaires.

Goldman Sachs at a glance

Employees: n/a
Annual staff attrition: n/a
Key locations: London
Annual graduate intake: n/a
Annual intake: n/a

An inside view

With Europe in the midst of a period of significant change in the business and regulatory environment, Goldman Sachs is capitalizing on the variety of opportunities and competitive challenges that have resulted. It is a multi-faceted organization operating many different divisions. Investment banking and global investment research undertake the structuring of public offerings and analyse companies' financial statements. The fast-paced transaction oriented environment of equities, fixed income, currency and commodities and asset management offer opportunities in sales and trading.

The divisions of operations, technology and finance are oriented around planning, developing and maintaining critical business systems that enable the firm to manage risk and ensure control. The firm is registered as a broker-dealer with the US Securities and Exchange Commission (SEC) and as a futures commission merchant with the Commodities Futures Trading Commission (CFTC).

As a prominent investment bank, Goldman Sachs is central to important and innovative developments in the financial markets. For example, in 1997 Goldman Sachs worked in conjunction with the Chinese government to achieve a $4.2 billion partial privatization of China Telecom, one of the largest cellular companies in the world. It was the first large-scale privatization in China, the largest-ever public offering by a Chinese entity and the largest-ever public offering in the global cellular telephone industry. The restructuring of Imperial Chemical Industries (ICI) illustrates how Goldman Sachs provides advice and multiproduct support that can assist a company in redirecting its business and add value for its shareholders. Among other things, it acted as joint advisor in ICI's acquisition of the speciality chemicals business of Unilever for $8 billion, the largest private market transaction ever in the UK. Leveraging its long tradition in the private equity markets, the asset management division launched its first private equity fund in 1997.

Goldman Sachs is a meritocracy, operating in a non-hierarchical management structure, where both analysts and associates find themselves working alongside managing directors daily. The firm-wide culture is committed to a dedicated, expert and collaborative effort on behalf of all its clients, forming the basis of its competitive advantage. Teamwork is stressed throughout the organization, as it has no room for those who put their personal interests ahead of the firm and its clients. Goldman Sachs has an intense and sometimes stressful working environment. This is generated by partaking in high-profile transactions and having contact with many powerful clients, even those employees at entry level. Professionalism is paramount, as Goldman Sachs displays an uncompromising determination to achieve excellence in everything it undertakes.

How does Goldman Sachs rate?

Pay:	excellent
Benefits:	excellent
Communications:	good
Training:	very good
Career development:	excellent
Morale:	very good

People and personnel policies

Training is most intense at the entry level. In addition to product and business training in the individual's division, new analysts and associates participate in inter-divisional programmes which offer a broader perspective on the firm's key businesses and deepen understanding on the firm's history and culture. For example, all incoming associates attend 'Worldwide Associate Orientation', a week-long global programme held in New York.

For recent graduates, entering the company as an analyst, training is slightly different from those people starting as an associate. As part of the training, analysts are given finance and accounting instruction by senior professionals, assigned a mentor or someone to help the newcomer learn the ropes and participate in various networking and social events. Interviewing, writing, management and presentation skills training are on-going. Then there is less formal, but critical, on-the-job learning specific to the employee's division.

Typically, the individual will be given a great deal of responsibility early on, whether for a product, client, industry or firm business function. Developing and maintaining client relationships is one of the more important roles, and therefore management and leadership development is another crucial part of the training. Technology training is mandatory for all new employees, from rudimentary to advanced generic software as well as the firm's proprietary applications. All individuals participate annually in an extensive review process, resulting in feedback that is used for an individual's continued professional development.

Most information technology opportunities are in the Information Technology department, but there are technology-related opportunities in other areas of the firm, such as investment banking and fixed income, currency and commodities. These positions are not necessarily part of a two-year programme, although all positions involve a comprehensive three-month training programme.

There are considerable opportunities for mobility within the firm. Professionals can move to other regions or other divisions for a variety of reasons. Employees can be invited to work for a period of time in a location other than where they were initially hired to work. Analysts in two-year programmes typically do not relocate until after their second year, and associates do not usually transfer until after two or three years. Goldman Sachs does not expect its employees to commit long-term to the firm, although it finds many do because they enjoy the work and opportunities provided.

Essentially promotion and reward are based entirely on performance, so for high achievers there is a huge incentive to work hard. The extensive appraisal system enables the employee and his or her managers to identify areas for career and personal development. Goldman Sachs does offer its employees the opportunity to move ahead more rapidly than at other organizations, if the employee is motivated enough to accept the responsibility.

Contact address

Goldman Sachs International
Peterborough Court
133 Fleet Street
London EC4A 2BB
Telephone and fax numbers vary by individual operating division.
Web site: http://www.gs.com

Halifax plc

Few high street names have as much direct impact on the lives of significant parts of the population as Halifax. At the time of its conversion from the UK's largest building society to a financial services company, it held the lion's share of British household mortgages. For many people the Halifax is bank, savings institution and mortgage lender. The company is active in most towns and cities, and enjoys a formidable reputation in its native West Yorkshire. It was founded 145 years ago at a local public house, and built on a reputation for fair dealing. Household mortgages remain a significant part of business following the merger with the Leeds and conversion in June 1997. The organization is ready to expand with more acquisitions and now offers a wide ranging and comprehensive spectrum of financial services with the accent on growth. Culturally, Halifax advocates meeting and exceeding customer expectations and employee achievement.

Halifax at a glance

Employees: 36,000
Annual staff attrition: between 10 and 14 per cent
Key locations: head office sites in Leeds and Halifax employing 7,000. Branches including estate agencies throughout Britain and Clerical Medical Insurance Group in Bristol
Annual graduate intake: 100
Annual intake: up to 4,400

An inside view

The financial services sector has experienced dramatic and widespread change in the last decade. The number of building societies has contracted rapidly and sector analysts say that fewer and fewer will avoid merger, takeover or conversion. Britain's two largest societies, Halifax and Abbey National, both converted into plcs and became broader based financial services combines. The industry's strategists saw, in the late 1980s, that a series of trends would influence the development of financial services. The number of businesses would become significantly smaller; the companies at the top end of the market would change into generalists offering a range of products including insurance, pensions, savings plans and current accounts; the sector would be increasingly dominated by a group of heavyweight players; and the quality of the marketing relationship with customers would become critical as businesses competed for profits.

The character of the market has also been transformed by the creation of millions of individual shareholders who were accountholders in mutual days and suddenly found themselves owners in businesses catapulted to the top of the FTSE100. In autumn 1998, Halifax plc was the third biggest bank and the tenth largest business in the UK by market capitalization. Its 1998 interim (six-month) financial figures showed a record £843 million in pretax profits. Assets under management reached the Halifax's highest ever at £134 billion.

Despite intense competitive pressure, the company's share of the UK residential mortgages market remains the largest of any provider at 20 per cent of the total market. Fixed rate mortgages account for 20 per cent of existing business and 60 per cent of new business. At the time of its 1998 interim results, Halifax was the market leader in liquid savings with £75 billion in balances. Halifax has 2.5 million borrowers, 15 million savers and 3.5 million money transmission account holders.

All of the companies in retail financial services have recognized the need to improve and develop customer service. More than 20 million people use Halifax for some part of their financial service needs, so the organization has tailored its marketing approach to meet the needs of these customers. Like many other companies in this sector, Halifax has worked to improve the range of products, enhance the design of its branches and introduce new services to make handling financial issues easier for the customer.

Halifax is committed to quality and efficiency with the minimum of fuss. Its commercial philosophy argues that by providing service that consistently exceeds expectation, it further enhances its relationship with the customer. Its product development programme utilizes a range of techniques to anticipate customer demand and so Halifax is able to market new packages which are ahead of its competitors. In doing this Halifax aims to build long-term and broadly based relationships with its customers. The result, it believes, will be enhanced shareholder return.

How does Halifax rate ?

Pay:	very good
Benefits:	very good
Communications:	excellent
Training:	excellent
Career development:	very good
Morale:	very good

People and personnel policies

During the 1990s the philosophy of people as the principal asset of a business has emerged as a commonplace idea. A decade ago, a small group of companies espoused individual and team empowerment, offered decent reward packages, provided good training and development features and created a positive environment in which employees could thrive. The growth in the concept has meant that the standards of employee management are constantly pegged higher. In the financial services sector, Halifax has made fostering its people a cornerstone of its strategy. In earlier days, Halifax was a solid if slightly unimaginative employer. Today it is a human resources leader in its market sector.

Central to its approach to personnel management is a belief in individual and personal achievement. It believes in equipping members of staff with a repertoire of professional skills that will enable individuals to meet and exceed personal targets. Training and development supports individual performance that feeds directly into individual rewards policy.Group Personnel and Services director John Lee says, 'We have created a new, more flexible pay and performance structure. The way in which we measure performance will be more structured and more consistent. It has moved away from the old grading hierarchy into new structure which is designed to encourage staff to respond better to the needs of our customers'.

Five new pay bands that were introduced in June 1998 replaced Halifax's grading structure. It changed the emphasis from measuring the job and its accountabilities to recognizing the person and the contribution each makes to the business. Personnel managers aimed to be able to reward positive performance more easily. The line manager is seen as a coach who takes the individual through a balanced scorecard approach to objective setting. The relationship with the manager is characterized by partnership, where objectives are agreed rather than imposed.

Halifax regards communications as a vital part of its corporate objectives. There is an in-house TV channel which is on air throughout the organization every two weeks with longer broadcasts when the occasion warrants. Internal e-mail is the preferred choice of business communication and a monthly magazine featuring personal and business issues is available for all employees.

The company is keen to support and encourage appropriate business education and training. Where it pays for a course of study, it offers successful candidates a tax-paid payment on successful completion. Numerous in-house courses are offered through in-house training and development departments.

Equally, Halifax regards graduate recruitment as a vital part of its ongoing process of excellence. A two-year programme is geared to a wide programme of on-the-job experience, with the objective of fast track promotion. It seeks genuine capability, flexibility and mobility. And it favours determination and ambition in successful candidates. Halifax receives around 10,000 applications a year for all posts.

Contact address

Alan McAvan
Employee Development Manager
Halifax plc
Trinity Road
Halifax
West Yorkshire HX1 2RG
Telephone: 01422 333333
Fax: 01422 335106
Web site: http://www.halifax.co.uk

Hewlett-Packard

Hewlett-Packard (HP) is one of the world's best known and most successful multinationals. The group, with global sales of some $47.1 billion, is the second largest American shipper of PCs and the world market leader in laser printers. It is ranked as the tenth most admired corporation in the US, as assessed by *Fortune* magazine, and operates the fifth most valuable brand name worldwide. HP is widely renowned for its innovation, originality, professionalism and people management, as well as the quality of its products. It is esteemed as an employer, offering excellent benefits, opportunities for further education and training, and is committed to encouraging an open and flexible working environment for its employees.

Hewlett-Packard at a glance

Employees: 125,300 worldwide, 23,000 in Europe and 5,600 in the UK
Annual staff attrition: 6 per cent
Key locations: HP is a US company, with headquarters in Palo Alto, California. The Company's first UK office opened at Bedford in 1961. Since then, the UK operation has expanded to include manufacturing, sales and support functions. Its main locations are in Bracknell, Bristol, Edinburgh, Ipswich and Manchester
Annual graduate intake: 100–150
Annual intake: n/a

An inside view

Hewlett-Packard is commonly considered to be one of the most successful computer companies in the world. Since its foundation in 1938, it has multiplied in size and scope, remaining a leading performer despite growing competition in recent years. The company's global sales currently total some $47.1 billion and it has been profitable since its inception five decades ago. HP is active in PCs, laser and ink jet printers, UNIX machines, information storage, test and measurement, wireless communication, chemical analysis and health care.

HP invests up to ten per cent annually in research and development, and one-third of this is expended in the UK. HP is understandably proud of its focus on future commercial and personal requirements from electronics and its ability to identify and fulfil the needs of potential markets. HP currently has nine futuristic projects under development, each seeking to produce new sources of profits in the twenty-first century. It is this initiative and recognition of the need to stay ahead of its rivals which has sustained HP's success and distinguished it from competitors.

HP's attitude towards its employees and its distinct culture is summarized in the concept of the HP Way. The key elements of this concept are the highest level of business ethics; trust and respect of employees; encouragement of flexibility and innovation; and recognition of employees' individual achievements. The values and objectives enshrined in the HP Way govern the way the company manages its dynamic business, and supply the guiding principles for all HP decision-makers.

HP expects a high level of commitment from its employees. In return, the company recognizes their efforts and contributions to the company by means of excellent rates of pay, extensive benefits and a positive and flexible work environment.

How does Hewlett-Packard rate?

Pay:	excellent
Benefits:	superb
Communications:	very good
Training:	excellent
Career development:	excellent
Morale:	excellent

People and personnel policies

HP works with its employees to create a safe, pleasant and stimulating environment in which they can thrive. Emphasis on the team is a fundamental aspect of HP's strategy. The company is organized into small manageable teams, each consisting of no more than 30 people, linked directly to a product or service. The objective is to encourage employees to contribute and work together to achieve common objectives. It aims to recruit employees with an innovative approach by its management style, maintaining an open line to the main board in Palo Alto, California for any unit with an innovative idea. HP believes that a diverse workforce is a business imperative and expects every employee to aspire to his or her full potential.

Clearly, intellectual capacity is a key consideration in staff recruitment. However, originality, energy and the ability to work within a team are also essential to HP. HP has strong links with top universities and research bodies worldwide to share ideas and expertise, contribute to the establishment of standards, influence the curriculum, and to help students to think about the requirements of global organizations and their place at work. Within the UK, HP offers around 350 student work placements of three to twelve months' duration, which provide opportunities to learn and develop.

HP believes it will only maintain its excellent business results by realizing the full potential of all employees and attracting a workforce which is representative of the customer base. HP considers personal development to be an investment and thus enthusiastically encourages continuing education of its employees and offers an exceptional range of courses and learning opportunities to develop personal, management and technical skills.

Employees wishing to take professional qualifications will receive financial support and management support. HP encourages flexible working wholeheartedly and continues to encourage a range of new working arrangements as part of its ongoing commitment to work-life balance. Every employee has a performance evaluation after six and twelve months, and annually thereafter. This is to discuss performance, development needs and areas of interest and concern. It occurs between individuals and managers throughout the year. HP encourages innovation and expects individuals to take the lead on their own career. It gives responsibility to all staff through its single status culture.

Employees of HP are entitled to an excellent range of benefits. Its pay philosophy contains four key elements: paying among the leaders; paying for sustained performance; ensuring employees understand how pay is determined; and striving for equality and fairness.

After six months' service employees become eligible for the Corporate Cash Profit sharing scheme which can be taken as cash or used to purchase HP shares. It has consistently achieved profit since its inception in 1939. Staff also benefit from life assurance, a non-contributory medical plan, 25 days' holiday a year, long service awards and the benefits of a large blue chip employer which include free beverage facilities and sports/social clubs, employee assistant programme, employee discounts and a secure and pleasant work environment. HP's maternity benefit packages are excellent and highly flexible in respect of return to work.

Contact address

Miss Denise C Mason
UK Graduate Programme Manager
Hewlett-Packard Limited
Cain Road
Bracknell
Berks RG12 1HN
Telephone: 01344 360000
Fax: 01344 362394
Web site: http://www.hp.com

HHCL and Partners

For marketing people, HHCL+P is one of the most exciting places to work for in Europe. Its approach to developing client campaigns is unique. It was founded in 1987 and is now the twentieth largest agency in the UK. HHCL+P is also the second fastest-growing business in the top 30 agency list. The extent of its success has been due to its commitment to excellent client-agency dialogue, high quality creative solutions and the business basis of the organization. In 1994 it was relaunched as a total marketing communications company, and in 1998 merged with Chime Communications.

HHCL and Partners at a glance

Employees: 160
Annual staff attrition: 19 per cent
Key locations: London
Annual graduate intake: n/a
Annual intake: 30 per cent (driven by growth)

An inside view

At any one time in creative market sectors, some businesses will be fashionable or attractive and others will be out of favour. Since October 1987 when HHCL and Partners was launched it has always been in demand. This organization has remained successful by being distinctive. Its creative approach, its relationship with its clients and also the commercial footing of its business activities mark out HHCL and Partners from its competitors.

In 1994 the company relaunched itself as a total marketing communications company. This reflected its belief that advertising should not always occupy centre stage. It has no bias towards one medium or another but brings together an original blend of marketing skills under one roof. Specialists work together collaboratively with a completely holistic perspective. HHCL+P says that it offers integrated thinking and marketing problem solving.

The freshness for which HHCL+P is synonymous is in great demand. In 1989 Campaign voted the company as Agency of the Year. In 1990 it dominated industry awards with its campaigns for Maxell tapes, the launch of First Direct and the relaunch of Fuji Film. In the following year Fuji received the title of Campaign's advertiser of the year with its HHCL+P-devised relaunch.

In 1992, HHCL+P's Tango and Mercury campaigns won widespread acclaim and HHCL+P was listed by the influential US publication *Advertising Age* as one of the leading international agencies. In the following year, the Tango project attracted Campaign's Campaign of the Year. Within 12 months it had become the fastest-growing agency in the UK. In October 1994, HHCL+P was joined by a team of ten people with direct marketing and sales promotions backgrounds in preparation for Marketing at a Point of Change, its new marketing agenda.

1995 was another busy year with the creation of In Real Life – a face-to-face communications company. In the same year HHCL+P was selected for Campaign's Agency of the Year. The judging panel made the award for 'the most interesting body of work in the UK, a steady accumulation of developing business from existing clients, and industry-leading stands on integration, remuneration and pitches.'

A year later the *Independent on Sunday* named HHCL+P as one of the top 50 fastest-growing companies in Britain for the second year running. And in 1997 the business again dominated the industry's annual awards with its Blackcurrant Tango campaign.

HHCL and Partners has distinguished itself by a range of creative and commercial initiatives. The company has never been prepared to sacrifice its integrity as a business to win a particular client or assignment. HHCL+P always demands proper remuneration for its expertise and talent. It continues to work with the best brands in the commercial world today including Allied-Domecq, Britvic, Guinness Ireland, Pearl, Thomson Holidays, The Automobile Association, BAA, BP, Bass, British Airways, ITV and Unilever. It coined the term *professional radicals* to describe the approach of the firm and the people who work inside it. The phrase has a precise meaning which defines an approach based on original, sometimes revolutionary, thought but which is also tempered by good judgement and practical experience.

Never content with a quiet moment, in November 1997 the company merged with Chime Communications plc. Chime was created by Sir Tim Bell and now embraces HHCL+P and the famous public relations agency Bell Pottinger Communications. WPP Group owns 29.9 per cent of Chime Communications. The merger with HHCL+P doubled the size of Chime and Rupert Howell, the first H in HHCL+P, became joint chief executive of the newly enlarged PLC. He told Chime's shareholders in early 1998, 'HHCL+P's merger with Chime Communications opens the door to an expansionary stage of development. The five founding partners Rupert Howell, Steve Henry, Axel Chaldecott, Adam Lury and Robin Price, together with Chris Satterthwaite (formerly chief executive of IMP) remain active hands-on managers of the business.'

How does HHCL+P rate?

Pay:	good
Benefits:	good
Communications:	good
Training:	very good
Career development:	good
Morale:	excellent

People and personnel policies

HHCL +P is a business which does not stand still for very long. It has a creative undercurrent which seeks practical and original form. It is a company which embodies the pragmatic and commercial values of a well-managed corporate integrated with fresh artistic and creative concepts. In short, HHCL+P started operations as an advertising agency which was determined to do things differently from the rest of the field.

The structure of the agency was markedly distinct from its competitors. The five founders came from diverse industry backgrounds but one of the partners – Robin Price – was a finance man. Rupert Howell always made clear that HHCL+P would be run as a business and it would be paid on time and in full measure. Importantly, a finance perspective on the board encouraged the creative directors to consider the commercial aspects of certain assignments. The business also aimed to be different in the closeness of its dialogue with its clients and in the extent of its relationship with those clients.

Through the succeeding 12 years, the company has adapted and changed its scope to meet new market demands. It has become a standard bearer for thoughtful change in its industry. The speed of ideas, the pragmatic experience and the concepts of involvement and participation are characteristic of HHCL+P – and therefore of people who come to work for the company. It has a phenomenally low attrition rate for the marketing sector and HHCL+P is a highly attractive career option for people in the field.

Lou Burrows, head of the People Team, says, 'We launched the new positioning of professional radicals. This is something that every member of staff can get behind. There is a responsibility for each and every person to meet the highest standards of professionalism, while constantly looking for new ways of doing things differently. It is in keeping with our objective to provide a fun and challenging work environment.'

HHCL+P grew from 120 to 160 permanent members of staff in 1998. It will continue to expand and the company estimates that it is on track for more than 200 employees by the end of 1999. The growth and development team (the company is not keen on the term 'human resources') has risen to four to meet the increasing need for training, development, recruitment and welfare.

'We involve people in as much of the business as possible and we are constantly looking at ways to innovate and improve. For examples, all existing partners are canvassed before the appointment of new ones. So the partnership determines the number and quality of people who join it. We operate a Balanced Scorecard mechanism to track client satisfaction, financial performance, staff satisfaction and creative excellent. This is managed by the operations team and fed back to staff quarterly with plans for how to improve in each area. We also have a budget for innovations. This means that new ideas are assessed separately from the assignment process and adopted if they add effectiveness for the business. We involve all staff in the tendering process – not just those people whom the partners consider the best for the assignment in mind.'

HHCL+P does not have conventional departments but disciplines. It appoints heads of discipline or HODs who may not be the most experienced or best paid people but rather the most effective people managers. The company regards training and development as vital to the process of attracting and keeping good people. Everyone takes part in a 360 degree annual appraisal which is managed by specifically trained Reflectors who assist with each member of staff's development.

'We run Appraisal Breakfasts each month where ten people due to be appraised are invited to meet to discuss the aims of the process. There is a great emphasis on helping one another develop. New joiners are appointed guardians and all staff have a finance buddy to help them navigate the company's financial systems. HHCL+P has an unusual training and development strategy. This ensures that its people do not learn from standardized methodologies. HHCL+P employs a permanent organizational development consultant who provides training which includes business management courses, the Mind Gym series with teachers from the US, and ongoing discipline development programmes.'

Contact address

Lou Burrows
Head of Human Resources
HHCL+P
Kent House
14–17 Market Place
Great Titchfield Street
London W1N 7AJ
Tel: 0171 436 3333
Fax: 0171 436 2677
Web site: http://www.hhcl.com

IBM UK Holdings Limited

In the pantheon of great enterprises IBM ranks among the elite. Until its spectacular problems in the early 1990s, Big Blue's writ ran across industry worldwide. Governments formed in a line at the corporate headquarters to tempt IBM to base manufacturing, sales or research establishments in their states. The creed of 'no-one here was ever fired for buying IBM' held multinationals and small companies alike in thrall. Then IBM missed a beat. It completely misunderstood the software revolution. Many thought the unthinkable – that IBM might not emerge from the other side of its horrendous difficulties. Yet the phoenix astonished corporate America. It created a new business out of the old. Though it remains true to its traditional values, it has recognized the imperatives of new market conditions and fashioned new approaches and products to meet that demand. It claims to be the most global company, and the most successful IT group in the world. Fresh colour and a renewed vitality have energized IBM.

IBM at a glance

Employees: 23,000 in the UK (permanents, fixed-term contracts, short-term contracts and students) plus several thousand people supplied by contractors
Annual staff attrition: 6.5 per cent
Key locations: Portsmouth (HQ), London and Greenock plus offices in major cities
Annual graduate intake: 550
Annual intake: c.2,300

An inside view

If you are going to make a loss why not go for the biggest in corporate history. IBM has never done anything by halves and when it hit the rocks in the early 1990s it recorded the largest deficit by any company – ever. Solid, reliable, powerful Big Blue personified corporate America, the institution of international capitalism, the global multinational. But inside the forces which had fashioned this towering monolith lay the seeds of its downfall. IBM was slow, blinkered and sclerotic.

A certain degree of smugness characterized the enterprise. IBM had always sold big boxes – and according to the upper echelons of IBM management always would sell big boxes – a market where it could always distinguish itself. Although IBM invented the PC, it did not capitalize on that market, which it considered small and unimportant. But this mis-reading of the biggest growth sector in hardware was minor in comparison with its total failure to appreciate that software would dominate the industry. IBM regarded applications as peripheral to the main market of selling mainframes.

It saw the results of this disastrous policy too late to do anything. And the bellweather of the US economy entered unknown territory, plunging catastrophically in the red. But like all good romances, this tale has a happy ending. IBM recreated itself entirely. It regained the respect of corporate contemporaries and international governments, and once again captured the imagination of computer buyers. The scale of the transformation from spent force to innovative, flexible and alert business is hard to imagine. Its only rivals in the UK for such thorough-going metamorphosis are BT and Unipart. IBM likes to be considered a benchmark company in quality production, excellent service provision, strong and supportive personnel management. It has also set the standard for corporate recovery.

A key to IBM's recovery was a genuine commitment to learn from its mistakes. Previously, the core of all decision making was its management committee in the corporate headquarters in the US. While rivals devolved power down the line, IBM reinforced the authority of top executives. This was changed in line with prevailing management philosophy, and had an immediate effect in releasing the talent and ambition of able IBM managers. The catharsis of going into the red focused management teams on an assessment of changing market conditions.

Another crucial change was the business approach. The aim was no longer solely to sell its hardware into clients. It moved to a greater consultancy role – understanding customer business issues, developing appropriate solutions, and offering IT services. Heavy investment has gone into developing new technology and establishing relationships with a much wider range of expert suppliers. As a telling sign of the new orthodoxy, IBM has also launched a series of joint ventures with rivals to share the costs of investment in new products and establishing common industry standards which are not purely IBM-driven. The company has evolved into a global, solutions and services driven company and the success of this transformation can be seen in its figures that are back where they belong – in the black!

How does IBM rate?

Pay:	good
Benefits:	excellent
Communications:	very good
Training:	excellent
Career development:	very good
Morale:	good

People and personnel policies

The UK companies of IBM have a reputation for being much more nimble than some of the parent's other national subsidiaries. Today, IBM employs around 23,000 people throughout the United Kingdom. These people are engaged in IT design and development, manufacturing, sales, marketing, customer service, technical and administration.

Human resources director Ann Grinstead says, 'Qualification is not the most important priority in recruitment. We still recruit a high percentage of arts graduates rather than science or computer science students. Personal qualities are more relevant to us. We want candidates to be able to demonstrate some degree of achievement in their studies or in their outside interests. IBM looks for people who have width in their activities, are articulate, mature in their thinking, and perform well in teams. In any event, most graduates today are computer literate to some degree.'

IBM operates a year-round graduate recruitment programme, with interviews taking place in February, May, August and November. Successful graduates at the initial interview stage are then invited to an assessment centre in the following month for further interviews, group exercises with fellow graduate applicants, and written tests. Successful candidates are contacted within five days of this assessment, with a range of jobs on offer.

Once inside the company, training is intensive. IBM majors on the quality of the expertise which it provides in extensive periods of detailed formal and on-the-job training. All employees are regularly updated on the IBM commitments (to win in the marketplace, to execute with urgency and to teamwork), its strategic imperatives, its principles and its vision. The IBM vision is to be the most successful and important information technology company by helping its customers to apply extraordinary technology, and for IBM to be the basic source for most of what is new in the industry. Its eight principles embrace its market focus, standards for success and commitment to teamwork, its people and its communities.

In addition IBM is constantly recruiting experienced professionals. Owing to the growth in the IT services sector and the current IT skills shortage, skills acquisition is a priority needed to sustain business growth. Recruitment is from a variety of sources and is in areas such as sales, project management, application design and development, service delivery and various support groups and covers skill groups from new media to year 2000 and mainframe knowledge.

In the past, people who reached the top in IBM had started at the bottom and worked their way up the organization. The company is now more flexible about recruiting from outside to fill more senior posts, and to acquire specific skills. 'We say to potential recruits: come and take advantage of our world-class training and the exposure to our business groups. Once they join us most want to stay,' says Ann Grinstead.

Contact address

Louise Hawkins
Recruitment Manager
IBM UK Limited
North Harbour
Portsmouth PO6 3AU
Telephone: 01705 561000
Fax: 01705 388914
Web site: http://www.ibm.co

The Intel Corporation

Intel is one of the great corporate success stories of the last 20 years. Global revenues increased from $5.8 billion in 1992 to $25.1 billion in 1997. In 1997 sales grew by 20 per cent and profits by 35 per cent to $6.9 billion. The company invested $2.3 billion in research and $4.5 billion in capital development. The company introduced two major new international products – the Pentium Processor with MMX technology and the Pentium II Processor. The company designs and manufactures microprocessors for major computer companies. As demand for chips grows in a variety of market sectors and geographical regions, the company has achieved a more equitable distribution of income. Some 44 per cent of revenues come from North America, 27 per cent from Europe, 19 per cent from Asia-Pacific and ten per cent from Japan.

Intel at a glance

Employees: 63,700 worldwide, 650 UK
Annual staff attrition: n/a
Key locations: Swindon
Average graduate intake: 20
Annual intake: 70

An inside view

Among its many other achievements, Intel can proudly boast that it introduced the world's first microprocessor. The microprocessor is the heart of a series of parallel revolutions in IT, telecommunications and electronics. The business environment has been changed radically by the technology which Intel pioneered. The speed and breadth of communications which we now regard as standard would not be possible without the microprocessor. Its creation has also substantially altered domestic life. The nature of household entertainment, for example, is entirely different from a generation ago. Digital television, satellite broadcasting, computer games and CD audio systems are all dependent on chips. Learning is now done on CD-ROM or on line through multimedia PCs.

The scope of cultural change which Intel has initiated is breathtaking. The company supplies manufacturers with the ingredients of computer architecture. These include the chips, boards, systems and software which create advanced electronic, IT and telecoms products. Intel's aim is to be the world's pre-eminent supplier of the building blocks to the computer industry worldwide.

The biggest development in recent years has been the launch of the Pentium II Processor. It enables the growth of visual computing for consumers, small businesses and corporate enterprises. It brings sharper audio, fluid video and dramatic 3D graphics to the desktop. Its take-up was equally dramatic. By the end of 1997, it represented about 25 per cent of Intel's microprocessor production. Throughout 1998, Intel introduced versions of the Pentium II at higher speeds reaching the top end of 450 mHz.

The impressive engineering skills required to produce Intel's principal lines can be grasped when it is understood that the human hair is 400 times wider than the circuitry on its most advanced chips. It was the first high volume producer to announce a new 0.25 micron manufacturing process and it is now working on the next generation 0.18 micron technology. For the non-technician, this means engineering at finer and finer levels to produce minute components with immense power. In 1997 it unveiled its 64-bit microprocessor architecture for the high end work station and server markets. This will result in the launch – during 1999 – of the Merced processor, which is the first using IA-64 architecture. The second IA-64 chip is scheduled for introduction in 2001.

Most businesses in this sector are quintessentially Californian in their laid back but creative approach or they are highly driven, commercial and sales orientated companies. Intel is different again. The core of this organization is its engineering and technical excellence. This underpins the personality of the business and gives Intel a distinctive market focus. Two apparently divergent cultural traditions – personal informality but demanding professional and technical standards – combine in a unique blend to define the Intel approach.

The company advocates constructive confrontation – a policy where ideas but not the individuals who champion them are regularly challenged. Meetings are conducted on an adversarial basis and the people who argue most convincingly and passionately often win the day. Given Intel's engineering bias, the company also depends heavily on data and it respects well-researched and well-argued proposals.

How does Intel rate?

Pay:	very good
Benefits:	very good
Communications:	superb
Training:	very good
Career development:	very good
Morale:	very good

People and personnel policies

Intel's value system plays a crucial role in the operational lives of its employees. This is not an amorphous set of statements but a framework within which everyone works. In the first six months all new employees take a series of courses which introduce them to the way in which the company thinks. 'These sessions cover the way we expect people to behave in Intel. These are typically taught by senior managers and cover such subjects as values, ethics, the way to behave with clients and constructive confrontation. It can be a little difficult when you are not used to Intel's environment to understand the way in which we do business. These courses show new recruits how we approach relationships both within and outside the business and we make extensive use of role play and case studies,' says Bidal.

These classes are compulsory and form a key part of the early career. From day one, the entrant will be given a line job and teamed up with someone more senior. A formal development plan is sketched out in terms of broad areas of activity which will be given more substance as more experience is gained. Once a month, there will be one-to-one discussions including performance review and career development discussions. 'Our performance management system requires one-to-one meetings to be held monthly for it to work effectively,' he says.

Most people work in a given team but increasingly Intel is building cross-functional groups on specific projects. Sales taskforces are not based on rank within a group but more loosely centred, and a hierarchy develops on the competence of individual members. The team leader is responsible for the running of the team and at the end of the project they disband with individuals moving back to their original groups. All training is done on a completely cross-functional basis, partly to reinforce networks within the company.

Communication is open and direct, and the company uses a variety of techniques to ensure that its messages are disseminated and that employee feedback is actively heard. If individual staff members believe that they are not being treated fairly by their immediate manager they can take any concerns to the most senior level in the company. In some organizations this exists as a policy but once an employee attempts to exercise it, then they find that their career collapses. In Intel it is a tenet of faith that this mechanism should work well and that no one should be penalized in any way for resorting to its use.

Contact address

Bill Bidal
Human Resources Director
Intel Corporation (UK) Ltd
Pipers Way
Swindon SN3 1RJ
Telephone: 01793 403000
Fax: 01793 641440
Web site: http://www.intel.com

John Lewis Partnership plc

John Lewis is a British retailing institution. Its eponymous department stores and the Waitrose supermarket brand are universally regarded as benchmark businesses. The company's culture is uniquely democratic and could easily be seen as foreshadowing the current vogue for stakeholder participation. The personal stake which employees have in the company and the quality of John Lewis training combine to give exceptional levels of customer service. Other enterprises shout loudly about their high standards of customer service but John Lewis is a practised master. Its style is quiet, understated efficiency. Sales in 1998 from the 23 department stores, 117 supermarkets and other elated businesses were £3.5 billion.

John Lewis at a glance

Employees: 45,000
Annual staff attrition: 16 per cent
Key locations: London (HQ), mainly southern half of the UK plus some in the North and Scotland
Annual graduate intake: up to 175 in stores, Waitrose and IT
Annual intake: 8,000

An inside view

Companies the length and breadth of the UK – acute to political sensibilities – have begun to talk animatedly about the stakeholder philosophy. At the core of this currently fashionable idea is the concept that a business enterprise has many communities of interest which influence its development. These include employees, suppliers, customers, shareholders and local populations. But the stakeholder economy is not new. Some companies – a handful in the UK – have been operating on the central premise for decades. Among its leading protagonists is John Lewis. Its principle of Partnership bears an astonishing resemblance to early stakeholder arguments.

The John Lewis achievement is remarkable because it has managed to reconcile two potentially divergent trends – the need for commercial prosperity and a desire for democratic accountability. The intimate involvement of employees in the management of the business has led to a workforce that cares about the service which the company provides. It is characteristically efficient, thorough, helpful, mature and fair. The quality of the department stores' buyers gives a good insight to the depth of the John Lewis management culture.

The Partnership ethos can be traced back to the early days of the business. Members of the workforce form branch councils that determine local policy in conjunction with branch management. There is also a 140-strong central council which is composed of one-fifth appointees and four-fifths elected from employees. Although this structure appears complicated, it is designed to ensure that employees are fully briefed about key issues which affect John Lewis and can influence management decision making.

The company's management believes that this distinctive approach to structure and employee involvement is one of its primary reasons for business success. Since the 1920s, John Lewis has referred to its permanent employees as partners. They are effectively co-owners of the business, and they have a direct financial interest in its profitability. Each year every John Lewis partner receives a share of the profits. In Spring 1998 this equated to 12 weeks' pay per partner. This is an arrangement of considerable financial worth for people working in retail. None of the other top class retailers offers anything as good as this in terms of straight pay deal.

Retailing includes striking examples of companies that are either very good employers or among the worst in industry. In fact the disparity between the best and worst is among the most graphically defined in the entire business world. John Lewis is a standard bearer among the top tier. And the strong ethical position which it adopts with the workforce is also seen in its approach to the customer. Chairman Sir Stuart Hampson, commenting on the Never Knowingly Undersold creed of John Lewis, says, 'This is a statement of our determination never to be out-thought, out-classed or out-performed. In short it is a commitment to think bigger.' He says that none of its recent expansion was achieved without regularly challenging its own standards and its assumptions about the business.

How does John Lewis rate?

Pay:	very good
Benefits:	excellent
Communications:	very good
Training:	excellent
Career development:	very good
Morale:	very good

People and personnel policies

In keeping with the partnership ethos of ensuring that people are informed about developments within the business, John Lewis is also an exemplary trainer. Training – in most retailers – tends to be on-the-job, brief and elementary. John Lewis, in direct contrast, is a benchmark company for training. Like all great enterprises, it puts considerable resources, thought and expertise to developing its training modules and ensuring that its people receive comprehensive and relevant training.

Its programmes must be relevant to both the employee and the company. The Partner will want training to develop skills and aptitudes for particular tasks. The company views training as a stimulus to improved profitability. John Lewis is first and foremost a commercial organization. 'We are in business to make profit, but it's what we do with the profit that is different,' says its personnel literature. After recruitment, a plan to cover the first 12 to

24 months is drawn up. This identifies the training and development which will be needed in the initial post.

The company is an active graduate recruiter. It draws around 120 people into the department stores and another 25 into the Waitrose chain each year. This has grown rapidly in recent years. Successful candidates must demonstrate a range of personal, practical and academic skills. Those who can put their intelligence, enthusiasm and drive to use in practical settings will be the ones who do best in the company. John Lewis, unlike many of its competitors, is committed to long-term relationships with its people. After the initial training period trainees are given their own department to manage. Managers who prosper inside the John Lewis culture can reasonably expect to reach the upper layers of management after ten years.

Graduate training schemes are extensive. The Waitrose scheme, for example, has three components: retail skills, management skills and personal development. Personnel manager Sally Carruthers says, 'It's because of our emphasis on personal development that we attempt to ensure that the programme is constructed and remodelled to meet individual requirements.' An individual joining Waitrose will be assigned a management trainer who will act as a mentor and steer individuals through the course. Off-the-job training is equally comprehensive and trainees can expect 40 days a year. There is also residential management development, technical training and regular forums where trainees can compare notes.

For retailing, the reward structure is impressive. Quite apart from competitive salaries, Partners receive an annual Partnership Bonus. They can also take advantage of subsidized dining rooms, free life insurance, non-contributory pensions and substantial discounts on John Lewis and Waitrose products. 'The benefits go further. Graduate trainees get a full five weeks' holiday in their first full year. Most organizations have some form of social club and social activity, but we do tend to outdo most of them.' The company owns five cruising yachts, three mature golf courses and two country clubs, among other amenities.

Contact address

Sally Carruthers
Head of Management Development
John Lewis Partnership plc
171 Victoria Street
London SW1E 5NN
Telephone: 0171 828 1000
Fax: 0171 592 6301
Web site: http://www.johnlewis.co.uk

J.P. Morgan

J.P. Morgan is an international financial services organization formed in 1838 with the opening of a merchant bank in London by George Peabody, whose partner Junius S Morgan later took over the firm. Although headquartered in Wall Street, New York City, the group is truly global with offices or subsidiary companies in more than 30 countries around the world, including more than 12 in North America. Employees number around 16,000, working in the three geographical regions of North America; Europe, Middle East and Africa; and Asia Pacific. Around 250 graduate recruits are taken on each year in Europe, and in London alone there are 62 nationalities working together. Almost two-thirds of the 15 top management positions are held by non-US nationals.

J.P. Morgan at a glance

Employees: 16,000 worldwide
Annual staff attrition: n/a
Key locations: New York (HQ) and major global centres in London, Amsterdam, Brussels, Frankfurt, Geneva, Madrid, Milan, Paris, Prague, Rome, Warsaw, Zurich, Johannesburg, Moscow
Annual graduate intake: 250 (Europe)
Annual intake: n/a

An inside view

Precision and quality typify J.P. Morgan's culture, which is one of efficiency based on the highest standards of personal and professional conduct. To J.P. Morgan everything is geared to providing the client with work of the highest standard and value. This is perhaps not surprising when clients include governments, multinational companies and central banks plus principals of privately owned companies, wealthy individuals and professional portfolio managers.

Its business sectors are concerned with providing help and expert advice to clients with complex financial needs. There are five such sectors: finance and advisory which assists clients to structure and raise capital to support current and future operating plans, and counselling on and helping to execute business strategy; sales and trading helps clients buy and sell a wide variety of securities, currencies, commodities, and derivatives in connection with their investment, risk management, and trade-related activities; asset management and servicing manages portfolios and provides other investment and financial services for institutional and individual clients; the equity investments sector invests and manages a diversified portfolio of private equity for the firm's own account; and the asset and liability management sector manages the interest rate risk and liquidity profile of J.P. Morgan's assets, liabilities, and off-balance-sheet exposures.

As an indication of the high profile work carried out by the business, during 1998 J.P. Morgan had a number of successes in its advisory business, including advising on Exxon and Mobil, and BP and Amoco on what are the largest and second largest industrial mergers ever, and also the joint venture of international business between AT&T and BT. The firm is one of the top six merger and acquisition advisers worldwide, ranking third in Latin America and fourth in Europe, and in the first half of 1998 completed 138 advisory transactions worldwide.

How does J.P. Morgan rate?

Pay:	excellent
Benefits:	excellent
Communications:	very good
Training:	excellent
Career development:	very good
Morale:	very good

People and personnel policies

Client-focused teamwork is the bedrock of work at J.P. Morgan. It believes that a team-orientated approach gives clients access to the firm's best thinking and the full benefits of all its capabilities, while making the firm a rewarding and professionally supportive place to work. Successful graduates, men and women, are not in general chosen because of the type of degree they have. The academic qualifications held by graduates at the firm's London office, for example, range from BAs to MBAs in subjects as diverse as mathematics to forestry or zoology. What is sought are people who can demonstrate a willingness to work as part of a team. Furthermore, the business wants graduates to work across all disciplines.

Incoming graduates need analytical skills; leadership, interpersonal, and communication skills; an interest in collaborating with internal business partners to contribute to the firm's business goals. Graduates join one of four business areas: Investment Banking; Markets; Asset Management Services; and Internal Consulting Services (ICS).

The Investment Banking training programme prepares trainees for a career at J.P. Morgan as well as for initial assignments. It provides the opportunity to build relationships with peers from its offices worldwide. During the first year, trainees attend the training programme at the firm's New York headquarters. The programme covers: Morgan's strategic direction, culture and values, business ethics and the regulatory environment; focused course work in accounting, financial statement analysis and forecasting, research and valuation techniques, and credit risk plus exposure to derivatives and financing; and the development of team and personal effectiveness.

Trainees in the Markets division gain team experience in a series of product areas. These are fixed income, capital markets, emerging markets, foreign exchange, commodities, futures and options, interest rate management and proprietary trading. After an initial period of on-the-job experience in sales, trading or research, each trainee attends an extensive training programme on Wall Street. This includes: an overview of the financial services industry and J.P. Morgan's business; an insight into J.P. Morgan's strategies, culture and ethics; and instruction on the firm's products and services, including financial markets analysis, global capital and currency markets, derivative instruments and risk management.

Asset Management Services offers opportunities in the private clients group or investment management. Training in the former begins with the European Asset Management course. Trainees learn about the asset management process and are then assigned to a specific team to gain practical experience in researching and synthesizing information on financial markets, performing financial and portfolio analysis, researching and evaluating potential clients, and preparing materials for sales presentations. Investment Management training starts with the asset management course and leads to work with a specific group. There is extensive on-the-job training with experienced colleagues and as careers progress product knowledge sessions and training seminars are identified for development purposes. This leads ultimately to investment management training in New York.

ICS trainees pursue either generalist track or specialist track opportunities, and the programme consists of formal training and rotational work assignments across the European region for up to two years, for periods of between three months and one year. First trainees attend the Morgan Core programme and then the ICS training programme, which focuses on building a common skills set applicable to assignments in all groups. This includes: project management, process improvement and problem solving skills; and financial and risk management knowledge such as the transaction life cycle and control awareness.

J.P. Morgan works in an industry of change and says standing still is not an option. Extensive continuous training is therefore provided and mobility is encouraged. This means there are many opportunities for working, during and after training, at the firm's offices in other parts of the world. J.P. Morgan pays competitively in what is a highly paid industry and pay levels are driven by personal performance. This performance is defined using a wide range of criteria spanning from bottom line contributions through effective teamwork. As one would expect from an organization of this size in a competitive marketplace, other benefits such as pensions and medical insurance are provided.

Contact address

Graduate Recruitment
J.P. Morgan
60 Victoria Embankment
London EC4Y 0JP
Telephone: 01753 608307
Web site: http://www.jpmorgan.com

Kellogg Company

Everyone is familiar with Kellogg's. It is the brand and market leader in ready-to-eat cereals including the eponymous Corn Flakes, Rice Krispies, Frosties and Crunchy Nut Corn Flakes. There are many different varieties which come in and out of fashion. Kellogg created, developed and pioneered breakfast cereals and is one of the world's great brand names. In the past it could be described as a classic American corporation which was conservative in approach but represented quality and good value. Today Kellogg is a global company which has two main product streams – ready-to-eat cereals and convenience foods which embrace delights such as Pop Tarts, Lenders Bagels, Rice Krispies Squares and Nutri-Grain cereal bars. The culture is in significant transition after experiencing commercial pressure from new sources. Kellogg has become a much more proactive business which is customer- and people-centred.

Kellogg at a glance

Employees: 3,500 in Europe including more than 1,500 in UK
Annual staff attrition: 10 per cent
Key locations: Manchester, Wrexham, Bremen (Germany), Valls (Spain)
Annual graduate intake: 10
Annual intake: 100

An inside view

Kellogg's Corn Flakes are part of the great British breakfast. Kellogg is the company which originally conceived the idea of making toasted flakes a staple food. The rosy image of families meeting at the breakfast table for a bowl of Corn Flakes has, for generations past, fixed itself into the marketing lexicon. It was, of course, an American invention but one that has travelled well and is even more popular at the end of the century than it was in the 1920s.

The Kellogg Company was founded in 1906 in Battle Creek, Michigan by William Keith Kellogg, business manager of the Battle Creek Sanatorium. Breakfast had been a fairly indigestible affair in the late nineteenth century. Kellogg pioneered a new and eminently more palatable product. The idea – and the company – were a roaring success. So much so that Kellogg became synonymous with breakfast. In 1924 the company began distributing its products in the UK and built its first factory in Trafford Park in 1938.

Kellogg today is a radically different company from the conservative US business which symbolized all that was wholesome about America. In 1999, Kellogg is a global business, divided into four regions. The European business is centred in Manchester with the world's largest cereals plant outside Battle Creek nearby, and a second factory in Wrexham. The rather reserved culture has been superseded by a more proactive, vital approach which instead emphasizes performance, people and customers.

The structure of Kellogg is moving to pan-European lines. Central functions such as Information Systems, Finance, Human Resources and Supply Chain Management are now run on a continental basis while sales and marketing retain a national flavour. Duncan Lindsay, HR adviser, says, 'Sales and marketing need to take account of local customer preferences and are effectively based in each country with 100 people in Manchester.'

The company now has four factories throughout Europe where it makes the trademark cereals and the convenience foods which have been introduced in recent years. Kellogg is constantly seeking new products to spark the imagination of its customers. Previously the company tended to rely on its principal products for its financial performance but the greater demands of the consumer and increased competition have prompted the business to take a more innovative approach.

The movement from a UK national operation to a European structure has been the major theme for Kellogg here in the last couple of years. A series of internal projects has been created to ensure that the transformation will be completed with speed and efficiency, and this focus has dominated the strategic and operational direction of the enterprise.

How does Kellogg rate?

Pay:	very good
Benefits:	very good
Communications:	good
Training:	good
Career development:	very good
Morale:	good

People and personnel policies

The cultural renewal at Kellogg has encouraged its human resources professionals to redefine the profile on an attractive recruit. Kellogg is moving towards people who are customer-focused, innovative thinkers, change orientated and proactive. For certain roles language skills are important. It has devised a map which shows the strategic and cultural direction of the company which has already triggered major changes in the way the company conducts its business. It was very traditional in managing the business but now there is genuine commitment to participation. There is also an enhanced emphasis on the team and greater flexibility for teams to discover the most effective way for them to deliver.

Kellogg is focused on innovative solutions to market conditions. It encourages its people to think beyond the scope of the limited framework of their current assignment. The launch of the cereal bars is a good example of how Kellogg people applied original thinking to changing market forces.

Recruitment is normally done through a group of consultancies which advertise for the company and screen the candidates. It receives a shortlist from whichever agency has been used and then the company conducts interviews on a competency-led basis. Sometimes – but not always – it uses psychometric testing. Kellogg has very low staff attrition so we are talking about comparatively small numbers of recruits in a normal year.

The company recruits graduates every year but it has no formal graduate recruitment scheme. However, Kellogg does have a detailed and sophisticated induction programme. It covers the history of the business, the culture of Kellogg, and the terms and conditions of employment. The core human resources department induction is then followed by a process which is specific to each department. This embraces the skill requirements for the principal tasks in that area and the scope of the individual assignment.

Training is a key part of the employment package in the company. Much of it is job and sector specific. Many of the key managerial courses are outsourced to leading specialists but the sales and marketing and production departments conduct a considerable amount of both formal and informal training in classroom and on-the-job settings. Kellogg has opened a learning resource centre which features a series of career progression courses on the skill requirements of managers and the qualities and characteristics of competent managers. Training and development opportunities and requirements are highlighted by the annual appraisal process. Everyone in the company is assessed at least once a year against performance criteria reflecting personal, team and corporate objectives.

Contact address

Human Resources Department
Kellogg Management Services (Europe) Limited
The Kellogg building
Talbot Road
Manchester M16 0PU
Telephone: 0161 869 2000
Fax: 0161 869 2100
Web site: http://www.kelloggs.com

KPMG

KPMG is a major global player in accountancy, tax and consultancy as one of the Big Five accountancy practices. It has an outstanding reputation for innovation and has regularly been the first large firm to introduce new approaches. It was the first Big Five firm to incorporate its audit business, for example, and was also the first practice to develop the concept of the audit being something more than a statutory obligation on companies. Despite an unsuccessful attempt to merge with Ernst & Young, KPMG continues to thrive and is growing its business in a range of sectors. Its latest annual results show substantial growth.

KPMG at a glance

Employees: 10,000 staff and 600+ partners
Annual staff attrition: 14–15 per cent
Key locations: London, all major UK cities
Annual graduate intaket: 600–700
Annual intake: 900

An inside view

'Only the strongest survive' could easily be the motto for the accountancy sector in the last decade. The profession has been characterized by merger, takeover, collapse and consolidation to an extent that it mirrors the most active industrial and commercial companies. Where there was a Big Eight and roughly 12 medium sized firms in the mid-1980s, there is now a Big Five and half the number of significantly sized smaller practices.

KPMG's recent history reflects the pace of the profession. It was the first – in recent times – to contract a major merger. In 1985, Peat Marwick Mitchell, one of the bastions of old school accountancy, absorbed KMG Thomson McLintock – at the time the UK's tenth largest practice and probably the biggest in Scotland. The merger was – in corporate finance speak – a perfect fit. McLintock brought a number of assets, not least its international affiliation network. Intrinsically, accountancy firms were national practices. To achieve international coverage, they needed to create alliances with other like-minded firms in significant territories. These alliances were the foundation stones of later international partnerships. While Peats was a member of Peat Marwick International, McLintock had joined Klijnveld Main Gordeler (KMG) which included the number one firm in the Netherlands and a top two practice in Germany. Furthermore, the KMG network was number one in continental Europe.

Peats – accountants to the Royal Family – was at that time the number one

UK practice and through the creation of KPMG overnight became the largest group of firms in Europe. It also consolidated its strengths in America. The KPMG initiative created a chain of mergers which are still taking place. And while the other larger practices were experiencing the vicissitudes of their amalgamations, KPMG was free to keep its eye on the ball, and to pick up clients driven away by a change in supplier. The story has been characterized by outstanding performance.

Since the early 1990s, KPMG has addressed a series of internal structural issues to create a more cohesive organization. For example, at the beginning of the decade, KPMG, in the UK, was a federation of regional partnerships. This is no longer the case. In fact, the experimentation with diverse corporate forms in KPMG has been among the most progressive in the sector. KPMG was the first accountancy practice of any note to incorporate its audit practice, and as this book was going to press the firm announced that it would consider floating part of its consulting business.

On the business side, KPMG was always a pre-eminent audit and tax firm with an impressive portfolio of blue chip clients. It gained a strong reputation for excellent corporate finance work especially in the area of MBOs, venture capital and top end greenfield ventures. The size of the UK network of offices is greater than any other Big Five firm and although refined from its dimensions in the early 1990s it has been valuable to detect new growth companies. Competitors speak enviously of the KPMG net which scoops up new businesses of potential before they become visible in the wider corporate environment. KPMG is an acknowledged player in the owner-managed business market and has a strong name for skilful selection of promising embryo businesses.

The firm is also known for its capacity to generate original product and service ideas. As long ago as 1985 it was the first accountancy firm to present the value-added audit. KPMG recognized that many CEOs and CFOs regard the audit as a compliance burden and little else. More than a decade ago it repackaged the audit as a product which would create value to business managers. It could provide not only assurance to shareholders but also an insight – for management – into the intricate functioning of the business. Consultancy has been a key area of growth for KPMG in the 1990s with revenues of $3 billion worldwide.

How does KPMG rate?

Pay:	very good
Benefits:	excellent
Communications:	very good
Training:	excellent
Career development:	excellent
Morale:	good

People and personnel policies

The shape of the larger accountancy practices is unrecognizable from 20 years ago. The influence of progressive corporate management is now unmistakable. Instead of a hierarchical group of partners who ascended according to length of service, today individuals achieve senior positions on merit. And now merit is clearly categorized and defined.

In the mid-1980s a shift was taking place. Managers were rarely made up to partnership purely on the principle of being a 'good chap' alone although there were some who did make it on the most unusual grounds. KPMG in common with all other firms developed criteria for the qualities which make a successful and effective partner. These have been refined and sharpened as the years have passed. They form the basis of the assessment centres for partnership selection.

The aim of many of the graduates who train as accountants with KPMG is to make partnership in the firm. Others see chartered accountancy as a passport to opportunities in investment banking, corporate finance or company management. The art of KPMG's personnel managers is to create enough sufficiently stimulating opportunities for the best to stay and develop longer-term careers inside the firm. The greater integration of KPMG, the growth of the international practice and the creation and expansion of new business areas means that the potential routes for career development are diverse.

The need for a large body of accountancy and audit trainees is as strong as ever. This necessitates an active process of milk round recruitment; the firm seeks people with a 2.1 degree or above. It enlists between 600 and 700 graduates into the firm each year. John Ashman, head of Human Resources, says, 'We recruit even more experienced hires. We look for people who have good business sense, who will be team players and who are well rounded. The subject of the degree is not especially important; intelligence and a high level of energy are the primary criteria.'

The intake, particularly of experienced people, is so great that induction courses are in operation every week throughout the year. New recruits are given a strong grounding in the firm's culture together with an understanding of the IT arrangements. Details of their disciplines and the programme for training for qualification are laid out. KPMG is keen that its trainees see a significant part of the business for the duration of their contract and cross-functional assignments are arranged.

There is now increased emphasis on individuals taking responsibility for their own development during training and beyond into a career with KPMG. The firm, however, also sees this as a key part of management. 'It is a shared responsibility. We help trainees plan their work and provide constructive guidance and advice. From the start we take care to address training objectives so that all trainees have a clear perspective of the tasks ahead. But we look to individuals to have the initiative to help organize their own career plan.' To support career development, KPMG runs a structured appraisal system which, for more senior staff and partners, includes 360 degree feedback ensuring valuable feedback from a cross section of colleagues.

Training is a central theme at KPMG and the business is active in encouraging its people to seek advanced levels of eduction where appropriate. It has created a package of leadership courses and an executive MBA cycle.

KPMG is alert to the market when setting salaries. Graduates come in at highly competitive starting rates. There is a wide portfolio of salary bands. Some of the pay package is a variable, performance related element. This is awarded based on performance against objectives and personal and team performance. Tailored bonus schemes can provide an additional annual five to six per cent on base salary. Benefits are flexible and substantial. The reward package is delivered in a cafeteria format which includes items as diverse as Sainsbury's and M&S vouchers, life insurance, healthcare insurance, top notch pensions and cars.

KPMG was the first accountancy firm to publish annual accounts which John Ashman argues demonstrates its commitment to transparency. It has developed as a practice by listening carefully to its people and aims to build on what it hears. KPMG believes strongly in the power of communication to create an effective culture. Feedback is used extensively to appreciate the value and effectiveness of particular policies and approaches.

'We believe that open knowledge and information is the root of success. It is a cardinal value of KPMG that we need to communicate clearly and effectively with one another so that we can all prosper. The quality of the dialogue is also important. We use several different techniques for communications. With more than 600 partners regular briefing, either face-to-face or electronically, is extremely important.'

Contact address

John Ashman
Head of HR
KPMG
8 Salisbury Square
London EC4Y 8EB
Telephone: 0171 311 1000
Fax: 0171 311 3311
Web site: http://www.kpmg.com

The Littlewoods Organisation plc

The Littlewoods Group is chiefly known for three landmark areas of business. Its retail clothing stores populate many high streets around the country. Catalogue services have been established for decades. And, for many, the Littlewoods name is synonymous with football pools. The late Sir John Moores founded the pools business in 1923. Having created a thriving enterprise in the gaming sector, this extraordinary man turned his attention to home shopping in 1932. Five years later he opened his first retail outlets under the Littlewoods brand. The home turf of the company is Merseyside even though it employs 27,000 people throughout Britain. The overall shape of the group has been broadly the same since it was controlled by Sir John but has always worked to ensure that it is organized to meet the needs of its customers and to provide a rewarding and innovative working environment.

Littlewoods at a glance

Employees: 27,000 (2,500 at head office with another 3,000 on Merseyside)
Annual staff attrition: +/– 20 per cent in stores; negligible in home shopping and pools
Key locations: Merseyside, Greater Manchester, 300 stores throughout the country
Annual graduate intake: 36
Annual intake: variable

An inside view

Littlewoods is one of the most distinctive names in British retailing. The company which is synonymous with department stores and the football pools was created out of the vision and enterprise of Sir John Moores, a formidable Merseyside businessman. His legacy in Liverpool and throughout the UK is a company which – sometimes against all odds – weathers the hardest storms. But the business today has evolved substantially from Sir John Moores' inspiration.

The composition of the group is the home shopping catalogue business, and the retail stores comprising 140 Index stores and 110 high street stores. There is also a small printing business, J & C Moores Ltd, employing 250 people. The leisure division encompasses both football pools and lotteries. In addition there is a thriving new book initiative called Index Extra which harnesses the best of home shopping and Index shops. The main challenge which faces Littlewoods is to sustain and grow its businesses in markets which are under massive competitive pressure and where margins can be tight. Retail in particular is a sector where leading names need constantly to reinvent themselves to keep pace with the relentless pattern of change in product quality and customer demand.

In 1998, the group launched an internal branding campaign called Changing with Pride. Littlewoods management aims to encourage employees to build on the traditions of the past while embracing the talents and skills needed for successful endeavour in the future. The primary objective of the initiative is to make Littlewoods the most admired consumer business in the UK. Group chief executive Barry Gibson has toured the country expounding his concept of shared vision reinforced by a set of corporate values which emphasize pride in every aspect of the business.

Renewal and focus is feeding through into all sections of the group. The last full year financials show a turnover of £2.29 billion and a pretax profit of £191.1 million. In the group's retail business, Littlewoods Home Shopping is the UK's second largest home shopping retailer, Index operates 130 catalogue shops in high streets across the country, and the group owns 110 of the familiar Littlewoods stores. The style of all these businesses is value-for-money, quality products at best price. In the leisure division, Littlewoods Pools and Lotteries is the world's premier operator of pools and charity scratchcards. The pools took a major hit with the advent of the National Lottery but, with characteristic vigour, it has fought back and this area of the group is finding new markets.

The group runs three prominent joint ventures which it believes will be important for the long-term development of its business. It is creating a series of niche catalogues around the Arcadia label, developed by what was formerly The Burton Group, and is also including Arcadia products in the main Littlewoods catalogues. Another famous name in the north-west is Granada Television. Littlewoods and the Granada Media Group are working on a joint home shopping channel for cable television called Shop! Thirdly, a group of US-style warehouse clubs called Costco is being rolled out in the UK. Littlewoods holds a 20 per cent stake in the venture.

A particular source of pride in the enterprise is Business Express which provides parcel delivery for home shopping and third party businesses. Business Express was voted carrier of the year in 1993–4 and 1994–5 by the Institute of Transport Managers. In 1997 it also achieved the Investors in People Award.

Home shopping is at the core of the business, employing 13,500 people mainly in the north of England with an annual turnover of £1.4 billion and an operating profit of £61.7 million. Now the company is preparing for new ways of bringing a full range of everyday merchandise to the armchair buyer. In addition to the long-established agency catalogues, it has moved into direct catalogues with Index Extra, the fast-growing UK direct book. Index Extra has been a phenomenal success for Littlewoods with considerable competitive advantage over its rivals. So remarkable has the achievement in this sector been that competitor businesses have struggled to keep pace. Electronic buying is high on the agenda for the future.

In 1997–8, the stores' business recorded a turnover of £483 million with operating profits of £23.4 million, partly thanks to Berkertex, a new brand launched three years ago backed by new support marketing initiatives. Another significant factor has been the re-engineering of the supply chain and a new purpose-built distribution centre.

How does Littlewoods rate?

Pay:	good
Benefits:	excellent
Communications:	good
Training:	very good
Career development:	good
Morale:	good

People and personnel policies

Littlewoods' HR team has re-evaluated the traditional ways of working and produced streamlined HR policies to provide new drive and fresh thinking. Now there is an atmosphere of application and dedication. It has also made the shift from traditional employer to modern, participative business.

Using the renewed commercial agenda as its focus, Littlewoods has restructured the principal functions in the group. A new management team will act as the backbone of the enterprise. Functional directors report directly to the group chief executive. As well as being heads of their own sections, they are expected to see themselves as part of the executive team and share a collegiate responsibility. To be appointed as a senior executive in a Littlewoods business unit, means an acceptance of the creed of unity and consensus.

Central to the new human resources philosophy is the idea of greater employee involvement in decision-making and a substantial adoption of the concept of stakeholder responsibility. Employee relations director Ford Graham suggests that HR must be commercially astute and be geared to best practice. The revitalized Littlewoods management argues that the stakeholders – employees in particular – are the main asset in the business. Building on the goodwill and commitment of well informed and motivated stakeholders is a critical factor in establishing and maintaining business prosperity.

In practice, Littlewoods has revolutionized HR to change both the nature of its function and the status of the company's relationship with its employees. In traditional companies the personnel department dealt with processing – locating people, training them and rewarding them. In modern businesses, the human resources department is a catalyst for achieving enhanced customer relationships and helping employees to make a stronger contribution. In return, HR assists individuals to find a new sense of purpose, structure and enthusiasm in their careers.

In addition to limited graduate recruitment, the company has recently recruited a quality, high potential team from both internal and external sources which is designed to promote original thinking and fresh drive to the business. They have been slotted in at middle management level to galvanize the middle reaches of the company. Littlewoods has also launched a package of initiatives to improve management effectiveness, communication and consultation. A managers' conference, attended by 850 executives, prompted an exchange of ideas with the emphasis on vision and values and changing business performance. In addition the group has opened a new monthly magazine and a series of issues-focused newsletters. Employees are encouraged to telephone new ideas to a dedicated hotline and Barry Gibson is accessible to all either on the phone or through e-mail.

Littlewoods has also understood that all the access, confidence-building and participation must be matched by a fair reward package. Recognition is via hard cash as well as positive personal reward. To this end the salary and wages structure is being revamped and a greater emphasis on assessing personal performance achieved through agreed targets. The company has a well established and good working relationship with the unions which have been a positive help through the process of change. Incentive measures and performance-related bonuses are a major feature within the organization. They are regarded as a vital part of the remuneration package, running alongside an excellent pension scheme and staff discounts on all goods.

Littlewoods has been at the vanguard of promoting equality, diversity and fairness since the inception of its very first business (Pools) in the 1920s. Equality and diversity have been embedded into the very heart of the organization, with board level commitment and an Equal Opportunities Strategy Committee, chaired by chairman James Ross. Senior managers are directly accountable to the chief executive and must ensure that issues of equality are threaded through every business function. This innovative approach brings the company closer to its customers, the communities in which it operates; ensures supplier diversity; enables the recruitment, retention and development of the best people which makes Littlewoods an employer of choice. An outstanding feature of the Littlewoods profile is its genuine understanding of the needs of its employees. It is a founding member and champion company for several initiatives where it is regularly cited as a case study of best practice. It offers maternity, paternity, adoption and family leave and flexible working. Littlewoods has made great strides in implementing diversity and has collected many awards for Equality Innovation.

Contact address

Ford Graham
Employee Relations Director
The Littlewoods Organisation plc
100 Old Hall Street
Liverpool L70 1AB
Telephone: 0151 235 2222
Fax: 0151 235 2927
Web site: http://www.littlewoods.co.uk (corporate)

Lloyds TSB Group

A survey in *The Sunday Times* in Autumn 1998 placed Lloyds TSB Group as the third most efficient organization in the UK in terms of shareholder value. For a financial services company this is a remarkable statistic. It complements data covering a decade or more which reveals that Lloyds TSB is a market leader in terms of profitability in the banking industry. While other British banks struggled in the late 1980s and early 1990s, Lloyds was acknowledged as one of the few banks which was efficiently managed. It is now larger – in market capitalization – than NatWest and Barclays combined, which makes it one of the largest financial services organizations in the world.

Lloyds TSB at a glance

Employees: 82,500 – including some 12,000 employed overseas
Annual staff attrition: 6 per cent
Key locations: London (HQ), Bristol (offices), most major towns and cities in the UK
Annual graduate intake: 100
Annual intake: 8,500

An inside view

In an industry given to fashionable diversions into exciting new markets, Lloyds has always stayed true to its principles and has never been lured away from its main markets. In 1993 a *Financial Times* management report 'Profitability for European Banks' concluded that few banks in the European region understood profitability like Lloyds TSB. In fact it was the only UK bank which merited a mention in the entire document. The bank uses a WEV (Warranted Equity Value) calculation to determine its business objectives and targets. Its governing principle remains Maximizing Shareholder Value.

Two significant corporate developments have radically changed Lloyds TSB's shape and scope. In the mid-1990s Lloyds Bank purchased Cheltenham and Gloucester. The two companies had many similarities. C&G drew the lion's share of its clients from individuals with greater than average net income and Lloyds had a strong private banking division, servicing people of high net worth. Also C&G was well managed, highly regarded in the financial services industry and enjoyed a good reputation for customer service.

In 1996 TSB joined the group. This was a different kind of banking operation and one with a savings bank tradition. The newly created Lloyds TSB Group had, overnight, much greater coverage and penetration. In many ways the two businesses complemented each other. TSB's regional strengths were different from Lloyds and TSB's market focus reached people in lower income groups.

The strategy of the merged group has three main aims: to be the first choice for its customers for all their financial services needs; to be a market leader in its chosen markets; and to facilitate investment by driving down day-to-day operating costs through increasing efficiency.

As one of the largest banks in the world, Lloyds TSB faces increasing commercial pressure. The group believes that to continue to be successful, Lloyds TSB must be distinctive. Top management appreciates that people are a key strategic differentiator to keep it ahead of the competition. Lloyds TSB wants a worldwide reputation for the quality of its leadership, its people and the way they are managed.

Lloyds TSB believes in providing service that will add value to its customers and that in the future the range of distribution channels will expand. At the moment telephone banking is a growing phenomenon but the group also sees a time when kiosk banking and Internet banking will become commonplace. The diversity of outlets will be a continuing theme and IT now offers many services in a single package, previously available from different locations. Personal banking will be enhanced and more focused to meet specific and often specialized needs of customers.

How does Lloyds TSB rate?

Pay:	very good
Benefits:	very good
Communications:	good
Training:	excellent
Career development:	very good
Morale:	very good

People and personnel policies

Some 60 per cent of Lloyds TSB's workforce is employed in the retail banking network. The group has around 2,500 outlets across the UK. Other members of staff work in Insurance, International, Treasury or Wholesale banking divisions.

The group recruits 100 graduates every year. Selection for one of the places in the graduate recruitment scheme is done through an assessment centre, and includes a range of tests. The centres also feature in the bank's internal career development programme, specially for managers eager to be considered for senior posts.

Graduate entrants join a two-year induction programme featuring four periods of six months in different departments. This is designed to give a rounded knowledge of the business. It takes them to the first step of the managerial ladder, when they become responsible for securing a full-time role in the group.

A high percentage of graduate entrants have more specialized careers in management, preferring to stay within a particular division in the bank. However, a small group of the graduates is identified during the induction course and is given a broader cross-functional training.

The bank emphasizes leadership skills as a key criterion for advancement and much of the training organized centrally focuses on creating new leaders.The Lloyds TSB Training Department spends £30 million a year on formally organized training. There is also a high level of on-the-job training and courses arranged by the individual departments. Lloyds spends 3.8 per cent of all staff costs on training which is higher than the national average for UK banks. It has also invested heavily in learning centres which are spread across the country in branches and departments where people can access a range of learning facilities including PC based tuition through CD-ROM, on-line facilities and also video.

Lloyds TSB is taking steps to ensure that talented people who are affected by restructuring in one sector of the business may be able to find new roles elsewhere in the group. 'Lloyds TSB is moving towards a competencies-based approach to career management. If, for example, a manager in Insurance Services is good at problem solving, client relationships and negotiation, he or she may have the competencies for a senior role in the branch-banking network. It is matching the skills required for a particular post with the qualities which a specific individual can bring to the task.'

The progressive nature of the group means that communications is a significant issue for Lloyds TSB. The group makes strenuous efforts to ensure that its people are kept informed and have the opportunity to ask questions about the changes which affect them. Given the extent of changes in recent years, staff morale is high. Mergers can bring dislocation and uncertainty but Lloyds TSB has characteristically planned the initiative methodically and employees have responded to the leadership that has been shown.

Contact address

Alan Houston
Head of HR Strategy and Policy
Lloyds TSB Group
Canons House
Canons Way
Bristol
Telephone: 0117 943 3407
Fax: 0117 943 3082
Web site: http://www.lloydstsbgroup.co.uk

Logica plc

Logica is a highly respected organization. It has grown strongly in the last few years and is on target to come an FTSE 1000 company by the year 2002. Logica is a leading UK-based international consultancy, software, IT solutions and systems integration business with a 1998 turnover of almost £473 million, achieving pretax profits of £41.8 million. The company provides information technology solutions to meet the business needs of leading organizations worldwide, mainly in the specialist areas of finance, telecommunications, energy and utilities, defence, industry, government, transport, industry, space and aerospace. Logica, with headquarters in central London, employs around 7,000 people and has offices in 23 countries throughout Europe, the Middle East, North and South America and Asia Pacific.

Logica at a glance

Employees: c.7,000
Annual staff attrition: n/a
Key locations: Logica's head office is in central London and there are 10 regional offices throughout the UK. The largest of the company's subsidiaries overseas are in France and the US
Annual graduate intake: 380–400
Annual intake: n/a

An inside view

The IT industry has been plagued by cyclical fluctuations during the last decade. In the last few years in particular the demands of customers have accelerated and the pace of competitive pressure has stepped up. Logica, like all of its serious competitors, has met the challenges head-on. It has reshaped its business and adopted a new approach.

Logica now brands itself as The Global Solutions Company with a mission to help leading organizations worldwide to achieve their business objectives through the innovative use of IT. Its market strategy is underpinned by five values: respect, innovation, challenge, value and fulfilment.

In 1993 when the current managing director and chief executive Martin Read took over the company, he was charged with revitalizing the business. 'At that time Logica was a relatively small UK-dominated company struggling to deliver a satisfactory return for its shareholders. However, it was also a company with tremendous potential, highly valued by its customers for its technical excellence and hugely talented staff.

'The strategy for the future which we set out five years ago was aimed at creating a world class IT solutions company which would deliver for its customers and its staff, and provide a superior return for its shareholders. The key elements of the strategy were to focus on value-added activities critical to the businesses of our customer; to offer reputable solutions which deliver economies of scale and faster time-to-market; to develop an international network to deliver solutions globally; and to broaden our offering to encompass strategic consultancy and support services in addition to our traditional strengths of systems integration and project management.'

The strategy has paid off. Earnings per share and pretax profits have increased by 500 per cent. The company now operates in 23 countries and the vast majority of its revenues are based overseas. Some 70 per cent of its business are in the fast-growing global sectors of telecoms, energy, utilities and finance.

Martin Read says that Logica is now poised to make another significant leap forward. 'We focus on value-added, mission-critical work in growth markets and establishing a global network. To supplement this we have begun a programme of selected acquisitions to add new territories, achieve critical mass in existing units, increase our portfolio of reputable solutions in chosen market sectors and broaden our service offering.'

At the time Logica was formed the computer hardware industry made massive mainframes operated by data processing managers and their staff, and visual record computers largely used by sales and accounting departments. The computer industry was dominated by IBM and the so-called seven dwarfs – most of which have either fallen by the wayside or merged. These companies also provided the operating software to run the machines and in so doing tied their customers to a particular manufacturer.

The original founders of Logica, the most well-known being Philip Hughes, still a non-executive director and admired for the paintings he continues to create, were among the first to see a niche market for providing custom-designed software which was not only more cost-effective than that supplied by hardware manufacturers, but usually more efficient. The added bonus was that customers were provided with the software they wanted, rather than what was thrust upon them, and very soon a series of healthy business partnerships were established by Logica through hand-holding and guiding its clients through what was becoming an increasingly complex industry.

How does Logica rate?

Pay:	very good
Benefits:	very good
Communications:	excellent
Training:	very good
Career development:	excellent
Morale:	good

People and personnel policies

Jim McKenna, Logica's director of human resources, is a pragmatist. Pointing towards the window of his sixth floor office at the company's imposing headquarters building in the Euston area of London, he says, 'My senior colleagues and I are under no illusion. Our business walks out of this, and other of our buildings around the world, every night. If they don't return, we have no business.'

He is, of course, referring to the company's employees – of which a staggering 87% are 'extremely bright, talented and ambitious graduates.' It is therefore understandable that when he uses that well-worn and over-exposed cliché, used in numerous annual reports and other corporate publications – 'our staff are our most vital assets' – he really means it.

It comes as no surprise, therefore, that Logica's human resources policy, set against the background of the competitive industry in which it operates, is aimed squarely at attracting the right sort of people and, importantly, keeping them. The average age of Logica's employees is 28. McKenna explains, 'We work in partnership with our customers. Relationships are established based on our long track record, trust and the ability of our people to relate to our customers. Inter-personal skills are a vital ingredient of the people we employ. The fact that 60 per cent of our customers were our customers 20 years ago is evidence that by putting the customer at the heart of everything we do is the right approach.

'We are totally committed to adding value to our customers' businesses; we give them what they want in order for them to succeed. In the process of achieving this customers do not like a procession of different consultants coming and going. That is one very good reason why we like to keep our people and we do everything possible to help them develop their careers to give them greater responsibility, job satisfaction and rewards.'

At the core of the company's philosophy is its structure, which is non-hierarchical, and heavily decentralized. Most people work in an open, task-orientated project environment, dealing with one or more client at any time, led by a project manager, and with or without direct support from colleagues, depending on the size and scope of the project.

However, almost all employees at Logica have a so-called staff consultant, who operates an 'open door' policy, with whom they can discuss all matters relevant to their current work and future ambitions. Nevertheless, as in most IT companies, employees need to be proactive about the development of their careers. There is a formal career structure where employees and managers plan careers in partnership.

Logica takes on up to 400 graduates a year. Although those with a good technical degree – such as computer sciences, physics or electronic engineering – are in particular demand, graduates with other degrees, such as economics or geography, are also sought. No matter what the qualifications, the company always looks for graduates with strong interpersonal skills.

Successful candidates spend their first year being developed and going through a mandatory induction programme. They are exposed to project management, quality assurances, finance and development of interpersonal skills. They start to work as a member of a project team almost immediately and will be given responsibility for smaller projects very early in their careers. Graduates with three to four years' experience currently manage some of the company's most prestigious and challenging assignments.

All employees are expected to develop their skills to help develop their careers. The company provides on-going training in strategic and general management, interpersonal skills, team-building, and of course in the ever-changing information technology sector where Logica says it spends 'an enormous amount of money'. Much of this training is in-house, using CBT (computer-based training) techniques. A series of lunchtime workshops, formal and informal, is also held continuously.

As an international company operating in four geographic regions – the UK, Europe, North America and Asia Pacific – the opportunities for working overseas or in various parts of the UK constantly occur, not only in project management but in general management, marketing and finance. Everyone has the opportunity to apply for such appointments as details of them are broadcast on the company's internal *Logica Visual News*, a network of television screens strategically placed in common areas of the company's premises. Here details of job opportunities are given together with general news about the company.

All employees are set annual objectives and are subject to an annual performance review. There are also more frequent reviews on the progress of particular projects. The company says it pays competitive salaries and operates a profit-sharing scheme. It provides free health insurance and a contributory pension scheme. One novel benefit is the company's house purchase plan through which pension contributions can be paid as part of the mortgage for as long as an employee wishes. This is to assist employees moving to London from other parts of the country to enter the housing market.

Contact address

Ms Margaret Little
Recruitment Manager
Logica plc
Stephenson House
75 Hampstead Road
London NW1 2PL
Telephone: 0171 637 9111
Fax: 0171 468 7006
Web site: http://www.logica.com

Marks & Spencer plc

Marks & Spencer is one of Britain's largest and most respected retailers. It has traditionally been a benchmark for good practice in human resources in the retail sector. Throughout the last few decades, the brand has strengthened and become synonymous with fair dealing and value for money. Its recent excursions into financial services and food retailing have proved fruitful and in the last few years it has begun a serious expansion of its network of stores into mainland Europe. In the autumn of 1998 the company's financial results were not as good as anticipated and it suffered an embarrassing succession battle in the full glare of public attention.

Marks & Spencer at a glance

Employees: 66,500
Annual staff attrition: 10 per cent
Key locations: 640 worldwide, 286 in the UK
Annual graduate intake: 200
Annual intake: n/a

An inside view

Marks & Spencer is the bell-wether for the UK retail sector. It enjoys a formidable name among the public, who regard it as a British institution more than a shop. M&S is also viewed with great respect among European business leaders. Almost every survey of chief executives and chairs of major international PLCs on the standing and integrity of companies puts M&S at the front of the field. Since this book first appeared in 1989 M&S has been a by-word for strong brand performance, quality of operation and reliability in personnel policies.

But 1998 was a troubled year for the company. It had a bad first six months of trading. Its optimistic forecasts of future trading – and £300 million from its £2 billion investment budget – were cut back. Questions were asked among analysts about whether M&S was experiencing a little local difficulty or that its strategy was more fundamentally flawed. Within hours of the interims being announced, a succession battle broke out in the City pages of the quality national press. This was all very unlike M&S, which in its public pronouncements has traditionally been on message.

In December chairman and chief executive Sir Richard Greenbury had his way. His deputy chairman, Keith Oates, who as a finance man was not on the chairman's preferred list, took early retirement. But Sir Richard had to give some ground and his role was split. As he retained the chairmanship, his candidate

Peter Salsbury stepped up to the role of chief executive. The surprise was not that M&S made succession plans, but that it was done – so graphically – in public.

However, for most people employed by M&S, beyond a little playful speculation, tiffs among directors have modest impact on their work. And regardless of their arguments M&S remains an exceptional employer especially for shop floor staff. In a way it has become public property. It is certainly an evocation of the nature of British shopkeeping. M&S stands for quality, value for money and reliability.

The company's touchstone is integrity and reliability. People who shop at Marks & Spencer believe that they will be treated fairly, the goods on sale will be value for money and if they are dissatisfied M&S will always take their purchases back. The flagship clothing stores have worked hard to overcome their long standing tendency to be rather unadventurous and its buyers have attempted to put some life into the collections. It has also opened up top end food retailing and in the 1980s ventured into financial services.

How does Marks & Spencer rate?

Pay:	very good
Benefits:	very good
Communications:	excellent
Training:	very good
Career development:	very good
Morale:	good

People and personnel policies

During the research for this book, its immediate predecessor and the original edition, and indeed in the interim, people throughout the company, the retail industry and across the business world have made similar observations. Marks & Spencer is a superb employer for people who work in its stores.

The support which shop floor staff receive is excellent. The training is among the best in the retail environment and the company is generous in its pay and benefits. In fact, M&S was always legendary for the extent of its benefits package. Communications is also good and it has been a trendsetter in the retail sector for its staff cascade briefings. M&S is perhaps a typical environment where team briefings succeed. Every Monday morning before the shops open new prices are announced through the cascade system. The system also updates staff on corporate, financial and personnel news.

It is the sheer quality of the M&S delivery to shop floor employees which has earned the company its outstanding reputation as an employer. During the exploratory work for the first edition, when our researchers asked 'Who are the best employers?', personnel directors would inevitably answer, 'Well, apart from Marks & Spencer, there is . . .' it is fair to say that there were not many exemplary employers in 1987 and 1988 and, in the minds of senior directors, excellence in employment often coincided with being a strong and thriving commercial enterprise. Nevertheless, at the heart of the M&S ethos there was a real sense of treating its people with equity.

M&S was the first company to treat its staff as individuals, and its primary personnel guideline is to treat all staff with respect and honesty. Integrity is a core value and this extends to the nature of the dialogue between managers and employees. Opportunity for all is a touchstone for M&S.

Some 83 per cent of the workforce is female and three-quarters of employees are part-time. Two-thirds of management positions are occupied by women. In the early 1990s, a major initiative to help women who work in the stores was launched by the company. The extent and flexibility of part-time employment has increased; a child break scheme is in operation which allows female employees to remain in touch with the company during the early years of child rearing. M&S is one of the UK's most active users of job sharing, which allows women with children at school to rejoin the business in stages.

Contact address

Human Resources
Marks & Spencer plc
Baker Street
London W1A 1DN
Telephone: 0171 935 4422
Fax: 0171 487 2679
Web site:
http://www.marksandspencer.co.uk

Mars

In the UK economy there is a group of benchmark employers. Perhaps 15 companies – many of them multinational businesses – define employment best practice in this region. Most are long-established practitioners in the art of human resources management. These companies excel in each of the component areas of human resources. When they compare approach and standards among themselves, Mars is one of only two or three which are leaders of this unique set. For decades this business which is principally known for its confectionery products, but which is also market leader in petcare, packaged foods, drinks vending, electronic payment systems and a form of highly specialized IT, has been a world class innovator in people management. Needless to say, it is also extremely successful commercially.

Mars at a glance

Employees: 30,000 worldwide, 5,500 UK
Annual staff attrition: 5 per cent
Key locations: Slough, Melton Mowbray, Peterborough, Kings Lynn, Reading, Leeds, Basingstoke
Annual graduate intake: 40
Annual intake: 250

An inside view

Mars to the general public means chocolate bars. To the business community it is a group of market-leading businesses in confectionery, petcare, packaged foods and niche IT. But to the human resources professional, Mars is synonymous with excellence in people management. At home in the US – but emphatically here in the UK – Mars is in the vanguard of innovative personnel policy. In fact, it is hard to underestimate the role which Mars has played in shaping the environment for best practice in British employment.

Many of the components of human resources policy which have become commonplace in Britain's better employers were introduced first at Mars. For example, it is the archetype for the flat structure company. Years before widely publicized hierarchies began to strip out layers of management, Mars operated on only seven levels. The Office of the President in America is at the top level, and shop floor staff producing Mars, Snickers or Bounty bars are a maximum of six layers away.

Mars has been a consistent pioneer of effective employee communications using a range of media to convey messages and solicit views. Its mechanism of briefings which cover every level in the space of 48 hours is the envy of many companies.

At the heart of its success as a widely admired enterprise, is its philosophy of business. The Five Principles of Mars enshrine the culture of the company and underpin all of its activities. These are: quality, responsibility, efficiency, mutuality and freedom. The company adheres strongly to these values and in seeking recruits looks for talented, ambitious individuals who can subscribe to and articulate these values in their work.

The demand for posts in the group is high and only a small percentage of applicants secure places each year. In universities and colleges the reputation of Mars is well founded over several decades. Careers information officers are aware that Mars is a popular choice but that competition for jobs in the group is intensive. It is a career choice which does not suit everyone. The culture is a demanding one and Mars people are expected to make a significant contribution to the business. Mars offers benchmark training, superb reward packages and significant development opportunities. But the company expects a return in commitment to the business, a willingness to work within co-operative teams and high quality output.

The company is one of the world's top three confectioners. It shares with Cadbury and Nestlé a commitment to best employment practice but Mars has strong meritocratic values, a belief in total integrity and respect for the individual. Mars appreciates that the company must invest in its people to remain a thriving enterprise. In recent years, the corporation's global growth has been exceptional. It has operations in more than 60 countries worldwide. It is particularly proud of its ventures in Russia, Eastern Europe, Latin America and the Pacific Rim. Mars has invested $150 million in Russia alone. Its salesforces now reach markets in more than 150 countries across the world.

All Mars businesses are worldwide in scope and have significant European regional management. The UK businesses are fully integrated into these international operations. Mars Confectionery, for example, is a core part of Snackfoods Europe. The electronics company MEI is a global operation.'Our strategy has been to integrate all our operations either at a European or global level. I think we have seen great benefits from working more closely at a regional level but there are aspects of operations which must remain national to achieve local competitive edge,' says one group personnel manager.

This is a brand-led group with an enviable portfolio of famous names. The confectionery business, based in Slough, produces Mars, Twix, Snickers, M&Ms, Maltesers, Milky Way, Bounty and Starbust. Pedigree Petfoods makes the market leaders in dog food – Pedigree Chum – and cat food – Whiskas. It also manufactures Pal, KiteKat, Sheba, Trill and Aquarian. Mars is also engaged in other areas of food manufacturing with brands such as Uncle Ben's, Dolmio and Yeoman. It runs the Four Square dispensed-drinks machine company and sector brands such as Flavia and Klix. This activity led Mars to develop and market a new coin acceptance mechanism which was the foundation of Mars Electronics International.

How does Mars rate?

Pay:	excellent
Benefits:	superb
Communications:	superb
Training:	excellent
Career development:	superb
Morale:	excellent

People and personnel policies

Mars is a role model for all of the companies in this book. Its tradition as a standard-setter for best practice is matched by its search for better ways to conduct business. It remains head and shoulders above the vast majority of employers in the UK because it has stayed true to its values and built on its considerable achievements of the past.

The principal lines of business are developed on global and regional lines but current and future skill requirement is determined on a regional and national level. As in any other multinational company, Mars produces in one location for marketing and distribution in several territories. Buying of materials, preparation and manufacture, and despatch is handled centrally. Marketing is shaped by regional and national teams, which share common approaches adapted to local circumstances. The structure of local businesses will vary considerably according to need on the ground. If operational demand dictates, specialist teams will be created on an entirely pragmatic basis.

Its flat structure – created in the early 1960s – is a foundation stone. Mars appreciated long before its competitors that quick decision-making and rapid response to customer and market demand led to commercial success. Short reporting lines facilitate the flow of new ideas and a business which can be flexible and highly efficient. What has changed is the remit of managers in the structure. Junior managers now have some European level responsibility and senior managers spend much of their time moving from site to site to monitor progress.

Mars has a long history of employing graduates. It is best known for the Mars Management Training Programme (MMTP), which brings in around 20 individuals directly from university. In addition, Mars brings a further 20 graduates on to more technically specific programmes, in areas such as IT, finance and software engineering. The company sources from colleges and universities all over Europe. It also likes to recruit another 150 plus recent graduates who have had two to five years' experience in industry. Mars has actively built links with certain universities, and student, careers guidance and recruitment associations. It also has summer and industrial placement schemes where potential recruits can get a feel for Mars and the company can assess whether particular individuals could be suitable for permanent roles.

The company looks for people who are strong on leadership, motivation, influencing skills and critical thinking. Beyond this Mars people are self-disciplined, enthusiastic, articulate and dedicated. If this makes them sound a little dry, they are also good humoured and recruitment managers seek people who are fun to work with. On the

Management Training Programme, a trainee performs a series of assignments in different areas of the business. Each of these lasts between six and nine months. The individual then takes up a full-time post in a specific functional area of the business.

The changing shape of the business as a global player has re-emphasized its commitment to diversity. In October and November 1998 Mars ran diversity workshops for all senior managers in the UK to give renewed impetus to these issues in the business. Mars has always been a meritocratic employer which encourages people of all backgrounds. It describes its approach to business as 'Distinctive voices working together within a common culture'. 'At our units and sites, we wish to facilitate the process of building a diverse workforce. All associates understand and accept that diversity is business-wise, culturally responsible and consistent with developing our franchises and customer bases. Cultural richness is a natural asset in doing business,' says the company.

Specifically, it has put in place a series of initiatives to ensure that diversity is fully expressed in Mars businesses. These include: a strengthened equal opportunities policy, a commitment to dignity at work and a series of special needs policies. Progress in diversity issues is actively monitored and Mars invests in training programmes to support the initiative.

Contact address

Mars Graduate Marketing
Dundee Road
Slough SL1 4JX
Telephone: 01753 514999
Fax: 01753 215559
Web site: http://www.snickers.com

Matsushita/Panasonic

Known in Europe through its market-leading brand names of Panasonic and Technics, Matsushita Electric Europe is part of the Japanese multinational Matsushita, one of the world's largest manufacturers of high-quality electric and electronic products for the consumer, business and industrial markets. Headquartered in Middlesex, Matsushita in Europe carries out manufacturing, sales, research and development and operational support functions such as financial support services in the UK and the rest of Europe. The company's philosophy is that the wellbeing of the company and society is inextricably entwined. It regards its people as its most important resource and, therefore, the development of individual potential has always been a cornerstone of its business philosophy.

Matsushita/Panasonic at a glance

Employees: 276,000 worldwide, 13,500 Europe, 4,400 UK
Annual staff attrition: 7 per cent
Key locations: European regional HQ: Uxbridge, Middlesex; Sales: two offices at Bracknell and Wokingham in Berkshire; Manufacturing: four in South Wales, Thatcham and Reading, in Berkshire, and East Kilbride, Scotland; Group Finance: London; R&D: Edinburgh and Wokingham, Berkshire
Annual graduate intake: 30
Annual intake: 300

An inside view

Matsushita Electric Europe, headquartered in the UK, is one of Europe's most successful electronics businesses. Since the establishment of its first sales office in Hamburg in 1962, the company has grown into a Europe-wide organization with 20 manufacturing sites, 22 sales companies, as well as local R&D and group support functions throughout the region. Matsushita designs, manufactures and markets a wide range of innovative and constantly evolving electronic products from industrial robots to mobile phones.

Under the brand name Panasonic, Matsushita supplies high-quality office equipment, audio and video products for the professional and domestic market, factory automation equipment and innovative digital technology and communications products. Under the Technics brand name it supplies high-grade audio equipment, hi-fi, component systems, CD players, amplifiers, speakers and electronic musical instruments. More than 50 per cent of Matsushita goods sold in Europe are produced at Matsushita European manufacturing bases.

In its 1997 financial year, Matsushita initiated its Progress 2000 Plan, a four-year strategic programme aimed at building a new, stronger management structure which will enable the company to achieve growth in its core businesses of consumer products, industrial products and components in the twenty-first century. Matsushita is at the forefront of product development to exploit the possibilities of the digital technology explosion, focusing on the acceleration of activities in its five priority businesses: digital TVs, optical discs, mobile communications equipment, display devices and semiconductors.

The culture at Matsushita stems from its Basic Business Philosophy (BBP), of which the underlying principle is that the company has certain responsibilities to the environment and to the communities, be they local or global, in which it operates. The company is committed to assisting the progress of society and people's wellbeing through its business activities and, in so doing, making the world a better place in which to live. Integral to this philosophy is the belief that in order to carry out its obligations, the company must be profitable and that this mutual prosperity of company and community is achieved by putting the customer first.

How does Matsushita/Panasonic rate?

Pay:	good
Benefits:	superb
Communications:	very good
Training:	good
Career development:	very good
Morale:	excellent

People and personnel policies

The commitment of high-calibre individuals at every level of production – from shop floor to management – is a vital factor in the Matsushita success story. The recognition of individual capabilities and development of personal potential have always been fundamental to Matsushita's corporate philosophy and are two of the company's particular strengths.

The company prioritizes investment in training of its employees through a comprehensive range of internal and external training schemes designed not only to improve on existing skills but to develop new ones. In-company training is provided in a long list of disciplines from computer and business skills to advanced engineering specialities, including arts and language studies in order to improve cross-cultural understanding. In addition, Matsushita provides self-development training and financial support for further education classes in work-related courses, languages or personal development, in accordance with the proportion of content associated with an individual's job.

In conjunction with the HR department, all employees have individual development plans designed to allow people to achieve their personal and company objectives. These include personal training programmes and a job rotation scheme to enable employees to broaden their experience. Matsushita's appreciation of excellent performance is illustrated by the remarkable advancement within the company of those individuals who can combine a number of characteristics, including the ability to implement the BBP, particularly through excellent co-operation and teamworking, diligence, communication and adaptability.

International management staff also need to be able to adapt to, and communicate in, a foreign environment and possess the capacity to perceive issues from a global viewpoint. Matsushita provides career opportunities, both within the UK and internationally, across a whole range of disciplines from manufacturing, sales and R&D to group support functions such as financial, legal, EU affairs and product certification.

With operations worldwide, Matsushita is culturally and racially diverse and the ability to adapt to foreign cultures is a definite advantage to an individual's career prospects. Matsushita has faced head-on the preponderance of non-Europeans at upper management level – in 1989 only 20 per cent of board members were European – by the implementation of a ten-year plan to increase the proportion of European board members to 50 per cent by the year 2000. The programme, which includes training to transform managers into directors, is proving extremely successful and is fully expected to reach its Millennium target.

Matsushita's policy towards part-time working makes it attractive to people with family commitments. It encourages requests for part-time working by paying salaries and other entitlements on a pro-rata basis and, provided they work for at least 15 hours, part-time employees are also entitled to private medical cover in the same way as their full-time colleagues.

Contact address

Tim Watmuft
Personnel and General Affairs Manager
Matsushita Electric Europe
(Headquarters) Ltd
3 Furzeground Way
Stockley Park
Uxbridge
Middlesex UB11 1DD
Telephone: 0181 899 1502
Fax: 0181 899 2214
Web site:
http://www.matsushita-europe.com

McKinsey

McKinsey is America's premier management consultancy firm and arguably its most powerful. It has consistently increased its share of the fast-growing and competitive consultancy market. The company prides itself on recruiting the brightest and most talented candidates and is the most popular choice of employer for business school graduates. It is distinguished by its roster of formidable clients and a culture which resonates with quality and discretion. McKinsey offers a hugely stimulating work environment, supplemented by exceptional training and development opportunities.

McKinsey at a glance

Employees: 4,000
Annual staff attrition: TBA
Key locations: 76 offices in 39 countries
Annual graduate intake: TBA
Annual intake: TBA

An inside view

McKinsey is widely recognized as being at the forefront of the management consulting profession worldwide. The firm advises some of the world's most prominent organizations including multinational companies and several national governments. Its work cuts across all business sectors including financial services, retail, consumer goods, pharmaceuticals, manufacturing, transport, energy, telecommunications, information technology and media.

Unlike some of its rivals, McKinsey focuses almost exclusively on issues of strategic concern to top management. Typically, this means advising on corporate strategy and organization, but also involves helping clients reduce costs and increase productivity. The firm is also strong in functional areas such as marketing, finance, manufacturing and distribution. McKinsey has also taken on a number of assignments free of charge, for example, for the young and homeless, and for the Tate Gallery.

In the 1990s, McKinsey led thinking about such issues as technological innovation, logistics, alliances and acquisitions, organization design and the role of the corporate centre. The company recognizes the need to constantly stay ahead of its rivals and each year spends between $50–100 million on research. Much of this takes place in special interest groups which have developed expertise in a particular field of management.

The company's hugely impressive reputation stems not only from its objectivity and independence, but also from the high-quality intellectual and analytical skills brought to bear on the challenges facing their clients. For this, McKinsey relies on the professionalism and dedication of its consultants worldwide, a team that currently consists of more than 4,000 colleagues in 75 offices and 38 countries.

No one will deny that working for McKinsey is highly demanding. The company has established its reputation over many years by producing consistently high-quality work for blue-chip clients in changing and challenging circumstances. Intellectual rigour and clear thinking are accepted as standard. It is these disciplines which makes McKinsey a special place to work.

How does McKinsey rate?

Pay:	excellent
Benefits:	very good
Communications:	good
Training:	excellent
Career development:	excellent
Morale:	excellent

People and personnel policies

McKinsey is committed to hiring exceptional individuals with outstanding intellectual ability and interpersonal skills – whatever their background and experience – who will make great consultants and stimulating colleagues. It seeks candidates with excellent records of academic, managerial, professional or scientific achievement and the capacity to continue developing and learning. Employees at McKinsey need to have drive and commitment, be comfortable with numbers and logical reasoning, capable of innovative ideas, and good at sustaining team and client relationships and communicating complex ideas clearly.

For the past decade, McKinsey has been pursuing a radical hiring policy that seeks to recruit brainpower regardless of its discipline. Where once a main criteria for a McKinsey recruit was an MBA from Harvard or another leading business school, now new recruits are just as likely to be graduates of economics, engineering, science or law. Few other management consultants have cast such a wide net for new talent as McKinsey. The company has one simple criterion in recruitment: it wants 'distinctive people' who are best equipped to solve the increasingly complex problems facing business in the global market. That means finding people with outstanding intellectual capability irrespective of what discipline it is in. So successful is McKinsey's non-traditional intake that it now makes up around 40 per cent of all new recruits, compared to less than five per cent 15 years ago.

McKinsey hires into one of three entry roles – Business Analyst, Junior Associate and Associate. All of these consulting roles involve working with clients, solving problems and contributing as a full member of the team. However, each role bears a different degree of responsibility and implies a different training and career path, reflecting the need of the individual. McKinsey aims to make each of its new recruits an excellent consultant, but recognizes the fact that no one path suits all individuals.

The opportunities to learn at McKinsey are exceptional. The company spends a lot of time and money training and educating its new recruits in the wider world of business and commerce. Learning takes place both on-the-job (in teams) and in training programmes. The atmosphere inside teams is open and honest. Team members exchange ideas, create and test hypotheses about the client's situation, and challenge each other's conclusions. Being on a McKinsey team is both stimulating and rewarding, but it is also demanding. Team members must be good both at logical analysis and at dealing with the human side of organizations.

In addition, McKinsey sponsors many individuals to attend leading business schools, such as Harvard or Stanford in the US or INSEAD in France, to study for a Master in Business Administration (MBA). Postgraduates who have already spent considerable time in further education often complete its three-week-in-house 'mini-MBA', an intensive course in business concepts and financial analysis. McKinsey places great importance in the belief that developing its people is just as crucial as serving its clients.

The company encourages its consultants to learn and grow continuously. An employee's progress is reviewed twice a year. Staff who have expanded their skills and developed leadership qualities can expect to progress quickly. Successful consultants normally advance to principal (partner) after a total of five to seven years at McKinsey. Advancement to director (senior partner) may be possible after another five to six years. If at any stage in an employee's career path, a consultant ceases to progress, he or she is asked to leave McKinsey. This 'up or out' policy applies throughout the firm, and ensures that it continues to motivate exceptional people and provide superior client service. Generally, consultants spend a few years of their McKinsey career broadening their skills and experience to new industries and different business problems. By the time they become senior managers, however, they often find themselves focusing on particular areas of interest in which they have built up a substantial body of knowledge and experience.

Contact address

Rachel Haynes (for those studying for an MBA) or
Louise Quayle (for undergraduates)
McKinsey & Company Inc
1 Jermyn Street
London SW1Y 4UH
Telephone: 0171 839 8040
Fax: 0171 873 9777
Web site: http://www.mckinsey.co.uk

Merrill Lynch Mercury Asset Management

Merrill Lynch Mercury Asset Management (MLMAM) is the envy of the City. It commands a formidable reputation as an excellently managed investment house and a forward-looking employer. It thrives on teamwork and a direct, quality approach to business. It is a part of the global Merrill Lynch & Co organization. Until 1995, Mercury was a central part of the SG Warburg Group, one of the most respected names in the City. Mercury's distinctive approach to asset management grew in attractiveness since its inception in 1939 and from the 1960s it was the leading firm in the sector. In 1986, one group embracing the entirety of Mercury and Warburg was created. A year later Mercury Asset Management Group plc was floated with a 25 per cent UK stock market holding. In 1995 it was demerged from SG Warburg and in 1997 it was acquired by Merrill Lynch. MLMAM is one of the quality names in the City, widely regarded by investors, professionals and clients.

Merrill Lynch Mercury Asset Management at a glance

Employees: 2,000 worldwide: 1,400 UK
Annual staff attrition: 5 per cent
Key locations: London, New York, Los Angeles, Tokyo, Melbourne
Active graduate intake: 30–35
Annual intake: n/a

An inside view

Few institutions in the City enjoy the pedigree of MLMAM. Its literature says that it is old enough to have a history but young enough for its early history to be relevant today. Founder Siegmund Warburg fled his roots in investment banking in Hamburg in 1933 to escape the increasing threat of Adolf Hitler. Within months of his arrival in London he was in business and within five years he created Mercury Securities. Immediately after the war he was granted a banking licence. His legacy is a formidable one. His companies are the cornerstone of excellence in the financial community.

At the end of 1997 Merrill Lynch acquired Mercury Asset Management. 'Merrill Lynch's rationale for buying Mercury Asset Management was straightforward. We were the largest fund manager in the UK at the time. Our position in the UK was strong and established, and in Europe – especially in Germany – the company was growing. In Japan we were the largest foreign fund manager. So, as far as Merrill Lynch was concerned, acquiring Mercury gave them a significant presence in global asset management business outside the US, and an expertize and presence in the institutional market,' says Christ Emmins, a director in human resources. MLMAM is characterized by a high quality, professional approach to meeting client expectations. The heart of its business is the management of client asset portfolios. It works on behalf of individuals and institutions, from all corners of the globe. It manages in excess of $450 billion of client money.

Merrill Lynch already had a predominantly retail, domestic asset management business but no significant institutional international presence. Mercury Asset Management, on the other hand, was established internationally but had no business in the US. 'The strategic fit was very good and that is the platform for our growth plan. Merrill Lynch Mercury Asset Management, as we are known globally, is responsible for all non-US domestic retail asset management businesses of Merrill Lynch. For Mercury it means access to the enormous distribution network of Merrill Lynch. It has 14,000 financial consultants worldwide: some 13,000 in the US, the largest savings market in the world. If we had attempted to establish that kind of presence in the US on our own without the support of an organization like Merrill Lynch, it would have taken us many years.

Within MLMAM, there are manufacturing and distribution businesses. Manufacturing divisions create investment performance and our distribution teams sell and market the products. Manufacturing divisions are split on broadly geographical and product lines.

The other key manufacturing parts of our business include the non-UK equities, Fixed Income; Retail and Private Client Management Group; and a fully integrated asset management business in Japan. MLMAM has a major Global Sales and Marketing division responsible for managing relationships and marketing products and services to clients around the world. Mercury also has a major team globally devoted to managing relationships for the company's wholesale clients.

How does Mercury Asset Management rate?

Pay:	excellent
Benefits:	excellent
Communications:	very good
Training:	excellent
Career development:	very good
Morale:	superb

People and personnel policies

There is no formula for the successful applicant to MLMAM. Graduates are drawn from a wide spread of universities in a diverse selection of academic disciplines. The company's recruitment campaign is not restricted to the UK,

Mercury sources its new people globally. 'We are looking for quality rather than volume, locating perhaps 30–35 in Europe and another 15 in the US. We seek people with a genuine interest in financial markets with a demonstrable passion for investing. We are looking not only to bring people in to be future fund managers but also to work in information technology and sales and marketing. We have a well-developed Internet site which we use to access all universities globally. We also make on-site visits to eight or nine universities in the UK as well.'

MLMAM uses different recruitment methods according to the type of vacancies it wishes to fill. For graduates, there is a dedicated process which involves face-to-face meetings and a full assessment centre. For experienced hires, it uses a range of methods. Emmins says that the company operates in a highly regulated market so the company goes to great lengths to ensure that its employees are fit and proper to manager other people's money. This is a judgement which Mercury makes throughout the careers of its employees as well as at engagement.

Training and development are essential requirements in the business. After company-wide induction, each individual is familiarized with the nature of work in the specific business area for which he or she has been recruited. In most areas of the business, employees will need to achieve professional qualifications. Senior management have long supported the policy of high quality training. They have invested heavily in the provision of relevant courses and the creation and expansion of a fully integrated training function for the company. Recognition of the results of this investment has come through its accreditation in the Investors in People scheme which has paid off not only in terms of direct employee advancement and development terms but also in enhancing client relationships.

In 1998 Mercury Asset Management was re-accredited under Investors in People – three months after a major reorganization. Emmins argues that this is evidence of the value of investing in the training and development of all staff, that such an award can be achieved during a corporate transition.

Mercury was the first independent investment house in the City to achieve IIP status and it has an outstanding reputation among investment professionals for its training.

At the time we were originally accredited in 1995 it was groundbreaking stuff because the City is not renowned for its people management. We have been fortunate to take up a marketleading position on this. This has been important in promoting Mercury to prospective employees but also for clients who realize that our people are well trained and motivated. Some of our clients in the UK are from the public sector – local authorities. Many of them are IIP-accredited and in the final analysis what tipped the balance in favour of Mercury being chosen as their fund manager was its IIP Status.

Career development at MLMAM is an individual responsibility. However, the organization is committed to providing the environment and opportunities for individuals to achieve their goals. 'In order to assist with the development of all our staff we have developed a "best practice" competency based approach to appraisal.

We also use 360 degree feedback for all of our team leaders which is a very powerful tool in developing people's skills.'

The company's reward packages are performance driven. It is keen to ensure that, over time, employees are given the opportunity to share in the success of the firm. It offers a standard City package of benefits including a non-contributory pension scheme, health insurance and subsidized membership of local gyms.

Mercury has been active in promoting and developing women. As well has a high profile female chief executive, it has 35 women as senior managers and directors, 29 as associate directors and 234 junior managers. The company is an active member of Opportunity 2000 and benchmarks against the best in the field.

Contact address

Chris Emmins
Human Resources – Director
Mercury Asset Management
33 King William Street
London EC4R 9AS
Telephone: 0171 280 2800
Fax: 0171 280 2820
Web site: http://www.mam.com

Microsoft Limited

Microsoft was founded less than 25 years ago but by 1998 it had become the largest company in the United States (overtaking General Electric in September of that year) with global revenues of $14.4 billion and a market valuation of $262 billion. The launch of Windows 95 consolidated Microsoft as the standard-setter in the software industry. Bill Gates, one of Microsoft's founders and its current head, always envisaged PC software as a great enabler for businesses, public corporations and individuals and his dream is in the process of being realized. His vision has now evolved to 'the idea of integrating the intelligence and interactivity of PCs with the video and sound of TV.' In 1997 Microsoft made its biggest purchase ever when it spent $425 million on WebTV, a company with a system for surfing the Internet via television.

Microsoft at a glance

Employees: 672 (Microsoft Limited) + 110 (global and regional staff based in the UK)
Annual staff attrition: 6 per cent, plus another 5 per cent go to other Microsoft companies
Key locations: Thames Valley Park (HQ), London, Manchester, Edinburgh, Southampton, Dublin
Annual graduate intake: n/a
Annual intake: 200

An inside view

A conviction that computer software could create a personal and commercial revolution provided the spark of inspiration to found the greatest post-war American business story. Two young computer nerds, Bill Gates and Paul Allen, growing up on the Pacific north-west coast, turned their hobby into a business and founded the Microsoft Corporation. They are now two of the wealthiest individuals in the world, and it is estimated that if Microsoft shares continue to rise at the current rate, Bill Gates will be worth $443 billion in five years and more than $4 trillion in ten years' time. The company's mainstream product, Windows 95, was – on launch – adopted as global standard by virtue of the sheer volume of uptake by businesses, and, at the time of writing, Windows 98 looks like building further on that success.

The culture of the nascent company immediately appealed to young software engineers. The environment in Seattle was similar to a college campus with casually dressed enthusiasts working 36-hour and

72-hour stretches in a driven atmosphere to break the barriers of software capability. Indeed, among the young software designers in the US this atmosphere continues to proliferate but the business is more broadly based today. 'In the early days we had many young and single people who worked very long hours,' says Stephen Harvey, Microsoft Limited's director of FA and HR. 'A decade later many of these people have married and now have families. They are still as enthusiastic about the company and our products, but our work patterns tend to be slightly more conventional.' Nevertheless, enthusiasm is the touchstone. Throughout the organization people are stimulated by what Microsoft is doing. The car park is often packed at 8 am with people staying until 8 or 9 pm in the evening.

Harvey recognizes that people management skills were as important to the company as its leading technical status. Almost every division within Microsoft requires its people to demonstrate intrapersonal skills and so the directors of the business realized that they would need a director to manage the company's human resources objectives and policy. The company identifies three broad classifications for the skill groups which it uses in its UK operation: sales and marketing, consultants, and product support. Much of the software and systems design is done in the global headquarters in Seattle. In three buildings at Winnersh Triangle, the company created three cultural patterns: sales and marketing has a traditional professional environment, product support is the heartland of the technologists, and consultancy is particularly business-focused.

How does Microsoft rate?

Pay:	good
Benefits:	very good
Communications:	good
Training:	excellent
Career development:	excellent
Morale:	excellent

People and personnel policies

Harvey says that Microsoft has a structured business model which is flexible and adaptable and responds to the needs of its customers, markets and employees. Project imperatives are often best served by a totally fluid environment where individuals can be brought together at a moment's notice, but this sometimes conflicts with wider strategic and operational goals for the business. Microsoft is a substantial multinational which is undergoing transformative change. It aims to lose none of its visionary technological prowess but it also plans to strengthen its structure, develop its people skills and enhance its functioning.

'We are one of the market leaders in terms of the technology. However, there is still room for improvement. People are so keen – and we have grown so fast – that we have concentrated on the outward-facing aspects of Microsoft.' Everyone in the UK operation is becoming more customer-aware. Whether that customer is external – a major corporate client or a personal user – or internal, the focus is on service supplied to the customer. So personal communication abilities are key and these are principal among the skills which the company seeks on recruitment. Foremost among the personal qualities which Microsoft expects in its new people is enthusiasm. 'We want people who are in love with the technology and are so keen that they want to make an impact on the company.'

The company is a competitive payer. Although Microsoft has participated in many of the major salary surveys, its approach to reward packages has been geared to its worldwide compensation policy. Pay is characterized by three components: base, bonus and stock options. Base pay will vary from country to country and is determined by market conditions. The bonus – and its value – is kicked in twice a year according to the six-monthly performance review. Employees can also take advantage of stock options and some of the people who have been around since the beginning are very wealthy as a result. (The Share purchase scheme enables employees to purchase shares in Microsoft Corporation at 85 per cent of their market value.)

The company runs what has been described as one of the best group pension schemes in the industry. All employees benefit from permanent and private health insurance and life insurance, 23 to 28 days' annual leave, stock purchase scheme and sports facilities. They get discounts on Microsoft products and free access to the MSN on the Internet. Maternity benefits are better than average and Microsoft is flexible about when new mothers return. The headcount is 60 per cent male and 40 per cent female; these statistics are replicated in the manager grades, but the more senior the manager the greater likelihood that an individual manager will be a man. Women are rising rapidly in the company and employees with high intelligence, deep enthusiasm for the technology, a talent for leadership and a capacity to get on with people will prosper in Microsoft.

Contact address

Stephen Harvey
Director of FA and HR
Microsoft Limited
Microsoft Campus
Thames Valley Park
Reading
Berkshire RG6 1WG
Telephone: 08706 010100
Fax: 08706 020100
Web site: http://www.microsoft.com

Milliken Industrials Limited

Milliken & Company, one of the world's largest textile concerns, is financially strong and privately owned. The foundations for the multinational's success were laid in Portland, Maine, US some 130 years ago, but it was not until 1964 that manufacturing operations began outside the United States in Bury, Lancashire. Since then additional manufacturing plants have been established in Belgium, France, Denmark, Spain, Germany, Australia, Brazil and Japan. There is sales back-up in all locations with additional sales offices in London, Paris and Bremen to promote total product offering. Milliken has 13 European plants including seven in the UK. Each Milliken location retains the best of a small company while gaining the strength of a world leader in the textile industry.

Milliken at a glance

Employees: 16,000 worldwide, 2,000 associates in the UK
Annual staff attrition: around 2 per cent
Key locations: Wigan, Bury, Burnley, London, Gloucestershire, Leighton Buzzard and Middleton, Manchester
Annual graduate intake: 20
Annual intake: 50

An inside view

Milliken is the largest independent textile manufacturer in the world. The name may be unfamiliar to many people outside the industry but inside the sector it is widely regarded as a key player and a strong employer. The company produces 48,000 products in the chemical and textile markets. It was founded in South Carolina in 1865 and now has more than 70 manufacturing facilities worldwide.

The company is highly regarded as an innovator, and it has accumulated nearly 2,000 patents. Milliken has a keen commitment to excellence and its textile research centre is the largest of its type on the planet. A major challenge for the business is its Pursuit of Excellence which runs through every aspect of the company. This is a process dedicated to quality and education. The company aims to find people of exceptional ability who anticipate change and find creative ways to improve the business.

The company is founded on core values and principles including uncompromising concern for the environment, safety as a number one priority, care for the community, dedication to research and innovation, emphasis on education and focus on customers.

David Littler, director of Recruitment, says, 'The idea of a complex team, a global team based on processes prevails across all the product ranges. But it's not a do-as-you-are-told environment. Personal growth is key. We're constantly improving and developing our products – and we apply the same rationale to people.'

He comments that the Milliken vision is to provide the best quality of products, customer response and service in the world through constant improvement and innovation with a bias for action. Blair Biggerstaff, director of Manufacturing, says, 'If you're looking for a place where you can sit down at a desk all day, then you ought to go somewhere else. Here you have to be active, you have to be involved, you have to interrelate with everyone from the production associates to the CEO of the company. And you need to be effective in both circumstances. Personality is very important.'

Milliken's European group consists of two operational divisions, supported by the American parent company. In Britain modular carpets are produced at Wigan on a site that comprises the manufacturing facility for European contract carpet design and sales. Wellington Mill at Bury manufactures synthetic textiles for the rubber, tyre and airbag industries. Plants in Stroud and Cam in Gloucestershire produce tennis ball and snooker table fabrics. Specially designed and engineered textile interior trim is made in Burnley for major automotive companies in the UK and Europe. Since the last edition of this book was published in June 1997, a new business has been acquired based at Leighton Buzzard and Middleton, near Manchester. This business manufactures dust control products and high quality speciality products for the rubber moulding industry.

Milliken is a company whose people, products and philosophies set the standard for quality. Its carpets provide comfort, style and wearability to hotels, business and public areas. Its fabrics keep astronauts safe, soldiers and youngsters warm. It claims, with some justification, that each of its 48,000 products reflects a company-wide commitment to excellence. Quality emanates from a philosophy called the pursuit of excellence – a process which starts at the very top and which became a watchword in 1979. Milliken was already renowned for its high performance products and state of the art technology. But executives wondered why some Japanese competitors achieved higher quality, less waste, greater productivity and fewer customer complaints.

The answer had more to do with management style and people rather than machines and automation. So Milliken undertook a new and basic strategy. All employees are called associates, work mainly in self-managed teams and, above all, are empowered with authority and autonomy. An associate in the line can halt any process if he or she feels that quality or safety is at risk. Collective action teams – teams are the company's hallmark in the pursuit of excellence – address specific manufacturing and business challenges, supplier action teams work to improve supplier relationships, process improvement teams continually analyse and improve products and services. Customer action teams work together to emphasize the partners for profit ethos. And to further maximize quality potential, Milliken makes education for associates, suppliers and customers – a priority.

The company invests heavily in education each year, and customers and suppliers attend comprehensive seminars in quality. An overriding approach, good housekeeping in business terms, is to reduce costs, improve profits and increase product and service quality. The basis of the company's operation is one of technological leadership with a value system which expects and demands nothing less than integrity, hard work, teamwork and effective communication.

How does Milliken rate?

Pay:	very good
Benefits:	excellent
Communications:	good
Training:	excellent
Career development:	very good
Morale:	excellent

People and personnel policies

A company which keeps its attrition rate at around two per cent come rain or shine really must have something going for it. And, of course, Milliken is a very impressive operation where people are central to its quest for excellence, high level customer service, dedication to community, social and environmental issues, and to be a responsible employer. This is a business which oozes quality from every pore.

The main objective at Milliken is simply to ensure that people perform effectively in a motivated and focused environment, at the same time feeling pleased that they are part of a forward-looking organization. The philosophy is a programme of change: changing people's hearts, minds and performance with the ultimate goal of eliminating non value-added cost. It is set out as harmony between process improvement and people improvement and Milliken believes in only recruiting those of the highest quality.

Littler says, 'We have a fully participatory environment designed to deliver a high quality customer fast response with a team ethos. Any issues are attacked as a team because that is our culture.' Milliken, like many other companies, sees its associates as front line troops. It demands regular feedback on the business from all its employees. There is, in fact, a requirement for them to speak up, emphasizing that the concern is not only a business seeking to make a profit, but a complete partnership.

The watchword is simple and straight to the point: OFI. This means opportunity for improvement. Littler comments, 'It gets our people involved. No matter how big or small a suggestion for improvement, we welcome it. The experts in this business are not the management but the people on the shop floor.' That simple and effective principle meant a change of management thinking. There were ten levels, now there are only four encouraging greater effectiveness. The levels comprise senior management, general management, administrative and shop floor. Graduates enter at management level with clear career patterns established.

And when Milliken recruits the brightest, the company seeks those with skill, capability and a spread of learning; it is determined to get the best. But above all, the company is about involvement, empowering those at the lowest level to contribute to the decision process which will help take the business forward. The company's HR strategy is committed to improving associate contribution and to take Milliken successfully to the year 2000 and beyond. HR is concentrating on working in an integrated manner with associates at all levels and it believes that the quality of service provided by HR should be high and valued by every associate.

It wishes to attract and retain the best graduates to satisfy the company's long-term plans. They spend seven weeks absorbing key issues with a leadership orientation programme in the US, having completed a thorough inter-site UK induction programme. They can expect to be in the middle management population within three years. For some newly recruited graduates and ambitious associates the opportunity to be posted overseas to improve their competence is a common occurrence.

A main thrust of the Milliken operation is communications with frequent cascade briefings. This is a two-way operation with a positive accent on feedback. 'We are a highly proactive concern, taking into account what everybody says or wishes to contribute in the pursuit of excellence.' Milliken is aware of its local responsibilities too with in-house social activities and support and sponsorship for a wide range of local charities, and involvement with football and rugby league.

Contact address

David Littler
Director of Recruitment
Milliken Industrials Limited
Hill Plant, Gidlow Lane
Wigan
Lancashire WN6 8RN
Telephone: 01942 612745
Fax: 01942 612739
Web site:
http://www.milliken.com/nextstep/europe

Motorola

Motorola is one of the world's leading providers of wireless communications, semiconductors and advanced electronic systems, components and services. Major equipment businesses include cellular telephone, two-way radio, paging and data communications, personal communications, automotive, defence and space electronics and computers. The fundamental objective of the company is total customer satisfaction. Motorola maintains sales, service and manufacturing facilities throughout the world, conducts business on six continents and employs more than 150,000 people worldwide.

Motorola at a glance

Employees: 150,000 worldwide
Annual staff attrition: 12 per cent
Key locations: Basingstoke, Slough
Annual graduate intake: n/a
Annual intake: n/a

An inside view

The corporate giant that is Motorola began in 1928 with the 'battery eliminator' that allowed consumers to operate radios directly from their household currents instead of the batteries supplied with early models. It has grown to become a leading force in military, space and commercial communications as well as consumer electronics. Motorola's presence is felt all over the globe, from its base in the United States to Israel, Hong Kong, Germany and the UK and its products are found in industries worldwide.

Throughout its history, Motorola has phased out businesses with limited potential to focus on new technologies and new markets throughout the world. While it takes significant risks to develop its new ventures, the company takes very little balance sheet risk. Motorola manages for long-term growth and profitability, while consistently and appropriately investing in technology to maintain competitive leadership.

The last two years has seen Motorola undergo a reorganization of its business structure, to position the company for competing in the next quarter century. The new organization includes four market-focused groups and a Semiconductor Components Group. The Consumer Systems Group covers the technology found in products ranging from games and digital cameras to computer printers, smart cards and high-definition television. The Transportation Systems Group focuses on automotive applications from engine and power train control to digital sound systems. The Wireless Subscriber Systems Group is driving Motorola's digital signal processing architecture. The move from analog to digital technologies will more than triple the amount of silicon used in wireless devices such as cellular telephones. Finally, the Networking and Computing Systems Group created the embedded silicon technology that is used by most major switch manufacturers.

Creativity is one of the key principles of the culture of Motorola, as it is the quality of the design and management teams that has been behind many of the company's ground-breaking innovations. The company requires a level of creativity from its employees that goes beyond the conventional approach to problem solving. Empowerment for all is prominent in the company's culture and is applied in a participative, co-operative and creative workplace. Motorola promotes a family atmosphere and is committed to uncompromising integrity and strict ethical conduct in all business-related matters.

Quality is also an important driver in the Motorola culture, which has become synonymous with the term Six Sigma throughout the company. This is a six-step methodology that initially aimed to improve the manufacturing standards and was then extended to non-manufacturing. Because the pursuit of Six Sigma quality has required dramatic changes in processes and the renewal of work flows, it has also driven new inventions.

How does Motorola rate?

Pay:	very good
Benefits:	excellent
Communications:	very good
Training:	excellent
Career development:	very good
Morale:	very good

People and personnel policies

New employees attend a three-week orientation on Motorola culture, values, goals and initiatives. Depending on the division they are posted to and their level of experience, new employees complete a training programme that can last up to 18 months. For example, a graduate beginning employment in software engineering undergoes prolonged training, whereas a qualified product engineer will be quickly assimilated into the department with a short course that outlines Motorola's production systems and technology. Motorola operates an intern programme which gives graduates the opportunity to gain real-world experience in the areas of engineering, information sciences and technology, marketing and finance.

Within the multi-faceted corporation of Motorola, there is plenty of scope for career advancement. Openings continually arise in software, electrical, computer and mechanical engineering, product, systems and product engineering, information sciences and technology, marketing, human resources, and finance. Motorola conducts business in 45 countries so there is potential for employees to work in new and stimulating environments and within different teams. Movement up the Motorola hierarchy is possible depending on the motivation, area of expertise and drive of the individual. The company supports continuing education and reimburses members of its workforce for any further education they undertake. The Motorola University provides each employee with at least one week of training per year to update skills on new systems and refresh his or her knowledge of current developments.

Motorola's remuneration package focuses on paying competitively in the marketplace and concerns itself greatly with benefits centred around the wellbeing of the employee and employee's family. Motorola's total benefits programme has a large amount of family-friendly benefits, including health care assistance that focuses on education and prevention as well as treatment. These cover a pension plan, childcare centres (located on or near ten of the Motorola facilities throughout the world), share option plans, and medical, dental and disability care and insurance. It leads the way in the industry for supporting healthy work, personal life and community balance, investing heavily in work/life and wellness solutions in each of the worldwide businesses. For example, a mildly ill childcare referral program covers 80 per cent of the Motorola workforce, allowing peace of mind for working parents, together with elderly care referral programmes, flexi time, and telecommuting.

Total Customer Satisfaction Teams are a concept unique to Motorola and were introduced in the 1960s. Training is made available to teams of employees on analytical techniques and teamwork. The company holds an annual competition to preserve and ensure high levels of customer service. Motorola has been honoured frequently for its employment policies and implementation. These awards include: 100 Best Companies for Working Mothers, Catalyst Award – American Business Collaboration for Quality Dependent Care, and US Department of Labour – Secretary of Labour's Opportunity 2000 Award.

Contact address

Human Resources Department
Motorola
Midpoint
Alencon Link
Basingstoke
Hants RG21 7PL
Telephone: 01256 790790
Fax: 01753 575555
Web site: http://www.mot.com

Nationwide

With assets of more than £47 billion, Nationwide is currently the world's number one building society, and the UK's fourth largest mortgage lender and ninth largest retail banking, saving and lending organization. Nationwide puts its customers first by providing a full range of top value, quality financial services that are widely available and delivered with speed, courtesy and reliability, backed by underlying policies of fairness, honesty, staff importance and corporate responsibility. Nationwide has adopted some of the most modern employment practices in the UK, placing particular emphasis on teamworking and is among the very best in its approach to equal opportunities.

Nationwide at a glance

Employees: 9,805 full-time equivalents (FTE) (society), 10,727 (FTE) (group)
Annual staff attrition: 13 per cent
Key locations: Swindon (HQ), Northampton (admin centre), plus more than 680 branches across the country
Annual graduate intake: 20
Annual intake: 1,357

An inside view

Nationwide is the product of more than a hundred mergers, most notably that between the Nationwide and the Anglia Building Societies in 1987. With its head office located in Swindon and a second major administration centre located in Northampton, the company operates from around 700 locations throughout the UK, providing a full range of personal financial services including mortgages, retail investments and banking products to 7.9 million customers. Owned by, and run solely for the benefit of, its members, Nationwide is managed by an executive team overseen by an elected board of directors. Like all building societies, it is regulated by the Building Society Commission.

Nationwide aims to offer its customers highly competitive rates and services in order to honour its commitment to deliver real value to its members. In a turbulent and increasingly competitive financial services world, Nationwide is currently experiencing unprecedented growth, achieving significantly increased shares of the residential mortgage and short-term savings markets in the UK. In each of its last two financial years, the society delivered £200 million of potential profit in benefits to members, principally through very competitive mortgage and saving rates. By operating on narrower margins than its main competitors,

Nationwide has achieved product pricing that rewards the loyalty of its existing members, and is continuously attracting new customers. The society's consequent strong performance in both the mortgage and savings markets has led to a notable increase in its assets to more than £47 billion, growth on a scale which has taken its constituent societies generations to achieve.

Nationwide emerged as the world's number one building society in 1997, following the Halifax's conversion to a bank, and there has been recent discussion on whether Nationwide should follow this move or remain as a building society. However, the society believes that its strong performance over the past year demonstrates more than adequately that there is no business case for change. As a building society, backed by reserves built up over the years, Nationwide can afford to offer better interest rates and services and to carry on providing these benefits to members into the future.

Nationwide is widening the range of services it offers members, taking in such areas as life insurance, unit trusts, and most recently, pet insurance and motor insurance products. Particular areas of growth have been pensions, personal equity plans and guaranteed equity bonds. In addition, the society has continued to invest in new ideas and technologies which offer practical benefits to members in the long term. In 1997 Nationwide launched the first UK Internet banking service and in 1998 it became the first organization in the world to pilot an iris recognition system in a cash machine. Since then, with more than 50,000 Nationwide customers now using its PC services, the society has become an Internet service provider. Nationwide plans to recruit 500 more employees across its retail operations in order to handle increased volumes of business and believes that it is very well placed to strengthen further its franchise as the world's number one building society.

How does Nationwide rate?

Pay:	good
Benefits:	very good
Communications:	very good
Training:	excellent
Career development:	very good
Morale:	good

People and personnel policies

One of the most important goals of Nationwide is to be an organization where employees want to work. To this end, the society has an outstanding approach towards its people, priding itself on its open communication of company objectives to employees, individual training and development and equal opportunities policies. In addition, it is the aim of the society for pay rates to be in the upper quartile of a comparison group of companies and to be linked to performance through bonus schemes in order to reward effort and achievement.

The society is committed to maintaining and developing systems for the provision of information to employees, and for their consultation and involvement, for instance by actively continuing to discuss issues with the Nationwide Staff Union. In addition, meetings, team briefings, circulars and newsletters ensure employees are aware of the society's performance and objectives, and the business environment in which it operates. Opinions and ideas of employees are valued and directors regularly convene with separate groups of staff to hear their views on business activities. Everybody who works for Nationwide has a performance agreement, outlining clearly what is required of them, and there are formal annual reviews of performance. All employees have the opportunity to discuss career aspirations using the company's career development review process.

Nationwide aims to move ahead of its competitors not only by helping its staff to fulfil their needs and aspirations, but also by ensuring its business has the correct balance of skills when and where they are needed. Nationwide has increasingly been moving away from a traditional approach of employing people from 9 to 5, Monday to Friday, aiming at developing more flexible working arrangements to best meet customer demand and ensure excellent customer service. Employees also enjoy more opportunities to work in cross-functional project teams and it is now possible for staff to be working for several different managers on more than one project at a time.

The ability to relate to a wide variety of people is one of the most important qualities Nationwide seeks in potential employees. The Society places great emphasis on customer satisfaction and thus regards such qualities as creativity, innovation and a set of skills involving control and quality to be just as important as intellectual expertise.

Nationwide is highly regarded for its exceptional policies towards equal opportunities for all its employees. More than half of Nationwide's branch managers are women. Women now hold approximately 47 per cent of middle management and more than 42.6 per cent of junior management positions. Its maternity policy has also been enhanced in order to attract and retain skilled and experienced employees. More than 80 per cent of Nationwide's maternity leavers return to work. In addition, Nationwide encourages flexible learning and self-development, allowing employees equal access to training regardless of their level of responsibility and hours of work.

Contact address

Denise Walker
Head of Corporate Personnel
Nationwide Building Society
Nationwide House
Pipers Way
Swindon SN38 1NW
Telephone: 01793 513513
Fax: 01793 455341
Web site: http://www.nationwide.co.uk

NatWest Group

NatWest Group is one of the largest financial services organizations in the UK. It provides a broad spectrum of financial services, principally in UK and Irish markets to customers ranging from individuals and small businesses to multinational companies. The group consists of 14 operating businesses which focus mainly on personal financial services, business and corporate banking, cards, private banking, electronic commerce, the long-term savings and investment market, treasury and dealing services and debt and corporate advisory services. In addition to the NatWest brand, the group's other principal brands are Lombard, Coutts & Co, Ulster Bank Group, Greenwich NatWest, Gartmore and its corporate advisory businesses – Hawkpoint in the UK and Gleacher in the US. In 1997 the group reported operating income of £6.97 billion and a pretax profit of £1.01 billion.

NatWest at a glance

Employees: 69,000
Annual staff attrition: n/a
Key locations: London (HQ) and locations in every sizeable town or city in the UK. Representation in more than 30 countries
Annual graduate intake: c.180
Annual intake: n/a

An inside view

The financial services sector is one of the great industries of the UK. It generates substantial external revenues for the British economy and provides a financial backbone for industry. Every company and the vast majority of individuals in the UK use banking services. The sector is highly competitive and has undergone significant change in recent years. Building societies, insurance companies and high street retailers now offer banking services, although NatWest, Barclays, Midland (HSBC Group) and Lloyds TSB remain the key players.

In 1997 the group's financial results were adversely affected by the poor performance of NatWest Markets, the group's investment banking business. Following a review of this business, the equities operation was sold, together with several smaller overseas activities. The strategy is to build on NatWest's role as the premier bank for business in the UK and Ireland, to be an innovative personal bank, to be a leading provider of cards and electronic commerce and to be a source of novel wealth management products.

In personal banking, NatWest serves more than six million customers through its 1,750 branches across the UK. New ways of delivering financial services, such as telephone and PC/TV banking continue to be developing alongside products and services to make the lives of customers easier. The group is currently testing one such product, known as Zenda. This is a personalized information service for customers on a whole range of matters from travel timetables and weather reports to planning a holiday or moving house. This is an example of how NatWest aims to build and develop strong relationships with its customers.

The bank continues to have a dominant position in the UK business banking sector. NatWest has more than 700,000 small business customers and it has relationships with more than 40,000 corporate customers. In addition to core banking services, the group has strong capability in debt markets through Greenwich NatWest, together with world-class treasury and foreign exchange operations through NatWest Global Financial Markets.

Cards and electronic commerce are an important part of the future of all financial services and NatWest is in the forefront of this area. It was instrumental in the development of both Switch and Mondex and this area of operation continues to grow strongly. NatWest believes that it is well placed to capitalize on the opportunities presented by the revolution in banking technology.

Wealth Management brings together the businesses that specialize in developing and managing customers' long-term savings and investments, and private banking needs. Its wide range of products enables the group to provide for customers in different circumstances from the smallest private saver to the largest pension fund.

Group managers argue that the strategy is paying off. After a difficult 1997, especially in the investment banking sector, NatWest reported pretax profit for the first half of 1998 at £967 million, up from £648 million in the same period of 1997.

How does NatWest rate?

Pay:	good
Benefits:	very good
Communications:	strong
Training:	excellent
Career development:	very good
Morale:	very good

People and personnel policies

Christ Wathen, director of Group Human Resources, says, 'The market conditions in each of our businesses are very different. In Greenwich NatWest, for example, the remuneration packages are higher but this is because investment banking requires a higher proportion of specialist skills which are in particular demand in that type of business. In the retail business we seek different people to fulfil a wide range of differing functions and the package will reflect market circumstances.'

Wathen says that establishing a centralized group-wide HR policy on many personnel issues would be inappropriate. 'The managers in the 14 businesses are alert to the people issues which have greatest impact on their operations,' he says. One initiative which has come from the group is the creation of worldwide Staff Council, which meets regularly. Elected members of the workforce and trade union representatives form this council where management puts forward issues and council members are invited to make their contribution to the agenda. The establishment of the council is a major step forward to improving communication and dialogue with employees.

NatWest has stepped up its commitment to training and development of its employees as a way of responding to the challenging market conditions which it faces. Again the operational aspects of training are administered by managers in the businesses. The training needs of a currency trader in Global Financial Markets will be different from a branch manager in Ulster Bank. Nevertheless, the group has emphasized its objective to make training relevant to the needs of the individual and business.

'The vast majority of our business units have achieved IIP accreditation and the group remains committed to the standard. But for me the important thing about IIP is not the achievement of accreditation but the spirit and processes which lead to accreditation. That means positive developments such as the involvement of staff in the business and the creation of teams.'

Graduates joining NatWest can expect to be recruited into a specific business role. However, individuals are encouraged to take responsibility for their own career development, to seek opportunities to experience the group's other businesses and functions, and to take advantage of the wide range of training and development support available. Traditionally, a banking career was very compartmentalized and highly structured. But with the pace of change, level of competition and impact of technology, banking has become a fast-moving environment with considerable opportunities.

Contact address

Graduate Recruitment Manager
NatWest Group
Heythrop Learning Network
Heythrop Park
Enstone
Chipping Norton
Oxon OX7 5UE
Telephone: 01608 673504
Fax: 01608 673598
Web site: http://www.natwestgroup.com

Nestlé UK Ltd

Nestlé is one of the world's largest corporations in the food and drink sector. Confectionery and beverages were its traditional strengths but the company also produces ice-cream, baby foods, pet foods, fruit juices, breakfast cereals, pasta and chilled frozen meals. One of the most significant recent UK milestones was the 1988 acquisition of the York-based confectioner Rowntree Mackintosh. Since then it has gradually integrated the Nestlé and Rowntree management structures. In 1997 the Nestlé corporation reported global sales of 69,998 million Swiss Francs. In the UK the company employs more than 11,000 people in three main trading divisions: beverage division, Rowntree division and food division. In addition, Nestlé UK incorporates Nestlé Ice Cream, a business development unit and various corporate functions – supply chain, production & technical, finance and administration (including IS), communications, sales and HR. Nestlé has two further food businesses in the UK, Friskies Petcare and Perrier Vittel, and a joint venture, Cereal Partners, which sells cereals under the Nestlé brand.

Nestlé at a glance

Employees: 220,000 worldwide, 11,000+ in the UK (including 1,800 managers)
Annual staff attrition: 10 per cent
Key locations: More than 20 factories, depots and sales offices. Group HQ is in Croydon, Nestlé Rowntree operates from York
Annual graduate intake: 25
Annual intake: 120 managers

An inside view

When Henri Nestlé started manufacturing the first powdered baby milk in 1867 in the small Swiss town of Vevey on the banks of Lake Geneva, he probably had little appreciation of the size to which his company would grow. Nestlé is one of the world's leading food companies with a broad sweep of brand leaders in food, drink and confectionery sectors. The company owns 495 factories in 77 countries worldwide. In the UK its brands include Nescafé, Kit Kat, Carnation Milk, Aero, Crosse and Blackwell (including Branston Pickle), Buitoni Pasta, Dairy Box chocolates, Quality Street, Sarsons Vinegar, Rowntree's Jelly and Sun Pat peanut butter.

The company was founded on children's and dietetic foods, and has spread by acquisition and organic growth into its current range. According to Nestlé SA, the parent company, the real thrust for brand diversity began in 1960 with the purchase of Crosse & Blackwell which was followed by a string of acquisitions including Findus, Vittel, Libby's, L'Oreal, Chambourcy, Carnation, Herta, Buitoni, Rowntree, Lyons Maid, Perrier and Spillers. Nestlé has stamped its imprint on each of these businesses as it has brought them into the group fold. Inherently, the personality of this outstandingly successful company is at once a strongly professional, hierarchical, instinctively private and well-ordered management culture.

On a day-to-day basis the culture is informal and open, with first name terms being used throughout, and regular briefings from senior managers with opportunities to ask questions. It ranks with Shell, ABB, Mercedes Benz and the other global businesses which started on mainland Europe. It is a reputable and highly structure world-class company. Continental market leaders often owe a great deal of their success to the efficiency of their management systems, the concentrated focus on their products, and the quality of their production and marketing skills. So it is with Nestlé.

'We look for real potential, people who show a capacity for assuming high-flying management positions. We look for certain characteristics beyond, obviously educational ability. These qualities include a capacity to communicate with other people, openness, honesty, objectivity and a preference for teamworking over a solo operation,' says Graham Prentice, Nestlé UK's director of HR Development and Remuneration.

How does Nestlé rate?

Pay:	very good
Benefits:	very good
Communications:	very good
Training:	excellent
Career development:	very good
Staff morale:	good

People and personnel policies

The company is similar to that other pre-eminent advocate of brand leadership, Procter & Gamble. Like P&G, Nestlé relies heavily on first appointment recruitment and appointment thereafter from within. 'Nestlé worldwide does this. And we either develop within markets or around markets to a great extent. We do some external recruitment at higher management levels and on a specific requirement basis. We tend to develop people from within and concentrate on the qualities and characteristics which we are looking for,' says Prentice.

Graduates typically move every six months during their first two years. They are employed by the company centrally but work in one of the business areas or corporate functions in a real job. The rationale behind this approach is to give potentially high-flying managers an overview of the company and a chance to experience work in production or vice versa.

'One of the virtues of Nestlé is that it is a truly international company which means that its 1,800 managers, potentially, can expect take assignments on any continent and in most countries. In particular, Nestlé is active in almost all of the developing countries where some of the most exciting work is emerging. Other companies are perhaps not investing as much in these markets. We have been in China and India for years, and we are hiring people locally. Management is often brought in from the developed world. In the last couple of years, we have exported 50 managers a year to the international structure,' says Prentice.

The company aims to be upper quartile in terms of pay. There is an increasing focus on reward being linked to the achievement of clearly defined business objectives. The Nestlé pension scheme is among the best in UK industry with a good investment performance. Private health insurance is widely available in the company but a remarkably generous scheme which has been extended into retirement has been capped. It also operates staff shops in many locations where employees can buy Nestlé products at discounted rates.

In addition, Nestlé provides what it calls an early years database. This gives new parents information on childcare facilities and contact names in their area.

Attrition rates are low for the sector. The annual resignation rate for managers is less than seven per cent so the company believes that it is good at keeping people.

A substantial proportion of the UK group's employees are long-term staff. Many have served 20, 25 or 30 years. There are even some who have been with the enterprise for 40 years. This, says Nestlé, is testimony to the loyalty that the company has earned from its people.

'Our focus is to recruit efficiently and well. The emphasis among staff is generally on staying with and growing in the company. We tend to treat employees as individuals rather than collectively. We do monitor turnover in a statistical sense but if someone leaves we ask if there is an issue here that we can do something about,' says Prentice.

Contact address

Personnel Department
Nestlé UK Ltd
St Georges House
Croydon CR9 1NR
Telephone: 0181 686 3333
Fax: 0181 681 1218
Web site: http://www.nestle.com

Nissan Motor Manufacturing

Faced with the twin challenges of Asian meltdown and ailing UK motor industry, Nissan has responded in characteristic fashion. It has invested heavily to develop a third model, the replacement for the Almera, and will create a further 800 new jobs in the depressed Wearside region by the year 2000. Nissan is a classic story of enterprise, commitment and energy. It is often cited as a primary example of intelligent industrial relations where an astute management reversed the employment history of the area by creating a positive environment through creative staff participation. Sunderland was chosen as the location for its British manufacturing operation in 1984 and the story since then has been one of unmitigated and unqualified success. The first car was made in 1986, and 12 years later the two millionth vehicle rolled off the assembly line. In September 1997 Nissan invested an additional £215 million to increase the UK commitment to £1.29 billion.

Nissan at a glance

Employees: 4,200
Annual staff attrition: 4 per cent
Key locations: Sunderland; also Cranfield, Rickmansworth
Annual graduate intake: 12
Annual intake: 150

An inside view

From the year 2000, Nissan will expand its range of cars to produce a third model – the replacement for the Almera. The company plans to increase its workforce by around 800 people to 5,000. This extra recruitment demonstrates the growing commitment by the car company to the Wearside region where it set up in 1984 and revolutionized industrial relations in the North East.

Nissan's achievement is not only to have created a vibrant company in an area of economic decline but to have pulled off this coup against a tradition of worker-management hostility. The death of the staple industries of the north east was, in fact, a significant element in persuading the Japanese car company to set up its operation on the former Sunderland airport.

Nissan's managers were astute enough to realize that there would be government inward investment grants available. The pits had closed, the shipyards shut, the steelworks phased out and there was a pool of skilled labour which welcomed any serious initiative to provide sustained employment.

Everyone is encouraged to work together towards the common goal of high quality and profitable production. Advanced management techniques ensure there are no costly buffer stocks on components because parts are delivered as and when required and Nissan rightly insists that Sunderland is far more than just an assembly plant. It manufactures engines and axles, presses body parts and produces aluminium castings and major plastics components such as fuel tanks and bumpers.

Total quality is a core philosophy which runs through every aspect of the business: the way in which the plant is run and the way in which the cars it produces are built. Quality is not something left to people called quality controllers. It is the responsibility of every single person in the organization from receptionists to employees working on the production line and all administrative staff including the managing director.

The company's main thrust is in the North East where the vehicles are made with around 80 per cent European content. Nissan's technology and design centre at Cranfield, Bedfordshire and the marketing and sales section based at Rickmansworth, Herts are ancillaries to the all important production operation. No European motor manufacturer since the early days of the twentieth century has grown with the speed that Nissan has developed its Sunderland plant. The company is now producing two models – the Primera, which has won 21 major European motoring awards, and the Micra.

How does Nissan rate?

Pay:	excellent
Benefits:	superb
Communications:	superb
Training:	very good
Career development:	excellent
Morale:	superb

People and personnel policies

When Nissan was looking for a symbol to define its corporate philosophical approach, the tripod seems most appropriate. The principle of three legs demonstrates the basis of a firm and stable operation. All legs are equal: flexibility which means expanding a person's capability to his or her limits; quality consciousness; and teamwork. The selection of staff has a crucial impact on the success of this approach and this process, which gives equal weight to its three core components, is regarded as all important. All prospective employees are interviewed by those under whom they would work and the watchwords are attitude, numeracy, verbal reasoning, manual dexterity and, above all, attitude.

The Nissan guidelines are simple to the point of expediency: a team of between 15 and 20 people make up the core activity under a supervisor who is pivotal to the wellbeing of the organization. Within that framework they are free to range within the whole area and width of their responsibilities. The plant's philosophy is to develop a high degree of teamwork with complete trust and co-operation between all staff.

Everyone is encouraged to work together towards the common goal of high quality and profitable production.

Culturally, Nissan tries to embody of the best of all traditions. Some of the people management techniques appeared somewhat unorthodox when introduced into the plain speaking North East. But after initial reservation they were absorbed and applied highly effectively. Central to the company's thinking is the concept of kaizen which means continuous improvement. It works like a spiral staircase with four basic principles: plan, do, check, action and improvement and then plan again and the system works well. The foundation for Nissan's regard and involvement for its employees is laid down in a comprehensive 34-page booklet of terms and conditions.

As Philip Ashmore, director of personnel explains, 'We believe we are a special company. We spend a lot of time talking about teamworking and flexibility. We have leadership courses, communication courses, workshop technique courses and all are geared to improving performance in the workplace.' Nissan does most of its own training from inside because it regards itself as a big family concern. Trainers from outside could easily be unfamiliar with the nuances of the Nissan culture and ethos. Graduates are recruited and run the whole gamut of operations but are, by virtue of their education, earmarked for eventual specialist roles within a management structure which has a minimum of tiers.

Ashmore says of graduate recruits, 'We take around a dozen a year. In the early days of our operation it was twice as many for obvious start up reasons.' Those who are hired take around 30 months to reach the engineer controller or supervisory level and there is no shortage of applications to join the company. 'We have a good reputation for the quality of training we give. We try to get them into decision-making roles as early as possible because they are high quality people. We attempt to give them an up front job and support them when they need support, but they are not regarded as an élite. They have to earn respect.

In fact Nissan regards all of its workforce as an élite and sings the praises of all the people who work for the company. It targeted the North East when setting up after extensive market research into attitudes throughout most regions of the UK. But Nissan spotted the inherent work ethic and generations of craftsmen and capitalized on that talent. The reward package is the envy of the area: competitive basic salaries with extra money based on an annual appraisal – typically two per cent in addition to an annual all round basic increase. In the last five years average pay has been ten per cent over and above inflation in real terms. Free health insurance means private healthcare for employees and their immediate family.

Contact address

Mr Philip Ashmore
Director – Personnel
Nissan Motor Manufacturing (UK) Ltd
Washington Road
Sunderland
Tyne and Wear SR5 3NS
Telephone: 0191 415 0000
Fax: 0191 415 2741
Web site: http://www.nissan.com

Nokia

Nokia was born over 100 years ago, and has been in the telecommunications business for more than 30 years – a long time in this industry. Its established reputation puts it at the forefront of the market, as a leading supplier of digital mobile and fixed networks, and as the world's largest mobile phone manufacturer. As a broad-scope telecommunications company, Nokia also supplies multimedia equipment, satellite and cable receivers, computer monitors, as well as other telecommunications-related products. Nokia strives for continued leadership in the fastest-growing global telecommunications markets by anticipating and fulfilling customer and consumer needs with alacrity, providing quality products and processes, and being open with people and their ideas.

Nokia at a glance

Employees: 42,000
Annual staff attrition: n/a
Key locations: Swindon, Huntingdon, Camberley, Farnborough
Annual graduate intake: n/a
Annual intake: n/a

An inside view

Nokia has pioneered many of the technologies that are in standard use today and is widely acknowledged as one of the most creative and dynamic collective minds in the industry. Originating in Finland, Europe is Nokia's home market and where most of its 42,000 employees are based. Recent years have seen offices set up in more than 40 countries with research & development centres in Finland, Hungary, Japan, Germany, the US and Australia. Nokia operates as a global network, where knowledge and experience is shared over national boundaries. The Nokia Group comprises Nokia Telecommunications, Nokia Mobile Phones, Nokia Communications Products, Nokia Multimedia Network Terminals, Nokia Industrial Electronics, and Nokia Ventures Organization plus the corporate research unit, Nokia Research Centre.

Nokia Telecommunications develops and manufactures infrastructure equipment and systems for mobile and fixed networks, and is currently the world's second largest supplier of Global System for Mobile phones (GSM) networks. In 1997 Nokia Mobile Phones was the world's largest manufacturer of mobile phones, with a global market share in excess of 21 per cent. In digital phones and pioneering wireless data products, Nokia is a world leader and introduced 31 new mobile phone models in 1997.

The Multimedia Network division is a pioneer in digital satellite, cable and terrestrial network terminals for multimedia applications. In 1997 Nokia introduced the world's first digital satellite receiver with a Common Interface. Nokia Industrial Electronics develops and manufactures computer and workstation monitors, including applications for professional desktop communication and new technology display. Nokia Ventures expands the company's scope with new promising areas in future communications solutions. The division is divided into three units. The Research Centre works in conjunction with all Nokia business units and focuses on GSM enhancement and third generation mobile technology, broadband communications and multimedia.

Nokia's style of operating is characterized by fast decision making, flat organizations, and the ability to promptly apply new technologies. Understandably, certain aspects of Finnish values are inherent in the corporate culture, but the company's globalization shows that it is largely compatible with other cultures worldwide. The four Nokia values – customer satisfaction, respect for the individual, achievement and continuous learning – are adopted globally, with emphasis on different aspects depending on the national culture. Understanding these dynamics is a continuous process at Nokia. Additionally, Nokia recognizes three fundamental principles in its operations: always operating according to strict, ethical principles; always serving the community in which you work, and always protecting the environment in which you work and live.

During the past three years, Nokia has recruited more than 17,000 people all over the world. Standards are high at Nokia, who look for graduates with a 2.1 degree or better in physics or maths, or equivalent qualification in computer science, information technology, electronic, mechanical or electrical engineering. It is a high-pressure environment, with tight deadlines and demanding targets.

How does Nokia rate ?

Pay:	very good
Benefits:	excellent
Communications:	very good
Training:	very good
Career development:	excellent
Morale:	good

People and personnel policies

Nokia recognizes that competence development is critical to success and shares responsibility for it with the individual. It provides continuous training, both locally and globally, ranging from induction, skills and technology training through to management and leadership development. In 1997, Nokia employees spent an average of 11 working days in training. The number of training days for an individual varies from four to more than 30. In their first years, new recruits usually receive at least one month of training each year. Nokia believes that most learning takes place out of the monitored learning environment and therefore promotes action learning in many of its programmes and provides new assignments and opportunities for growth and job rotation.

Nokia is a growing company, operating in a rapidly developing field of technology, and every employee has the opportunity for career development. Employees may move up, down or sideways, locally or internationally, depending on available opportunities and individual ambitions. Nokia stresses the importance of each manager knowing the skills and skill levels of all team members. The development of employees' abilities is integrated into the performance management practice and each year every member of the workforce has at least one performance management discussion with their senior manager.

Nokia offers competitive and flexible compensation and benefits packages, which take account of the individual's level of skills and capabilities and local conditions. Total compensation aims to be externally competitive and to achieve a balance between cash and other forms of compensation, in order to meet diverse employee needs. Basic pay is reviewed annually in relation to performance, taking account of factors such as market rates, qualifications, skills and expertise, responsibilities and inflation. After six months' service, all employees are eligible for incentive plans, such as the Connecting People Bonus plan and the Stock Option plan.

Nokia's other benefits are extensive and range from company cars to life assurance and a comprehensive pension scheme. Benefits include private medical cover for the individual and family, maternity and paternity leave, short-term sickness benefit and long-term disability schemes. The annual holiday entitlement is 25 days per year, plus recognized public holidays.

Contact address

Human Resources
Nokia Telecommunications Ltd
Lancaster House
Lancaster Way
Ermine Business Park
Huntingdon
Cambs PE18 6XU
Telephone: 01480 434444
Fax: 01480 435111
Web site: http://www.nokia.com

Nortel Networks

With more than a century of research and manufacturing experience, Nortel Networks has an assured place among the world's leading telecommunications companies. As one of the world's largest suppliers of digital network solutions, Nortel (Northern Telecom) has recently increased its worth through the 1998 merger with Bay Networks, a leader in the worldwide data networking market. Nortel Networks was thus created. It now occupies a unique position in the industry, having the technology to unify packet and circuit switching, and deliver IP-optimized Unified Networks. Starting off in Canada in 1896, the company has steadily gained momentum, spreading into the US, Europe, Asia and South America.

Nortel Networks at a glance

Employees: 80,000 worldwide, 6,800 Europe
Annual staff attrition: 4 per cent
Key locations: Maidenhead (HQ), New Southgate, Harlow, Monkstown, Paignton, Cwmcam
Annual graduate intake: 250
Annual intake: 1,000

An inside view

The merger of Nortel and Bay Networks is currently in the process of reshaping the Nortel of old. It is no longer just a telecommunications backbone provider. Nortel Networks works with customers worldwide to design, build and deliver communications and IP (Internet Protocol)-optimized networks – Unified Networks that create greater value for customers by delivering integrated network solutions spanning data and telephony. Unified Networks can help public carriers deploy data networks on their time line and revenue stream without sacrificing voice quality and carrier-grade services. Enterprises can strengthen their business performance by better supporting such applications as electronic commerce, supply-chain integration, work-at-home applications, and Internet telephony. For wireless service providers, Unified Networks enables third-generation wireless networks (i.e. IP-centric data and voice networks).

As the first liberalized European market, the UK telecommunications environment has changed considerably since Nortel Networks' 1991 acquisition of STC, one of Britain's foremost telecommunications companies. More than 140 licenses have been awarded to operators delivering a wide range of residential, mobile and business services. Nortel Networks has invested substantially in the United Kingdom, upgrading manufacturing and R&D and now employing around 6,800 people. The company is a major supplier to the established telecommunications operators, for example BT, and to new carriers such as Energis and the CATV industry. Nortel Networks generates UK exports to more than 35 countries around the world.

The last six years have seen great change in the corporate culture of Nortel Networks as the company has expanded through acquisition, but its underlying principles have stayed the same. 'Our people are our strength' is one of the core values of Nortel Networks, reflecting the importance of ensuring that, as a knowledge-based organization, the company aligns its people management processes, policies and systems with its business plans to maximize competitive advantage in the industry. Nortel Network's key quality driver is putting the customer first, expressed in another of its core values, 'We create superior value for our customers.'

The current strategy of the organization is to develop a culture of virtual and geographically dispersed teamworking. It is an intense working environment as managers are aware of the competitive nature of the industry and the rate at which it grows and changes. Nonetheless, employees find they are supported by a concerned team of co-workers and management, and a constant dialogue that ensures the employees' opinion is acknowledged and acted upon.

Graduate recruitment is a critical part of Nortel Network's resourcing strategy. Graduate trainees are recruited through relationships with a number of strategic universities, identified from a review of the company's previous graduate recruitment trends. As one of the largest employers of engineering graduates in the UK, it employs twice as many female engineers than the national average. Along with technical and professional expertise and business acumen, employees need to have the ability to operate in teams and build good working relationships.

How does Nortel Networks rate ?

Pay:	very good
Benefits:	very good
Communications:	good
Training:	excellent
Career development:	very good
Morale:	good

People and personnel policies

Effective employee management is high priority at Nortel Networks, reflected in the extremely detailed people management handbook that covers everything from training and recruitment, to reaching targets and manager-employee dialogue. Nortel Networks is renowned for its excellent training, as the company believes it to be its lifeblood. A local induction course is carried out within the first week and a corporate induction programme is generally attended within the first three months. This is a three-day residential programme for all new starters and provides an overview of the marketplace, the competition, products, career development, performance management, etc.

Nortel Networks tailors its training scheme to the individual rather than putting everyone through the same programme, enabling people to gather experience in a timely and appropriate way. New recruits consult with their manager on technical training needs. Marketing, HR and Finance require the graduates to rotate around a number of locations to gain a breadth of experience. A significant aspect of people development activity is not addressed by formal courses, but in project and assignment work that extends employee knowledge and skills, and provides a broader talent base. For example, employees can be sent on secondment to non-UK markets and a repatriation process exists that enables the organization to apply new skills learnt away from home.

Career development is supported by a number of processes, recently instigated after assessing the results of employee surveys. All positions are openly advertized throughout the organization using CareerNet, an intranet tool, Careerline, a telephone enquiry service, and notice boards. Nortel Networks strongly promotes continuous learning, driven by regular development reviews. Many of the businesses within the company have introduced open learning facilities and resources at their sites, including language training in anticipation of increased growth in international markets.

The benefits at Nortel Networks are numerous and are set according to external survey activity. Because of the diverse nature of benefits, the total benefit packages are surveyed and each individual benefit is also benchmarked to maintain a balance. The Nortel Networks Pension Scheme is managed by a consultative committee that includes employee representatives as well as managers, and is responsible for the ongoing review and refinement of the scheme. A healthcare plan, company cars or cash option, an employee stock purchase plan, sickness benefit, maternity and paternity leave, relocation assistance and Connections! discount scheme combine to provide an extensive package. Depending on where the employee is situated, facilities and services are provided that secure employee satisfaction, for example, childcare and restaurant facilities, subsidized travel to work and flexible working hours.

Contact address

John Cartland
Human Resources VP
Nortel Networks
Westacott Way
Maidenhead Office Park
SL6 3QH
Telephone: 01628 432000
Fax: 01628 432810
Web site: http://www.nortelnetworks.com

Oracle Corporation

Oracle Corporation is currently the world's second largest software company, and leading supplier of software for enterprise information management, despite being relatively new to the computer industry scene. Its rise in the echelons of the US corporate arena has been characterized by intense drive and unwavering focus on results and new solutions. Its annual revenues exceed $8 billion. It offers database, tools and applications products and related consulting, education and support services in more than 140 countries. The UK subsidiary of this dynamic company was founded in 1984 and has ten regional locations.

Oracle at a glance

Employees: 4,032
Annual staff attrition: 14 per cent
Key locations: Reading (HQ), Bracknell and other sites in the Thames Valley plus the City of London, Bristol, Manchester, Edinburgh, Aberdeen
Annual graduate intake: 140
Annual intake: 1,200

An inside view

Oracle has a reputation as a company on the move, constantly developing new technologies, finding new solutions and supplying new services. The financial results reflect the positive outcome of this culture – they have grown by around 30 to 40 per cent every year. Originally the company concentrated on providing software but has swiftly progressed into the domain of established companies, such as Microsoft and IBM, becoming a major player in the global information industry. A significant feature of the company management organization is its level structure, resulting from the high level of specialist expertise and interaction with clients necessary in most positions in the company. Its employees are generally young, innovative, highly motivated people who capitalize on the potential to make a difference within the company.

The company has two major businesses: one providing low-cost information technology infrastructure and the other supplying business and competitive advantage through high value applications. Oracle is currently expanding into the area of network computing, a form of database server utilized by larger companies. It provides a common platform that integrates client software with Web application servers and database servers, supported by communications technologies that allow software components to work together, even if they are built using different standards. Competition is strong between Microsoft and Oracle in this industry sector, but the two companies are diverse enough for Oracle to prosper in its core applications and database business.

Oracle is a results-orientated business, which invests in employee strengths and in which advancement is based on ability, contribution and productivity counts. The individual is the focal point and intense individual creativity is the root of success in vital areas such as product development. Oracle fosters career self-management and a self-directed learning environment, which allow the employee immense scope for fulfilling his or her ambitions. Flexibility is another key word in the culture of the company. A major proportion of work can be carried out in a solo setting. Oracle permits flexible work schedules, individual environments and direction to encourage the employee's entrepreneurial nature.

A high percentage of the annual intake is graduates, with qualifications in an ever increasing range of technologies. Relationships have been developed with technology-based universities, such as Staffordshire and Southampton, which enables early identification of potential recruits with the intellectual capabilities and other skills necessary to succeed in the company.

Initiative is a primary asset of future employees. Oracle seeks people who do not need to be led by the hand and who enjoy using their own knowledge and expertise to provide solutions to their clients. The emphasis is on interpersonal skills, empathy and client handling, given the requisite level of intellectual know-how. The environment is highly competitive and the ability to work under pressure is an essential quality. Working in Oracle is not for the faint-hearted.

How does Oracle rate?

Pay:	good
Benefits:	very good
Communications:	very good
Training:	excellent
Career development:	very good
Morale:	good

People and personnel policies

Graduates spend their initial two months on induction, which combines corporate and technical skill training. 'Class Of', a course specifically designed by Oracle for graduates, provides an introduction to Oracle technology, the corporate culture, team building and related business skills. Recruits then progress to a project team as an assistant consultant under the supervision and instruction of a manager. A mentoring system operates at Oracle and the new graduate has both a senior manager and the previous year's graduates as backup support. Psychometric testing is used to define the strengths and weaknesses of each employee and ongoing training is individualized to their specific needs.

After spending the first year familiarizing themselves with the way in which Oracle operates, new employees are able to apply for other positions within the company. There are numerous training courses available to all employees as well as clients and users through the Oracle University virtual campus, a Web-based learning system. These range from product development and related technologies training, consulting, support, and sales training as well as management training.

Oracle is a veritable playground for career development. The company freely encourages the employee to explore opportunities for change and advancement as long as they have been in a position for a reasonable period of time. This time period varies depending on the job and department but is generally between one and two years. People transfer frequently to new projects within their departments and between organizations and countries. Oracle does not expect long-term commitment to the company, although it is keen to retain top performers. It is willing to act as a training ground for talented and entrepreneurial people and hopes to reap the returns when employees realise the capacity for innovation within the company. There are educational reimbursement options for job-related training provided the applicant acquires a satisfactory grade. Undertaking a MBA is one possibility.

Oracle's remuneration policy links pay closely to performance. It is at very competitive rates and a large proportion is variable. The company operates a discretionary bonus scheme, a contributory pension scheme, an employee share purchase scheme and a health scheme, which covers employees plus their children and spouses.

Contact address

Vance Kearney
Human Resources Director
Oracle Corporation
Oracle Parkway
Thames Valley Park
Reading RG6 1RA
Telephone: 011892 40000
Fax: 011892 43882
Web site: http://www.oracle.co.uk

PepsiCo

PepsiCo, headquartered in New York State in the US, is among the most successful consumer products companies in the world, generating revenues of nearly $23 billion in 1998 and employing around 140,000 employees worldwide. Following the divestment of its restaurant operations in 1997, the company consists of Pepsi-Cola Company, the world's second largest beverage company; Frito-Lay Company, the world's largest manufacturer and distributor of snack crisps and the recently acquired Tropicana Products Inc, the world's largest marketer and producer of branded juices. Apart from the obvious, Pepsi-Cola and Tropicana, well-known brand names include Walkers, Doritos and 7-Up. Truly believing that the company is only as good as its people, PepsiCo's stated strategy is to attract the best and brightest people available whom it rewards accordingly.

PepsiCo at a glance

Employees: 142,000 worldwide
Annual staff attrition: 10 per cent
Key locations: SW London
Annual graduate intake: 30
Annual intake: 120

An inside view

Since 1997 PepsiCo has re-created itself as a formidable packaged goods company through a strategy of vigorous investment in its soft drinks business, the strengthening of Frito-Lay and by focusing on improvements in cash flow. In 1997 PepsiCo disposed of all of its restaurant businesses including Pizza Hut, KFC and Taco Bell and, at the same time, made changes to its snacks and beverages businesses including the restructuring of some operations and the disposal of others. The new entity is an organization with a simpler structure, fewer distractions, greater continuity and it is expanding – as recently as August 1998 it acquired Tropicana – and its long-term prospects are exciting. If the company continues its excellent record of satisfying consumers and customers and continuing to invest in growth, in the words of chairman and chief executive Roger Enrico, 'PepsiCo will rank among the great companies of the twenty-first century.'

Since PepsiCo was formed in 1965, by the joining together of Pepsi-Cola and Frito-Lay, the company has grown faster than almost any other large corporation on earth – a remarkable feat in such a competitive industry. PepsiCo considers that its success is a result of a combination of superior products, high standards of performance, distinctive competitive strategies and the high level of integrity of its people.

PepsiCo ranks marketplace performance equally with financial performance and puts consumers and customers first by selling them products which are excellent in terms of quality, customer service and brand image. The biggest factor in the success of the company is the creation of products which become consumer favourites; a prime example being the Walkers brand of potato crisps which, as regards brand equity – a combination of brand recognition and consumer regard for a product – is the highest-scoring brand in the UK, doing better than Kellogg's and Levis.

The PepsiCo philosophy is that its people thrive, both personally and professionally, by being set stretching targets. In a company culture which is informal and team-driven, employees are encouraged to pursue profit energetically and to seek business solutions in creative and innovative ways. At the same time, PepsiCo prides itself on another key component of the company culture – that of integrity – which, as well as encompassing the courage of individuals to act honestly and fairly, Enrico defines as people's responsibility to speak openly to their colleagues at all levels within the organization and for their views to be listened to and treated with respect.

How does PepsiCo rate?

Pay:	very good
Benefits:	very good
Communications:	excellent
Training:	excellent
Career development:	excellent
Morale:	very good

People and personnel policies

The excellent training and development opportunities offered to employees by PepsiCo are fundamental to the company's strategy of attracting and retaining the best people in the industry. PepsiCo recognizes that in order for people to be able to give of their best the company is obliged to provide its employees with the necessary know-how, skills, resources and freedom to do their jobs. Individuals are provided with continuous training and development programmes. The majority of training is on-the-job, frequently taking the form of challenging assignments, which PepsiCo considers is the most effective type of training. This approach is supported by formal training programmes which are usually run internally and are divided into three categories: functional and technical skills, leadership and understanding the business.

At PepsiCo, individuals are expected to plan and manage their own careers in a company environment which promotes success and provides remarkable opportunities for personal and professional development. The company's performance management system provides valuable information on achievements, strengths and development needs which are fed back to employees. With PepsiCo's decentralized company structure, people are encouraged to develop a wide range of business skills and experiences at local, national and international levels. PepsiCo offers individuals great opportunities for advancement, which depends on talent and excellent performance, commercial ambition on behalf of the company and the ability to work as a member of a team in a stimulating, fast-moving business environment. It is possible for individuals with the right set of experience and skills to go far in the company: witness Roger Enrico who began with PepsiCo as an accountant, and the vice-chairman who was once a clerk in the personnel department.

PepsiCo provides its people with an excellent remuneration package and for those who perform exceptionally well, the rewards can be great. The pay package depends very much on an individual's performance and includes highly competitive basic salaries, broad salary bands offering room for salary growth, bonus opportunities at many levels and wide stock options eligibility. Other superb benefits include a pension plan paid for by the company and a flexible employee insurance programme with benefits such as life, accidental death and disability insurance schemes, medical plans, dental schemes and legal services, which allows employees to choose the benefits which best suit their circumstances. Overall, the company's highly competitive total compensation package offers employees the opportunity to share in the prosperity of a great company and provides them with the potential for significant rewards.

As a global company with a presence in virtually every corner of the world, PepsiCo has a positive policy of fostering diversity in the workforce, which it accomplishes through a combination of teamwork and excellent communications initiatives and programmes throughout the company. This approach is aided by the informal, decentralized structure of the company in which people must be able to work in teams with all different kinds of people.

Contact address

Magda Nowak
Frito-Lay
2 Sheen Road
Richmond
Surrey TW9 1AE
Telephone: 0181 334 1000
Fax: 0181 334 1010
Web site: http://www.pepsico.com

Peugeot Motor Company plc

The Peugeot Motor Company is among the top three carmakers in the UK. In 1997 it recorded sales of £2.3 billion and improved its share of the diesel and fleet markets. In the diesel sector, it is the number one producer in Britain, capturing more than 20 per cent of a fragmented market. Based predominately in Coventry, Peugeot employs 3,500 people on three sites. Most of the workforce is located at Ryton in the 206 assembly plant, but other staff are sited at Stoke and Tile Hill, as well as in its network of 25 wholly owned distributors employing a further 1,700 people.

Peugeot at a glance

Employees: 5,300
Annual staff attrition: 2.3 per cent
Key locations: three in Coventry plus 25 distributors nationwide
Annual graduate intake: 20
Annual intake: 80

An inside view

Peugeot has traditionally defied motor industry norms. The company has a workforce whose commitment, enthusiasm and energy is redolent more of a West Coast software house. Peugeot people are great believers in the product. In autumn 1998 the employees – rather than the management – launched the new 206. The entire staff of Peugeot in the UK went to the official launch of the car at the Birmingham International Conference Centre, where 206 team members drove away their own 206s.

The company has been transformed in recent years into a stable and secure business. It plays an increasingly influential role in Peugeot worldwide. And the level of morale in the British business is outstandingly high. Michael Judge, personnel director, says the workforce is treated with a high degree of respect. 'The most tangible aspect of this is the company charter which identifies the commitment of the business to its people. The charter leads to a series of communications initiatives where people are informed about UK developments within the UK company, the group and the industry.'

This degree of consultation contrasts markedly with the days when the business was owned by the Chrysler Corporation of America. Industrial disputes then were a daily occurrence. 'Long-term planning then was the day after tomorrow. If you asked me when the last dispute was, I would have looked at my watch. We had 800 disputes a year. Now we have a role in the next car and the one after that. We have never been in that position before. Our visibility within the group grows larger and larger. Now we are consulted and drawn into the development processes.'

Coventry, for decades, has been a city which existed for the motor trade. In the

1960s Rootes operated out of Ryton. Rootes was one of the great brand names of the British car industry. Eventually Rootes became part of Chrysler and Chrysler – unable to find an appropriately successful management style – sold it on to Peugeot. Each owner has had a profoundly different approach to running the enterprise. Peugeot has been – by far – the most participative. Its style has captured the imagination of the employees who now regard the business as their own as much as the shareholders.

Peugeot was the first of the slimmed down car companies to achieve such an extensive level of employee support. The management philosophy is personified by a series of initiatives led by and involving employees, such as the 1995 Gala Day, the creation of the Peugeot employee rally team, and the autumn 1998 launch of the new 206.

Two areas of human resources policy particularly instrumental in maintaining growth are communications and training. Peugeot is a benchmark communicator. 'The focus for this is the internal team briefing,' says Judge. 'We send out red and green communications bulletins. The reds are for urgent releases and are normally distributed on the day of issue. The green are for less time-sensitive issues.' Management at local level brief staff regularly and at the beginning of each year senior management reports to all employees on the objectives for the coming 12-month period. The spread of communications media also includes an employee newspaper and annual employee reports.

The company works with the trades unions on an assisted development programme. Employees can attend non-vocational training courses at the company's expense – to a maximum of £250 per person. Around a fifth of the workforce take up this option for life. The aim of the exercise is to build a greater bond between the business and its people. When Peugeot started this programme, it was years ahead of today's creditable initiatives such as learning centres and learning for life.

How does Peugeot rate?

Pay:	very good
Benefits:	excellent
Communications:	superb
Training:	excellent
Career development:	excellent
Morale:	superb

People and personnel policies

Peugeot's conviction that the act of encouraging employees to acquire the habit of learning has direct benefits for the company is now recognized by many leading blue chips. In the industrial heartland of the West Midlands, where industrial relations had been less than sparkling, some members of staff required convincing that the exercise was genuine. But even the more sceptical discovered that the learning process has a positive impact on both the individual and the company.

'So we asked ourselves how could we encourage the process of lifetime learning among our people. These courses show an individual's personal flexibility and the capacity to adapt. The French view is that a manager is a manager is a manager. You do not need a technical discipline to be a manager. But you rarely get to the top of the company without an understanding of, and experience of, people management.'

Peugeot believes that a company cannot function without the active co-operation of its people. Judge is dismissive of the concept of human resources management. He argues that his department is personnel which deals with people. 'The only constant in the business is change and our role is to prepare our people for that change.' People issues are at the top of the agenda of the British company and are central to decision making in the group.

Taken in isolation, pay in Peugeot is average for the sector but the reward package, as a whole, is impressive. The company has a profit-related pay scheme which paid 1.43 per cent in 1998. Its pension scheme is commendable.

Employees can buy the company's products at 25 per cent discount on run-out models and are offered reductions on spare parts which are attractive compared with high street retailers. People with five years' experience can own a new Ryton-built car for around £100 a month (including tax, insurance and servicing). Peugeot has a large sports and social club where it stages a variety of entertainment for employees. It is the only large company which still has its own cricket pitch and among a handful of businesses which continue to operate an internal radio station. Like other large car companies, Peugeot has employed in-house video and computer bulletin board facilities.

The low attrition rate in the company is underscored by the results of frequent employee attitude surveys. The most recent showed that two-thirds is very satisfied with the company as an employer. Another 17 per cent said they were satisfied. The combined effect of the portfolio of initiatives which the business has created is to build a bond between management and employees.

Contact address

Mr Michael Judge
Director of Personnel
The Peugeot Motor Company plc
Aldermoor House
Aldermoor Lane
Coventry CV3 1LT
Telephone: 01203 884000
Fax: 01203 884288
Web site:
http://www.peugeotcareers.co.uk

Pret A Manger

Pret A Manger is one of those remarkable businesses which apparently arrived from nowhere and was suddenly everywhere. It is a highly distinctive fast food retailer with trademark shop fittings. It sells freshly made sandwiches and beverages in a striking chrome setting and has managed to capture some of the best positions on the high street. Its strategy is to become established very quickly as one of the reliable brand names in main shopping streets and in key public locations. The breathtaking speed with which it has arrived is redolent of the high tempo inside the business itself. Pret is regarded by many including BP, Deloitte & Touche and the BBC as the benchmark for modern retail.

Pret A Manger at a glance

Employees: 1,800 UK, an average of 20 per shop
Annual staff attrition: 20–60 per cent, seasonal
Key locations: London and most major cities – 74 shops
Annual graduate intake: n/a
Annual intake: 1,000, 900 shop staff and 100 managers

An inside view

Pret A Manger was started in 1986 by a couple of property developers, Julian Metcalfe and Sinclair Beecham, who saw an opportunity for a high quality, consistent and attractive chain of sandwich shops. They own the business today and are respected by their employees not only because they used to make the sandwiches and serve behind the counter in the original shop in Victoria. The explosive growth did not come until the mid-1990s but the turning point arrived in 1990 when stores two to five were opened all in the same year. Now there are 74 shops.

Part of the original engine for growth was franchising because the company needed capital to expand but now all the outlets – bar seven – are wholly owned. During the next five years a further 200 branches are proposed, many in shopping centres and out-of-town retail parks. Pret A Manger is a private company and so does not publish accounts in the same way as a major PLC but it does report an annual turnover. In 1998 this was around £70 million.

One of the great achievements of its remarkable growth during this decade has been its capacity to secure prominent high street locations which, perhaps, would have evaded other more experienced hands. Sally Adair, management development manager, says, ‘Sinclair had substantial experience in property development before he and Julian created the company. They realized that if this was something which was going to be successful on a large scale they had to get the key locations.' In every case, except one in Slough, they have managed to secure by adept negotiation the most favourable sites for the brand.

The company's booklet Food for Thought says, 'We trade successfully on the high street, paying prime pitch rents adjacent to the country's leading fashion retailers. Pret A Manger's average sales per store are £968,000, among the highest sales per square foot in the country. The company's rent, rates and service charge represent just under nine per cent of turnover. Pret cannot pay more than ten per cent of a store's turnover in property costs. In places where capital investment is high, this may be reduced to eight per cent.'

Adair says that the formula for rents is important especially as the company grows outside London because it is presenting a complete package to landlords. 'We have a strong reputation for developing our staff and making a positive contribution to business in every high street. For the long-term development of the business we need to be sure that we will have room for profitable investment.'

Another significant marketing and profile boost has been the company's acceptance by leading public institutions. Pret A Manger, for example, provides the catering facilities at the National Gallery, Heathrow Airport, The Tower of London, Eurotunnel at Folkestone and Selfridges Food Hall.

At the moment Pret is concentrating on expanding its brand beyond London where it has previously focused on the office worker business. 'We are opening what we term E grade facilities in all the major cities. These are the high volume, multi-shift shops which turn over between £70,000 and £90,000 a week,' says Adair. 'Some of the newer outlets like Bicester Shopping Village will be serving an entirely different market from our traditional City-based branches. Without compromising the brand we will need to adapt our hard floor and tall stools for family use. We are gearing our growth in a different way. We are forming clusters of shops in the big cities rather than opening one large outlet in each city. Our smaller stores like Richmond or Beauchamp Place will turn over between £8,000 and £10,000.'

Pret distinguishes itself by not compromising on the quality of its food. 'We are passionate about not using additives and preservatives in our food. Pret creates handmade, natural food. We have menus for breakfast, lunch and tea at an average spend of £3 a head. Pret started as a high quality sandwich maker and now we are a fast food retailer of luxury sandwiches. We never carry sandwiches over to the next day. If we are going to have a surplus we collect the excess to give to the charity Crisis for distribution to the homeless.' The company serves more than 20 million customers a year who buy 10 million cups of coffee and 14 million sandwiches.

How does Pret A Manger rate?

Pay:	good
Benefits:	good
Communications:	very good
Training:	very good
Career development:	good
Morale:	good

People and personnel policies

Pret is in the vanguard of the ethical businesses movement. It regards the quality of its relationship with its customers and its people as core to its operation. It is as important to the business as its financial wellbeing and operational efficiency. It emphasizes repeatedly that without its people it would be unable to deliver its unique proposition to its customers.

The company employs around 1,800 people. On average there are 20 people working in each shop, although some outlets employ around eight and others up to 60. Pret has 170 managers, 74 are termed general managers – the rest are assistant managers or assistant general managers. Staff attrition is relatively high – between 20 and 60 per cent a year – but this is largely because many young people are not looking for a career. Pret aims to keep, develop and promote the best candidates and provide early opportunities for talented people.

The company's human resources function is currently introducing a graduate recruitment and career development programme. This will be rolled out during the course of 1999. At present Pret recruits around 100 managers a year, which can be expected to increase as the relentless expansion continues to gather pace. It recruits around 900 non-managerial employees and is subject to seasonal fluctuations in demand and availability of employees.

For team members there is an assessment centre in Holborn which is partially a shop but there are also offices at the site. A team of four people screen people through CVs and one-to-one meetings. This recruitment team will be fed details of vacancies from each shop manager in need of staff. The candidate will go to a specific shop for an interview and spend a day in the shop, where they will be supervised by the manager and assessed by the team in the shop. 'It is up to everybody in the shop – not just the manager – whether they keep that person or let them go. It is an essential part of the process. Teams then realized that they needed colleagues whom they could rely on and get along with, people who will turn up on time. The majority of our people get up at 5.30 and are at work at 6.30. So they need colleagues who will do the same.'

The company has developed a competence-based approach which includes assessments for leadership, facility for taking action, problem solving, developing people, passion for excellence, talent for motivation, planning and organizing, communicating, listening and integrity. The company runs what it calls The Academy which provides support for people across the business and embraces the people management aspects of recruitment, training and human resources functions.

Contact address

Sally Adair
Management Development Manager
Pret A Manger
16 Palace Street
London SW1E 5PT
Telephone: 0171 827 8000
Fax: 0171 827 8787
Web site: http://www.pret.co.uk

PricewaterhouseCoopers

The autumn of 1997 could be characterized as the season of accountancy mergers. Some succeeded, others did not. The proposal to bring together the practices of Price Waterhouse and Coopers & Lybrand was the most visible – and the most successful. Today PricewaterhouseCoopers is, by far, the largest of the Big Five consulting firms. While it is still in the process of fully integrating these two major international firms much progress has already been made in creating a new business with a single approach to strategic development, human resources, business policy and IT. PricewaterhouseCoopers operates through global service lines, three regional theatres and national country management. This means that strategic decisions about its services and products are taken at a world level while national teams operate cross functionally to deliver local client services.

PricewaterhouseCoopers at a glance

Employees: 145,000 worldwide, 16,500 UK
Annual staff attrition: 15–17 per cent
Key locations: 40 offices nationwide
Annual graduate intake: 1,650
Annual intake: 2,000

An inside view

The dynamics of the accountancy and advisory sectors took a quantum leap forward in this decade. In the 1980s the largest firms ceased to be professional partnerships secure in their oak panelled offices, resting on thick pile carpets. The rapid development of the global economy in the 1990s demanded that the top end practices responded to the challenges of their leading blue chip clients. This meant that all their services would be available at any location in the world where clients have operations. The standards needed to be uniformly high – and improving. Directors of client companies expect to secure greater value from audit and tax compliance services to give them an enhanced appreciation of the strengths and weaknesses of their enterprises.

The challenges for the Big Five firms, as they are now, lie in anticipating what services and products clients are likely to buy in the future. So, in that they are no different from any other large multinational. But to a certain extent, it is incumbent upon advisers to be several steps ahead of their clients so there is greater competitive pressure to achieve real advances in service quality and delivery within ever tighter timeframes. Clients want increasing value for money. They also expect that however good today's service delivery was, it should be exceeded tomorrow.

This is the underlying reason why PW and Coopers were driven to combine. Both firms already had plans for expansion to meet or anticipate client need, but believed that by bringing the two practices together, a formidable new partnership would be created. Consulting firms tend to argue that critical mass is vital both geographically and in service discipline. The PricewaterhouseCoopers merger is the ultimate expression of this thesis. The founding partners were both convincingly strong in a wide range of service divisions and believed the benefits of their merger would come in the enhanced levels of innovation, service delivery and cross-functional synergies.

The integration of two international brands of formidable reputation in the business environment, coupled with potential cost efficiencies and opportunities for significant capital investment, has created an organization of unprecedented force. 'The change has been remarkable,' says Charles Macleod, recruitment manager for PricewaterhouseCoopers. 'The increased scale of the operation has, from an HR viewpoint multiplied the career opportunities available in the business. There is a real sense of excitement among people throughout the firm that we are creating something different. Mergers often breed insecurity but not this one. The sheer scale and scope of the resources available to us is of real value to our clients and they share in our excitement. We have already been able to refresh our advertising approach and to explore new methods of internal communications.'

The firm is structured into five service lines. The largest is Assurance & Business Advisory Services which includes the audit practice. This service line also contains a number of IT and accounting-related consulting activities. Management Consulting is also a major business as is Tax & Legal Services, which includes associated legal firms; Financial Advisory Services embraces Corporate Finance, insolvency and forensic investigative services; and Business Process Outsourcing. Each business has its own global and regional management while each nation within PricewaterhouseCoopers has country management across the businesses. 'We are operating as a global business with global service lines. But the local country management includes a cross-functional element to allow us to take account of national cultural patterns and variations.' Like many multinationals, the global service lines are divided into three theatres: The Americas; Europe, Middle East and Africa; and Asia Pacific.

'If you have a client who has interests in all three theatres, you are able to say with confidence that you can deliver consistent service in all locations because our global framework provides for common training to uniformly high standards. Wherever your people are based you can communicate with them in a common language and through common technology which makes service delivery so much easier. For smaller clients who may operate at a more local level, we are able to draw upon unrivalled resources to help them solve their business problems.'

How does PricewaterhouseCoopers rate?

Pay:	very good
Benefits:	excellent
Communications:	excellent
Training:	excellent
Career development:	very good
Morale:	very good

People and personnel policies

PricewaterhouseCoopers has a very open recruitment policy. Most of its trainees come through a graduate entry scheme where personal characteristics and quality of performance matter more than the specific subject of the degree.

Experienced hires are drawn from a broad commercial background and although most will have studied in higher education it is what they have achieved and what individual talents they can bring which is important to the firm.

Inevitably, as such a huge recruiter of graduates, PricewaterhouseCoopers is a full participant in the milk round. It visits all of Britain's senior academic institutions and considers people of talent from whatever background. Macleod says the most impressive people are those who have shown evidence of leadership and organising capacities while at college, who possess the ability to communicate with others, who are self-confident and take responsibility, who display an aptitude for problem solving and are individuals whom the firm can trust to deliver quality client work.

The majority of the annual graduate intake goes into professional training for accountancy. This is generally a three-year programme. Trainees will work in an audit or advisory function gaining experience which is directly relevant to their qualification. Other graduate entry points exist in each of the service lines. All new entrants to PricewaterhouseCoopers are engaged on an induction programme. In the audit and related divisions this is called Starting in Business and covers the firm, its activities, its culture and approach. Participants are told how the firm operates and their place in the organization as well as receiving technical business training. Management Consultancy runs its own course which contains similar elements but which reflects the different orientation of that sector of the business. For more experienced hires there are more advanced induction courses run internationally by the different service lines.

Longer-term success in PricewaterhouseCoopers derives in part from a capacity to work in a variety of different cultures. Inevitably with an organization which builds service teams from a selection of geographical markets, travel is an inherent factor of the job. This is easier for some than others. Where a team is providing a service that is more or less the same worldwide, expertise is necessarily international in nature. For people working in other areas of the business, their knowledge is more country specific and so for them international assignments can be harder to come by. Tax is a good example where the work is complex and stretching but often essentially national in character.

Compared with audit work therefore, overseas assignments in Tax may be harder to come by.

'There is a fair degree of mobility between service lines. The Assurance & Business Advisory area trains the majority of graduates. On qualification, some may seek new opportunities. Many of these are found in PricewaterhouseCoopers in different divisions in the UK or perhaps for one of our office overseas. It is natural for consulting work to draw people together from different locations in the firm. The degree of opportunity for internal moves will be defined by the nature of the expertise you offer. An IT consultant, for example, would probably have more scope in management consultancy than in corporate finance.'

The training development ethos is one of self-development. 'There is a very active process of performance appraisal, identifying the skills which people need and then filling the gaps with whatever training is appropriate. There are many different vehicles. Perhaps someone might need to go on a course with 25 other people or they might need to work through a series of training modules on their own. We train for the skills that people actually require rather than the ones they might need. More than simply a learning culture we see ours as a coaching culture. We conduct a lot of training on-the-job and believe in helping people get things right. We give as much responsibility as we are able to do as early as possible. We assign responsibility not on grade but on ability. There is also a strong self-development ethos beyond our approach to coaching. People should want to get on. They should feel free to put themselves forward for training if they feel that they need it.'

From April 1999 there will be a flexible benefits scheme called Choices. Instead of getting base pay and certain fixed benefits, each person's total reward package is valued and employees can consider which benefits they wish to select. They are obliged to accept a certain minimum percentage in cash but they can commute the rest into a range of alternative benefits. 'Everyone has a package which equates with their value in the marketplace but the detail of how they would prefer to take that package is up to them.' From the firm's perspective it is valuable because it maximizes the value of the total reward to the individual and also breaks the link between seniority and eligibility for certain benefits.

Contact address

Charles MacLeod
Recruitment Manager
PricewaterhouseCoopers
Southwark Towers
32 London Bridge Street
London SE1 9SY
Telephone: 0171 804 3000
Fax: 0171 804 3030
Web site: http://www.pwcglobal.com

Procter & Gamble Limited

A combination of deep consumer understanding and leading edge science and technology has made Procter & Gamble the global success it is today. The company manufactures an enormous range of high quality products from chemicals to health and beauty products, detergents to foodstuffs, household cleaning goods to pharmaceuticals. Procter & Gamble originated in Cincinnati in 1837 and now markets its products in 140 countries around the world, selling more than 300 brands of well-known goods. Employing over 103,000 people worldwide, the company plans to double its size every ten years, creating a high demand for exceptional people.

Procter & Gamble at a glance

Employees: 103,000 worldwide, 5,500 UK
Annual staff attrition: 4 per cent
Key locations: 12 (7 manufacturing), Gosforth (HQ), Weybridge, Staines
Annual graduate intake: 130
Annual intake: 200

An inside view

The average consumer may not be so familiar with the name Procter & Gamble, but they will certainly have heard of some of their products and every household in the UK is likely to use at least one. For example, Ariel, Britain's best-selling detergent, Fairy Liquid, the first antibacterial washing up liquid, and Pampers, the leading disposable nappies, are all P&G products. Other prominent brands include Oil of Ulay, Pringles, Clearasil, Max Factor, Flash, Crest, Pantene, Daz, Head & Shoulders, Vicks Formula 44 and Sunny Delight. P&G is very consumer driven and was one of the first companies in the world to hire full-time professionals to study consumer needs. The world and North American headquarters are in Cincinnati, Ohio, US and regional headquarters in the major cities of Europe, Asia and Latin America.

With 140 manufacturing plants around the world, tight business structure and unified goals unite P&G. The company focuses on developing brand names, leading innovations in the field, and building relationships with consumers based on their needs. Advertising is the principal way P&G reaches its consumers, spending more than $3 billion a year on marketing. World brands are at the core of the company's overall marketing strategy. P&G is ranked amongst the most innovative companies in the world, filing for nearly 20,000 patent applications every year and able to boast of more than 200 technologies that can be found only in P&G brands. The company interacts with more than 7 million consumers a year worldwide to obtain feedback on what today's consumers want and believe. The product sector with the highest return, 40 per cent of P&G's global income, is laundry and cleaning products, followed by paper products (nappies and sanitary towels) at 25 per cent, 20 per cent from beauty care, 10 per cent from food and 10 per cent from healthcare.

In the past P&G has been portrayed as a secretive and manipulative institution, whose employees were personally and professionally restricted. The company culture, in recent years, has undergone a major transformation. Among key strategic priorities is a commitment to make P&G a more people-friendly organization – one obvious manifestation being the recent switch to casual attire.

Despite this softer, kinder image, P&G is unlikely to become any less aggressive. The company aims to create a high-performance culture where the emphasis is on creativity. This attitude has given P&G a reputation for challenging convention in product development and business management, and it regards innovation as the cornerstone of its success. P&G believes that the interests of the company and the individual are inseparable and the quest for mutual success binds the business together. Stock ownership is encouraged.

P&G aims to recruit for long-term careers. The long-standing policy is to recruit at first stage only, as the company wants people who will commit and invest in their careers and P&G as a whole. It seeks out top-level graduates with a balanced profile who fit the criteria mapped out by five key attributes: intelligence, energy, leadership, creativity and ambition. The current policy is to recruit from internships and vocational business courses, which provide a clearer indication of the talent and standard of applicants. Internships operate over the university summer vacation, a period of two to three months, and every year each sector of P&G operates a one-week vocational business course. Applicants therefore have the opportunity to find out what it is really like to work at P&G. The company has built its organization from within, promoting and rewarding people without regard to differences other than performance.

How does Procter & Gamble rate?

Pay:	very good
Benefits:	excellent
Communications:	very good
Training:	excellent
Career development:	excellent
Morale:	very good

People and personnel policies

Training at P&G is primarily on-the-job, as the company does not advocate training that is superfluous to the employee's function. A new recruit is given a job, which is his or her sole responsibility, but supported by the necessary supervision. There is emphasis on new employees taking a full, active and creative role early on in their employment. Consequently the ability to handle pressure and adapt to change are important qualities of applicants. If an employee decides that he or she requires more training in order to complete a project to the required standard, P&G will ensure it is supplied. There is corporate training to instruct employees in managerial skills, such as how to run a meeting, project management and report writing. More than 90 per cent of training is carried out by the internal workforce to ensure that it is relevant and to promote team building.

Catalyst, a New York-based advocacy and research group, honoured programmes created by P&G to raise awareness of the need for women in the executive ranks. P&G's 'Advancement of Women' initiative used a task force that focused on such issues as cultural change, work/life balance, coaching and mentoring, and networking for women. According to the company, the number of women at the general manager/vice president level has more than tripled from five in 1992 to 18 in 1997.

The benefits that P&G provide to employees are among the best in the world. The company was a pioneer in the establishment of benefits programmes that make employees true owners of the business. The most significant retirement benefit is locally defined benefit pension plans. Performance related pay is the norm and is based on the work and development plan. It is specific to the individual and there are no across the board settlements. P&G pay competitively, benchmarking themselves against those in the industry who do comparable work.

Contact address

Simon Brocket
Director of Human Resources
Procter & Gamble UK
The Heights
Brooklands
Weybridge
Surrey KT13 0XP
Telephone: 01932 896000
Fax: 01932 896200
Web site: http://www.pg.com

Reader's Digest

Reader's Digest Limited is the UK subsidiary of a US multinational, Reader's Digest Association, and is a household name in the UK. It publishes the eponymous magazine which has the highest readership in the UK, selling 1.4 million copies monthly. Its ancillary publishing activities include condensed books, high quality illustrated non-fiction books, special interest magazines, CD and cassette collections, videos and related publishing activities. It is a renowned direct sale publisher with an aggressive and persuasive marketing approach. Annual global revenues are $3 billion.

Reader's Digest at a glance

Employees: 550 UK
Annual staff attrition: 5 per cent
Key locations: London (Canary Wharf) and Swindon
Annual graduate intake: none
Annual intake: 40

An inside view

Founded in the USA in1922 by DeWitt and Lila Wallace, the first issue of Reader's Digest had a print order of 5,000 copies. By the late 1930s circulation had risen to more than 1 million copies. The first overseas edition was published in 1938 in the United Kingdom and since then overseas editions have been introduced in numerous countries and languages. It is currently published in 48 editions and 19 languages and has a global circulation of 28 million copies per month. In 1950 Reader's Digest Condensed Books were launched. These two products represent the foundation of the now vast publishing empire.

Reader's Digest used the mailing lists, which resulted from the publishing business to develop direct sales. The company's direct sales techniques are sometimes criticized for being too aggressive, but they have, nonetheless, been highly successful. A fundamental reason for its success is the company's dedication to quality in respect of its products.

The company has been quick to react to new technologies and to diversify publishing projects from the written word to audio, video and computer-based technologies. The latest developments include 11 linked worldwide web sites through which browsers can access many elements of Reader's Digest, while at the same time being subject to the selling techniques of the company's and other approved advertisers' products and services.

The UK operation publishes specifically for the UK market. A very successful example of this is the magazine *MoneyWise*, which is the largest personal financial magazine in the UK. The company's marketing continues to be almost exclusively by direct mail, although it recognizes that other media, such as newsstand advertising and the worldwide web, may be the future direction.

How does Reader's Digest rate?

Pay:	excellent
Benefits:	very good
Communications:	good
Training:	very good
Career development:	very good
Morale:	very good

People and personnel policies

The fundamental personnel policies and employment philosophy are determined by the parent company in the US. Staff attrition in the UK is exceptionally low in the marketing and journalism sectors, which normally have high staff turnover.

The company pays very well for the publishing sector. Its salaries compare favourably with almost any blue chip commercial enterprise in London. Benefits are also good, especially the pension scheme.

The reward system is only a part of the loyalty and morale policy of the company. It is supported by training and communications programmes. Internal communication is aimed at all levels in the company. Regular informative bulletins and newsletters are prominent features of company life and active contribution is encouraged through monthly meetings between managers and staff. The meetings start as briefing meetings based on a paper circulated to all managers. Following the briefing, general unrestricted debate is encouraged and managers pass useful comments up the line.

The move to Canary Wharf has brought all London-based staff together in an open plan environment to encourage communication and awareness. The management has also created less formal areas where staff can meet on an informal basis to enhance communication and bonding between team members.

The company regards training and development as an important foundation for the long-term wellbeing of the company, because people are publicly identified as the company's most important asset. Providing staff with the skills, experience and insights necessary to perform their jobs in a rapidly changing and competitive world is believed to be essential.

All managers are expected to accept responsibility for the basic training of their staff. At the same time each member of staff is expected to take personal responsibility for his or her own development. The human resources department provides a formal framework for ensuring these simple ideals operate within the company. A performance review sets objectives, identifies development needs and training priorities and records career aspirations. HR then plans and organizes individual, group and company training plans. This training may be in-house or external depending on the requirements and the availability of training staff. Annual performance reviews monitor progress, achievement, further requirements and update human resources plans. A key course for new employees is the induction course. This is a short course on the first morning for all new employees and a two-day course during the first three months for newly recruited managerial, professional and specialist staff.

Career development is not restricted to the UK. As part of a global organization, the UK company offers opportunities in other parts of the world for employees with appropriate skills and experience, although such opportunities are more likely to be by assignment rather than application.

The company has women in many senior positions, including two on the UK board of directors. The maternity benefits package is one of the best in the UK and the company also offers a degree of flexible working for women who return from maternity leave.

Reader's Digest terminated its graduate recruitment scheme in 1990. The company decided to actively recruit at the second job stage because of its previous experience of providing training and development to graduates only to lose them to other employers. The company considers this new policy to be more in line with its basic strategy of recruiting for long-term commitment.

Contact address

Lila Campbell
Human Resources Director
Reader's Digest Association Limited
11 Westferry Circus
Canary Wharf
London E14 4HE
Telephone: 0171 715 8000
Fax: 0171 715 8181
Web site: http://www.readersdigest.com

Rentokil Initial plc

Rentokil Initial is a highly successful group which lays claim to the title of the world's largest business services company. In recent years the group has grown rapidly and purposefully to a point where it has 1.5 million customers in more than 40 countries in North America, Asia Pacific and Europe. Its commercial interests are diverse. They include cleaning, hygiene, personnel, pest control, distribution, plant, property and security services. Annual turnover is nearly £3 billion with pretax profits at £190 million. The group's corporate target is to provide growth for shareholders of at least 20 per cent a year in profits and in earnings per share, while not detracting from long-term growth. Rentokil Initial is no stranger to accolades from the press and the City.

Rentokil Initial at a glance

Employees: 140,000 worldwide, 80,000 UK
Annual staff attrition: variable
Key locations: HQ at East Grinstead, West Sussex; more than 500 branch offices across the UK. Main overseas offices: throughout Europe, North America and Asia Pacific regions
Annual graduate intake: 20 (company trainee management scheme) plus numerous directly into local branches
Annual intake: n/a

An inside view

Rentokil Initial is a favourite of City analysts. It is perceived by the financial community as a growing business which is well managed and continues to provide enhanced returns. To the general public it is viewed as a company which provides pest control, office maintenance and hygiene services. In fact, it is much wider.

The company breaks down into a series of divisions embracing cleaning, hospital services, medical services, textile services, personnel services, conference and training centres, pest control, catering services, leisure services, environmental services, facilities centres management, roofing, timber preserving, tropical plants, distribution and plant services. The company is active in more than 40 countries worldwide including every major economy in Europe, North America and Asia Pacific.

Sir Clive Thompson, chief executive, says 'Our strategy is to develop a global business services company with a range of high growth and quality driven services which can be marketed in the major developed countries of the world using the combined strength of the Rentokil and Initial brands.

'This successful strategy was established in 1982 and during the following 17 years profits have increased by an average of 23.2 per cent a year and earnings per share by 22.8 per cent a year. In Rentokil Initial the company culture is commonly described as The Rentokil Initial Way. It exemplifies rigorous control of costs with high quality service. It has acquired some 300 businesses during the last 16 years and the culture has been adopted readily by the many thousands of people who have come into the company.'

'All Rentokil Initial services worldwide have the same organizational structure. Central to this structure is the branch which is a profit centre. We have around 1,000 branches and they share the same administration, management structures and financial reporting systems. This facilitates comparison between the performance of branches and the identification of best practice.'

Rentokil was renamed Rentokil Initial in October 1996, and gave rise to the development of two equal brands. All services were rebranded from October 1996 as either Rentokil or Initial. 'In determining areas for new services we aim to utilize our core competence which is the ability to deliver consistent, high quality service through well-recruited, well-trained and well-motivated blue collar staff working on other people's premises with relatively low levels of supervision.

How does Rentokil Initial rate?

Pay:	good
Benefits:	very good
Communications:	good
Training:	excellent
Career development:	excellent
Morale:	very good

People and personnel policies

Despite the broad scope of operations and market sectors, there is a clarity and coherence about the Rentokil Initial approach to management. Its strategic vision and practical application have both worked well to create an extremely profitable and valuable company.

'The rapid expansion of Rentokil Initial – at least 20 per cent a year – places even greater emphasis on our need to continue helping people to do better the things which they already do well. We have a deserved reputation for growing our management talent and the challenge for Rentokil Initial is to maintain this supply. Our purpose in developing people is clear. By providing training, career opportunities and the environment for the interchange of views and ideas, we prepare our people for ever-increasing responsibility in a company which is committed to achieve,' says Thompson.

He says that the company continues to favour promotion from within – especially those employees who demonstrate the capacity to be flexible and deploy business and management skills irrespective of discipline. 'Management will continue to be a company-wide resource rather than that of any subsidiary. And managers will be considered for vacancies not only within their own division but elsewhere in their country and, in many cases, worldwide.'

Ken Bowman, management development director, comments, 'Talent is recognized quickly and the best people progress rapidly into management. They will be thoroughly grounded in the business and trained through management training courses, developing essential skills – especially in people and financial management. All training is cross functional to give young managers experience of key issues across all the business streams and national boundaries. Throughout the career path, the management development programme will monitor progress, counsel and coach to ensure that individuals make the most of opportunities.'

Branch managers are not particularly concerned with previous academic performance when they recruit for more junior positions. They stress that anyone, graduate or non-graduate, can apply to join the company, which operates a meritocratic policy. The point of entry is at branch rather than central level where new recruits join a closely knit team of between 40 and 60 people in one of the specialist services.

Bowman says, 'The most senior positions in the company are open to those people who demonstrate ability and we attach great importance to developing the careers of those people who show talent. All development programmes are held at our UK corporate training facilities including our international senior managers' programme. Delegates discover key learning points for themselves by participative discussion, case study exercises and the use of CCTV where relevant. All courses are multidivisional, allowing delegates to exchange ideas and experiences with colleagues from other parts of the company.'

Contact address

Ken Bowman
Management Development Director
Rentokil Initial plc
Felcourt
East Grinstead
West Sussex RH19 2JY
Telephone: 01342 833022
Fax: 01342 326229
Web site: http://www.rentokil-initial.com

Reuters Holdings plc

Reuters supplies the global financial markets and the news media with the widest range of information and news products, including real-time financial data, collective investment data, numerical, textural, historical and graphical databases plus news, graphics, news video and news pictures. Reuters also designs and installs enterprise-wide information management and risk management systems for the financial markets as well as providing equity and foreign exchange transactions systems. It exclusively uses Internet technologies for wider distribution of news and information.

Reuters at a glance

Employees: 17,000
Annual staff attrition: 4 per cent
Key locations: London, New York, Hong Kong and Singapore
Annual graduate intake: 100 worldwide, 50 UK
Annual intake: 700

An inside view

'We have two main divisions around which our products are organized,' says Ivan Newman, university relations manager. 'On the one hand we have a group of products which are called financial information products. This is not solely financial information but a huge component of this area provides information for the financial and business markets. This gives our clients market-led information on which to make key decisions about the operations of their companies. That information may be generated internally by our own journalists in text, multimedia or television or it can be sources from 5,000 financial institutions around the world telling us what is happening in their markets. It can be sources from governments and major financial institutions as an outlet for their research departments. We also draw on information from journals of record.

'Our other division is trading systems mechanisms that allow our financial services customers to buy and sell various sorts of financial instruments and to establish the risk profile of their transactions or proposed transactions. The company is now organized around these two axes and through this structure products are conceived, developed and launched. The customer contact on a day-by-day basis is made by local geographic units organized in account teams. These account teams will include specialists from both axes. The customer sees a single integrated team while we have product responsibility from the top of the company to the customer account professionals.'

As a global business, Reuters devises strategy at an international level and implements its approach through local geographic units around the world organized in account teams, called the global sales and operations groups. These account teams will include specialists from both divisions, while retaining product responsibility from the top of the company to the customer account professionals.

'The divisional and global sales and operations approach is the biggest transformation in Reuters' organization in nearly two decades,' says Newman. The group has changed from a horizontal business managed by area and country units to a vertical business driven by products and measured by their profitability. The reorganization is the result of responding to the changing markets in which it operates. It is a highly diverse organization in terms of professional skill and culture.

'The culture of the business will vary enormously depending on the time horizon of the area you are in. Different buildings have different tempos. If you are in Gray's Inn Road, where our main editorial operation is based, the time horizon is minutes. When you speak about hours, you are talking long-term. It is a creative environment where journalists are observing and then creating in some medium – text, stills, film, graphics TV. In another part of the building where we take numerical information from 5,000 banks and stock exchanges about what is being traded now, the horizon is fractions of seconds. A minute is a lifetime. It is not creative in the sense that a journalist would use the word. But a creative process has been used to capture the information and distribute it to half a million professional users.'

How does Reuters rate?

Pay:	very good
Benefits:	very good
Communications:	very good
Training:	excellent
Career development:	very good
Morale:	very good

People and personnel policies

'Increasingly we are looking for the graduates we bring in to get early exposure to a series of technical and product disciplines,' says Lesley Cox, human resources manager UK and Ireland. 'When we recruit we seek a capacity to achieve in our environment. This means a group of attributes. Our business is subject to ongoing change, change among customers and in their markets. A key ability is the capacity to cope with change – indeed initiate change – and manage projects in a fast-moving environment. Five years ago we were looking at projects with a three-year delivery horizon; people now have to manage projects of a similar complexity in 18 months. To be effective they must ask themselves the question Why?'

Reuters recruits from a limited pool of universities – more because resources are finite than any positive policy to exclude. 'We tend to concentrate on those universities from where we have recruited successfully in the past. These include the two Manchester universities, Strathclyde, Bath, Exeter and UCD Dublin.' Many graduates enter the business in September each year when they are gathered together and given an induction course. They are grouped as a defined unit within the business for the first two years of their employment and come together at various points for training and development initiatives. Individual employees work for specific product groups.

Cox says that training has an inward and outward face. 'The internal training will promote greater understanding of products, develop interpersonal skills and encourage people to integrate better and be more effective. The externally focused courses will examine our markets and the type of business our customers conduct. Advanced financial sector qualifications which give clients confidence in the integrity of our products and services are important. We tend to favour industry qualifications rather than purely academic ones.

'We have an internal training department and in addition we do a considerable amount of external training offsite. We also have a learning centre and a policy of encouraging lifelong learning. If we do not keep employees up to date they will lose their competitive edge and their effectiveness. The impact of this on the business is self-evident. We regard training schemes as fully integrated into the business.'

Cox says that the application of the appraisal and review process may vary according to the business area where the individual employee is located. 'If, for example, someone is doing a sales role where there are monthly or quarterly fixed targets, that is the basis on which they will be reviewed. The basis will be the deliverables in terms of sales and the behaviour in achieving those sales. If someone is working on a longer-term project, the assessment will probably be more formal and reflect that achievement can be measured over a longer duration. We tend to be a company that says "What does the business need to develop?" and create policies to suit.'

Contact address

Lesley Cox
Human Resources Manager
UK and Ireland
Reuters
85 Fleet Street
London EC4P 4AJ
Telephone: 0171 250 1122
Fax: 0171 542 5262
Web site: http://www.reuters.com

Richer Sounds

Richer Sounds is a breath of fresh air. In a world dominated by strategic matrices and complex human resources approaches, Richer Sounds is a straightforward business. It is the UK's largest hi-fi retailer. The business operates from compact premises at the unfashionable end of town in more than 20 locations throughout the UK and Ireland and is now beginning to venture across the North Sea. The business is wholly owned by Julian Richer who, as an owner-manager, has put a distinctive imprint on the company. He advocates the Richer Way, a set of value statements which defines how the company does business. At the heart of this is its people.

Richer Sounds at a glance

Employees: 280
Annual staff attrition: 10 per cent
Key locations: London, Stockport and most major cities. Now also in Amsterdam
Annual graduate intake: n/a
Annual intake: 50

An inside view

Richer Sounds stores are compact, busy and packed to the ceiling with hi-fi units. They are rarely to be found on the high street and more likely to inhabit cost effective premises which instead have good access. The branding is simple and direct. Where Richer Sounds succeeds is in unparalleled customer service.

Managing director David Robinson, a Richer man to his fingertips, says that Julian Richer has always objected to poor customer service in whatever sphere. So he was absolutely determined that customer service would be an absolute priority in his stores. And the growth in business and profits has come from employee involvement and management encouragement of staff potential.

Julian Richer started the enterprise in 1978. 'Our start was humble from a small unit piled high at London Bridge. We now have 29 stores around the British Isles. We have a committed workforce of 250 which is without doubt our greatest asset.' He says that he has stuck to what he knows best which is hi-fi retail. The group also owns the Audio Partnership, which makes and markets audio equipment. That business is run by a former London Bridge store manager.

Richer says, 'I passionately believe that if you treat people well, genuinely respect them and work hard at constantly motivating them, it should result in a group of people who value their jobs and feel valued themselves. This will inevitably result in improved service for the customers and, in turn, increased profits.'

Businesses like Richer Sounds depend – to their roots – on a confident, friendly and informed salesforce. So many sales-driven companies miss the point and base their businesses on a fear culture. Richer took a completely opposite view and has enshrined this in numerous publications including his book *The Richer Way*. Few observers have any doubt that this group of companies depends heavily on the inspiration and direction of its owner. But his vision is based on employee participation and personal achievement.

'A primary measure of a business' success should be customer satisfaction. It is this, along with great value for money, which drives our business and I am sure has led to success. Continuous improvement is vital and we really strive to improve, listening to our customers and to our colleagues. A healthy organization feeds on ideas, suggestions, comments and criticisms.'

The current sales of the business stand at £46 million with pretax profits of more than £2 million. It made its first step outside the UK in 1993 with the opening of a store in Dublin. The company has opened a store in Amsterdam and over a longer period will roll out into Belgium, Luxembourg and perhaps Germany, says Robinson.

How does Richer Sounds rate?

Pay:	very good
Benefits:	good
Communications:	very good
Training:	excellent
Career development:	very good
Morale:	very good

People and personnel policies

If you work for Richer Sounds there is a good chance that you will have been recruited by one of two novel, innovative and cost effective routes. Instead of running large recruitment campaigns, the company provides an information sheet on employment prospects in the company in the stores and it also carries details in its product catalogues.

The typical customer – and likely recruit – is 18 to 40. Many people buy their first hi-fis in Richer Sounds. The location of the stores is designed to attract students and young people in their first jobs. The exciting atmosphere and the immediate contact with many other young people is a direct incentive for people in this age bracket to apply. Richer Sounds pays well for a sales environment, and although it has a looser structure than many retail groups the career development prospects can be attractive. Each new employee is given a shadow who can show them the ropes.

Each new recruit receives a welcome pack on or before the day of arrival. This ranks with some of the best put out by leading blue chip businesses. It includes a benefits guide which is outstandingly good compared with its sector and includes discounts, free vouchers, medical advice, hardship loans, giving up smoking initiatives and weekly competitions.

Robinson says, 'Sales commission is paid to colleagues on most items, and on all complimentary questionnaires and correspondence. Our customer service index rates the customer service performance of each sales assistant and engineer in each month. On questionnaires, we pay £3 for each excellent rating, we deduct £2 for each mediocre and deduct £5 for each poor. For each good letter, positive We're Listening customer response card returned, and complimentary phone call the company pays between £5 and £10. For each negative it takes away – from the monthly sales commission – between £5 and £10.'

Bonuses are also paid in a range of other situations. Colleagues receive £50 if they secure a photograph of a celebrity in a Richer Sounds store holding a Richer Sounds bag or mug. An innovation scheme has been launched. New ideas are submitted to Julian Richer and if he likes them he awards up to £25 tax free. An employee who introduces a family member or a friend who stays for more than six months is paid £100. Equally, someone who reports a colleague for dishonesty is given a substantial loyalty bonus. The company also runs a mystery shopper scheme where each store is rated by an anonymous individual. This attracts an increasing scale of awards according to performance. If an employee finds a location which the company then turns into a store, he or she wins £250. Golden aeroplanes are awarded to employees who provide a contribution which is over and above the call of duty. Exceptional performers can cash in five golden aeroplanes for one platinum.

Richer Sounds places great emphasis on training. 'We are fortunate enough to have an excellent training centre in York,' says Robinson. New recruits are given three days' induction training there within the first six weeks of their employment. It covers the history of the company, what it believes in and its culture. During the courses, they will receive a one-hour presentation from Julian Richer or David Robinson. The accessibility of senior directors is a key feature of the Richer Sounds culture. Employees will be briefed regularly by Richer or Robinson, and career counselling is often done by these two directors.

Contact address

David Robinson
Managing Director
Richer Sounds
Hankey Street
London SE1 4BB
Telephone: 0171 940 2222
Fax: 0171 940 2211
Web site: http://www.richersounds.com

Rolls-Royce plc

Life is good at Rolls-Royce. This technically excellent engineer has record sales and full order books. It enjoys a global reputation for market excellence and commands formidable market shares. In recent years the management team has been making adjustments to the composition and structure of the group to ensure that it plays to its strengths. The core gas turbine technology of the company has created one of the broadest product ranges of aero engines in the world. Its products are familiar to any frequent flier on civil aviation. The technology is also deployed in the defence and energy sectors.

Rolls-Royce at a glance

Employees: 40,000
Annual staff attrition: 3 per cent
Key locations: London, Virginia (US), Derby, Bristol, Indianapolis, Newcastle-upon-Tyne, Coventry, Gateshead, Montreal
Annual graduate intake: 300
Annual intake: 1,000

An inside view

Rolls-Royce enjoys a certain cachet among the world's top companies. It is synonymous with technical excellence, flair, reliability, the quality of its relationships with its clients and its high level of commitment to its employees. In the last couple of years, Rolls-Royce has made structural changes to ensure that the company is fully able to exploit the opportunities of the coming decade. In March 1998, it introduced a new organization which recognized that strategy and structure stem directly from customer requirements.

This change followed a year when sales reached £4.3 billion and pretax profits £276 million, a record year for the company. Chairman Sir Ralph Robins told shareholders, 'We achieved record sales and profits and our best ever share of the commercial aero-engine market. More than 90 per cent of all of our business activities are now built around our gas turbine products. We have won a 34 per cent share of the world market for civil turbofans and more than 80 per cent of the market for large new twin-engined aircraft in 1997. Our strategy to offer a broad and competitive product range has led to new developments across the range. We are confident of continuing success.'

Rolls-Royce engines power more types of civil aircraft than any other manufacturer – some 32 in all. John Rose, the group chief executive, says, 'Our core business is the gas turbine and our strength in the technology generates more than 90 per cent of our business in the growing markets for civil and military aero engines, power generation, oil and gas power systems and marine power. Our success in winning orders in 1997 led to a 50 per cent increase in manufacturing, and engineering productivity has risen by 17 per cent in two years. It is a fundamental part of our strategy that the quality of engineering is matched by commercial and business excellence.'

A new initiative to spearhead this approach is Better Performance Faster which was launched in the aerospace business in 1996 and rolled out into the entire group in 1997. 'We recognize that we need to develop products and services better and faster to stay competitive and to improve our profitability. We began this programme to transform our business performance by streamlining our processes and beating our competitors on cost, quality and delivery. Better Performance Faster covers everything we do from procurement and product development to supporting our customers in the marketplace,' says Rose.

He adds that the underlying principles are focus and integration. Rolls-Royce is concentrating more rigorously on the skills, products and activities which bring the company its best possible reward. Combined with a capital investment of £200 million in 1997, the Better Performance Faster initiative has already brought tangible benefits. One example is the V2500 engine, with assembly times cut from 30 to 15 days.

At the heart of the business is the aerospace sector. In late 1998 there were more than 55,000 Rolls-Royce engines in service with 300 airlines, 2,400 corporate and utility operators and more than 100 armed forces. In the civil sector, Airline Business covers the hugely successful Trent family of engines, the RB211 family, including the RB211-524 and the RB211-535 and V2500. The Corporate and Regional Aircraft sector is served by the BR700 series, AE2100, AE3007 and Tay.

In terms of management structure, Rolls-Royce is much more streamlined than it used to be. However, since many of the company's activities have vital safety and security implications, a hierarchy of approvals and controls is inevitable. As a result, therefore, the company is much more traditionally structured than companies in, for example, the service sector.

How does Rolls-Royce rate?

Pay:	good
Benefits:	good
Communications:	good
Training:	excellent
Career development:	excellent
Morale:	very good

People and personnel policies

Given the highly competitive nature of the aerospace industry worldwide, Rolls-Royce has placed a strong emphasis on the importance of recruiting and developing a high-calibre workforce. The company aims to establish an environment in which continuous learning can take place, and is placing a much greater responsibility on the individual to specify the type of training he or she wishes to receive.

Since 1995, Rolls-Royce has been carrying out a continuous review of training and its role within the group. As a consequence of this review, significant new training and development initiatives were launched. These include the Rolls-Royce business leadership programme, a suite of technical programmes in support of a major investment in electronic product definition and multi-skilling programmes. In addition, learning centres have been established to provide computer-based training for employees to upgrade their skills, both through work-based projects and study in their own time.

In recognition of the quality of the group's training for young people, one Rolls-Royce employee recently won the New Graduate Engineering Prize from the Royal Academy of Engineering. Training also plays an important part in support of sales and marketing internationally. Various long-term training initiatives have been established with governments and institutions in a number of developing countries.

The group's remuneration policy is to set salaries based on market rates. However, Rolls-Royce is increasingly keen to reward employees based on their performance and see the workforce share in the success of the company by introducing a variety of incentive schemes. Building on the success of its Sharesave scheme (which has been in existence since 1987), the company has recently introduced a performance-related pay scheme for all employees, in order to align their interests more closely to the group's performance. The company has created a closer identity of interest between shareholders and senior management by developing a long-term incentive plan.

One of the major benefits of the company's wider international representation is that it offers much greater opportunities for developing its management team through overseas postings. Similar opportunities are offered by the number of joint ventures and alliances in which the company is entering. International experience is increasingly seen as a pre-requisite for a senior management position.

Traditionally, engineering has been a male-dominated profession, and to a large extent it remains so, not least through the general reluctance of females to take engineering and other scientific disciplines at university. Both through its recruitment policy, and by offering flexible working arrangements such as career breaks, Rolls-Royce is trying to retain and promote women within engineering. There are a handful of senior women within the organization who can act as role models, but progress is slower than the company would like.

The company employs a variety of techniques to communicate information through the organization. As well as the standard written forms of communication such as employee newspapers, there are also briefing and focus groups which are designed to communicate change to lower levels.

Contact address

John Rivers
Human Resources Director
Rolls-Royce plc
65 Buckingham Gate
London SW1E 6AT
Telephone: 0171 222 9020
Fax: 0171 227 9178
Web site: http://www.rolls-royce.com

The Royal Bank of Scotland plc

The Royal Bank of Scotland is the largest company based in Scotland and is widely respected as a European innovator in banking strategy and products. It offers a wide range of financial services in Britain and overseas. With assets of £80 billion the group is the UK's seventh largest commercial bank and consistently rated as a leader in customer services. As with the 1997 full year profits (up 15 per cent at £801 million), the 1998 full year profit of a record £1.001 billion shows RBS as developing its future businesses from a solid base.

Royal Bank of Scotland at a glance

Employees: 30,000 worldwide, 20,000 UK
Annual staff attrition: 11 per cent
Key locations: Edinburgh (HQ), with regional headquarters in London and Manchester. More than 700 high street branches throughout England, Scotland and Wales
Annual graduate intake: 100
Annual intake: n/a

An inside view

Banking is a sector which both urgently needs and regularly lacks innovation. Its tradition as a solid, steady market sector which inherently dislikes volatility and abhors risk is slowly, almost painstakingly, being eroded. The leading high street operators appear to have difficulty understanding what efficient management and quality of customer service really means. Well-managed operations in the banking sector are few and far between. There are notable and outstanding exceptions – and the Royal Bank of Scotland is one of them.

Characterized by serious financial journalists in Scotland as the most commercial and innovative bank in its markets, RBS has often startled its rivals with enterprising vision and a flexibility of approach uncommon in financial services. Its partnerships with mainland European bankers, its launch of telephone banking and the formidable success of Direct Line insurance are all examples of RBS going where others fear to tread.

The group's chief executive, Dr George Mathewson, is confident that UK Bank, Direct Line and the US based Citizens Financial Group, will continue its profitable expansion in the years to come. He does of course have good reason to say this. For more than a decade the Royal Bank of Scotland has shown a willingness to lead the way against its competitors.

The bank was the first in the UK to have all its branches connected on line to a central computer; the first to introduce full Internet banking services; play a prominent role in launching the switch debit card, and was first to introduce laser-etched photographs of customers on plastic cards, thereby helping to cut fraud by 99 per cent. Indeed during 1997 a new company, RBS Cards, was set up to lead the development of new products, with its first launch being the Au Gold MasterCard. The card is attracting substantially new balances from its target market of low-risk customers.

In 1985 RBS's Direct Line insurance service was set up, offering motor, home, life and travel insurance, as well as personal loans and mortgages. It had a major impact on the general insurance industry which it continues to out perform. Another subsidiary, Direct Line Accident Management, has created a network of motor accident repair centres throughout the UK.

UK banking remains the engine room of the group's frontline business. In all three sectors – retail, corporate and institutional, and offshore banking – substantial earning growth has been achieved. A continuing pattern of increased profits is expected during the next five years although the UK Bank's chief executive, Iain Robertson, admits that this will only happen with improved cross-selling, better marketing, concentration on good quality business, further investment in training and systems, and creativity and flexibility. As with other financial institutions further exposure to an unsettled Asian market is not being ignored although the recent turmoil there has had little impact on the bank.

How does Royal Bank of Scotland rate?

Pay:	good
Benefits:	very good
Communications:	very good
Training:	very good
Career development:	good
Morale:	good

People and personnel policies

To become a first choice employer in a highly competitive sector the Royal Bank of Scotland's managers in the two main arms of the group – retail and corporate – have sought to employ the best people, with ability, initiative and ambition. In principal employee groups are customer service personnel, relationship managers and the lending function, with a career structure for each.

The bank's managers are well trained in staff selection techniques. Their aim is to achieve results through training, skills planning, improved resources while at the same time closely monitoring employee development and performance. Innovation, creativity, and teamwork and collaboration are seen as essential to the group's business success in the eyes of both the bank and its customers. The bank has also opted to introduce new reward packages based on an individual's performance level. To this end internal human resource policy is designed to highlight what RBS views as critical to its future. HR director Neil Roden stresses that the ultimate aim is to transform his division's function from being administration-focused to getting people to consider how best the business itself can be transformed.

'At present, the vast majority of our activities are about providing services as efficiently as we can. We are not yet in the business of proactively contributing to the bank's success in partnership with line management. That will have to change,' he says.

As part of that re-framing process he sees nine key objectives: values and behaviours; leadership capability; performance management; employment costs; reward strategy; skills base; employment relationships; HR development; and human resources. As to the last initiative, Roden, admits there are some concerns.

'There are significant regional variations in labour supply and a specific skills shortage. London continues to present problems in the attraction and retention of high calibre staff, while IT staff are commanding greater premiums in the run up to the Year 2000 and European Monetary Union. There is also a shortage of quality executive talent.'

The Royal Bank of Scotland can hardly be called inward looking. It is utilizing the experiences of some of the world's most innovative companies in reshaping its HR strategy. Through its membership of the Corporate Leadership Council, a globally sponsored research initiative involving 700 companies, the bank has access to a wealth of case material. Roden stresses that the bank will not be seen as an organization heading into the twenty-first century clinging on to old ideas and practices. He adds that it is vital RBS takes note of what is happening in the external world, interprets the information, tailors it to the bank's own circumstances and uses it as a focus for action.

The Royal Bank of Scotland has also introduced a benefits choice plan – RBS*elect* – which gives employees the option to tailor their existing benefit package to meet their unique individual needs. Some of the options include health benefits, i.e. private medical insurance, health screening and dental insurance. There are various lifestyle features such as personal lease car, and retail and childcare vouchers. Needless to say this new plan also benefits the employer, allowing the bank to continue attracting the right people and maintain a competitive pay structure.

Contact address

Neil Roden
Director, Human Resources
The Royal Bank of Scotland plc
PO Box 31
42 St Andrew Square
Edinburgh EH2 2YE
Telephone: 0131 523 2022
Fax: 0131 551 3084
Web site: http://www.rbs.co.uk

Safeway plc

Safeway is one of Britain's most dynamic and innovative retailers. The business has been strengthened in recent years by its successful implementation of the Safeway 2000 strategy taking annual sales in 1998 to £7.5 billion. This places Safeway firmly among the key players in the grocery industry, currently operating more than 470 stores, with 76,000 employees. Safeway's priorities now are sales growth, efficiency and shareholder value with the Customer Promise being at the core of business strategy. The Customer Promise provides the main point of difference between Safeway and its competitors. The Safeway Customer Promise is: 'Making shopping easier for families with young children'. Safeway sees its people as key to helping achieve the Customer Promise; a strong emphasis is therefore placed on being a good employer and investing in the training and development of its staff.

Safeway at a glance

Employees: 76,000
Annual staff attrition: 28 per cent
Key locations: HQ in Hayes, Middlesex and over 470 stores including Isle of Man, Gibraltar, Channel Islands and Northern Ireland
Annual graduate intake: 100–150
Annual staff intake: 25,000

An inside view

Safeway along with Tesco, Sainsbury and ASDA, has revolutionized the retail food market in the last 20 years. There has been a massive switch to supermarket shopping with the leading food retailers now accounting for more than 60 per cent of the market. Safeway has been responsible for a number of successful initiatives and innovations, many of which have since been imitated by competitors. The company is now concentrating on sales growth, efficiency and shareholder value. Its aim is to meet the family shoppers' expectations and demands in respect of range, availability, value and service. The Customer Promise is the driving force behind creating a better shopping environment for the family shopper with friendlier, more attractive, and better laid-out and stocked stores.

The company aims to match the industry leader across all its ranges of products, and to be the best in the sector in those product categories which are identified as particularly important to its customers. To achieve this the company is applying the principles of category management to identify how it can better meet the customer's requirements. This has resulted in revised product ranges, new products, improved merchandising and store layouts and specialist service and advice in key product categories.

Product availability, a key factor in retailer success, has improved as a result of the Fill that Gap! strategy which revolutionized shelf replenishment practices. The benefits were achieved through more effective communication between stores, depots and central divisions and a better understanding throughout the business of the factors which affect availability.

Safeway believes that its Customer Promise distinguishes it from its major competitors. Its focus on making shopping easier for families with young children was the most important single outcome of the Safeway 2000 programme. The company responded to customer feedback which indicated that it was trailing behind other supermarkets in terms of value by launching a number of initiatives. Price Protected has now been applied to around 500 products and guarantees that if any of the products covered by the scheme can be bought cheaper elsewhere the customer can have the product for free, or their money back. The Baby Discount scheme offers a ten per cent discount for six months to ABC cardholders with babies under 12 months old.

How does Safeway rate?

Pay:	good
Benefits:	good
Communications:	excellent
Training:	excellent
Career development:	good
Morale:	very good

People and personnel policies

Colin Smith, chief executive, is determined that Safeway should continue to provide its people with the same level of care given to its customers. He is committed to ensuring that the best people are recruited and equipped with the skills they need to do their jobs effectively, while being rewarded for achievement. He also sees effective two-way dialogue as an essential feature of the workplace.

Basic remuneration is set against an organization structure of ten levels across the whole company ranging from chief executive to check-out operator, and is very competitive. The ten-grade structure has made decision making quicker and more effective and, by widening individual spans of control, has given managers more accountability. The company also operates a profit related pay scheme.

Safeway has a three- and five-year savings related share option scheme, a pension scheme, life assurance and accident insurance schemes for all staff. Healthcare insurance is provided free to most managers and at a heavily discounted rate to all other employees. In November 1997, Safeway launched a share option plan for everyone in the business linked to Customer Service Standards.

The company is highly committed to staff training and communications. It recognizes that its employees represent its public image and that staff attitudes, knowledge and helpfulness encourage or deter customers. Each store has appointed a manager responsible for in-store customer service and ensures that staff are fully briefed on both strategic and operational issues. The company has a recognition system which encourages prompt awards to individuals for exemplary service. Managers make an immediate award of, for example, chocolates or flowers when a member of staff has done something exceptionally well. This represented a major change in management philosophy by rewarding employees for achievement rather than catching them out and admonishing them for doing something wrong.

The Safeway training programme focuses on the customer. It also emphasizes the importance of good internal communications to ensure that employees are fully briefed on strategic and operational procedures. Safeway prides itself on the informal culture within its stores which are supported by professional systems and training and which therefore encourage employee participation.

The company recruits between 100 and 150 graduates each year and has a strong management development programme. Graduates are moved around the organization and across disciplines to broaden their experience. They are also given demanding roles early in their career, rather than entering lengthy training programmes.

Safeway was the first retailer to introduce behavioural assessment and development centres more than 15 years ago. The centres have been adapted and modified as demands have changed. The company has identified a framework of 16 competencies which it regards as essential for the effective development of its managers. These competencies provide individuals with a focus to identify what behaviours they need to develop to fuel their progression through the organization. Safeway does not dictate the pattern of careers but expects the employee to take an equal level of responsibility for the direction of his or her personal career.

Contact address

Jim White
Director of HR
Safeway plc
6 Millington Road
Hayes
Middlesex UB3 4AY
Telephone: 0181 756 2489
Fax: 0181 573 5101
Web site: http://www.safeway.co.uk

The Sage Group

Sage is the UK's undisputed market leader in PC-based business software. Based in Newcastle-upon-Tyne, the group's software portfolio is based on 18 years of continuous product development. Sage continues to expand its international presence, moving into France, Germany and the United States in recent years. The group markets itself towards small and medium-sized businesses and, by means of its respected brand name, aims to provide a sense of security and reassurance in the complex world of computer technology.

Sage at a glance

Employees: 2,800 worldwide
Annual staff attrition: 5 per cent
Key locations: Newcastle-upon-Tyne plus companies in the US, Germany and France
Annual graduate intake: 5
Annual intake: 100–150

An inside view

Sage Group is one of the UK's most dynamic and successful IT companies. Eighteen years of continuous product development, organic growth and expansion through acquisition, and dedication to the customer have driven its evolution. In 1985, the business reworked an old CPM accounting package which it then sold at £100 a unit. Within four years, the company had been listed on the London Stock Exchange. Today, the group has over 2 million customers worldwide.

Sage Group offers accounting and payroll software and related products for personal computers, with a comprehensive range of products designed to offer solutions for small- and medium-sized businesses. It is currently broadening its range by developing new business software products, including solutions for electronic banking and commerce. One of the primary reasons for its success has been its attention to customer service. Sage views customers as the single most important aspect of its business approach, setting out to be loyal to its customers throughout their business life.

It also recognizes the vital importance of the relationship between accountants and its customers, and has a dedicated division to support accountants in practice. A significant development for the group in 1998 was the acquisition of State of the Art Inc (SOTA), a leading US accounting software publisher which sells its products through the Value Added Reseller channel. The purchase gave Sage a strong strategic presence in the important US market. Three other important acquisitions in the UK were PACS, suppliers of final accounts production software, and PASE, suppliers of cash flow forecasting software, based in Berwick-on-Tweed.

The group uses nationwide training centres not only to offer training to customers but also to update accredited Sage resellers with the latest information on Sage software and other developments. All courses are run by full-time, fully trained Sage personnel. In a wider context, Sage has established links with the education sector to promote excellence in the fields of accounting, payroll and information technology.

Sage employs people in a range of disciplines: software development; support; product management; sales and marketing; distribution and administration. Many of those work closely with the company's clients, so good communication skills are vital. Most importantly, however, Sage recognizes it has to be a responsive and innovative organization – employees must demonstrate that they have the mental agility and initiative to satisfy the needs of increasingly demanding customers.

The Information Technology sector is characterised by a rapid and constant rate of change, and Sage needs people who can prosper in such a dynamic environment. Team skills and a positive 'can-do' approach are also valued, as is a proven track record of completing large projects. A knowledge of accounting, tax, payroll or vertical markets such as manufacturing is generally considered an advantage.

How does Sage rate?

Pay:	good
Benefits:	good
Communications:	good
Training:	very good
Career development:	excellent
Morale:	very good

People and personnel policies

Over the last 12 months or so, Sage has undertaken a number of initiatives designed to retain its status as one of the industry's preferred employers. In particular, HR directors have been appointed to all of the group's main operating companies. Sage has also improved recruitment processes, invested in career planning programmes, developed a broad range of internal training programmes, and effected a number of exchange programmes within the group, all with the aim of improving recruitment, retention and development of its workforce.

In order to sustain its growth, Sage needs constantly to recruit high-calibre software development professionals. Much of its recruitment tends to be from reputable software houses, consultancies and blue-chip end-user organizations. Importantly, the group's focus is on an individual's relevant experience rather than his or her relevant skills. It is more than happy to train employees who have the right experience, but who may simply lack knowledge of the latest technology.

Ensuring staff have access to the latest market knowledge is fundamental to Sage's success, and consequently, training is accorded the highest priority within the group.

Throughout its development, Sage has been a proponent of promotion from within, and this policy extends to any role in the company. It regularly asks those who are not in a management position to put themselves for management assessment. In addition, managers are asked to identify those who they feel have the potential to progress further within the company and are assessed on their own team-building capabilities. Through measures such as these, Sage has successfully developed its own management culture.

In common with other leading companies, Sage is moving increasingly to performance-related remuneration packages. In recent years, the demand for IT services has grown strongly, forcing wages higher: by keeping pace with these developments, however, Sage has not experienced some of the staff shortages which have afflicted other companies in the sector.

Contact address

Karen Geary
Human Resources Director
Sage Software Limited
Sage House
Benton Park Road
Newcastle-upon-Tyne NE7 7LZ
Telephone: 0191 255 3000
Fax: 0191 255 0309
Web site: http://www.sage.com

J Sainsbury plc

J Sainsbury is one of the world's leading retailers, operating three separate store chains in the UK, a supermarket chain in the US and a bank in the UK. Through these operations it serves 14.2 million customers a week. As Britain's oldest major food retailing chain – it was formed in 1869 – and retailer of clothes, household goods, do-it-yourself and hardware products, the company places great emphasis on high quality, value for money and responsiveness to customer needs. Sainsbury's aims to be seen as a world-class retailer. This will be achieved by planned expansion, and the continuous implementation of pace-setting training and career development programmes for its workforce, linked to personal targets for managers and teams.

Sainsbury's at a glance

Employees: 180,000 worldwide, 160,000 UK (70 per cent part-time)
Annual staff attrition: 20 per cent
Key locations: 750 UK stores; 130 in the US
Annual graduate intake: 650
Annual intake: 40,000

An inside view

By any measure, Sainsbury's is a retailing success story. Operating in the fiercely competitive retailing sector, the company has emerged from its historical position as a chain of high street grocery shops, mainly in the south of England, to become a dominant player at the forefront of the national retailing revolution. At the end of March 1998 its annual turnover had reached £15.5 billion.

The supermarket network forms the largest part of the group, serving 9 million customers each week at 380 outlets from Cornwall to Scotland, Wales and Northern Ireland. Around 60 per cent of these are in shopping centres or edge of town developments, in line with Sainsbury's commitment to urban regeneration.

Typically, one of the larger Sainsbury's stores will sell 23,000 products, with own brand labels accounting for 40 per cent of sales. In addition to food and grocery products, many stores also offer freshly baked bread, delicatessen, fresh meat and fish counters, pharmacies, coffee shops and restaurants, and petrol stations. A total of around 127,000 are employed in these stores. Some 70 per cent are part-time. Women make up 65 per cent of the workforce. Sainsbury's opened 20 new stores in 1997 and a further 18 were planned for 1998-9. Major extensions were scheduled at 21 existing stores.

The quality of food and the responsiveness to customer requirements are paramount in the company culture. Managers carry out benchmark exercises on own label products as a matter of systematic practice, and buyers and food technologists make ongoing improvements. This process has earned the company many prestigious awards. In the industry-standard A C Nielsen Homescan consumer survey, Sainsbury's was rated top for the second year running. The award was given for range of product, quality, service and fully-stocked shelves. Tesco attained second place, and ASDA was third.

Sainsbury's also carries out its own survey among customers to discover what new products they would like to see on the shelves. This innovation led to more than 1,100 new own label products being introduced in 1998. Also, the number of organic lines doubled to 320.

The 13 Savacentres are large stores which offer the biggest range available in the group. They embrace clothing, household goods, toys, gardening and electrical products. More than 1 million customers use Savacentres, which in total employ more than 10,000 people. In addition there are 300 Homebase D-I-Y stores, which sell home improvement and gardening products. The current focus for development is on the home-enhancement side of the business with the addition of decorative items, such as lighting, and bathroom-fitting and garden design services. Homebase employs 17,000 people.

Shaw's Supermarkets Inc, is the wholly owned US subsidiary with 130 stores in New England. It has a workforce of 20,000. Back in the UK, Sainsbury's Bank was inaugurated in 1997. This is a joint venture with the Bank of Scotland (55 per cent Sainsbury's, 45 per cent Bank of Scotland). Sainsbury's was the first UK supermarket group to offer 24-hour telephone banking. In the space of a year it had won 700,000 customers and has more than £1.5 billion in deposits. It is currently expanding its portfolio of financial services products.

How does Sainsbury's rate?

Pay:	good
Benefits:	good
Communications:	excellent
Training:	very good
Career development:	very good
Morale:	good

People and personnel policies

Like any other major retailer, Sainsbury's recognizes that to succeed and grow in an increasingly competitive marketplace where customers demand and expect higher and better standards, it must have excellent people. To meet its corporate goal of being 'The customer's first choice', it is committed to motivating and developing its employees to meet and exceed customer demand.

Sainsbury's is conscious of the reputation of the retail sector as an employer – and is determined to set standards which will make it an attractive choice for people choosing between careers. It has faced the problem head-on by creating a climate where everyone is valued and personal contributions are encouraged and respected. The impact of this approach is a workforce which is responsive to the diversity of customers. It has also been creative in its use of a range of workplace techniques which make optimum use of the skills and talents of all employees. It positively encourages the team ethos in which hard work and opportunity go hand-in-hand, and individual effort is rewarded. Some store managers, for example, are individually responsible for businesses valued at £50 million a year.

The large food retailers offer a portfolio of career paths which are attractive to people with diverse interests. These include store management, routes in distribution and pharmacy or head office functions in finance, logistics, scientific services, trading and IT. For its future generation of managers, Sainsbury's seeks out A level school leavers, graduates or mature managers. There are also opportunities for vacation training, and business placement for penultimate undergraduates researching career possibilities.

The group spends around £40 million on staff training and career development – and the potential for progression is excellent. For example, the retail management training scheme, which lasts approximately 12 months, is designed to provide a strong business focus and early exposure to management responsibility. It also develops technical skills, leadership potential and team building as well as core retail requirements such as customer service, merchandising and display. Trainees will identify learning needs, undertake technical skills development, work shadow, understand personnel management, and complete project work. On completion of each training module, performance is reviewed by a departmental manager. At the end of the scheme, a panel including a district manager, line and personnel officers assess progress. The successful candidates are then appointed as managers of their own departments.

No one is left in any doubt about the realities of working in retail: long hours, weekend working, early starts, late finishes, varying customer demands, and the flexibility to move from store to store. Sainsbury's returns this commitment by supporting the Investors in People standard, which reaffirms the commitment to training and development of all employees throughout the group. Investors in People status is a constant reminder of the importance of high standards in the working environment, its commitment to performance management and effective communication.

Along with other leading retailers, Sainsbury's is an active member of CORTCO, a voluntary organization dedicated to presenting the industry in a positive light to attract talented graduates with both the intellectual and personal qualities needed to maintain the growth of the industry.

Contact address

Resourcing Department
J Sainsbury plc
Stamford House
Stamford Street
London SE1 9LL
Telephone: 0171 695 6742
Fax: 0171 695 8149
Web site: http://www.sainsburys.co.uk

Schlumberger

Since its inception more than 70 years ago, the US oil industry multinational Schlumberger has grown into a world leader generating annual revenues of more than $10 billion. The company enjoys an enviable reputation as a leader in new technology in the sectors of oilfield services, and measurement and systems, and although Schlumberger may not be a household name, its products and services are at the heart of our day-to-day activities. With operations in 100 countries, employing 60,000 people at some 930 facilities, Schlumberger is a truly global company of great cultural diversity.

Schlumberger at a glance

Employees: 63,500 worldwide (60 per cent oilfield services, 40 per cent measurement & systems), 4,700 UK (43 per cent oilfield services, 57 per cent measurement & systems)
Annual staff attrition: 4 per cent
Key locations: Some 930 in 100 countries. UK: 11 onshore sites plus various offshore. Oilfield services at London, Aberdeen, Great Yarmouth, Shetlands, Gatwick and Cambridge. Measurement & Systems at Felixstowe, Port Glasgow, Manchester, Blackburn, Dundee and Ferndown
Annual graduate intake: 100
Annual intake: 150–200

An inside view

The sole activity of the company for the first 30 years of its existence, and the original foundation for Schlumberger's success, was the revolutionary application of wireline logging to the detection of oil-bearing formations deep in the ground. Since then, the company's development has been fuelled by the growth of its wireline services and its expansion into other oilfield activities such as seismic, drilling, pumping, testing and data processing businesses. Today, Schlumberger Oilfield Services is a world leader in the development and supply of virtually every type of oil and gas exploration and production service including hardware and software.

Schlumberger's remarkable growth has led to diversification into other areas. Resource Management Services provides water, gas and electricity industry clients with metering technologies and solutions worldwide. Test & Transactions supplies technology, products, services and systems, such as smart and magnetic stripe cards and associated terminals, as well as automated testing and handling equipment, to the semi-conductor, banking, telecommunication, retail petroleum, transportation and health care industries. Omnes provides information technology and communications services to oil, gas and other companies operating in remote areas of the world.

First and foremost, Schlumberger's business is based on its ability to develop and apply new technological solutions in ways suited to clients' needs. A key factor in the company's success is its flat organizational structure and the way in which it operates through highly decentralized business units, enabling autonomy and responsibility to be devolved to those closest to clients and daily business challenges.

With a wide range of activities all over the world, Schlumberger values mobility, both geographical and functional, and in fact considers it essential for the growth of its business and for people's personal and career development. The company sees its cultural diversity as a distinct advantage in the development of creativity and flexibility and in providing people with a different outlook and approach to problems. Its employees operate as members of teams which can be made up of various functions, cultures, nationalities and management styles, and such interaction between different types of people leads to creative and imaginative ways of doing business.

How does Schlumberger rate?

Pay:	excellent
Benefits:	very good
Communications:	good
Training:	superb
Career development:	excellent
Morale:	very good

People and personnel policies

Schlumberger is renowned for the quality of training provided to its graduate entrants. In wireline and testing, which is part of Schlumberger's core business of oilfield services, field engineers spend their first month in a 'pre-school' at a well site, where they gain an understanding of what the work involves and the culture of the company. There follows an intensive three-month training programme – up to 11 hours a day, six days a week – where trainees learn and are tested on the operation of particular tools, how to repair them and how to understand what the equipment reveals and explain this to clients.

Trainees are expected to succeed at both programmes in order to continue with the company. While the success rate of 90 per cent at the pre-school is high, a significant proportion of trainees do not complete the subsequent stage, which has a drop-out rate of around 25 per cent. Trainees then work for a while on a project with another engineer and the client. In Measurement and Systems, recruits are employed immediately as part of a project team, perhaps working in development, marketing and sales or manufacturing. They take part in an induction process followed by training courses over a period of time with the support of a mentoring programme. Generally speaking, the atmosphere is less dynamic and more stable.

One of Schlumberger's key beliefs is that individuals develop when they move away from where they are comfortable and it encourages geographical and functional mobility by providing extraordinary opportunities for travel and movement between business units as long as the individual can perform. It should be said that there are definite career advantages to being mobile and flexible in outlook and that the better a person can handle change, the better he or she will progress within the company.

One of Schlumberger's essential policies is to promote from within. The proof of the success of its superb training and career development strategy, combined with a very good pay and benefits package, is found in the fact that most of its senior managers have grown through the company. The open structure encourages communication within the organisation.

Schlumberger is a truly diverse, multi-cultured global company, which encourages individualism as a key factor in the generation of new ideas. There are genuinely no barriers due to religion, race, colour or language. The company realizes that to make use of the best talent available it cannot exclude any parts of the world, including women who make up half of the population. For the past seven years, Schlumberger has been actively encouraging women to join the company through a programme which includes the running of seminars with AWISE (Association of Women in Science and Engineering) and other initiatives. Not so long ago, out of an induction class of perhaps 12 field engineers only one might have been a woman, but now perhaps half will be women.

Schlumberger describes its personnel approach as being one of 'borderless careers'. It operates at the cutting edge on technology which will fundamentally change the way in which we live. Groundbreaking projects include research to increase the oil recovery rate from 35 per cent to 70 per cent and the smart card which will be used in the near future to provide a multitude of services from shopping and banking to security access. For people who are creative and flexible, can handle responsibility and are prepared to take the initiative at the same time as enjoying problem solving and dealing with people from diverse backgrounds, Schlumberger offers highly prized opportunities to broaden their horizons as they move between locations, functions and product lines within the entire Schlumberger group.

Contact address

Mr Hugh Fordham
Schlumberger University Relations & Recruitment
UK & Ireland
High Cross
Madingley Road
Cambridge CB3 0EL
Telephone: 01223 325214
Fax: 01223 311523
Web site: http://www.slb.com

Schroders

Backed by more than 200 years of experience, Schroders is widely recognized as one of the leading investment banks working in the City. It distinguishes itself from its competitors by leading the way in high-quality internal management and is renowned for its productivity, independent stance, profitability and professional competence. Although based in the UK, Schroders is a global company and has a range of offices in all the important financial centres. Schroders is popular both with graduates, drawn by its training programme and fast-paced lifestyle, and more experienced personnel.

Schroders at a glance

Employees: 6,600
Annual staff attrition: 10 per cent (UK)
Key locations: City of London (HQ) and all major financial centres
Annual graduate intake: 60 (UK) in 1998
Annual intake: 300 (UK) to June 1998

An inside view

Other investment banks frequently endeavour to make a name for themselves in every market, but Schroders employs a somewhat different, and highly successful, strategy. It focuses on the business areas and opportunities where it has particular skills, consequently producing outstanding results in certain market sectors. The company is split into the investment banking division (encompassing securities, corporate finance and financial markets) and the investment management division. The UK has leasing and a global venture capital operation. Schroders' reputation as one of the finest and most effectively run banks in the industry can also be credited to its thorough understanding of its business and skilled management.

Within the period of the last three years, Schroders' securities business has gone from virtually nowhere to the top ten of both the pan-European and Japanese broking houses. The securities division is recognized for its expertise in sales, research, sales trading and trading and headway is being made into the United States, selling European equities to American fund managers through the New York sales desk.

Celebrated as the investment banker's banker, Schroders corporate finance teams have been involved in many of the major banking mergers for the past five years. It is consistently ranked in the top three players in the European mergers and acquisitions market. In the first half of 1998 Schroders was ranked first with 11 transactions valued at £15 billion. In the Financial Markets Group, the financing team has advised on £26 billion of acquisition finance over the past three-years, and the division is working on key projects including advice to the government on its Channel Tunnel rail link.

Schroders Investment Management division is international with 27 offices in 26 countries, managing balanced portfolios founded on investments in equities, bonds, cash and property. As one of the top three fund management houses in the UK, the firm's success is strengthened by a flourishing reputation in specialist portfolios, concentrating on smaller companies and international bonds.

One of Schroders' greatest assets is the respectful and co-operative working culture which it has cultivated amongst employees. In the intensely competitive business environment of the investment banking world, support systems are highly valued by employees. A full network of support services including financial control, compliance, IT, and personnel assists Schroders' main market sectors but more importantly each individual is guaranteed the consistent backup of team leaders and co-workers.

Schroders looks for top graduates, taking only the best of a select group of energized, intelligent and very hard-working people who will be able to fit quickly and competently into the fast-paced environment. Personality plays a vital role in which area the newcomer to Schroders is placed. Attributes required to be a successful dealer on the trading floor are going to be markedly different from those needed to do well in corporate finance.

How does Schroders rate?

Pay:	excellent
Benefits:	good
Communications:	good
Training:	good
Career development:	excellent
Morale:	very good

People and personnel policies

All new recruits to Schroders have to undergo a three-month induction course of intensive study. Part of it is a broad programme that covers the essentials and every graduate has to complete it, regardless of which area of the company they hope to go into. In the first week trainees learn about each business area and then the training for the individual divisions begins, detailing an increasingly meticulous and technical analysis of the processes, tools and techniques that will be needed.

Schroders is structured in small teams specific to certain divisions and their sub-groups, so an essential part of training is team building. New recruits meet with senior managers, newly appointed executives and with graduates from overseas offices to establish vital working relationships. Training objectives form part of an annual assessment that all employees undergo and responsibility is put into the hands of each individual to achieve their targets. Schroders also offers a comprehensive summer internship programme to undergraduates in their penultimate year, giving practical experience in the field before final career decisions are made.

The prospects for career developments within Schroders are excellent for highly-motivated people. Employees are expected to work hard, be very committed to projects and achieve early success. In return, early responsibility is given readily along with the opportunity to have your views heard and acted upon, even in a junior position. Schroders is a young environment and rapid advancement is possible, depending on performance and ambition.

While there is little cross-functional movement between disciplines, for example from capital markets to the trading floor, the company is flexible within divisions so an employee can transfer from a corporate finance team to the equity capital markets team with full company support. There is some migration between countries. For example, the joint managing director of financial markets, currently based in Asia, originally came out of the Australian business. Development is increasingly on-the-job and self-directed, in a supportive environment where the 'star culture' is not prevalent.

Schroders pays extremely well in what is already a highly paid industry and revenue earners are rated favourably in the company. Performance related pay is the norm defined using wide-ranging criteria spanning from on-line contributions to effective teamwork. As one would expect from a firm of this size in a competitive marketplace, a generous benefits package is offered.

The personnel department is vital to the success of the company as it creates the culture of people for which Schroders is renowned. Its focus is on getting the best people to fit the criteria for each different task that arises. It constantly reviews the selection process to ensure the right person is found for the job in the ever-changing environment of investment banking. Schroders uses only highly qualified recruiters and selectors and regularly benchmarks against the best in the business. Schroders is an intensely business-focused company with exacting standards of professionalism which retains its staff through commitment to the personal growth of each individual.

Contact address

Graduate Recruitment Officer
Schroders plc
120 Cheapside
London EC2V 6DS
Telephone: 0171 658 6000
Fax: 0171 658 3950
Web site: http://www.schroders.com/graduaterecruitment

Shell Transport and Trading Company plc

Shell, like all the petro-chemicals giants, faces a challenging future. In summer 1998 the company announced that it was preparing to close its London headquarters. In what appears a remarkable departure, the Anglo-Dutch oil company has taken a decision which recognizes the realities of its commercial environment. It says that its commitment to the UK is unaffected but that running twin headquarters was wasteful. The Shell Transport and Trading Company, a publicly quoted UK company together with Royal Dutch Petroleum, owns (in proportions of 40–60 respectively) the Royal Dutch/Shell Group of Companies. It is one of the world's largest and most successful businesses, and has operated here since its inception. The group reported net earnings of $4.7 billion in 1997. Shell recently completed an internal reorganization of its activities to improve its responsiveness and business focus.

Shell at a glance

Employees: 100,000 worldwide, 10,000 UK
Annual staff attrition: 2 per cent
Key locations: London, many others around the UK. HQ in The Hague
Annual graduate intake: 250
Annual intake: n/a

An inside view

For many years Shell has been regarded by the corporate world as a benchmark employer. Its holistic commitment to professionalism, integrity and quality stems from decades of structured, polished multinational management. In every area of the group's operation, Shell is viewed as a standard-bearer for enhanced shareholder value, creative innovation, efficient salesmanship and competent management. In many ways, the group is a model of modern international commercial leadership.

Its planning and corporate development skills have formerly been regarded as awesome – among a party of perhaps only five multinationals with equivalent depth of business understanding. But Shell has also been like one of its tankers, slow to turn. A recent restructuring attempted to address Shell's long-term market objectives in a world where the last big oilfield – in the former Soviet Union countries – takes the company and its main rivals only to the middle of the twenty-first century.

Shell is now divided into five basic business areas: exploration and production; oil products (covering refining, trading, shipping and marketing); chemicals; renewals; and gas and power. Each of these business areas incorporates a series of underlying operating companies and is also responsible for performing its own research (whereas previously research was carried out centrally). It is the operating companies which remain the principal entities through which business is conducted. Shell's philosophy is that managers should have as much autonomy as possible and that decisions should be made close to the customer interface. Supporting the entire business structure is a series of service companies, and the general rule is that bureaucracy should be reduced wherever possible.

Shell's core values are professionalism and integrity. In addition, it attempts to engender in its workforce a sense of pride in working for Shell and, increasingly, a respect for diversity in colleagues, other people and the environment. Within this framework, however, the company is also trying to foster a more entrepreneurial spirit which it hopes will more successfully exploit the innate talents of its workforce. In return, Shell is introducing a much greater element of recognition and reward for individual performance.

Another characteristic which distinguishes Shell is that it attempts to take a long-term view of its business and people. While the company can no longer be considered as providing jobs for life, given the current trends in the labour market and the global economy, no responsible company can offer this. Although Shell has actually been reducing its headcount over the last five years, it does take career development issues more seriously than most companies and makes a conscious effort, where possible, to satisfy employee aspirations, especially through its open resourcing approach. Here, 95 per cent of openings are posted on the Shell intranet.

How does Shell rate?

Pay:	very good
Benefits:	good
Communications:	good
Training:	excellent
Career development:	excellent
Morale:	good

People and personnel policies

To reach the highest levels within Shell, candidates must be graduates who capture the imagination of managers and personnel officers. It looks for a series of specific qualities in its employees. Four of the most important are intellectual capacity, a record of achievement, and strong interpersonal skills and leadership. Shell rates managers against these criteria. Information on the high-fliers within Shell is held on a central database, allowing them to be easily matched against opportunities within the group. Increasingly, individual performance and personal skills – ability to work within a team, initiative and flexibility and talent for leadership performance – are seen as critical to ultimate success within the Shell organization.

At a central level, Shell has set up a Learning Centre based in the UK and the Netherlands where employees from across the group can come together and solve real-life business problems. It is hoped that this Learning Centre will also prove to be a successful way of improving communication and developing leadership skills within the organization. Through a variety of initiatives, Shell is attempting to place a greater onus on the individual to take responsibility for his or her own training and development.

A further key element is the company's value creation teams, whose function it is to drive change through the organization. The company is determined to unleash the potential inherent in its people and sees one of the principal ways of doing this as delegating authority down to the lowest possible level. Another increasingly common feature is the movement of individuals between different parts of the company and around the world, both to create multi-disciplinary skills and give them a wider appreciation of the business as a whole, and cross-cultural experiences.

Shell's policy is that its levels of remuneration should be in the top quartile. While this basic philosophy has remained unchanged, its approach to the way in which employees are remunerated has done so significantly. In particular, the variable pay element of the overall package has become much more important relative to salary. Bonuses are being introduced throughout the company based on business performance. At higher levels, executives are being rewarded through stock option schemes. Where necessary, Shell recognizes that it must pay very competitively to attract and retain the best people.

Given that the group operates in more than 120 countries, there is a rich diversity to Shell's workforce at lower levels. More importantly, however, this is now also being reflected at more senior levels in the organization. One area where the company acknowledges it is weak, and on which it is focusing attention, however, is in the number of women holding senior jobs within the workforce. Shell tries to encourage women to remain in the workforce by offering flexible working arrangements wherever possible.

Probably more so than most large companies, Shell is painfully aware of its responsibilities within the community. One of the key lessons of recent years was that the company needs to be much more effective in communicating reasons for its behaviour to people outside the company. For example, although ensuring that products and operations are safe and environmentally acceptable is now an integral part of all research programmes, this is not always widely appreciated. The Shell Report, a groundbreaking externally audited report on Shell's record on social and environmental dilemmas, makes Shell unique among the oil majors. In a further attempt to improve its profile, various members of the group are also heavily involved in arts and educational initiatives and sponsorship.

Contact address

Shell Global Recruitment
Shell Services International Limited
Shell Centre, London SE1 7NA
Telephone: 0171 934 3630
Fax: 0171 934 7606
Web site: http://www.shell.com

SmithKline Beecham plc

SmithKline Beecham is one of the world's great healthcare companies with considerable market share in the professional pharmaceutical and the consumer products sectors. The company is regularly included among the top five UK businesses in terms of creating shareholder value. SmithKline Beecham regards itself as stronger than ever and able to move ahead with confidence. It has a variety of new drug compounds in the pipeline – always vital for the long-term vitality of a healthcare company. Underlying sales were up 7 per cent in 1998 to £8.1 billion.

SmithKline Beecham at a glance

Employees: 58,000
Annual staff attrition: n/a
Key locations: London, Philadelphia
Annual graduate intake: n/a
Annual intake: n/a

An inside view

Healthcare is among a handful of industries which are growing at an exponential pace. Alongside software, telecommunications, media and entertainment, it is a rapidly expanding sector in an increasingly global market. The main players in healthcare realized – probably earlier than operators in most other disciplines – that the economics of the world market would hit their industry. They appreciated that to survive they would need to be more competitive, better at what they do, operate on a global scale and produce innovative – and lucrative – new products more efficiently than others. The writing has already appeared on the wall for some businesses that could not manage the global scale or the translation of ideas into new products.

SmithKline is destined to be a survivor. It is the product of a UK–US merger in 1989 which assembled America's SmithKline Beckman and Beecham from the UK. During the 1990s it has been boosted by a twin-track approach of solid organic growth and appropriate acquisition. The company has also earned notable respect among industrialists for the quality of its vision, the integrity of its management culture and its capacity to attract high calibre staff.

Almost every company in the healthcare and pharmaceutical fields says that it needs to attract top drawer people to compete globally against the best. They need lively minds, great robustness of character, a personal talent for enquiry and the ability either to work alone or in teams. SmithKline gets its fair share. It is an enormously attractive environment for scientists and researchers who are seeking out compounds to ease pain and conquer disease. Salespeople too have direct contact with healthcare professionals and their work can make a difference to many patients.

Each global healthcare company has a distinctive profile and SmithKline has widespread activities in the consumer field. Many of its consumer products are familiar to anyone shopping in supermarkets and chemists. It is a brand-led culture and not surprisingly with familiar names such as Panadol, Lucozade, Ribena, Aquafresh, Nicorette and Contact. Among its leading para pharmaceutical products are Augmentin, Infanrix, Coreg, Kytril and Seroxat/Paxil. These are major market products in anti-infective medicine, paediatric vaccines, cardiopulmonary conditions, neurological medicine and treatment of depression and panic respectively.

Key to a prosperous future for healthcare companies is to have a series of blockbuster compounds in trials as future income streams. Product development can take as long as a decade so these companies need to invest heavily in potential new products. The art is discovering potential winners at an early stage. Part of the process is continuing multilevel dialogue with healthcare professionals to anticipate likely future demand and developmental work both in-house and with biotechnology and biopharmaceutical discovery and development companies.

How does SmithKline Beecham rate?

Pay:	excellent
Benefits:	very good
Communications:	good
Training:	excellent
Career development:	very good
Morale:	superb

People and personnel policies

SmithKline Beecham is a textbook example of how a demanding and competitive business achieves improved efficiencies, remarkable innovations and exceeds increasing commercial targets while keeping its people on side. This is primarily because in a market sector defined by global standards and performance, SmithKline Beecham is a class act.

Across industry there are perhaps a dozen companies in the UK which are in a premier league of multinationals. These are the businesses that set the benchmarks for all other operators. When assessed by a variety of financial and non-financial indicators they emerge as top level players. In the legitimate annual surveys of shareholder value SmithKline Beecham is normally in the first three companies. And as an employer it would be in the top ten. Testimony to this is the low staff turnover and the considerable employee loyalty to the business.

In all measures of employment – pay, benefits, training, communication, career development – the company is a market leader. The culture is one of quality and excellence blended with a hard commercial drive. It should be said that the demands of the global healthcare market are so high that in order to compete, the real operators need to exceed their previous best standards on almost a daily basis.

The organization is leadership-driven. It aims to build leaders not only at management level but through the business. Its corporate literature encourages every member of the workforce to become a leader in his or her own area. Leadership and other personal targets are tied into a continuous improvement campaign for employees called Simply Better. This is based on a genuine and widespread desire for everyone to regularly outperform his or her own personal bests whether operating alone or as part of a team. One of the key values is to help employees to achieve more.

It is an uncompromising marketplace where products need to be excellent, the distribution channels and marketing skills have to be top notch and the investment and foresight in the long pipeline of research and development must be at a peak. Against that, a well-managed business must seek greater efficiencies and to get more out of its people.

This vigorous climate requires people of spirit, determination, energy, vision, vitality of thought and the capacity to get on with others. To recruit these people for roles in research, sales and marketing, production and professional functions, it invites applications from the top universities worldwide for its graduate recruitment scheme. The management access programme allows graduates to join a two-year initiation course, which includes assignments in various departments. Alternatively, graduates can join departments directly.

Pay and benefits in SmithKline Beecham are among the highest in the UK. Leschly says, 'We offer highly competitive pay and benefits packages that are, as much as possible, tied to performance.' Most employees are also part of share ownership plans and all members of staff join the corporate pension scheme. Communications are high quality and both global and local. These include newsletters, briefings and televised and video programmes.

Contact address

Human Resources
SmithKline Beecham plc
New Horizons Court
Brentford
Middlesex TW8 9EP
Telephone: 0181 975 2000
Fax: 0181 975 2001
Web site: http://www.sb.com

Sony UK Sales Company

Sony is the one of the world's largest electronics companies – and perhaps the most famous. The company's development since its foundation by the legendary Masaru Ibuka and Akio Morita, is a modern-day success story. It is active in broadcast, audio, visual, music, television and film production. Many of the world's leading television and radio stations operate predominately on Sony equipment, a high proportion of homes use Sony televisions, Walkman personal stereos, VCRs and camcorders, and many arenas and stadiums depend on Sony's display screens. The company is also a major supplier of computer monitors, computer peripherals, semi-conductors, electronic storage devices and other electronic components. It is a multi-billion dollar global company, employing 173,000 people.

Sony at a glance

Employees: 173,000 worldwide, 7,000 UK
Annual staff attrition: 9 per cent
Key locations: Sales head office at Weybridge, Surrey; manufacture of television sets, display monitors, cathode ray tubes and key components at Bridgend and Pencoed, South Wales; broadcast and professional European headquarters at Basingstoke, Hants
Annual graduate intake: 20–30
Annual intake: 300

An inside view

Sony has many different faces. It is a manufacturing company, a music company, a pictures company, an international marketing organization, and a sales company. Opportunities for graduates occur throughout the organization including within the sales company, based in Weybridge. The sales company is split into many different sales divisions, some with UK territories, and others with European responsibilities. The company's culture is dominated by the need to be a customer-responsive sales organization. The need for achievement is balanced by the unwritten need to maintain relationships. In a culture where people often have two or more 'bosses', having good business relationships, and maintaining good communications, in what would otherwise be regarded as an extremely confusing situation, becomes vital.

A remarkably frank appraisal of what being a 'Sony person' entails comes from Stephen Barrett, divisional director, human resources development. He says, 'The need to achieve objectives is balanced by a requirement to achieve them properly. Not all people are comfortable with this idea. Behaviour, the manner in which we go about things, the impression we leave with someone lasts much longer than the memory of what specific objectives we have achieved. However, if we fail to achieve, without good reason, no amount of 'good behaviour' can make up for it. Being creative and innovative, doing something better first, is important to us, not only in the products we bring to market, but also in our services and the way in which we do business. If you are not number one in a particular marketplace you cannot rest until you are. If you are already number one, then you cannot afford to give the position away by being complacent.

'People do feel under pressure working in such an environment. It seems you have to work harder each year just to stay where you are, and so everyone is trying to work smarter and is increasingly using technology to help speed up things. It is not that we are constantly demanding things of our people – their pride in what they do and in their contribution to the brand, encourages them to volunteer sometimes for unrealistic deadlines. In this respect there is a strong 'psychological contract' which provides for superior performance – but the price can be long hours and hard work, and in some cases the increasing momentum created by this can be unhealthy,' he says.

To many outsiders Sony is the quintessential Japanese multinational – it combines expertise in production and marketing, it is highly alert to the nuances of a vigorously competitive sector, it has developed original and thoughtful people policies and it consistently outstrips its rivals at home and throughout the world. Certainly the scope of Sony's vision in its sector is breathtaking. There is no other electronics company which has become brand leader in so many disciplines within its markets as Sony.

A common misconception of Japanese subsidiary companies is that they are rigidly structured, highly controlled by Tokyo, and that all they do is assemble kits manufactured in Japan. This is not the case with Sony. It was the first major Japanese company to establish a presence in the UK and it has enjoyed increasing autonomy, over the years, from the centre. The UK business is a component of the European region of the company, which is a fully fledged division of the global corporation, and to a large extent sets its own agenda in consultation with the rest of the Sony world. Increasingly, the British operation has provided its employees with remarkable freedom to rise within the business and to take on fresh areas of responsibility. The company genuinely has no barriers to ability. Regardless of gender, culture or background, people can make their mark on the business.

How does Sony rate?

Pay:	excellent
Benefits:	very good
Communications:	superb
Training:	excellent
Career development:	very good
Morale:	excellent

People and personnel policies

Many Japanese employers are perceived, falsely, to be ritualistic in their approach to human resources management, as some of the methods were different from what British employees had been used to, even though most served to empower the employee, and to give greater freedom in the job. At the core of the majority of Japanese-owned businesses lies a substantial respect for their staff. Wherever they have been based, Japanese businesses have served to revitalize local economies and they have, in the main, earned the respect of local workforces.

The fairness with which Sony has treated its people has been repaid with a high degree of personal loyalty. As a matter of core policy, Sony reflects the national culture of its local operations. The social structure of the parent is not evident in the daily operation of the British company. Sony UK is a European enterprise that gives its people remarkable freedom to make a creative contribution to the management and operation of the organization. Sony's respect for the individual employee is genuine and the absence of restriction on personal mobility within the business is remarkable. The company wants its employees to achieve and it allows scope for any individual to make a contribution to the success of the enterprise.

This is based on the company's HR policy that is framed around a mission statement that has remained the same for the last five years: 'to promote the effectiveness of Sony's most vital resource, our people, in achieving business objectives. Our goal is to support by providing a centre of expertise that meets our customer's needs and encourages innovation in recruitment, development and reward.' The value of this statement can only be measured by the actions and the changes in behaviour it promotes, and the company's HR short-term and mid-range objectives are all designed with this in mind. To further this, the company has introduced its performance management system RAP – Recognizing and Assessing Performance.

This system has three main aims: recognize and reward performance; maximize potential; and work smarter. The aims are achieved through a continuous feedback on individual performance, through which the contribution to corporate and divisional goals is measured and rewarded accordingly. An essential part of RAP is the Outstanding Performance Awards, given at the time of the annual salary review. These awards seek to recognize people, especially those who have stepped out of the confines of their job, who have volunteered or who have performed well beyond their job definitions.

The British business is a key component in Sony Europe and many of the daily management issues that emerge are settled at a European, rather than a corporate level. Contact with headquarters in Tokyo is substantially less now than it was before a regional operational framework was created. Despite its global scope, the company remains an entrepreneurial business. It is an extremely positive organization, which, while being shaped by an overriding commitment to quality and excellent performance in every sphere of its activities, also sees into the future of customer demand. Each individual who works for the business is part of The Sony Family, which may seem somewhat coy to British observers but indicates the strength of company team-working and fellow feeling.

Contact address

Stephen Barrett
Divisional Director
Human Resources
Sony UK Sales Company
Sony United Kingdom Limited
The Heights
Brooklands, Weybridge
Surrey KT13 0XW.
Telephone: 01932 816000
Fax: 01932 817000
Web site: http://www.sony-europe.com

Standard Chartered Bank

Until recent years the Standard Chartered Bank would be familiar only to businesses dealing with key overseas markets and a few people in the City. But its reputation in the wider commercial world has advanced rapidly and it gained standing by producing strong results against a background of upheavals in key regions. Standard Chartered has delivered a concerted programme of upgrading to maintain a leading role within the group's traditional Asian, African and Middle Eastern markets. And despite several recent economic earthquakes, the bank has continued to perform strongly. This is reflected in 1997 trading profits, up 11 per cent to £904 million. Half-yearly results in 1998 revealed further strong advances with profits before provisions up 27 per cent to £607 million.

Standard Chartered at a glance

Employees: 26,000, 2,500 UK
Annual staff attrition: 10 per cent
Key locations: London (HQ), Hong Kong, Singapore, over 500 offices worldwide
Annual graduate intake: 250 (50 Europe/US)
Annual intake: n/a

An inside view

The UK financial services sector is one of the largest net contributors to national income. In large measure this is due to the global reputation of The City as Europe's principal financial industry location. This pre-eminent position in international finance underscores the key role which British banks play in the prosperity of the UK economy.

Several of Britain's banks constructed their formidable success in overseas markets and none more so than Standard Chartered. But whereas many were unable to meet the challenge of modern practice in banking, Standard Chartered has survived and – in recent years – it has thrived. At once it represents the best of the UK's traditions in global banking and a vigorous up-to-date approach to commercial management.

It is profoundly more than a bank and is correctly characterized as a highly successful multinational financial services corporation, with a pre-eminent position in Asia, Africa, the Middle East and latterly in Latin America. Headquartered in London, the bank maintains strong local links through its network of over 500 offices in more than 40 countries.

Founded as the Chartered Bank of India, Australia and China, the group took on its present form following a merger in 1969 with The Standard Bank. Standard

Chartered, with its primary focus on the emerging markets, has won more awards for service and excellence than any other bank in Asia. The bank is also an active member of the communities in which its customers and staff live. The group has set aside £6 million to be spent during a three-year period (1998–2000) assisting those most in need, including youth, health and education orientated projects.

Recent years of structural change and economic growth have been overshadowed to some extent by economic and political crises in Asia, especially in Thailand, Indonesia and Korea. Nevertheless a long tradition of loyalty and investment within its principal markets, allied with sound risk management, have enabled Standard Chartered to effectively manage the turbulence when others have suffered. Whilst the group remains cautious in the short-term, it is confident about future progress in its own markets, bringing with it further expansion and development.

The internal changes that have been made have centred on the consolidation of Treasury, Consumer Banking and Corporate and Institutional banking into three distinct business groups. At the same time management within each country has been simplified and strengthened, to ensure a greater response to market shifts and adjustment to group policies and initiatives.

The bank's confidence in doing business in the emerging markets was highlighted in early 1998 with the purchase of a 67 per cent interest in Extebandes. This Latin American bank, renamed Banco Standard Chartered, has operations in Venezuela, Peru and Colombia. Further acquisitions are envisaged particularly in Asia and the Middle East.

Standard Chartered's chief executive, Rana Talwar, is optimistic of continued success even if he is under no illusions that there are major challenges ahead, including European Monetary Union and Year 2000 compliance, to further enhancing the bank's position in its core markets.

How does Standard Chartered rate?

Pay:	good
Benefits:	very good
Communications:	good
Training:	excellent
Career development:	excellent
Morale:	very good

People and personnel policies

Standard Chartered values good relationship skills as a cardinal quality in its prospective employees. And it actively recruits good communicators, especially people who work well in a multicultural environment. Self-motivation and a focus on personal achievement also figure highly in the checklist of employee success factors. Like many multinationals, Standard Chartered likes its people to find a career path that demonstrates a capacity to contribute to and build team success while exceeding ambitious targets for personal achievement.

International finance is a highly competitive environment and Standard

Chartered, in common with many impressive businesses in this sector, knows that it must have a distinctive and attractive package to offer recruits. Standard Chartered majors on benchmark training. It has created well-established training, assessment and development programmes for all employees. All are closely tracked through an Executive Review process that ensures talented individuals are provided with the right opportunities. The prevailing multicultural aspect of the group provides a wide source of graduate expertise and a standardized selection methodology helps maintain a consistent quality of recruit.

Group head of human resources, Andrew Hunter, says that although formal training courses play a key part in bridging competency gaps, greater emphasis is also placed on flexible learning opportunities, such as team-based activities and project work. He believes strongly that a business is only as good as its people.

'If a graduate starts in a particular part of the bank it doesn't mean to say he or she will be confined there for the rest of his or her career. We encourage graduates to experiment. We try to create open opportunities while promoting a mix of maturity and experience. We want a blend of specialists and generalists, team-workers, innovators, people who are at ease working, not only in their own national markets but also those who can operate comfortably in and across other markets of the world.'

Besides the main businesses there are a variety of roles and challenging career opportunities at Standard Chartered from Audit, Cash Management and Custodial Services to Finance, Human Resources, Risk Management and Trade Banking. Two other examples of the bank's operations are Consumer Banking and Consumer Finance.

From current accounts to investment services and mortgages, Consumer Banking focuses on customer segmentation, financial needs analysis and service delivery. With nearly 12,000 staff in 410 branches serving more than 4 million customers, Consumer Banking is most active in Asia, Africa and the Middle East. Major locations include Hong Kong, Singapore, Malaysia, India, Indonesia, Kenya and Zimbabwe, where Standard Chartered is a household name. Priority Banking, which provides tailor-made financial services for affluent individuals, is yet another aspect of the overall operation.

From its UK head office in Cardiff, Wales, Consumer Finance is run by a subsidiary – Chartered Trust plc. With nearly 80 offices and over 1,500 staff Consumer Finance offers everything from credit cards to consumer loans; the majority of the business, however, is dealer-introduced vehicle leasing and operating finance

A series of groupwide initiatives complement the activities of the businesses, including a Business Leadership Programme, aimed at developing management skills of the bank's present and future leaders. Successful participants receive a post-graduate level Certificate & Diploma in Management, awarded by Nottingham Trent University. Also available is the London Business School Global Consortium Programme for those just below Board level, providing over a nine-month period the opportunity for those involved to work with five other consortia companies on strategic issues impacting multinational organizations.

Since 1992 Standard Chartered has offered an in-company MBA in Strategic Management. The degree, delivered by Henley Management College, is a three-year flexible learning programme with participants coming together on four occasions for residential development at the college and in various locations worldwide. When in their respective home countries, participants are linked together via the Henley Email network. During two of the residential weeks those taking part are required to undertake a 'live' consultancy analysis of a corporate customer's business. In 1998 there were 20 sponsored MBA participants from 14 countries.

A Group Development Programme for high potential employees at middle management has recently been introduced. Besides having an excellent track record of achievement, participants are expected to be geographically mobile and to have the aptitude to move between different parts of the business. They are career managed by the chief executive and members of his senior executive team.

There is a competitive basic salary and other benefit packages, bolstered by the continual performance monitoring. In particular Standard Chartered takes pride in an award-winning preferential share scheme for its employees.

Contact address

Andrew Hunter
Group Head of Human Resources
Standard Chartered Bank
1 Aldermanbury Square
London EC2V 7SB
Telephone: 0171 280 7500
Fax: 0171 280 7791
Web site: http://www.standardchart.com

Sun Microsystems Limited

Sun Microsystems is regarded as a doyen in the fast-moving global IT industry. This is a position it has achieved in the short space of some 16 years through its foresight in recognizing that the future was in network computers. Sun™ is a leading supplier for global enterprises that use information to achieve competitive advantage. It specializes in network computing-based systems including enterprise servers, multiplatform storage, technical workstations, network computers, telco systems and enterprise software. In a volatile industry, where companies rise and fall in a remarkably short space of time, Sun™ continues to be highly successful with a loyal and expanding customer base. Globally, Sun™ generated around $10 billion in turnover in 1998.

Sun Microsystems at a glance

Employees: 2,000+
Annual staff attrition: 5 per cent
Key locations: Bagshot, Camberley, Farnborough, Slough, the City of London, High Wycombe, Cambridge, Manchester, Bristol, Coventry and Consett, with Linlithgow, in Scotland, as its manufacturing base
Annual graduate intake: 30–40
Annual intake: 200–300 a year

An inside view

Sun's™ history lies in business information and software applications based on UNIX® systems and it is a true pioneer of open and distributed computing in UNIX® environments. In 1985 when the network computing concept was emerging Sun™ produced global revenues of $115 million. By 1998 its sales had exploded to $10 billion – with the US responsible for half, and Europe a quarter. By almost every measure of profitability, Sun™ has experienced rapid and sustained growth. In terms of employee productivity, for example, it has quadrupled the contribution of each member of the workforce in ten years and enjoys productivity rates which are envied by its peers in the industry.

Based on the success of its early workstation business, Sun™ has developed its ideas and expertise into other sectors. Essentially Sun™ is structured into several businesses, the biggest being Computer Systems, a hardware operation for commercial application rather than the technical environment, that concentrates on selling network computing. The Enterprise Services division provides software support, hardware support, professional services and education. Sun's™ software strategy has been the opposite of the proprietary approach which dominated the industry in the 1980s. The company works hard to license its technologies to other companies at peppercorn rates to ensure their establishment as industry standards. For example, its Solaris™ package accounts for 50 per cent of all UNIX® operating system sales.

Sun's™ appreciation that open systems define current and future markets led to a remarkable 25 per cent share of the units shipped for the entire UNIX® workstations market, shipping nearly four times the number of units than the second-ranked vendor, according to Dataquest. Translated into the software environment, Sun's™ technicians applied the same logic to create Java – a powerful computing language that allows developers and users to gain the benefits of software written once running on all platforms from smartcard to supercomputer.

It is – at its heart – several companies under one roof, each distinctive but all linked by a common approach. This is a business where the quest for profitability is matched by creative inquiry and passion for ingenuity and invention. Without all of these qualities, Sun™ would not be what it is – one of the most attractive IT companies in the world today.

How does Sun Microsystems rate?

Pay:	very good
Benefits:	excellent
Communications:	excellent
Training:	excellent
Career development:	very good
Morale:	superb

People and personnel policies

Sun's™ dramatic rate of growth has resulted in a continual growth of the UK workforce. The company is recruiting as many as 200–300 people a year – a trend that is likely to continue. Its direct recruitment of graduates from university is growing annually and is not just interested in technical graduates.

The company's graduate recruitment programme is called Shine. As its name suggests, it opens up a fast-track career development path for those with the enthusiasm, intelligence and ambition to succeed. This development is backed by a personal mentoring and development plan, and it is not unusual for a graduate to be in a 'real' job within three weeks of joining the company.

The Sun™ corporate style is informal but committed. 'We put a lot of emphasis on management as a discipline,' says Paul Harrison, Sun's™ human resources director for Europe. 'A lot of people tell us that we appear quite relaxed, even though we are deadly serious about winning in the marketplace. Our managers always seem very friendly and approachable. Beneath that they are organized and dedicated to what they do. We do not have many people with massive egos, which can be commonplace in the IT industry. We have an approach that says everyone here works very hard but we will respect the role that you play and we will empower you to do that to the best of your ability. If we can get every individual in the company to perform their role to the peak capacity, then we will beat the competition.'

One of the more compelling aspects of the Sun™ culture is that policy is conducted subtly. The company has a mission statement and values but these are not forced on employees. They are used as guidelines. When managers are appointed, they attend a five-day training course which outlines precisely and practically what Sun™ expects from someone in that role. 'Management means creating a shared vision in each team so everyone is clear what they have to do. They then set objectives, review progress and initiate a programme of on-going improvements. A Sun™ manager must also relate to other teams in the business and take a whole company-wide view about the targets of their group,' says Harrison. Sun™ managers speak of the values as the DNA in the business – unseen but definitive in ordering the way the organisation works.

This is an understated, warm, positive and good-humoured company. Its team ethos is a natural and spontaneous expression of the company's approach to business. Sun™ has adopted flat structures not because they are currently fashionable, but rather that this is the way the company has always operated. It retains this intimate but disciplined style by choosing its managers extremely carefully. 'It is the number one area of failure for many companies,' remarks Harrison. 'They say because someone is good at sales, for example, they must be made a manager. Management involves completely different skills. We profile what we need in our managers. Candidates for management positions are assessed for their capacities in defined skills. For example, they will be self-confident and good communicators.'

The company also maintains a dynamic intranet enabling job vacancies to be logged and viewed internally, linked to its worldwide recruitment Internet web site. Updated daily, an on-line CV-builder allows candidates to submit their CV directly to Sun™. Other sections of the web site include graduate/student opportunities, Sun's™ locations, culture, vision and rewards, and training and development.

Contact address

Paul Harrison
Human Resources Director
Sun Microsystems
Bagshot Manor
Green Lane
Bagshot
Surrey GU19 5NL
Telephone: 01276 451440
Fax: 01276 451287
Web site: http://www.sun.co.uk

Trademark legend

Tesco

Tesco continues to reign as the leading supermarket chain in the UK and recently acquired the top ranking in food and drink sales in European grocery retailing. Underlying its success is a philosophy of providing high levels of customer service, good quality products, innovation and real value for money. This is supported by the exceptional calibre of its employees who are motivated by an exemplary pay and benefits package, and a company that shows them respect. Tesco is continually expanding, cornering emerging markets in Central Europe and Thailand, and diversifying into non-food sectors.

Tesco at a glance

Employees: 163,000 UK
Annual staff attrition: 20 per cent
Key locations: more than 570 stores in the UK and Republic of Ireland, 100 in Eastern Europe
Annual graduate intake: 150
Annual intake: 30,000

An inside view

Tesco has been a major retailer for some time, but in the last ten years it has emerged with a new image; a competitive and single-minded force to be taken seriously. In 1995 it acquired the Scottish supermarket chain William Low and has grown to an operating capacity of 570 stores in Scotland, England and Wales. More recently, Tesco acquired the Stewarts and Quinnsworth businesses in Northern Ireland and the Republic of Ireland. Late in 1997 Tesco sold most of its interests in France in order to concentrate on expanding operations in Thailand and Central Europe, which currently include Hungary, Slovakia, Poland and the Czech Republic. Tesco states that its core purpose is 'to continually increase value for customers to earn their lifetime loyalty.'

There are a number of key elements at the root of Tesco's achievements. Value for money is vital and achieved through enterprising pricing initiatives and consistently lowering prices of principal products. Paramount to the business is excellent customer service, an example of which is the extension of its opening hours with 65 stores now open 24 hours.

Tesco also endeavours to provide more choice in food and non-food products. It continues to extend its range of food lines, and is increasingly targeting non-food markets that are close to its core business such as clothing, health and personal care, home entertainment, mobile phones and cut-price electrical goods. Its goal is to be as big in non-food as it is in food retailing.

Trials have been underway for some time on Home Shopping, via the Internet. In 1997 Tesco embarked on a joint venture with The Royal Bank of Scotland to provide a range of financial products and services under the guise of Tesco Personal Finance. Finally, customer loyalty is essential and schemes such as the very popular Clubcard and more recently Clubcard Plus, an interest-bearing current account, ensure customer retention.

The supermarket industry is extremely competitive, which in turn makes it challenging and demanding in all aspects. Tesco believes that 'First is First, Second is Nowhere', demonstrating the relentless and determined attitude which has elevated it to its leading position. The culture, which achieves such success, revolves around the employees. The company maintains that 'the quality of our people defines the success of the business' and employees are considered to be as important as customers. There is considerable scope for innovation at an individual level and employee participation is encouraged. This is assisted by the fact that the management structure has been streamlined and now has fewer levels.

How does Tesco rate ?

Pay:	very good
Benefits:	very good
Communications:	good
Training:	good
Career development:	very good
Morale:	good

People and personnel policies

Historically, training and career development for employees was low on the list of priorities in food retailing. Tesco has acknowledged its importance and addressed the subject in a comprehensive manner. Graduates are sent on a 12- to 18-month training programme, during which time they gain experience on the retail floor, which is compulsory for all employees, and are given projects and key tasks to execute.

Responsibility is delegated early and graduates are promoted to a position in senior management when they have completed their training. In 1997 9,000 people in management teams were put through the Tesco Core Skills programme to learn effective management skills. This course programme aims to develop managers to drive performance through their teams through such techniques as effective team building and problem solving. Continuing expansion overseas provides ever-broadening opportunities for executives. More than 100 UK managers are currently enjoying 'development moves' to the European and Far East operations. In the UK, Tesco encourages executives to move between functions, locations and businesses, with the aim of developing highly skilled well-rounded managers for the future.

To develop employee loyalty, Tesco encourages its employees to share in the success and wealth which they help to create. Nearly 55,000 of employees are already shareholders, owning 50 million of the company's shares, worth almost £300 million. All staff with two years' service gain shares through the company's profit share scheme and in 1997 profit-related pay linked to the company's success was introduced for all staff. In 1998 45 per cent ran a company Save As You Earn scheme.

More than two-thirds of the workforce is women, and incentives designed to encourage women to remain with Tesco include career-break schemes. As it is a predominantly female business, it is important that women are well recognized in the company structure. Of the top 100 executives, 30 are women. The company's selection, training, development and promotion policies ensure equal opportunities for all employees regardless of gender, age, race, marital status or disability. All decisions are based on merit.

Internal communications, which include a staff magazine, videos and staff briefing sessions, ensure that the workforce is well informed about the business. Employee attitudes are frequently researched by means of surveys and store visits. For example, the annual questionnaire, Viewpoint, regularly achieves an industry-beating response rate of more than 60 per cent. Line managers are encouraged to communicate regularly with their employees, evaluate their opinions and respond appropriately.

Contact address

Maya Brown
Group HR
Tesco Stores Limited
Southcourt Building
Edinburgh Gate
Edinburgh Way
Harlow
Essex CM20 2JE
Telephone: 01992 658291
Fax: 01992 658695
Web site: http://www.tesco.co.uk

3i Group plc

3i is Europe's leading venture capital group, with more than 50 years' experience of investing in unquoted, growing businesses. Formerly known as ICFC and Investors in Industry, 3i is respected for its intellectual rigour, professionalism and integrity. The company operates in every major regional centre as well as nationally and it is seen as a key component of the financial community throughout the UK. Its dedication to continual improvement and innovation allow it to offer a uniquely challenging and rewarding career.

3i at a glance

Employees: 771
Annual staff attrition: 9 per cent
Key locations: Central London (HQ), Solihull and major UK and European cities, Singapore and Japan
Annual graduate intake: 0
Annual intake: 80

An inside view

3i is by far the largest and most successful company involved in the provision of corporate capital in the UK. Since its establishment in 1945, it has invested over £9.5 billion in more than 13,000 businesses: over 950 businesses backed by 3i have subsequently achieved a stock market flotation. The company has a network of 28 offices in the UK, France, Italy, Germany, Spain, Singapore and affiliated operations in Japan.

As Europe's leading venture capital company, 3i is much more than a portfolio of investments in small businesses. The businesses it invests in are diverse, representing all sectors from general industrials to consumer goods, and from small manufacturing to technology-based businesses. Typically, most are small or medium-sized enterprises with a turnover between £1 million and £100 million. 3i tends to invest at times of transition in the life of a company and investments in emerging businesses, management buy-outs and management buy-ins account for around half the ventures in which it participates.

3i is regarded in the investment community as a company that has remained highly professional and the atmosphere within the company reflects the high standards of integrity which it regards as essential in business. Accordingly, it has developed a set of core values which it expects its employees to respect. These are to be commercial and fair; to respect the needs of shareholders, employees and clients; to maintain integrity and professionalism; and to strive for continual improvement and innovation.

Significantly, 3i does not select graduates for recruitment, believing they do not possess those sufficient levels of maturity or experience which the company expects of them. Instead, staff are generally recruited after developing substantial professional or commercial experience elsewhere. They will then receive further training and development to help them develop their capacities as investment or professional executives.

There are three particular qualities which the group looks for in new recruits – intellectual capacity, drive and resilience, and the ability to build relationships. Most of the people with whom executives are dealing on a day-to-day basis are directors so staff must be capable of establishing and maintaining relationships with senior people.

How does 3i rate?

Pay:	good
Benefits:	very good
Communications:	good
Training:	excellent
Career development:	excellent
Morale:	very good

People and personnel policies

3i enjoys a reputation for offering an excellent training programme with bespoke technical courses designed to support learning on-the-job. This is intended to give each employee a thorough grounding in the business to enable him or her to handle the complex transactions frequently undertaken at 3i. Training depends largely on individual needs, and falls into the following categories: technical and IT; management; and personal development. After an initial training period, employees become involved in three core elements of investment activity: generating investment opportunities; structuring and completing new investments; and managing a portfolio of existing customers.

3i seeks recruits with drive and determination. In order to meet the broad demands of the role, it looks for people with a real passion for the business world. The mental agility to absorb and analyse complex information is of paramount importance, as is the ability to solve a wide range of complex problems effectively.

Equally important are interpersonal skills to build mutually productive working relationships with customers. With 3i's growing network of international offices, the ability to speak more than one language is also a major asset. 3i takes into account the particular interests and strengths of each potential employee, and opportunities permitting, seeks to place individuals in the office most suited to their career development. In light of this, staff need to be flexible and keen to make the most of the opportunities available.

The group operates in the highly lucrative financial services industry, and thus the company's basic salaries and benefits are excellent, determined in the light of the need to attract, retain and motivate individuals of the calibre required. As with other financial services providers, pay is heavily influenced by performance. 3i also offers a wide variety of benefits such as a non-contributory pension scheme and subsidized mortgages.

All employees are eligible for substantial cash bonuses which vary according to local circumstance and individual performance. Its frontline investment sales staff receive the highest bonuses – possibly up to 90 per cent of salary. In addition, each head of department has a pool of money available to reward exceptional individual performance, as well as situations when employees perform a service beyond the normal demands of their role.

Employee appraisals and informal consultations, which are the company's principal means of keeping in touch with the views of its employees, are held regularly. Employees are assessed each year by their immediate manager and every two years they have a career development discussion with their senior manager. This covers the individual's career ambitions and the options which are available to them. In the investment stream, executives generally spend around five years developing as investors after which point they may either continue as senior investors or become team leaders. This is itself dependent upon performance and the results of a developmental workshop which explores the skills needed for evaluation within the company.

Managers throughout 3i are responsible for keeping staff fully informed of developments and for communicating financial results and other matters of interest. This is achieved by structured communications including regular meetings of employees.

Contact address

Human Resources Department
3i Group plc
90 Waterloo Road
London SE1 8XP
Telephone: 0171 928 3131
Fax: 0171 928 0058
Web site: http://www.3i.co.uk

3M

The Minnesota Mining and Manufacturing Company, better known as 3M, is one of the world's great companies, a global industrial group which invents, manufactures and sells many thousands of products to almost every imaginable market. These products – and there were more than 50,000 at the last count – are based around a diverse range of industrial and commercial sectors. The foundation of the company's success is innovation and 3M places great store by its capacity to generate original new products and markets. That same thirst for innovation has brought products as diverse as CFC-free medical inhalers, structural adhesives, flexible electronic circuits and even the ubiquitous Post-it Note to the world.

3M at a glance

Employees: 74,000 worldwide, 4,300 UK
Annual staff attrition: 5 per cent
Key locations: Bracknell, HQ; plus 17 sites across the UK and also Dublin
Annual graduate intake: 20–30
Annual intake: n/a

An inside view

Based in St Paul, Minnesota in the United States, 3M operates on 30 main technology platforms, including films, fluorochemicals, fibre optics, pharmaceuticals, adhesives, nonwoven materials and microreplication, supplying a variety of markets such as consumer and office products, traffic and personal safety, industrial, medical, automotive, chemical, electronic and communications, aligning its businesses closely to the markets which it serves. Microreplication alone – the construction of ultra-precise surfaces – has the potential to be used in up to a quarter of 3M products in the future. From its UK headquarters at Bracknell, Berkshire, and its Dublin office, 3M operates 12 manufacturing facilities and six laboratories and technical centres in the UK and Ireland.

Since its establishment in 1902, 3M has come to epitomize the innovative spirit essential to entrepreneurs and businesses, as it consistently breaks fresh ground in every aspect of its business. Within the company, there is a strong emphasis on the will and talent to innovate and every employee has the time to innovate built into his or her work schedule, on a daily or weekly basis.

In addition, the company has a fast, responsive decision-making process, based on teamwork, which is low on structures and remarkably quick at bringing ideas to fruition. This is all the more remarkable considering that each new product is thoroughly researched and no product is launched without active and detailed analysis of market possibilities. 3M's capacity for innovation extends to its structures and systems which are overhauled regularly. Throughout the world, this approach to the creation of new products and the development of business processes has won widespread respect for 3M; so much so that it is used as an example of good working practices in the training material of other multinationals.

The values of the company underlie and drive its activities. The 3M culture encourages individuals and teams to work together effectively with one aim in mind – to develop new products that make the lives of their customers easier and better. And some of the best products have been generated by transferring technologies from one business to another.

How does 3M rate ?

Pay:	excellent
Benefits:	very good
Communications:	very good
Training:	excellent
Career development:	good
Morale:	very good

People and personnel policies

Since its launch, 3M UK has striven to be an innovator, not only in its products and the way in which it conducts its business, but also in people issues. 3M UK offers superb working conditions and, together with a handful of US multinationals based in the UK such as Mars, IBM, Xerox and Hewlett-Packard, is one of the best when it comes to the management of human resources.

The company is a standard-setter for a wide range of human resource issues and considers that, in order for its people to be able to give of their best, they must have freedom and flexibility in their work and be well rewarded for their talent and effort. The approach to pay and benefits is a typically straightforward one. Pay is pitched at a high standard point, with an increasingly variable element according to grade within the company. There is a broad range of benefits, with strong pension, life and health cover and generous holiday and sick pay entitlements.

With an apparently innate ability for simple and direct expression, 3M attaches great importance to the quality of its communications, making open, frank and honest communication a priority. Employees are provided with information about the performance of the group through regular management briefing notes. More specific issues, such as major policy decisions, are communicated quickly and effectively by means of corporate or divisional publications and videos. Regular consultation takes place with employees concerning work methods and organization and the business encourages feedback which will assist in the improvement of ideas, processes and output.

3M places a great emphasis on the personal and career development of employees, believing that this approach is for the benefit of the company as a whole. For many years training has been seen as an important element of its human resources policy and the company has invested heavily in both courses and on-the-job training. More recently 3M has developed an assessment and development programme which aims to develop the potential of individuals through a clear understanding of personal strengths and development needs, at the same time as improving the company's ability to predict the potential of its employees, resulting in more effective people and organizational development.

There is a high graduate intake at 3M, as the company sees this as an efficient way of drawing intelligent and able people into the company. It is a favoured choice of graduates, particularly those with scientific backgrounds, who are attracted by the opportunities for developing new product ideas and 3M's reputation for personal headroom. Once within the organization, many activities are inter-disciplinary and there are numerous opportunities to move to different areas of the business.

3M expects its candidates for employment to have a strong commercial instinct. As well as new products, the company often creates completely new markets and highly values those who are able to identify new markets and ways in which products can be sold to them. 3M looks for people with a range of skills in addition to an understanding of markets – candidates must be able to communicate effectively and have the capacity to work on their own initiative and as a member of a team. In return for commitment, high quality and original work, speed of thought and action and fresh thinking, 3M provides pay and benefits in the upper echelons and employees have total integrity and remarkable latitude and freedom to make a contribution.

Contact address

3M United Kingdom plc
3M House
PO Box 1
Market Place
Bracknell
Berkshire RG12 1JU
Telephone: 01344 858000
Fax: 01344 858278
Web site: http://www.3M.com.uk

TNT UK Limited

In the last decade TNT has become a prominent example of management excellence, commercial quality in action and thriving enterprise, which encourages innovation, customer service and direct, pragmatic operation. In Autumn 1998 it was the winner of the European Quality Award for business excellence. Its latest figures show record annual profits of £37.5 million, which have grown steadily since its UK foundation two decades ago. The British business traces its origins back to its Australian post-war parent but owes most of its success to the grit, determination, expertise and good sense of its UK team. TNT is Britain's premier deliverer of parcels and a larger range of goods with a 24-hour door-to-door guarantee. It does not boast a monopoly, merely a desire to improve its already excellent customer services and build on a superb track record.

TNT at a glance

Employees: 10,000
Annual staff attrition: 5 per cent
Key locations: HQ at Atherstone, Warwickshire, employing 1,000 people. More than 300 branches and depots nationwide
Annual graduate intale: 25
Annual intake: 500

An inside view

One word defines TNT: passion. Its cultural imperative is greater than commitment, drive, energy or determination. The company is characterized by all of these qualities but passion best describes the TNT approach to business. If you are half-hearted about your work you will not survive long at TNT. Passion is expressed through TNT's absolute search for enhanced service quality, original and creative solutions to commercial problems and an aching desire that every employee exceeds yesterday's personal best.

There is no doubt that TNT has a performance-based culture – and individual achievement is central to the ethos. But there is also a remarkable degree of co-operative spirit – unusual in such an atmosphere – where colleagues genuinely want their teammates to do well. The result of such focused energy is scores of corporate awards for quality, achievement and high standards of management. Hundreds of businesses across the UK use TNT and its practices as a definitive benchmark.

TNT is its people. This is not a business, which relies on structure for its output. It depends virtually entirely on the zeal of its employees.

TNT keeps 4,000 vehicles and a fleet of 24 aircraft in constant use to ensure that its strict self-imposed demands are met. It delivers 80 per cent of Britain's national newspapers every day, 60 per cent of all magazines and is therefore the country's biggest carrier of the printed word in the country. In addition it is the largest carrier of automotive parts, tyres and oil; there is a daily delivery of a million loaves of bread. TNT operates around the clock 365 days a year. Nothing is too large or too small to take from one end of the country to the other, to Europe or even the rest of the world.

Atherstone in North Warwickshire became the company's headquarters for one simple reason: expert mathematicians and geographers decided that the town lay at the centre of the country – a base at Nuneaton, just a few miles up the road, would have meant an extra £8,000 a week in fuel costs. It is attention to detail such as this, which helps make TNT a major player. That is why a new state of the art parcels distribution centre designed to speed distribution and increase efficiency by harnessing the latest technology is on stream. It has been designed to increase TNT's share of Britain's express delivery market together with the company's extensive range of unique services.

TNT's success is geared to organic growth, word of mouth recommendation and reputation. This successful UK company has not expanded by acquisition. It reacts swiftly to changing conditions, hence a smooth and widely hailed operation. For example, on the night of the 1998 general election, enormous distribution challenges were posed by constantly changing print runs of the national newspapers but TNT ensured that people throughout Britain had up-to-date editions on their breakfast table.

How does TNT rate?

Pay:	very good
Benefits:	very good
Communications:	excellent
Training:	excellent
Career development:	superb
Morale:	superb

People and personnel policies

Personnel management in TNT is the achievement of results by cultural imperative. In other words, the company's management creates the right atmosphere that allows individual members of the workforce and dedicated teams to thrive. It is an environment where exceeding yesterday's best performance is considered normal. TNT believes that by liberating the talent in its people, individual and team success will be turned into a vibrant and profitable company.

This positive ethos reaches every corner of the enterprise and underpins its commercial, strategic and human resources targets. In TNT it is hard to understate the positive impact of its cultural energy. Various other strands of personnel policy are net contributors to the complete picture but the TNT quality enterprise ethic is the holistic vision.

And so when it says that it believes in

empowerment, the reality is that only the best person to make a decision will – in practice – take it. The best person will often be the individual at the front end – a lorry driver or a depot manager. He or she will be expected to tackle any situation as circumstance demands. One employee was lauded recently for chartering an airliner to ensure that a vital parcel was delivered. The Wild West's motto was that the mail must get through. It is the same with TNT. The company builds on a make-it-happen policy through clear direction, support and accountability. Promotion comes quickly to those who can demonstrate that they understand and can apply this particular style of management.

Pay is good for the sector and a key element is performance-related, as might be expected with an accountant for a managing director. Money-purchase pension and healthcare plans are also available and continue to improve as each year progresses. Attrition is tiny. Some do leave but after experiencing periods elsewhere are keen to return. One of TNT's biggest problems is to create enough opportunities to meet the aims of staff wanting promotion. In total, there are 200 profit accountable managers and eight senior directors, including the boss, who are at the centre of strategic decision making.

Contact address

Alan Jones
Managing Director
TNT UK Limited
Holly Lane
Atherstone
Warwickshire CV9 2RY
Telephone: 01827 303030
Fax: 01827 301301
Web site: http://www.tnt.co.uk

Ulster Carpet Mills

Owned by Walter, John and Edward Wilson, Ulster Carpet Mills is one of the world's most technically advanced manufacturers of woven carpets. Based in Northern Ireland, this privately owned company is a leading player in the carpet industry and has a presence in the UK, South Africa, the US, France and Germany. Ulster Carpet Mills is still a family-run firm and has preserved a concerned and caring atmosphere attractive to many employees.

Ulster Carpet Mills at a glance

Employees: 1,100
Annual staff attrition: 5 per cent
Key locations: Portadown, Kidderminster, London, Germany
Annual graduate intake: 6
Annual intake: 100

An inside view

Ulster Carpet Mills began life in the late 1930s and since that time has become a very profitable and successful company, shaped by the hand of the late George Wilson. His sons, Walter, John and Edward remain at the helm, now employing more than 1,100 people and expanding the business internationally. With the acquisition of Crossley in Durban, South Africa, in 1992, Ulster Carpet Mills became one of the world's few woven carpet manufacturers with production facilities in both hemispheres. Sales offices, along with fully staffed and computerized design studios, circle the globe. It is a vertically integrated company managing each different level of the production process.

The company is the second largest producer of Axminster carpets in the world and also produces Wilton carpets, both high-quality carpets famous for their design. Ulster purchases the raw wool and dyes and spins the yarn itself to ensure consistency in colour matching and thread quality. The next stage is the responsibility of the design team, which is instrumental in developing designs for clients. These can include corporate identities, patterns relating to fabric and soft furnishings and motifs to highlight special themes. Computer-aided design (CAD) facilities translate ideas into workable formats.

Ulster Carpet Mills has an electronic jacquard weaving system, trademarked as Uniweave™. It works on the principle of designing and weaving an entire piece of carpet for a room as a single concept. The latest weaving technology in operation is the high speed Axminster looms. Ulster currently employs the fastest Axminster broadloom in the world. The company operates from three sites in Portadown with 52 Axminster and Wilton looms and a computer-controlled warehouse with 300 different designs in stock. Leading luxury cruise-liners, including Cunard, North Sea Ferries, P & O European Ferries, Seafrance/Sealink and Airtours, are among Ulster Carpet Mills' most important customers.

The culture of the firm is based on Ulster Carpet's mission statement, which is primarily customer-centred, with a focus on delivering superior quality products. Particular emphasis is given to creating a harmonious working environment – especially relevant in a locality characterized by religious division. The owners like to retain a family feel about the business and feedback from employees, with regard to the working environment, is very positive.

How does Ulster Carpet Mills rate?

Pay:	good
Benefits:	good
Communications:	very good
Training:	excellent
Career development:	very good
Morale:	good

People and personnel policies

Ulster Carpet Mills has neatly combined both a personal and professional approach to its personnel policies. Drawing on its legacy as a family-owned organization, Ulster Carpet treats its employees with an almost intimate respect. This is coupled with an up-to-date human resources policy to form an extremely proficient, quality-motivated international enterprise. Edward Wilson elaborates on Ulster Carpets' commitment to its employees – 'care for our people forms one of our four principal objectives from the company's mission statement. We have a strongly supportive workforce prepared to adjust to new and changing technologies. We enjoy a reputation in the trade for the integrity, openness and friendliness of our staff.'

As a growing company with a distinguished reputation in both its region and field of expertise, Ulster Carpet Mills has no difficulty in recruiting new employees. Recognized for its technical innovation and design excellence by others in the industry, it is an ideal company to work at for those wanting to get a thorough grounding in the trade. Within the first six weeks of employment all new employees attend a company induction which is a two-day programme covering health and safety, terms and conditions, equal opportunity awareness, quality, training opportunities and the production process.

Training and ongoing development are important elements of business practice at Ulster Carpet Mills. Training courses are both internal and external and there is a dynamic employee and management development programme. Personal development plans are used throughout the company at all levels to map progress and performance of individuals. It is customary for every employee to complete a minimum of three days per year of on-the-job training. An annual personal performance review pinpoints areas of training which require development.

The company actively encourages further education and in many cases financial assistance is provided for employees who undertake a course of study at a recognized institution. Directors and managers who show potential are supported on an MBA programme. Ulster Carpet Mills are enthusiastic about investing in its future managers and therefore offer a comprehensive leadership course to all managers, to be completed over a period of 18 months. Some of the instruction is presented internally and some on residential training courses.

Particularly in the context of Northern Ireland, the pay is very good and the benefits offered are considerable. An excellent pension scheme is supplemented by healthcare insurance for every employee as well as sickness benefits, maternity and bereavement leave. Profit related pay is a recent development. Communications have always been vital to the culture of Ulster Carpet Mills and all employees now use e-mail and lotus notes as a mode of communication and means of reducing paperwork. A range of internal publications keep employees informed of company developments and progress, and team briefings are a regular occurrence.

Female employees are encouraged to take up roles in management, as part of Ulster Carpet Mills' strong commitment to equal opportunities. The last few years have seen a 30 per cent rise in female group leaders in the company. It is involved in charity and community initiatives such as the Give As You Earn Scheme and sponsorship of local events.

Contact address

Caroline Whiteside
Personnel Manager
Ulster Carpet Mills
Portadown
Craigavon
Northern Ireland
Telephone: 01762 395123
Fax: 01762 395170
Web site: http://www.ulstercarpets.com

Unilever plc

The component brands and companies within the Unilever group are some of the world's best-known names. The business, as it is presently constituted, came together in the early 1930s and has developed into a highly polished and respected multinational. Around 50 per cent of the company's income is derived from foods – frozen items, ice-cream, tea and margarine. It also produces: detergents, personal products – cosmetics, toothpaste, shampoo and conditioners – and fine fragrances. Targeted expansion will come in developing countries – the focus of the group's strategy. Unilever has long been regarded as one of the finest employers in the UK. Its graduate entry scheme is widely praised and places on it are keenly sought. Despite its size and influence as a global product and marketing force, Unilever is a friendly place to work and positively encourages individual initiative and creativity.

Unilever at a glance

Employees: 270,000 worldwide, UK, 20,000
Annual staff attrition: not recorded
Key locations: 88 worldwide
Annual graduate intake: 150 (UK)
Annual intake: 1,000 (worldwide)

An inside view

Throughout UK industry, the Unilever management-training scheme has emerged as an excellent role model. Since the late 1940s, many other businesses have modeled their graduate entry programmes on those evolved at Unilever. This is hardly surprising since Unilever is a company that enjoys a global reputation for quality, innovation and good stewardship. Its constantly expanding portfolio of brands include Magnum, Persil, Ponds, Elizabeth Arden, Omo, Lipton's teas, Flora and Vaseline – household names throughout the world.

In January 1930, the washing powder manufacturer Lever Brothers and the Dutch Margarine Union combined to form Unilever. The scope of the new union was widespread, both geographically and in product terms. The Union and Lever Brothers shared a common customer in the householder and both owed their success to the growing prosperity of the European working classes. Two separate companies, Unilever PLC and Unilever NV, operate effectively as an integrated business and are managed by a common management team.

British graduate trainees will normally spend their first five years in the UK before being considered for international assignments: nearly all senior managers have worked abroad at some stage in their careers. The focus of attention within the group is on the developing markets – Asia, Africa, Latin America – and its management believes that the potential for business growth in these areas is substantial.

Despite its acknowledged status as one of the largest and most successful global multinationals, Unilever in the UK is said to be one of the most friendly and personable organizations in the British commercial sector. The company places great reliance on the talents of individuals and so gives employees – and especially managers – considerable personal freedom in the conduct of their assignments. Although the business has a clear and centrally defined corporate strategy, individuals have much more freedom to develop business, and relationships with clients, than some of its competitors.

How does Unilever rate?

Pay:	excellent
Benefits:	very good
Communications:	superb
Training:	excellent
Career development:	good
Morale:	very good

People and personnel policies

Among personnel professionals, Unilever is regarded as one of the top performers. This is partly historic because Unilever was the first of the UK's major businesses to establish a management training facility and a graduate trainee scheme. Since those developments, the company's reputation as a trainer has, if anything, been further enhanced. Its trainee scheme was the template for many in British industry and has been adapted to take account of changing conditions and demands as the company has grown.

Unilever styles itself the 'multi-local multinational' that emphasizes the local and brand orientation of the business. Although there are certain guiding principles in place in personnel policy – upper quartile pay and benefits, high commitment to training, teamwork, and room for personal contribution – the stress lies in local management responding to local customer demand. Like Hewlett-Packard in the computer sector, Unilever managers enjoy the support of the centre and the strength of the international brands, but also remarkable freedom to manoeuvre. Each year Unilever introduces more than 1,000 graduates worldwide. Traditionally, these individuals would have worked mainly in the national businesses but with added commitment to learning from other territories, they can in the future be expected to take up managerial positions anywhere in the world.

The company places increasing importance on international project teams. Employees in one country will link with experienced people in other territories. It is one of the most obvious examples of the skill and knowledge interchange that is taking place at all levels to revitalize the culture. A Unilever university has been set up in central Europe where people from all over the world attend courses on the latest events in product development and marketing.

Management trainees will move from role to role roughly every 18 months to two years. Individuals destined for senior management positions will certainly take assignments overseas. Unilever is focusing much of its energy on the developing markets around the world – China, Latin America, Africa and Asia. High profile graduate trainees are being given the opportunity to contribute to the territories where Unilever is placing its greatest efforts. Managers who take placements in these regions will be at the forefront of the development of the global business.

The rules for Unilever managers are clear: the company will provide opportunity, good rewards, and room for creativity. It demands – as it always has – total integrity. This is the ultimate bottom line. If there is a problem, people are there to help, and the culture supports managers who, when experiencing difficulties, are totally open. This is normally a friendly and informal atmosphere in which to operate but managers who conceal their difficulties will quickly lose the sympathies of their colleagues.

Beyond the managerial grades, Unilever has a strong, if somewhat paternalistic, reputation for looking after its shop-floor staff. Pay is excellent and employees report that they enjoy good working conditions and a positive environment. Despite local variations in approach, Unilever facilities are standard-setters within their industries. But the decentralized culture of the Unilever group gives local management the opportunity to develop the quality and depth of their own personnel.

As can be seen, despite its size – the group's worldwide turnover was almost £30 billion in 1997 – the company is no lumbering giant. It responds quickly to change, identifies and seizes opportunities to expand, and is not afraid to pull out of a product area if it suits its strategic plans. With the advent of 'open' markets, it moved swiftly into countries such as Russia, China, Vietnam, and the central European states, where many of its products are now market leaders.

This same ability to change also applies to organizational structures. For example, in 1997 the company replaced its traditional job classification system with a structure of work levels. This helped to design flat and simpler organizations and allowed greater flexibility in remuneration. It also moved to an integrated approach to performance and potential assessment. This is likely to lead to more focused individual career planning and development programmes.

Contact address

Unilever Recruitment
PO Box 1538
Slough SL1 1YT
Recruitment hotline: 0541 543 550
Web site: http://www.unilever.com

Unipart Group of Companies

The Unipart Group of Companies (UGC) is one of the great success stories of privatization. Instantly familiar to accomplished managers throughout industry, Unipart demonstrates how – with a high degree of vision, intelligence and dedication – an unproductive relic can be converted into a pan-industrial benchmark. Today UGC is one of Europe's leading independent logistics, automotive parts and accessories businesses. A management buyout team quit British Leyland in 1987, and quickly established Unipart's comprehensive reputation for innovative treatment of employee and customer.

Unipart at a glance

Employees: around 4,000
Annual staff attrition: 4 per cent
Key locations: Oxford (HQ, manufacturing and university), with 16 other sites in the UK and Europe
Annual graduate intake: around 20
Annual intake: 150

An inside view

Several case studies are regularly quoted of British enterprises, formerly state-owned, which are graphic examples of how the translation to the private sector can be achieved with abundant success. Some of them are included in this volume because they realized that a key element of sustained commercial progress is the talent to be a good employer. Elsewhere in this edition you can read of the voluminous success of BT, British Airways and British Steel.

Yet for all their achievements these and other giants of the UK economy could not match the perception of employee involvement of Unipart. Its inspirational vision hinged on employee participation as core to the delivery of the business. The idea of stakeholder companies was pioneered, even hot-housed, at Unipart. It rose from the broken bits of British Leyland in a romantic rags-to-riches story. Chief executive John Neill's crusade for effective management has already assumed the aspect of legend; Neill's message is clear: if the UK is to survive the potentially awesome challenge from the very low-cost economies of the Far East, then business has to adopt radical, new working practices. And Unipart has done precisely that – particularly as change relates to the employee.

The group provides a full-spectrum demand chain management service for UK vehicle manufacturers, and produces a complete range of parts under the Unipart brand for all makes of cars on European roads. It has also created a cellular telephone service supplier (UniqueAir), an information technology company (UIT) and a creative communications agency (Complete Communications). Unipart has a significant investment in Railpart, which provides parts and services for rolling stock and in National Railways Supplies, which supplies parts and services such as signalling and telecommunications. In 1997 it acquired the Burden Group, which owns companies in the camping, caravanning and marine leisure industries. It also launched a new company, SureStock Health Services.

In 1997 Unipart also made a massive investment in manufacturing when it built four new factories – three in the Midlands and one in Kent. In 1997 turnover increased by 6.6 per cent to £1.1 billion with an operating profit of £28.6 million. The stakeholder philosophy, which Neill has raised from dusty textbooks to active workplace, is an economic theory which mixes partnerships and social responsibility with specified investment policy. Part of the stakeholder partnership is connected to the shareholder, and in 1997 the group paid a dividend for the full year of £7.7 million, nearly 150 per cent more than the £3.1 million paid just five years before in 1993.

The heart of its human resource philosophy is on the ground floor of the company's headquarters at Cowley where a training university (Unipart U) was created in 1993. Neill believes that training and inspiring employees to learn is essential to survival. 'We now have abundant evidence of the dramatic and beneficial impact which the Unipart U has had on every one of the group's companies,' he says.

How does Unipart rate?

Pay:	good
Benefits:	excellent
Communications:	excellent
Training:	superb
Career development:	strong
Morale:	good

People and personnel policies

'Human resources are always the most important part of any business in any part of the world,' says Neill. Central to the active implementation of this philosophy is training and the Unipart U sets a new industry standard for the preparation, composition and delivery of training courses. There are around 260 courses on offer at the Unipart university, and every employee takes ten basic courses, adding up to ten days every year. The courses are designed to be practical so that people who attend can apply the morning's learning to afternoon work. They are run mainly by line managers who have themselves been taught how to teach and encourage employee involvement in continuous improvement, customer service and the elimination of waste.

The group's corporate goal – to make the UGC logo the mark of outstanding personal customer service – is mainlined through the Unipart U programmes such as 'Our Contribution Counts Circles' (OCC Circles), which is the Unipart approach to the so-called Quality Circles, providing a framework for team problem solving using techniques taught in the university. These continuing improvement principles encourage employees to improve quality and reduce cost – the only way that Neill believes companies like Unipart will survive and prosper.

OCC Circles were first launched in the Unipart Group in 1991, being developed from the successful best practice experience of industry in Japan and North America. The programme has been designed to reflect the culture of Unipart, and is designed to give power to the employee, allowing him or her to solve challenges faced at the workplace. There are hundreds of circles operating at Unipart currently involving almost a third of the company's workforce. It is estimated that around £5 million in costs has been saved through this initiative.

The company's £2.5 million investment in the Unipart U, which now has an Internet Discovery Centre, reflects its commitment to put continuous learning at the core of the company's strategy for competitiveness. Neill says that 'the question is whether we can deliver continuous learning and upskilling. Learning is the way we do business; it is not a bolt-on activity.'

As you would expect from a company dedicated to continuous learning, graduate recruitment and training plays an important part in its philosophy. The two areas that offer most opportunities for graduates are Unipart International (UI) and Unipart Demand Chain Management (DCM). Both have graduate development programmes. UI is the sales and marketing division, responsible for the Unipart range of car parts, and is now the largest single-branded all-makes car parts supplier in Europe. It operates through a network of Unipart wholesalers and Express Factors, who in turn sell to the independent motor trade and other sectors. The division also comprises The Burden Group (see An inside view) and Truck And Trailer Components. DCM is the largest division within the Unipart Group, employing 1,200 people at four national sites, including the Oxford-based HQ, and three international locations – Spain, France and Italy. DCM provides a full-spectrum parts service, from identifying sources and processing parts, to pricing, marketing, and delivering to major contract customers at sites in around 30 countries.

The list of attributes required by graduates seems daunting, and is probably meant to be. As well as a relevant 2:1 degree, ideally business orientated, candidates are expected to be innovative in achieving objectives; be motivated to overcome obstacles; have the ability to work in a team; possess analytical skills to think through complex problems; display leadership qualities in planning and organizing the actions of others; and be flexible enough to alter an original approach to adapt to changing circumstances.

Each graduate has a mentor – someone who has been through the graduate development programme – to provide help and advice based on their own learning experience; and a senior management mentor, who is responsible for the graduate's career interests. Regular reviews are also arranged with the graduate's reporting manager, Personnel, and with the relevant managing director.

UGC also offers a training programme for graduates interested in careers in finance. Trainees work in a range of finance departments throughout the group during their time in the scheme and this is a precursor to finance management opportunities within the group. 'The company puts tremendous effort into direct communication with the employees, both upwards and downwards,' says Neill. 'Unipart has created a culture built on teamwork across all traditional boundaries. People are motivated by their high level of personal involvement in aspects of the business that make a real difference to the customer,' he says.

Chief executive Neill, always at the centre of change in the company, is well aware of the pressures that change brings. 'We are told that change in this decade will be ten times faster than in the past. Consider what this means for employees who must adapt quickly and welcome change. This rapid pace of change means that employees are facing more and more stress which can manifest itself in physical and mental problems. In the Lean Machine, they can not only get fit so that they can cope with stress, and receive treatment to deal with some of the problems created by stress, they can also learn how to manage stress . . .'

Contact address

Unipart Group of Companies
Unipart House
Cowley
Oxford OX4 2PG
Telephone: 01865 778966
Fax: 01865 383763
Web site: http://www.unipart.co.uk

Vauxhall Motors Limited

Vauxhall is one of the most famous brands in the UK motor industry. It is highly successful and profitable and is regarded among its peers as a leader in human resources policy. The company operates from four sites: two in Luton, one in Dunstable and another in Ellesmere Port. Vauxhall is a wholly owned subsidiary of General Motors, integrated into GM Europe in terms of its products, manufacturing processes and information channels. It is extremely lean and relies heavily on the quality, commitment and expertise of its employees.

Vauxhall Motors at a glance

Employees: 10,100
Annual staff attrition: 2 per cent
Key locations: Luton (HQ and manufacturing), Dunstable (parts and service support), Ellesmere Port (manufacturing)
Annual graduate intake: 30
Annual intake: n/a

An inside view

No industrial sector better depicts the transformation in attitudes towards employee management than the motor industry. Two decades ago it lived with a consistent background noise of employee-management mistrust and active hostility. Today it is in the forefront of advanced practice in human resources. And few businesses can rival the commitment to its people of Vauxhall. Fewer still can match the results which Vauxhall achieves.

The financial and corporate performance of the company is direct testimony to the success of its highly developed people policies. Candidates for jobs in Vauxhall show a series of characteristics in common. These are energetic, creative people who work well in teams but also demonstrate the capacity to run with original ideas. It is a testing environment. The modern automotive business is a competitive marketplace and Vauxhall, like other leading car-makers, daily challenges the core assumptions of the sector.

The UK business embraces a range of motor industry functions. In Luton and Ellesmere Port more than 9,000 people are engaged in manufacturing cars and the V6 engine. Some 750 work in a massive parts warehouse of a million and a half square feet in Bedfordshire. More than 250 work in the sales and marketing activity including co-ordination of dealership networks in the UK and Ireland, and around 290 are employed in central functions such as finance, PR, IT and personnel.

In many ways Vauxhall is a textbook company of the turn of the century. It is true to its values, indeed is probably more true to the spirit to the early days of GM now than at any stage in recent decades. It believes passionately in its people; it genuinely sees diversity as a basic tenet of its creed. As a business it invests heavily in originality, creativity and vision, while it is a benchmark producer and distributor. But perhaps the most valuable and engaging quality is its capacity to interpret its own strengths and weaknesses. Vauxhall is refreshingly free of pomposity.

Personal development planning leads employees to make appropriate career choices. The most significant new opportunity to open up for Vauxhall's employees in recent years is the growth in international career potential. As well as being an autonomous unit within General Motors, Vauxhall is a key player in GM Europe. 'Brands are now a common feature throughout Europe and the identity of the GM businesses is a worldwide phenomenon. Manufacturing is global, our financial operations are conducted on an international basis and our technological systems and processes are more or less common. We have established centres of excellence in designated locations all over the world,' says director of personnel, Bruce Warman.

How does Vauxhall rate?

Pay:	very good
Benefits:	very good
Communications:	excellent
Training:	superb
Career development:	excellent
Morale:	very good

People and personnel policies

There are few genuine meritocracies in industry but Vauxhall is one of them. Its system of locating and developing high fliers from within its own ranks is a case in point. Vauxhall differs from many employers is that literally anyone can become a high flier.

The company's approach to recruitment demonstrates its belief in expertise and ability rather than solely academic background as a key criterion for success. Rather than campus graduates, as it calls them, Vauxhall looks for people with a track record of achievement in industry. It does take on some graduates straight from college each year but the company also recruits people who have had some experience of the pace and scope of work in the real world.

This also makes their transition to Vauxhall's performance-based appraisal and reward system somewhat easier. Many companies now have systems which bear comparison with that in place at Vauxhall. But it is important to appreciate that the personnel management and development system is synonymous with the business functioning of the company. It is central to the way in which Vauxhall conducts its business. All the 1,640 salaried employees are appraised, many receiving comment via the 360 degree model. Assessment leads to a personal development plan for each employee.

It also provides the basis for the reward system. Management wants the package to be attractive and competitive with the best in the sector. It also wants a significant part of the deal to be performance related. So employees have the opportunity to be among the best paid in the industry. The principles of consistency in approach influence pay and benefits policy throughout Europe. Warman says that the company operates to certain fundamentals but it recognizes that market conditions are different in specific territories.

A notable factor in the package is the continuing commitment to the final salary pension arrangements. Final salary pensions are perceived as generous by many in human resources circles but Vauxhall aims to keep and develop many of its employees for the duration of their careers. 'People will leave but we value experience and industry knowledge. Our training systems are designed to give people better opportunities within the company – and internationally – and so we want them to stay and fulfil their potential.'

Every 18 months Vauxhall conducts an employee attitude survey. This allows the company to take the temperature of attitudes across the business – and it provides a basis for action.

In addition the company engages in extensive communications activities and its staff newspaper has won external awards for the quality of its reporting and design. The company also encourages employee involvement in a range of sporting and community activities.

Contact address

David Peters
HR Planning and Projects Manager
Vauxhall Motors Limited
Griffin House
Osborne Road
Luton LU1 3YT
Telephone: 01582 426684
Fax: 01582 426927
Web site: http://www.vauxhall.co.uk

Virgin Group

In a recent poll, 96 per cent of British consumers said they had heard of Virgin and 95 per cent could correctly identify Richard Branson as its founder. Such brand recognition, fronted by the personable face of Branson, is the result of more than 20 years of innovation and outstanding business management. The Virgin Group, comprising an array of companies and their joint ventures, operates in a wide variety of business sectors from retailing, publishing and media to travel, entertainment and merchandising. Virgin's management style empowers and encourages fresh ideas and the group is a popular employer, especially among the younger generations.

Virgin at a glance

Employees: 15,000 worldwide, 11,000 UK
Annual staff attrition: 5 per cent
Key locations: mostly Central London and Crawley (Virgin Atlantic)
Annual graduate intake: none
Annual intake: varies significantly

An inside view

It all began with a small mail order record company and the vision and energy of Richard Branson. Over a period of two decades he has built an enterprise that encompasses a diverse range of cultural interests, and has acquired a reputation as an ambassador of the people. Virgin's target markets are often those where the customer has been consistently under-served, or where the competition is complacent. This is in line with Branson's eclectic approach, which particularly appeals to young, upbeat individuals. His talent for creative marketing has blended well with a remarkable business instinct that has seen him produce his own music label and record shops, cinemas and radio station, an airline and a brand of cola.

One of the reasons for the popularity of the Virgin Group is its modernity. It is a group of companies with a global presence yet there's no head office, virtually no management hierarchy and minimal bureaucracy. The group's topmost managing board is tiny and just as likely to meet in one of the member's homes or at the local pub as in the boardroom. Therefore the terminology 'group' is slightly misleading. It is more like a community of companies which function autonomously but regard themselves as allies with shared ideals, interests and goals. The benefit of such grouping is that it predisposes the managers of each company to co-operate with the others in varied alliances and ventures.

The Virgin Group has eight main divisions: Virgin Radio; Virgin Retail Group (including its chain of Megastores and Our Price record shops); Voyager Investments (in effect a range of stand-alone investments); Virgin Travel (including Virgin Atlantic Airways, Virgin Holiday and the group's budding rail interest); Virgin Communications (which incorporates the publishing arm); Virgin Cinemas; Virgin Hotels; and Virgin Direct Personal Financial Services.

Embedded in the culture of Virgin are four key values. The first three – quality, competitiveness and innovation – are fundamental to the image Virgin aims to create in the minds of its consumers. Service and value for money stem from these values and are incorporated into the Virgin 'promise'. 'The Virgin promise means delivering value – first-class value at business-class prices – providing unusually high service levels and constantly being innovative and modern in all we do,' says Steve Ridgeway, managing director of Virgin Atlantic Airways. Fun is the remaining value and extremely important to the culture and representation of Virgin, setting the corporation apart from competitors. Fun is an experience enjoyed by customers and employees alike.

Virgin employs exceptionally motivated and enterprising people, who are dynamic and possess a keen sense of humour. The group is a unique employer and finds that people either stay at Virgin for the long haul or leave after six months. Some people thrive in the fast-paced working environment, dedicating themselves zealously to the group goals and becoming closely involved with the Virgin family, however the company's unconventional style does not suit everyone. Staff turnover varies enormously by business. For example, it is high in the airline industry at eight – ten per cent, but is a very low five per cent in the management sector.

How does Virgin rate?

Pay:	average
Benefits:	good
Communications:	excellent
Training:	good
Career development:	very good
Morale:	excellent

People and personnel policies

As it is such a diverse operation, Virgin does not have group-wide personnel policies. Each company decides upon its own terms and conditions – and also has separate bonus schemes – that are specific to each industry, locality and size. Nor is there a distinctive graduate recruitment programme. In keeping with Branson's practical approach to business management, preference is given to those university leavers who have had some experience in the business sector after finishing their education. Employees are made accountable early on in their career at Virgin, partly due to the flat management structure. Says Branson, '. . . cutting out hierarchy gives people the space to use their judgement and make their own decisions. We like to encourage our managers to be entrepreneurial. It's probably why we attract the best people.'

To be successful within the company, an entrepreneurial nature is essential. While the atmosphere is informal – you rarely see an executive in a suit – professionalism underpins all corporate activities. The opportunities for career development are continuously expanding within the group. Within companies there is potential to move around and up in the business structure. Historically, shifting between the different companies of the group was uncommon due to the dissimilarity between industries. This is changing as the group's interests continue to multiply and skills become more easily transferable. New and innovative ideas are the bread and butter of Virgin's success so if an employee presents the management team with a feasible concept which will enhance the group's value, promotion can be swift – to the point of playing a prominent role in new business development.

Communication is a high priority at Virgin, being the glue that binds this vast corporation and providing uniformity to the concept that is Virgin. Despite the fact that Virgin is continually expanding, employees are kept up to date with group events. In addition to newsletters, corporate videos and electronic interactions, the group organizes functions and outings in order to improve communication and morale.

Women have a high profile in the Virgin Group – an estimated 40 per cent of its senior executives are female. At Virgin Atlantic, for example, 50 per cent of executive positions are filled by women. The Virgin environment is inviting for many women, as it is characterized by relaxed and flexible working arrangements and democratic management practice.

Contact address

Ms Lily Lu
Group Personnel Manager
Virgin Management
120 Campden Hill Road
London W8 7AR
Telephone: 0171 229 1282
Fax: 0171 229 3234
Web site: http://www.virgin.com

Vodafone

The first commercial cellular telephone network operator in the UK was Racal Telecommunications Group, which began life in January 1985. Vodafone broke away from Racal in 1998 to concentrate on expanding the mobile telephones market. It is now among the top 20 companies of the FTSE 100 Index, no mean feat for a company which is only 14 years old and was floated just 11 years ago. Despite strong competition, it remains the market leader with over 4 million subscribers in the UK and a presence in 13 countries worldwide. Vodafone proposed a takeover of Air Touch Communications which would create the largest mobile phone company in the world and the third largest company in the UK.

Vodafone at a glance

Employees: 12,000 worldwide, 7,000 UK
Annual staff attrition: n/a
Key locations: Newbury, Banbury, Croydon
Annual graduate intake: 50
Annual intake: 2,000

An inside view

The growth and diversity of Vodafone is impressive. The Vodafone Group Plc consists of the following major subsidiaries: Vodafone Limited, Vodafone Distribution, Vodafone Value Added Services, Vodafone Paging, Vodafone Data Network and Vodafone Group International, each of which offers a range of mobile telecommunications services to business customers and the consumer markets. The group's principal activities include cellular radio network operation, cellular radio service provision, data transmission over cellular radio networks, digital cellular systems and equipment, packet radio operation, radio paging and value added network services.

The hi-tech, cutting-edge nature of the telecoms business means that change is the overriding feature of the business. Reassessment of Vodafone's products, services and skills, is continuous and flexibility is essential to sustain its commitment to innovation and improvement.

The Vodafone Group is one of the top 20 companies in the UK and is currently valued at over £15 billion. It employs more than 12,000 people around the world and has operations on four continents. Outstanding growth has become a key characteristic of Vodafone. Profits exceed £0.5 billion a year and in 1997 annual turnover grew by 41 per cent. Quality of service is of paramount importance and the company is approved to quality standard ISO 9000 for all its activities and consistently outperforms its competitors in independent network trials.

It is a young company with a young workforce – the average age of employees is 34. The culture is one of openness, enthusiasm and relative informality. The company encourages employees at all levels to put forward new ideas. It believes its working environment is exciting, because change brings with it new challenges and new successes. The atmosphere at Vodafone is friendly, professional and extremely productive. There is emphasis on maintaining high energy levels, which are vital in maintaining a competitive edge in a fast-paced industry.

Somewhat surprisingly, just 7,000 UK employees serve the 4 million customer base. Vodafone seeks to employ high quality people who can identify and take advantage of opportunity as it arises. The group values relevant qualifications, skills and work experience, highly developed written and oral communication skills and real-life problem solving and decision-making abilities. The ability to work effectively in a team, self-motivation, imagination and the flexibility to cope with the unexpected are all important requirements. Potential applicants must be prepared to act on their own initiative, because a high level of responsibility is given early. It is a rapidly expanding corporation and employees should find that the only limitations on their progress are self-imposed.

How does Vodafone rate?

Pay:	very good
Benefits:	very good
Communications:	good
Training:	excellent
Career development:	excellent
Morale:	very good

People and personnel policies

Initial product and company training is given at work locations or at the large training centre in Newbury. On-the-job training is supplemented by technical training in specific areas and the company offers support in related formal qualifications. Vodafone offers graduates a development programme and real responsibility from day one. According to Ranjit Sisodyia, Vodafone Group Services, senior financial accountant, 'There is some hand-holding at the beginning, but graduates are expected to learn fast and we expect them to start demanding further training and more responsibility pretty early on.' On-going training is of prime importance, to ensure that every member of staff is fully aware of the latest developments within the industry.

Annual appraisal provides the opportunity for all employees to assess their performance against set objectives and consider personal development either within their current role or by advancement. A management development programme aims to ensure that the skills and expertise of staff are employed in the most effective way to guarantee the continuing success of the business. Vodafone has a number of training schemes which lead to recognized qualifications and/or membership of a professional body. For example, employees in human resources are encouraged to achieve professional status by studying for the IPD (Institute of Personnel and Development) qualification.

Career opportunities are numerous and cover the following: engineering operations, i.e. network services, operations and implementation, finance, computing, IT and project management, customer services, corporate communications and publicity, personnel and training, and legal services. Vodafone's young culture encourages early career advancement.

Vodafone aims to pay above market rates and achieves this by constant reference to sector salary surveys. Remuneration takes account of individual merit. Annual leave entitlement is a generous 28 days for full-time staff, increasing with service. Most jobs are in normal office hours, but an increasing number involve shift working, which earns extra payments. The flexible company car scheme allows selection of a car above or below the benchmark car, with an employee contribution or cash refund to cover the difference. There is also a total cash alternative. Vodafone offers a pension scheme, which includes free life assurance.

An employee introduction scheme was launched in 1998 whereby current employees receive a fee for introducing a new permanent employee to the company. The fee they receive for the introduction is weighted in accordance with the scarcity of the skills of the new employee.

Contact address

The Group Personnel Department
Vodafone Group plc
The Courtyard
2–4 London Road
Newbury
Berkshire RG14 1JX
Telephone: 01635 502664/503001
Fax: 01635 507290/47069
Web site: http://www.vodafone.co.uk

Whitbread plc

Whitbread is a textbook example of how to manage a family of brands in the retail sector. It combines positive brand identification and coherent central strategic management with business unit devolution and a participative forward-looking culture. Across the board, Whitbread exceeds industry standards in almost every area of its commercial operation. Among its best-known brands are Marriott Hotels, Pizza Hut, David Lloyd Leisure, TGI Friday's, Café Rouge and Thresher. Its 1998 sales were £3.2 billion with profits at £355 million.

Whitbread at a glance

Employees: 90,000 (81,000 full-time)
Annual staff attrition: variable across the businesses
Key locations: London (HQ), Luton, Uxbridge, Milton Keynes, Welwyn Garden City, Borehamwood. Branches throughout the UK
Annual graduate intake: n/a
Annual intake: 5,000

An inside view

Every year Whitbread chief executive David Thomas meets with the group's senior executives to identify the business objectives for the coming 12 months. In 1998, he had three principal themes. But this set of imperatives reflected in a more general sense the core business philosophy of the group in the 1990s. During this decade the Whitbread group has transformed itself and initiated a process which is running through every operating unit of the organization. Whitbread is committed to a culture of service to customers. But it is abundantly aware that almost every commercial organization now says that customer service is its top priority.

So Whitbread has determined that it must exceed expectation in each aspect of its delivery to the customer. The standard which it achieved yesterday is the foundation for improvement today. It operates in a conceptual framework which encourages the 70,000 customer-facing employees to provide enhanced quality of service. The corporate centre is a backbone which enables investment and resources to be shared and which provides coherent stimulus for the direction of the business but it also facilitates the individual businesses to express commercial success in their own ways.

Thomas told senior managers that the company has three targets: enhanced brand development, creating a positive working environment, and improved return on capital employed. Like most other modern businesses, Whitbread is concerned about shareholder value. But these three targets nearly address its triple stakeholder groups: shareholders, customers and employees. It is possible to add a fourth in its local communities because Whitbread has a systematic approach to developing relationships in the places where it operates.

The company has worked hard to understand the changing dimensions of its markets and so to meet the expectations of its customers. It would be hard to understate the commitment which Whitbread exhibits to anticipating demand. On the macro level, it conducts continuous research into the lifestyle and leisure interests of its customers, both potential and existing. At a personal level, where it aims to be most visible, Whitbread seeks to please its quests to such an extent that they become repeat customers. This involves high level foundation training of its staff, the application of innovative technology and the desire by its employees to discover – for each guest – the elements which will make service personal and relevant.

The group now has eight business units which demonstrate the broad base of the enterprise. These comprise: Beefeater Restaurant and Pub – more than 250 outlets in the UK; Inns with 1,700 managed pubs and restaurants including Brewers Fayre, Wayside Inn and Hogshead; Restaurants with Bella Pasta, Costa, Pelican (embracing Café Rouge, Dome and Mamma Amalfi), Pizza Hut, TGI Friday's and German restaurant brands Churrasco and Tascaria Maredo; David Lloyd Leisure, the UK's largest operator of private health and fitness clubs; Pub Partnerships, which manages the company's leased pub operation; The Beer Company with brands such as Stella Artois, Murphy's Irish Stout, Boddingtons Bitter, Heineken and Labatt ICE; The Hotel Company with the Marriott and Travel Inn chains; and off-licences embracing almost 3,000 shops managed by the Thresher and Victoria Wine joint venture.

Whitbread is predominantly a brand-led organization which has grown through the acquisition and development of group brands. Considerable emphasis is placed in Whitbread in getting the best out of its brand portfolio and much of its market strategy is designed to make full use of its formidable catalogue of well-known names.

The group's aim is that each brand, although distinctive in the eyes of the public, will become a market leader in its segment and many of Whitbread's operations already dominate.

How does Whitbread rate?

Pay:	very good
Benefits:	very good
Communications:	very good
Training:	excellent
Career development:	excellent
Morale:	excellent

People and personnel policies

A transformation has occurred in the culture of Whitbread and its operating businesses in the last few years. The focus has reversed from senior management and its priorities to a predominately customer-facing strategy. The 70,000 employees who deal directly with customers are the people who deliver the business and the role of senior managers is to support them. It is a radical shift when the origins of the business are considered.

Whitbread was a brewer. Brewing was one of the most traditionally hierarchical sectors in British industry. But as Whitbread has moved to what is mainly a retail culture it has also changed its style. Today 90 per cent of Whitbread's profits come from retailing. Its largest chunk of turnover at £996 million comes from beer but the return from brewing is only £44.6 million. Inns alone turn in £807 million which generates £172 million.

Retailing requires different skills and a people-centric approach. The recruitment, development and retention programmes are designed to create fulfilling careers in a fast-moving and demanding environment. Much of the people development is done in the individual business units and is tailored to meet the skill and career needs in each unit. Investment in training is very high for the leisure sector and the results are seen in strong staff retention.

Chris Bulmer, human resources director for the group, explains, 'Whitbread believes in respect, teamwork, integrity and pride. We appreciate that employees will not give their commitment unless they are genuinely respected. We want them to share our pride in a well-managed business which aims to exceed our customers' expectations. Whitbread is a people business and our greatest assets are our employees.'

She explains that the business units are painstaking about recruiting the right people. 'We want them to live and breathe our values and the specific values of the individual businesses, so we need to locate the right people. They will have energy, imagination and an overriding commitment to excellent customer service.'

This is a direct, warm and personable environment where employees are encouraged to be brilliant at their work. She speaks about the three rings of customer service which is central to the people management philosophy across the group. One ring is the delivery of the basic product or service, another is supportive systems and practices that ensure customer expectations are met and the third is the commitment by each Whitbread employee to translate excellent service personally for each separate customer.

There is a real enthusiasm about Whitbread establishments and the passion, efficiency and intelligence which each staff member shows is measured in performance appraisal. 'We are introducing 360 degree appraisals across the business,' she says. Reward and development is linked to personal, unit and group output, so that individuals can share proportionately in the success of the business. Pay is above average for the sector and the company has an excellent pension plan. Employee share ownership is encouraged in various schemes and the company offers free medical advice.

Bulmer is a strong advocate of gaining experience in all aspects of the business unit. So someone might come into Marriott and start in bookings. They can move into finance, administration, catering or room service and progress through the ranks. 'If someone shows talent and aptitude we promote them very quickly.'

A personal initiative is the Pathways project. This is a complex but remarkably beneficial programme which allows people to move around Whitbread finding the right assignments for them. In common with many other organizations, Whitbread is a great supporter of the notion that the individual plans his or her career. However, it actively supports personal endeavours. Pathways provides assistance on the opportunities which are available, the type of career challenges which would be useful in terms of long-term ambitions and where specific vacancies lie. More importantly, it is designed to exploit cross-functional development across the group so that an employee from one group business will be able to transfer to another with ease.

This illustration depicts a great deal about the positive aspects of the Whitbread culture. Everyone is encouraged to help everyone else to grow. Training is structured but people also learn from experience and from each other.

The continuing and growing success of the Whitbread culture is revealed in the Views survey. This shows attitudes by employees to various aspects of the job and it also benchmarks Whitbread against other leading employers in the sector. Whitbread scores phenomenally well on every criterion. Whitbread has provided a broad-based framework where its people can excel at what they do best – pleasing customers.

Contact address

Chris Bulmer
Human Resources Director
Whitbread plc
Chiswell Street
London EC1Y 4SD
Telephone: 0171 606 4455
Fax: 0171 615 1009
Web site: http://www.whitbread.co.uk

WH Smith Group

The WH Smith Group is the leading retailer and wholesaler of books, news and magazines in the UK. In common with many leading names in the British high street, the group has experienced a series of changes to its shape and format. It is focusing on its principal brand of WH Smith and has recently made several acquisitions and disposals to reorientate the group on the lines of popular news vendor and bookseller. Its flagship stores have striven to re-emphasize their identity as the preferred source of family entertainment and educational materials.

WH Smith at a glance

Employees: 30,000 (21,000 full-time equivalents)
Annual staff attrition: n/a
Key locations: London (HQ), Swindon, throughout the UK and US plus some outlets in mainland Europe
Annual graduate intake: 80
Annual intake: n/a

An inside view

For many years WH Smith has been regarded as a benchmark employer. Despite apparent shifts in trading direction, the group has consistently maintained a well-earned reputation for developing its employees and providing a supportive culture. Ten years ago this was founded on a paternalistic ethic to look after its people. Today it has more or less completed its transformation to a commercially led enterprise which appreciates that for convincing success, the group's employees should be motivated, adaptable, well trained and well remunerated.

Although the perspective has changed, the values remain similar. It is a business which appreciates individuality, especially in retailing. Barely a handful of its intake each year are graduates. WH Smith looks instead for personal communication skills, intelligence, the capacity to inspire others and that most cherished of retailing qualities – resilience. It is a rapid promotion path for the talented branch manager. The group has never been slow to spot ability.

It is also distinguished by a true belief in diversity. Many companies advance their credentials in this most fashionable category but few have done as much as WH Smith to reflect its customer base in age, gender and racial background. At present only one of the five executive directors of the group is female but 20 out of the 50 seniors at the level below are women. The group has also worked with the Commission for Racial Equality to improve the racial mix in the businesses.

Gill Chapman, group human resources director, says that the move to a more commercial environment has taken a decade to implement. The last couple of years have been difficult but the group now has a new strategy which promotes the core WH Smith brand. It enjoyed great success with both Waterstone's and Virgin Our Price but sold both of these businesses this year in order to focus on WH Smith. It has been looking for the right formula for WH Smith stores for a long time and the group believes that it may have found it by concentrating on books, stationery, newspapers and magazines.

The group now comprises five businesses: The WH Smith stores; The WH Smith Travel Retail stores at stations and airports in the UK; WH Smith News, the newspaper and magazine wholesaler; WH Smith Inc, the airport and hotel retail business based in the US; and IBS, the Internet Bookshop.

The group recently acquired The John Menzies Retail stores and the 230-strong chain is now being integrated in to the WH Smith business. The group has also acquired the Internet Bookshop, which gives signposts to the future. Ainley says that the WH Smith Group vision is in development but it will concentrate on the core brand as the favourite source of education, entertainment and information.

Innovation has been lacking in the past but it has relaunched many stores with an attractive and welcoming design. It was this failure to reinvent itself which in the past has led to a lack of focus but which now appears to have been overcome.

The group is now an exciting place to be – especially for young retailers. The opportunities for personal career advancement are better than ever. Its emphasis on news and the WH Smith brand means that the group is looking for creative people with resilience, ambition and the capacity to inspire.

How does WH Smith rate?

Pay:	good
Benefits:	very good
Communications:	very good
Training:	excellent
Career development:	excellent
Morale:	very good

People and personnel policies

Whatever its corporate rationale, WH Smith has always held its people in high regard. And despite difficult periods of trading and even crisis in confidence, the group has always treated its employees with respect. The group demonstrated that through Waterstone's and Virgin Our Price it was able to run highly profitable businesses. It remains one of the few UK-owned retailers which has turned a profit in America. Its principal concern was that it was unable to renew its flagship brand.

The new management team – at least – appears to have found the spark of originality which was missing. Much of the focus has now gone into the elements which make up the identity of WH Smith. News retailing and wholesaling, popular and educational books, stationery and music/video are the staples. The purchase of Menzies was a long-overdue step; travellers at least probably assumed that they were already part of the same group.

For employees, the new strategic direction allows them to work to their strengths. These days WH Smith recruits leadership candidates who enjoy customer service and building sales. The pay and benefits systems have been restructured over the years to reflect the emphasis on personal, team and divisional performance.

Pay is set after 360 degree performance assessment. The top 50 executives in the group undergo annual 360 degree assessment. The belief is that anyone – at whatever level in the company – can improve from input from colleagues. Annual 360 degree assessment involves written commentary from a wide range of colleagues who deal regularly with the employee being assessed. The idea is that from an analysis of all of these different views an accurate appreciation of strengths and weaknesses can be assembled. Individual training needs and pay and benefits programmes are then tailored from this procedure.

Pensions have been reformed. Everyone taken on before 1995 took part in a non-contributory final salary scheme. Since then, a new money purchase scheme which equates more with contemporary practice has been introduced. This involves an employee as well as an employer contribution and offers more flexibility than the old scheme.

WH Smith remains its old self when staff ask for time off for a variety of reasons. Sickness, parenthood, personal emergency – no one blinks an eyelid. Experiments with job sharing have gone well – WH Smith has a high number of part-timers – but flexitime does not suit the culture.

Contact address

Gill Chapman
Group Human Resources Director
WH Smith plc
Greenbridge Road
Swindon SN3 3LD
Telephone: 01793 562801
Fax: 01793 562999
Web site: http://www.whsmithgroup.com

WPP Group plc

With offices in 91 countries, the WPP Group provides communications services to clients throughout the world – including more than 300 of the Fortune Global 500. Every WPP company is a distinctive brand in its own right, and some are considerably more famous than the parent, for example J Walter Thompson and Ogilvy & Mather. All the group's companies have their own identities and their own areas of expertise. That is their strength. What they have in common, says the group, is that 'they harness intelligence, talent and experience to bring competitive advantage to their clients.' The group's people are its main assets, and its investment in people accounts for approximately 50 per cent of revenues.

WPP at a glance

Employees: 30,000 worldwide; approx 3,600 UK
Annual staff attrition: 15 per cent
Key locations: 835 offices worldwide; 270 offices in Western Europe including UK
Annual graduate intake: 100 UK
Annual intake: 850 UK

An inside view

What has become the world's largest advertising and marketing services organization started life 14 years ago by acquiring a company called Wire and Plastic Products. By 1998 WPP, as it is now known, had a turnover of £8 billion with pretax profits of £177 million – up 19 per cent on the previous year. Its 1998 figures show earnings per share up by 20 per cent and dividends up by 20 per cent – all this despite the strength of sterling and economic difficulties in Asia. But as chairman, Hamish Maxwell, and group chief executive, Martin Sorrell, have jointly said, '. . . the numbers are no more than a measurement of the value delivered to our clients; and that value is created, account by account, project by project, discipline by discipline, by the talented people who work in WPP Group companies.'

The group is split into five different disciplines: advertising; media planning, buying and research; public relations and public affairs; information and consultancy; and specialist communications. Some of the companies are world famous (J Walter Thompson, Ogilvy & Mather Worldwide, Hill & Knowlton) but all are highly respected in their own sphere of influence.

One of the group's recent objectives has been to develop the role of the centre from a financial holding or investment company – concentrating solely on financial planning, budgeting, reporting and control, treasury, tax, mergers and acquisitions, and investor relations – to a value added organization that contributes to the management of both clients and talent inside the group. Consequently, over the past seven years or so important new roles have been created within the parent company in human resources, property management, procurement, information technology and, most importantly, practice development. At the same time the head-count at the centre has remained low, at approximately 90, with most staff located in London and New York.

The cost of property is important to WPP as it represents approximately 10 per cent of its revenue (or $250 million) each year. Therefore the parent company has focused on the elimination of surplus property and, more importantly, on enhancing the design and layout of its premises. To this end it developed its 'space program' with one of its own companies – BDG McColl.

Through procurement initiatives the group has also encouraged more effective purchase of goods and services. This has resulted in worldwide arrangements for travel and accommodation, computer hardware and software, recruitment and telecommunications. In particular, with a spend of more than $65 million a year on computer hardware, software and information management people, the parent company sought to develop a coherent strategy and framework, as well as to cut out wasteful duplication in various parts of the organization.

How does WPP rate?

Pay:	good
Benefits:	good
Communications:	good
Training:	excellent
Career development:	excellent
Morale:	very good

People and personnel policies

WPP is increasingly complementing the professional activities of individual operating companies through cross-group initiatives and programmes which provide greater value to clients as well as opportunities and rewards for its own people. In the field of human resources the strategy, according to Brian Brooks, WPP group human resources director, is to develop and manage talent, to apply that talent throughout the world for the benefit of clients, to do this in partnership with the operating companies, and to do this profitably. While there is concern throughout the industry about the shortage and calibre of entry-level recruits, WPP is determined to be an employer of choice. Its philosophy is that all its recruits should be 'best in class' and according to Brooks it is the only marketing services company to actively recruit MBAs from leading business schools in North America and Europe.

Although most career development continues to be performed at an individual company level – J Walter Thompson, for example, has long been regarded as the university of Advertising – there is an increasing focus on group-wide training initiatives. For example, the group has developed a Marketing Fellowship programme in which both first degree and MBAs participate in a three-year cross-disciplinary work experience programme. Additionally, more than 1,200 group company professionals have participated in an on-going programme of cross-company forums, workshops and seminars.

A series of Knowledge Communities has been developed by the group. These consist of professionals working in a specific sector – or with a particular skill such as retail or interactive media – who can share non-confidential insights, case studies and best practice. Also, for top management and senior professionals within the group, there are the 100 and 300 Clubs which provide senior executives with the opportunity to participate in customized development programmes and WPP's Stock Option Awards.

Other group initiatives include the Atticus Awards which honour original published thinking in communications services; the Group Navigator, a pocket reference book, which enables all 30,000 staff to source group companies, resources, capabilities and contacts; and the Worldwide Partnership Program – introduced in 1997 – that encourages teamworking across group companies which demonstrably enhance client service. Subsequently a portfolio of integrated case studies has been established.

No group in the communications business and operating worldwide can ignore the latest IT developments and, at the time of writing, the major hubs of a group-wide internal network are installed and operating. Further strategic initiatives, including an electronic job exchange, are in hand. Some individual companies are more advanced in their on-line environments than others, but ultimately everyone will be connected as part of the WPP Intranet, making it a vital source of worldwide knowledge.

Apart from the WPP Intranet, communication within the organization is primarily a matter for the individual operating companies. However, the group policy is one of openness and the effective communication of group strategy and progress by the operating heads is encouraged. To help implement this policy of openness, the group's worldwide newspaper, *The WIRE*, keeps individuals up to date with group news and developments. The WPP Web site also does this.

The creation of a more distinct WPP culture means that careers are no longer limited by the company which the individual joins, and inter-company moves within the group are now increasingly common. Clearly an important factor in attracting and retaining staff is remuneration. As befits a results-oriented organization, the career progress and personal rewards of an increasing number of people within the group are linked to agreed company and group financial objectives.

Contact address

Brian J Brooks
Group Human Resources Director
WPP Group plc
27 Farm Street
London W1X 6RD
Telephone: 0171 408 2204
Fax: 0171 493 6819
Web site: http://www.wpp.com

Xerox Europe, The Document Company

Xerox Limited is a wholly owned subsidiary of the Xerox Corporation. It began life in 1956 as Rank Xerox – a joint venture between the Xerox Corporation of the US and The Rank Organization in the UK. Xerox gradually increased its stake in Rank Xerox and in 1997 bought out Rank's interest entirely for $1.5 billion. In 1990 'The Document Company' was adopted as a trading name. Xerox International is based in Marlow, Buckinghamshire and manufactures and markets Xerox products and services across Europe. These include copiers, printers, digital publishing systems, and complete document outsourcing solutions, meeting the needs of all markets from personal users to the print room.

Xerox at a glance

Employees: 7,200 UK (4,500 in field sales and marketing, 1,800 in manufacturing, 700 in customer engineering and product development, and 200 in shared services at HQ)
Annual staff attrition: 5 per cent
Key locations: HQ at Marlow, Bucks; manufacturing at Mitcheldean, Gloucestershire; technology centre at Welwyn Garden City; research centre at Cambridge, customer support offices in major centres in the UK
Annual graduate intake: 20 (including students 120)
Annual intake: 360

An inside view

Xerox Europe has experienced a transformation since the early 1990s. The company has undergone a radical re-configuration of its business and a substantial reorganization of the way in which it is structured. It has broadened the scope of its operations, invested heavily in technology and emphasized its commitment to quality, its customers and its people. The benefits are legion and each year since the early 1990s it has improved its performance by the measures which Xerox regards as key. It tests itself on four principal criteria: customer satisfaction, market share, growth and improved employee standing. The combination of a strong track record in these areas has flowed through to excellent financial results. Sales and profits in each business area have flourished year-on-year in the 1990s.

Since 1990 when the name The Document Company was adopted, Xerox has focused its business approach on commercial documents rather than simply selling photocopiers. Executive director, group resources, Stephen Cronin, explains that 90 per cent of all corporate information is stored in documents of one sort or another. Some 60 per cent of employee time is spent in document production; and, after payroll costs, documents are the largest single item of expenditure in a company's budget. Five billion documents are created every day in Europe alone and a growing proportion of these will be in electronic formats. This prompted Xerox to become the premier document specialist and represents a major shift from only a few years ago when paper was the principal vehicle for documents.

'We realized that to meet and anticipate market changes and to become more effective and profitable, we had to make changes ourselves. We had to restructure our entire organization from top to bottom and become customer-focused and market-led. We had to communicate to the business world that no one understands the business document better,' Cronin says. Xerox's outstanding technological expertise in this field needed to be broadened to be world leader in document production through the use of emerging digital systems. In addition, the company wanted to demonstrate to customers its capacity to provide solutions to customer issues in a bewildering array of market conditions and circumstances. Some 800 staff at its technical centre in Welwyn Garden City grapple with scores of customer problems such as efficient document production through networks which are composed of systems originated by different manufacturers.

How does Xerox rate?

Pay:	very good
Benefits:	excellent
Communications:	superb
Training:	very good
Career development:	very good
Morale:	very good

People and personnel policies

The Xerox approach to employee management is underpinned by eight basic principles: honesty, trust, respect, openness, professionalism, teamwork, initiative and humour. It has also defined nine cultural dimensions in which each employee is expected to perform. These range from customer focus to team orientation. The company has equally assembled a set of 23 leadership attributes against which management competency is rated. These attributes form the basis of a series of personal, manager and direct report assessments to evaluate performance and provide a structure for personal development.

Individual employees are responsible for their own career and personal development which is linked into business requirements. Graduates are enlisted into an organized recruitment programme. Xerox aims for at least a 2.1 result at first degree level. 'We look for candidates who can demonstrate high energy, a capacity to integrate with others, a good leadership style, respect for others, and a results-orientated approach,' says human resources director Lis Barnes.

The company encourages entrants to gain experience across the organization and, in the longer term, to enter the management development programme. 'The aim is to bring in high calibre people and take them through the organization quite quickly,' Barnes says. Cronin remarks that the restructuring created a much flatter organization. People are now much closer to the decision-making process. Xerox's extensive communications programme is geared to high quality dialogue and feedback. As well as formal printed material and cascade briefings, it also holds regular cross-functional breakfast meetings to ensure that a wide group is aware of current business issues. 'These allow employees to get to know the directors better and us to take the pulse of the organization,' says Cronin.

Each job is part of a job-family and is graded according to the skills and competencies required for that post. Individuals are then encouraged to compare their own performance against those required for the putative assignment. 'At a higher level we are able to roll these competencies up to see what skills we need across the company,' says Cronin. Nearly all employees experience a variable element to their pay. The further up the organization, the greater the variable element. This part of the remuneration is conditioned by performance at a personal, team and corporate level. Sales people are on a high variable (60 per cent variable, 40 per cent fixed). The benefits package is excellent: an excellent pension scheme, health insurance for all employees, profit related pay, life insurance and subsidized high quality restaurants.

In 1996, Xerox launched its X-teams initiative which focuses on high achievement teamwork. Hundreds of teams have registered for the process which will direct them towards personal and collective growth through working together to push back the boundaries of their assignments. As well as sharpening their commercial edge, it brings a dash of fun into the workplace. Xerox is also at the forefront of the learning culture approach and has learning centres where employees can go to boost their understanding of a wide range of disciplines. The centres are networked so that what is available in one centre can be shared throughout the company. Diversity is another major area of focus for Xerox. 'We have looked at it in two ways,' says Barnes. 'The Document Company had established policies, goals and frameworks for equal opportunities and we broadened these to encompass diversity. We also examined the way we work and took an educational approach. We want to be active in encouraging diverse opinion, as well as background, in the company.'

Contact address

HR Department
Xerox Europe
Parkway, Marlow
Buckinghamshire SL7 1YL
Telephone: 01628 890000
Fax: 01628 892001
Web site: http://www.xerox.co.uk